Fachwörterbuch für Hotellerie & Gastronomie,
Reisebüros & Reiseveranstalter

Edgar E. Schaetzing

Fachwörterbuch für Hotellerie & Gastronomie, Reisebüros & Reiseveranstalter

deutsch — englisch/englisch — deutsch

bearbeitet von Antje Haritage und Fritz Neske

Deutscher Fachverlag

CIP-Kurztitelaufnahme der Deutschen Bibliothek

Schaetzing, Edgar E.:
Fachwörterbuch für Hotellerie & [und] Gastronomie, Reisebüros & [und] Veranstalter: dt./engl. · engl. / dt./Edgar E. Schaetzing. Bearb. von Antje Haritage u. Fritz Neske. — 2. Aufl. — Frankfurt am Main: Deutscher Fachverlag, 1985.
 1. Aufl. im EOS-Verl., Sankt Ottilien
 1. Aufl. u. d. T.: Schaetzing, Edgar E.: Tourismus dictionary
 ISBN 3-87150-221-9
NE: Haritage, Antje [Bearb.]; HST

Quellenhinweise für Titelfotos:
Britische Zentrale für Fremdenverkehr, Frankfurt am Main
Fotoatelier Deutscher Fachverlag, Frankfurt am Main

2. Auflage
ISBN 3-87150-221-9

© 1985 by Deutscher Fachverlag GmbH, Frankfurt am Main.
Alle Rechte vorbehalten. Nachdruck, auch auszugsweise, nur mit Genehmigung des Verlages.

Gesamtherstellung: poppdruck, 3012 Langenhagen

Vorwort

Das vorliegende Fachwörterbuch ist für die Mitarbeiter von Hotels und Restaurants, Reisebüros und Reiseveranstaltern, wie auch für den Weltenbummler bestimmt.

Die Tourismus Terminologie ist einem ständigen Wandel unterworfen, und eine Sammlung der gebräuchlichsten Fachausdrücke kann niemals „fertig" werden. Bewußt habe ich dieses Tourismus Management Dictionary nicht nach philologischen Richtlinien zusammengestellt; es setzt deshalb auch Grundkenntnisse in beiden Sprachen voraus.

Für die Übersetzung verschiedener Fachausdrücke bin ich Herrn Professor Karl Englisch und Herrn Professor Wolfgang Leiderer sehr verbunden. Mein besonderer Dank gilt auch Herrn Professor Robert A. Beck, Dekan der Cornell Universität und Herrn John P. Daschler, Director Industry Relations des Amerikanischen Hotel- und Motelverbandes, die mit wertvollen Ratschlägen bei einer Reihe von Übersetzungsschwierigkeiten zur Fertigstellung des Wörterbuches beigetragen haben. Danken möchte ich meiner Frau Ilsa, die die Kartei für die gastronomischen Ausdrücke erstellt hat.

Für Anregungen zur Verbesserung und Ergänzung bin ich besonders verbunden.

Edgar E. Schaetzing

Preface

This Tourismus Dictionary is meant for the staff of hotels and restaurants travel agencies and touroperators but also for the globetrotter.

The terminology of tourism is under constant change and a collection of the most common terms can never be completed. I should like to point out, that I have refrained from applying linguistic considerations; it, therefore, requires basic knowledge in both languages.

I am greatly indebted to Prof. Karl Englisch and Prof. Wolfgang Leiderer for a large number of English terms and wish to express my gratitude to Prof. Robert A. Beck, Dean of the Cornell University and Mr. John P. Daschler, Director Industry Relations – Educational Institute of the American Hotel & Motel Association whose valuable advice in a number of difficult translation problems has contributed so much to the completion of this dictionary. I should also like to thank my wife Ilsa, who prepared the card index of food and beverage terms.

Any suggestions for improvements and additions are welcome.

Edgar E. Schaetzing

Teil I

Deutsch — Englisch

Part I

German — English

Abkürzungen — Abbreviations

(f) feminine, weiblich
(m) masculine, männlich
(n) neuter, sächlich
(pl) plural, Mehrzahl

A

A la carte a la carte
Aal (m) eel
Aal (m) **grün** boiled eel
Aal (m) **in Dill** (m) eel in dill-sauce
Aal (m) **in Gelee** (n) eel jellied
ab Schiff (n) ex ship
abändern modify
Abänderung (f) modification
abbestellen cancel
Abbestellung (f) cancellation
abbiegen turn off
Abbildung (f) figure
Abc-Flug (verbilligter Flug) (m) abc-flight (advanced booking flight)
Abendessen (n) dinner, supper
Abendessen (n) **mit Tanz** (m) dinner dance
Abendkleidung (f) evening dress
Abendkonzert (n) evening concert
Abendmusikparade (f) tat-too
Abendvorstellung (f) evening performance
Abfahrt (f) departure
Abfahrt (Ski) (f) downhill course, downhill trail, trail, run
Abfahrt (Schiff) (f) sailing
Abfahrtshang (m) ski slope
Abfahrtslauf (m) downhill race
Abfahrtsstelle (f) place of departure
Abfahrtsstrecke (f) run
Abfahrtstafel (f) departure timetable
Abfahrtstag (m) sailing date
Abfahrtszeit (f) time of departure
Abfahrtszeit (Schiff) (f) sailing time
Abfall (m) rubbish, waste
Abfallbeseitigung (f) rubbish removal
abfallen fall of
Abfertigung (Flug etc.) (f) check-in, check-out, registration
Abfertigungsformalitäten (f) check-in formality
abfinden, sich put up (with)
Abflug (m) departure, start, take-off
Abflugtag (m) day of departure

Abflugzeit (f) time of departure
Abfluß (m) drain
abgabefrei duty-free
Abgangsbahnhof (m) departure station
abgelegen off the beaten track, out of the way, remote
abgenutzt worn out
abgrenzbar accruable
abhängen depend on
Abhang (m) slope
abheben draw out, withdraw
abheben von der Bank (f) draw out of the bank account
Abhilfe (f) relief
Abhilfemaßnahme (f) relieve measure
abkochen (Milch) scald
Abkürzung (f) short cut
Ablagefach (n) pigeon hole
Ablagekorb (m) tray
Ablaufdiagramm (n) flow chart
ablaufen expire
Ablauforganisation (f) method and procedures
ablegen (Akte) file
ablehnen refuse
Ablehnung (f) refusal
Abmagerungskur (f) reducing diet, slimming diet treatment
abmelden, sich check out
Abmeldung (f) notice of departure
Abnahme (Entgegennahme) (f) acceptance
Abnahme (f) decline, decrease
abnehmen (entgegenehmen) accept
abnehmen decrease
abnutzen depreciate
Abnutzung (f) depreciation
Abnutzung (f) **durch Gebrauch** (m) wear and tear
Abonnement (n) subscription

abonnieren subscribe
abräumen clear away
Abrechnungsstelle (f) clearing office
Abrechnungszeitraum (m) accounting period
Abreise (f) departure
Abreisedatum (n) date of departure
abreisen (Hotel) check out
Abreisetag (m) day of departure
Abruf (m) call
abrunden round off
Absatz (m) sale
Absatzgebiet (n) market
Absatzlehre (f) marketing
Absatzmarkt (m) outlet
Absatzplan (m) sales forecast
Absatzuntersuchung (f) sales analysis
Absatzweg (m) distribution channel
abschätzen evaluate
Abschaffung (f) abolition
abschalten turn off
Abschied (m) farewell
Abschiedsessen (n) farewell dinner
abschlagen (Golf) tee, tee off
Abschlagstelle (Golf) (f) tee
Abschlagszahlung (f) instalment, partical
Abschleppdienst (m) payment car-tow, recovery service
abschleppen take in tow, tow
Abschleppseil (n) tow-rope
Abschleppwagen (m) breakdown lorry, wrecking car
abschließen negotiate
abschließend final
Abschluß (m) closing, negotiation
Abschlußsumme (f) grand total
Abschmierdienst (m) greasing

9

service
abschmieren greasing
Abschnitt (m) coupon
abschöpfen skim off
abschreiben depreciate, write off
Abschreibung (f) depreciation
abschüssig slopy
abseilen rope down
abseits der Straße (f) off the road
absenden despatch, dispatch
absetzen deduct
absetzen (verkaufen) market
Absetzung (f) deduction
absinken fall of
absperren lock off
abspülen wash up
Abstammung (f) ancestry
Abstecher (m) detour
absteigen put up
Absteigequartier (n) house of accomodation
Abstieg (m) descent
abstimmen reconcile
Abstimmung (f) reconciliation
Abstinenzler (m) teetotaller
Abteil (n) compartment
Abteil (n) **zweiter Klasse** (f) second-class compartment
Abteilungskoch (m) chef de partie
Abteilung (f) department, division
Abteilung (f), **technische** engineering department
Abteilungsleiter (m) department head
abtreten assign
abtrocknen wipe
abwälzen pass on
Abwaschküche (f) dishwashing area
abwechseln vary
abwechslungsreich diversified, lively
abweichend vom üblichen out-of-line
Abweichung (f) variance
Abwertung (f) devaluation
Abwesender (m) absentee
Abwesenheit (f) absenteeism
Abwesenheitsrate (f) absence rate
abzahlen amortize
abziehen deduct, discount, subtract
Abzug (m) allowance, deduction, discount, subtraction
Abzug (Druck) (m) print
abzugsfähig deductible
abzugsfähig, nicht nondeductible
Achse (Auto) (f) axle
Achselhöhle (f) armpit
Achterdeck (n) after-deck
Achtung (f) attention
Administration (f) administration
Adreßbuch (n) address book, directory
Adresse (f) address
Adressliste (f) mailing list
adressieren address
Adressiermaschine (f) addressing machine
ändern alter, amend, change
Änderung (f) alteration, amendment, change
Änderungen (pl. f) **vorbehalten** subject to alteration
ärgern annoy
Ärmelkanal (m) **und Irische See** (f) narrow seas
Aerosoltherapie (f) treatment with aerosols
ärztliche Betreuung (f) medical care
ärztliches Attest (n) doctor's certificate

ärztliches Zeugnis (n) medical certificate
Äsche (f) grayling
äußerlich exterior
Affinitätsgruppe affinity group
Afrika (n) Africa
Agentur agency, travel agency
Ahornsirup (m) maple syrup
Akte (f) file, record
Aktenmappe (f) briefcase
Aktenschrank (m) filing cabinet
Aktentasche (f) briefcase
Aktion (f) capaign
Aktiva (pl.n), **sonstige** other assets
Aktiva (pl.) **und Passiva** (pl.) assets and liabilities
Aktivkonto (n) asset account
Aktivposten (m) asset
Aktivum (n) asset
aktualisieren bring up to date
aktuell up-to-date
Akzept (n) acceptance
akzeptieren accept
Alarmglocke (f) alarm bell
Ale (Bier) (n), **dunkles** mild ale
Ale (Bier) (n), **helles** bitter ale, pale ale
Alkohol (m) alcohol, liquor, spirits
Alkoholausschankzeiten (pl.f) licensed hours, licensing hours
alkoholfrei non-alcoholic
alkoholfreies Getränk (n) soft drink
alkoholisches Getränk (n) alcoholic drink
Allee (f) avenue, boulevard
Alleinvertreter (m) sole agent
Alleinvertretung (f) exclusive agency
allergisch allergic
Allerheiligen All Saints' Day
Allerlei (n) mixture (of food)

alles inbegriffen all included, everything included
Allgemeiner Deutscher Automobilklub (ADAC) German Automobile Club
Almwiese (f) alpine meadow
Alpenpaß (m) pass in the Alps
Alpenstraße (f) alpine road
Alpinist (m) alpine climber
Alse (f) shad
alt old
Altar (m) altar
Altersheim (n) home for old people
altmodisch old-fashioned
Altschnee (m) base snow, old snow
Altstadt (f) old town
am Apparat (Telefon) (m) **bleiben** hold on, hold the line
Amateur (m) amateur
Amerika America
Amerikaner (m) American
Amerikanerin (f) American
Amerikanisch American
Amerikanische Gesellschaft (f) **der Reiseagenturen** (pl.f) American Soiety of Travel Agents (ASTA)
Amerikanischer Hotel- und Motelverband (m) American Hotel and Motel Association
amerikanisches Frühstück (n) American breakfast
Aminosäure (f) amino-acid
amortisieren amortize
amtlich official
anstelle von instead of
Analyse (f) analysis
analysieren analyze
Ananas (f) pineapple
Ananaseis (n) pineapple ice
Ananassaft (m) pineapple-juice
anbieten bid, offer

11

Anblick (m) sight
anbraten parboil, sear
Anchovis (f) anchovy
Anchovisbutter (f) anchovy-butter
Anchovispaste (f) anchovy-paste
Andenkengeschäft (n) souvenir shop
Andrang (m) rush, throng of people
Aneignung (f) occupancy
anerkennen acknowledge, recognize
Anerkennung (f) acknowledg(e)ment, recognition
Anfängerhang (m) ski nursery slope
Anfängerkurs (m) course for beginners
Anfahrtsweg (m) approach road
Anfall (m) attack
Anfangsbuchstabe (m) initial
Anfangsgehalt (n) initial salary
anfassen handle
anfechten avoid
Anfechtung (f) avoidance
anfliegen land at
Anforderung (f) requisition
Anfrage (f) inquiry
Angebot (n) bid, offer, supply
Angebot (n), **verstecktes** hidden offer
Angebotserweiterung (f) diversification
angebrannt burnt
  Angelegenheit (f) concern, fact, matter
Angelfischerei (f) line-fishing
Angelgelegenheit (f) fishing facility
Angelgerät (n) fishing-gear, fishing-tackle
angeln angle, fish
Angeln (n) angling, fishing
Angelschein (m) fishing license

Angelsport (m) fishing
angemessen adequate, fair, reasonable
Angemessenheit (f) adequacy
Angestelltenverpflegung (f) employees meals
Angestellter (m) employee
Angestellter (m), **leitender** top executive
Anglerverein (m) angling club, fishing club
Angliederung (f) affiliation
angrenzend adjacent
Anhängezettel (m) tag
Anhang (m) appendix
Anis (n) anise
Anisplätzchen (n) aniseed cooky
Anker (m) **lichten** weigh anchor
Anker (m) **werfen** cast anchor
Anklage (f) accusation
ankleiden dress
ankochen parboil
ankommen arrive
ankündigen announce
Ankündigung (f) announcement
Ankünfteanzahl (f) number of arrivals
Ankunft (f) arrival
Ankunftsbuch (n) arrival book
Ankunftsdatum (n) date of arrival
Ankunftshalle (f) arrival hall
Ankunftstafel (f) arrival timetable
Ankunftstag (m) day of arrival
Ankunftstermin (m) date of arrival
Ankunftszeit (f) time of arrival
Ankunftszeit (f), **voraussichtliche** probable time of arrival
Anlage (Beifügung) (f) enclosure
Anlage (f) appendix

Anlage (f), bauliche structure
Anlagevermögen (n) capital assets, fixed assets
anlaufen (Seefahrt) call at
Anlaufhafen (m) port of call
Anlegehafen (m) port of call
Anlegen (Geld) invest
Anlegen (Schiff) make fast, moor
Anlegen (Schiff) (n) mooring
Anlegeplatz (m) landing dock
Anlegestelle (f) landing-place, mooring pier
anlernen train
Anlernen (n) training
Anmeldeformular (n) registration form
Anmeldegebühr (f) registration fee
anmelden declare, register
anmelden, sich (Hotel) check-in
Anmeldung (f) declaration, registration
Anmeldung (Hotel) (f) reception
Annahme (Entgegennahme) (f) acceptance
Annahme (Vermutung) (f) assumption
annehmen (entgegen-, hinnehmen) accept
annehmen (aufnehmen) adopt
annehmen (vermuten) assume
Annehmlichkeit (f) amenity
Annonce (f) advertisement (Abk.: ad)
Annulierungsgebühr (f) cancellation fee
Anorak (m) anorak, parka
anordnen arrange, direct
Anordnung (f) arrangement, direction
Anordnung (f), räumliche layout
Anpassungsfähigkeit (f) flexibility
anregen suggest
anregen (Appetit) whet
Anregung (f) suggestion
Anreise (f) journey
Anreisemöglichkeit (f) possibility of travelling
Anreisetag (m) day of arrival
Anreiz (m) incentive
Anruf (m) call
Ansager (m) announcer
ansammeln accumulate
Anschlagbrett (n) bill-board,
Anschlagbrett (n) bulletin board,
Anschlagtafel (f) poster board
anschließend an adjoining
Anschluß (m) connection
Anschlußfahrt (f) connection
Anschlußflug (m) connecting flight
Anschlußstrecke (f) connecting line, connecting route
Anschlußzug (m) connecting train
anschnallen bitte! fasten seat belts
Anschuldigung (f) accusation
Ansehen (n) reputation
Ansichtskarte (f) greetings card, picture postcard
Ansporn (m) incentive
Anspruch (m) cause, claim, demand, requirement, right
anspruchsvoll discerning
anstatt in lien of, instead of
anstellen employ, engage
Anstellung (f) employment, engagement
ansteuern head for
anstrahlen floodlight
Anteil (m) participation, quota, rate
Anteilszahl (f) ratio
Antenne (f) aerial, antenna

Antiquität (f) antique
Antiquitätengeschäft (n) antique shop
antizipative Schuld (f) accrued liability
Antrag (m) application, proposal
Antragsformular (n) application form
Antwort (f) answer, reply
antworten answer, reply
Antwortschein (m), **internationaler** international reply coupon
anweisen direct, instruct
Anweisung (f) direction, instruction
anwendbar applicable
anwendbar, nicht inapplicable
Anwendbarkeit (f) applicability
Anwendersoftware (f) application software
Anwesenheit (f) attendance
Anzahlung (f) deposit
Anzahlung (f)
  verlangen demand a deposit
Anzeige (Inserat) (f) advertisement (Abk.: ad)
anzeigen (inserieren) advertise
Anzeigenspalte (f) avertisement column
Anzeigentarif (m) advertising rate
Anzeigenwerbung (f) press advertising
anzeigepflichtig notifiable
Anziehungskraft (f) appeal, attraction
anzünden kindle, light
Anzug (m) suit
Aperitif (m) aperitif
Apfel (m) apple
Apfel (m) **im Ofen** (m)
  gebacken baked apple, oven-baked apple

Apfel (m) **im Schlafrock** (m) baked apple in puff paste apple turnover
Apfelauflauf (m) apple souffle
Apfelgelee (n) apple jelly
Apfelkompott (n) stewed apples
Apfelkonfiture (f) apple jam
Apfelkuchen (m) apple pie
Apfelküchlein (n) apple fritter
Apfelmus (n) apple sauce
Apfelreis (m) apple rice
Apfelsaft (m) apple juice, sweet cider
Apfelsine (f) orange
Apfelspalte (f) apple fritter
Apfelstrudel (m) apple strudel, covered apple pie
Apfelstückchen (pl. n)
  gewürfelt diced apples
Apfeltasche (f) apple-stuffed turnover
Apfeltorte (f) apple tart
Apfelwein (m) cider, hard cider
Apotheke (f) chemist's shop, pharmacy
Apparat (Telefon) (m) line
Appartement (n) self-contained flat
Appartementhaus (n) apartment house, block of flats
Appartementhotel (n) apart-hotel
Appetit (m) appetite
Appetitanreger (m) appetizer, whet
appetitlich appetizing
Applaus (m) applause
Apres-Ski (n) apres ski
Aprikose (f) apricot
Aprikosenauflauf (m) apricot souffle
Aprikosenröllchen (n),
  warmes baked aprikot roll
Arbeit (f) job, labo(u)r, work
Arbeiter (m) blue collar worker

Arbeitgeber (m) employer
Arbeitgeberverband (m) employers' association
Arbeitnehmer (m) employee
Arbeitnehmervertrag (m) employees' representative
Arbeitsablauf (m) flow of work
Arbeitsablaufanalyse (f) flow process chart, work flow analysis
Arbeitsablaufbogen (m) flow process chart
Arbeitsablaufdiagramm (n) process chart
Arbeitsanalytiker (m) job analyst
Arbeitsanreicherung (f) job enrichment
Arbeitsanweisung (f) instruction card
Arbeitsbedingung (f) working condition
Arbeitsbedingungen (pl. f) work terms
Arbeitsbelastung (f) work load
Arbeitsbereich (m) work area
Arbeitsbewertung (f) job evaluation
Arbeitsbogen (m) work sheet
Arbeitserlaubnis (f) work permit
Arbeitsersparnis (f) labor saving
Arbeitserweiterung (f) job enlargement
Arbeitsfähigkeit (f) ability to work
Arbeitsgemeinschaft (f) association
Arbeitsbegriff (m) grasp
Arbeitsgruppe (f) team
Arbeitshäufung (f) peak load
Arbeitskraft (f) manpower
Arbeitskräfte (pl. f) labor force, work force

Arbeitskräfte (pl. f), **gelernte** skilled manpower
Arbeitsleistung (f) output
arbeitslos unemployed
Arbeitsmarkt (m) labor market
Arbeitsmoral (f) employee morale
Arbeitspapiere (pl. n) working papers
Arbeitsplatz (m) work place
Arbeitsplatzbeschreibung (f) job description, job specification
Arbeitsplatzbewertung (f) performance appraisal
Arbeitsplatzgestaltung (f) work place layout
Arbeitsplatzrotation (f) job rotation
Arbeitsplatzsicherheit (f) job security
Arbeitsplatzstandardisierung (f) job standardization
Arbeitsproduktivität (f) labor productivity
Arbeitsstreitigkeit (f) grievance
Arbeitsstudie (f) job analysis
Arbeitsstunde (f) man hour
Arbeitsstunden (pl. f), **geleistete** hours worked
Arbeitstag (m) man-day
Arbeitsunterlage (f) work sheet
Arbeitsunterlagen (pl. f) working papers
Arbeitsunterweisung (f) job instruction
Arbeitsvereinfachung (f) work simplification
Arbeitsvertrag (m) contract of employment
Arbeitszufriedenheit (f) job satisfaction, work statisfication
Architektur (f) architecture
Arena (f) arena, circus-ring
Argentinien Argentina
Argument (n) argument

argumentieren argue
Arie (f) aria
Arkade (f) arcade
Arm (m) arm
Aroma (n) aroma, flavo(u)r
aromatisch aromatic, spicy
Arrest (m) arrest
Art (f) kind
Artikel (m) commodity
Artischocke (f) artichoke
Artischockenboden (m) bottom of artichoke
Artischockenherz (n) heart of artichoke
Arzt (m), **behandelnder** doctor in attendance
Arzt (m), **diensttuender** doctor on duty
Asche (f) ash
Aschenbecher (m) ashtray
Aspik (n) aspic, jelly
Assistent (m) assistant
Assistent (m) **der Geschäftsleitung** (f) **(Empfang)** assistent manager (front)
Asthma (n) asthma
Atemgymnastik (f) breathing exercises
Atmosphäre (f) atmosphere
Attraktion (f) attraction, appeal, feature
Au-pair-Aufenthalt (m) au pair stay
Auerhahn (m) mountain-cock, wood grouse, grouse, black cock
Aufbau (m) structure
Aufbewahrung (f) **von Wertgegenständen** (pl. m) safe deposit of valuables
Aufbewahrungsschein (m) baggage check
Aufbewahrungsstelle (f) chekkroom
aufbrechen set off

Aufenthalt (m) stay, stop, halt
Aufenthaltsdauer (f) period of stay, time of stay, duration of the stay, length of stay
Aufenthaltserlaubnis (f) residence permit
Aufenthaltsgenehmigung (f) residence permit
Aufenthaltsgutschein (m) board and lodging voucher
Aufenthaltskosten (pl.) cost of board and lodging
Aufenthaltsort (m) residence, whereabouts
Aufenthaltsraum (m) day-room, lounge, hotel lounge
Aufenthaltstag (m) day of stay
Aufenthaltsverlängerung (f) extension of stay
Aufenthaltsvisum (n) temporary residence visa
auferlegen impose on
Auffahrt (f) upward journey
Auffahrunfall (m) nose-to-tail collision
auffordern request
Aufforderung (f) request
Aufführung (f) performance
Aufgabe (f) task
Aufgang (m) way up
aufgeben quit, renounce, give up
aufgeben (Post) mail
aufgliedern itemize
Aufguß (m) infusion
aufheben lift up
aufheben (ungültig machen) avoid
Aufhebung (f) **(ungültig machen)** avoidance
aufhören cease
aufklären (Wetter) clear up
Aufklebezettel (m) sticker
Auflauf (m) souffle
Auflauf (m) **aus Hackfleisch** (n)

und **Kartoffeln** (pl. f) shepherd's pie
auflaufen (ansammeln) accumulate
Auflaufkartoffeln (pl. f) puffed potatoes, souffle-potatoes
Auflaufomelett (n) omelet souffle
Aufmachung (f) make up
aufmerksam attentive
Aufmerksamkeit (f) attention
Aufmerksamkeiten (pl. f) **für Gäste** (pl. m) guests' supplies
Aufnahme (f) reception
Aufnahmekapazität (f) capacity of accomodation
Aufnahmepotential (n) potential of accomodation
aufnehmen raise
aufräumen clean-up
aufrechterhalten maintain
aufrunden round up
aufschieben postpone, defer
Aufschlag (m) surcharge, extra charge, additional charge
aufschließen (Schloß) unlock
Aufschnitt (m) assorted cold meat
Aufschnitt (m) **kalt** cold cuts, cold meat
Aufschnitt gemischt (m) selection of cold cuts, selection of colf meat
Aufschub (m) delay
Aufschwung (m), **geschäftlicher** boom
Aufsicht (f) supervision
Aufsichtsperson (f) supervisor
Aufsichtsratvorsitzender (m) chairman of the board
aufstehen arise, get up
Aufstellkosten (pl.) installation cost
Aufstellung (f) schedule, statement

Aufstieg (m) ascent, rise
auftauen thaw
Auftauen (n) thaw
aufteilen subdivide
Aufteilung (f) subdivision
Auftrag (m) order, commission
Auftrag (m) **erteilen** place an order
auftragen serve
Auftragsgröße (f) lot size
aufwachen wake up
aufwärmen reheat
Aufwand (m) expenditure, expenses
Aufwand (m) **und Ertrag** (m) income and expense
Aufwand (m), **sonstiger** miscellanious expenses, other expenses
Aufwandskonto (n) expenditure account, expense account
aufwendig expensive
Aufwendungen (pl. f), **direkte** departmental expenses
aufwerten up-value
aufzählen enumerate
aufzeichnen note
Aufzeichnung (f) note
aufziehen wind up
Aufzug (m) elevator, lift
Aufzugsschacht (m) elevator shaft
Augenzeuge (m) eye-witness
ausbessern repair, darn
ausbilden train, educate
Ausbilder (m) trainer, training manager
Ausbildung (f) training, education
Ausbildung (f) **am Arbeitsplatz** (m) training on the job
Ausbildungsleiter (m) training manager
Ausbildungsmethode (f) training method

17

Ausbildungsvertrag (m) contract of apprenticeship
Ausbildungszeit (f) apprenticeship
auseinandergehen part
auserlesen exquisite
Ausfahrt (f) outing, way out, exit
Ausfall (m) deficit, deficiency
ausfindigmachen trace
Ausflügler (m) tourist, tripper, day-tripper, excursionist
Ausflug (m) outing, excursion
Ausflugsdampfer (m) excursion steamer
Ausflugsfahrpreis (m) excursion fare
Ausflugsgebiet (n) tour region, excursion area
Ausflugskarte (f) tour ticket, excursion ticket
Ausflugslokal (n) roadside cafe
Ausflugsmöglichkeiten (pl. f) touring facilities, excursion facilities
Ausflugsort (m) place of interest
Ausflugsprogramm (n) tour program, excursion program
Ausflugstarif (m) excursion rate
Ausflugsverkehr (m) tourist traffic, holiday traffic
Ausflugsziel (n) day-trippers' goal, excursionists' goal
ausführen export
Ausführung (f) performance
ausfüllen fill in
Ausfuhr (f) export
Ausfuhrbewilligung (f) export permit
Ausfuhrsperre (f) embargo
Ausfuhrzoll (m) export duty
Ausgabe (Geld) (f) expenditure
Ausgabe (f) issue
Ausgabebüro (n) issuing office

Ausgaben (pl. f) **persönliche** personal expenses
Ausgaben (pl. f) **unvorhergesehene** contingencies
Ausgabenkontrolle (f) control of expenses, expenditure control
Ausgabetag (m) day of issue
Ausgang (m) way out, exit
Ausgangsinterview (n) exit-interview
Ausgangsort (m) point of origin, starting-point, touring centre
Ausgangspunkt (m) starting-point, touring centre
ausgeben (Geld) spend
ausgeben issue
ausgebucht full
ausgelassen (Fett) melted
ausgenommen exempt
ausgestattet mit equipped with
ausgesucht assorted
ausgezeichnet excellent
ausgleichen balance
Ausgrabung (f) excavation
aushändigen hand over
Aushangfahrplan (m) train indicator
Aushilfe (f) extra help, part-timer
Aushilfskellner (m) extra waiter
Aushilfskellner (m) für **Veranstaltungen** (pl. f) banquet extra waiter
auskernen stone
Auskunft (f) **auf Anfrage** (f) information on application
Auskunft (f) **erteilt** information apply to
Auskunftsstelle (f) inquiry office
ausladen unload
Ausland (n) foreign country
Ausland (n), **im** abroad

18

Ausländer (m) alien, foreigner
Ausländerfremdenverkehr (m) international tourist traffic
ausländisch foreign
Auslandsaufenthalt (m) stay abroad
Auslandsflug (m) international flight
Auslandsgast (m) foreign guest, foreign visitor
Auslandsgast (m) oversea(s) visitor
Auslandskrankenversicherung (f) health insurance for abroad
Auslandsreise (f) journey abroad, trip abroad
Auslandsreisender (m) tourist abroad
Auslandstarif (m) foreign rate
Auslandstelegramm (n) oversea(s) telegram
Auslandstourist (m) foreign tourist, oversea(s) tourist
Auslandswerbung (f) advertising abroad, publicity campaign abroad
Auslaß (m) outlet
auslasten utilize
auslaufen (ausrinnen) leak
auslaufen (Schiff) put up to sea, leave port
Auslegung (f) construction
ausleihen lend
Auslöser (m) shutter-release, trigger
Ausnahme (f) exception
ausnehmen exempt
auspacken unpack
Ausreise (f) **bei der** on leaving the country
Ausreisesichtvermerk (n) exit visa
Ausreisevisum (n) exit visa
ausrollen (Teig) roll
Ausrüstung (f) outfit

Ausschank (m) pub, public house, saloon, saloon-bar, tavern
Ausschank (m) **alkoholischer Getränke** (pl. n) sale of alcoholic drinks
Ausschanklizenz (alkoholische Getränke) (f) licence, fully licensed
ausscheiden eliminate
Ausscheidung (f) elimination
Ausschiffung (f) debarkation
Ausschiffungsgebühr (f) disembarkment charge
ausschreiben write out
ausschütten distribute
Ausschuß (m) committee
Außenbord-Motorboot (n) outboard motor boat
Außendienst (m) field work
Außenkabine (f) outside room
Außenseiter (m) outsider
Außenvertreter (m) outside representative
Außenwerbung (f) outdoor advertising
außer Kraft ineffective
außerhalb exterior
Aussicht (f) view
Aussichtsfenster (n) observation window, wide-vision window
Aussichtsturm (m) observation tower
Ausspannen (n) relaxation
Ausstattung (f) equipment, make-up, outfit
Aussteigebahnhof (m) arrival station
aussteigen alight, get off
aussteigen (Flugzeug) deplane
ausstellen display, exhibit
ausstellen (Dokument) issue
Aussteller (m) exhibitor
Ausstellung (Dokument) (f) issue
Ausstellung (f) exhibition

Ausstellungsgelände (n) exhibition grounds
Ausstellungsort (Dokument) (m) place of issue
Ausstellungsstand (m) exhibition stand
Austausch (m) exchange
austauschen swap
Austauschgutschein (m) exchange voucher
Auster (f) oyster
Austernbank (f) oyster-bank oysterbed
Austernpark (m) oyster-farm
Australien Australia
Ausverkauf (m) sale, sellout
ausverkauft full, sold out
auswählen select
auswärts outward
Auswahl (f) assortment, choice, range, selection
Ausweichangebot (n) alternative offer
Ausweichstelle (f) passing-place
Ausweis (m) admission card, identification card, legitimation, membership card
Ausweispapier (n) identification paper
Auswertung (f) evaluation
Auszahlung (f) payment
Ausziehbett (n) pull-out bed
ausziehen (Mantel) take off
ausziehen, sich undress
Auszubildender (m) apprentice, trainee
Auszug (m) abstract
Auto (n) car, motor-car
Autoabfahrtsstelle (f) town terminal
Autoanhänger (m) trailer
Autoausfahrt (f) exit drive
Autobahn (f) driveway, freeway, motorway
Autobahneinfahrt (f) access road
Autobahnausfahrt (f) exit road
Autobahngebühr (f) motorway toll, toll
Autobahnhof (m) bus and coach station
Autobahnhotel (n) motorway hotel
Autobahnraststätte (f) motorway restaurant
Autobahnzubringer (m) feeder road, motorway feeder road
Autobeförderung (f) conveyance of cars
Autobus (m) bus
Autobusbetrieb (m), **städtischer** urban bus service
Autodach-Gepäckträger (m) roof rack
Autoeinfahrt (f) way in
Autofähre (f) car ferry
Autofahrer (m) motorist
Autofahrt (f) car ride, motor ride, motoring trip
Autoführer (m) motoring guide
Autogepäckträger (m) luggage rack
Autohilfe (f) motorist's roadside assistance service
Autohupe (f) hooter
Autokarte (f) road map
Autokino (n) drive-in cinema
Automat (m) penny-in-the-slot, slot machine
Automatenrestaurant (n) self-service restaurant with slot machines
Automatenverkauf (m) automatic selling
Automation (f) automation
automatisieren automate
Automobildienst (m) automobile service
Automobilclub (m) motor club
Autonummernschild (n) licence

plate
Autorallye (f) motor-rally
Autoreise (f) motoring journey, motoring trip
Autoreisender (m) motoring toursit
Autoreisezug (m) car-carrier train
Autoreisezug (Schlafwagen) (m) car sleeper train
Autoreisezug-Service (m) motorail
Autorennen (n) motor race
Autoschlüssel (m) car key
Autostopper (m) hitch-hiker
Autostraße (f) driveway, motor road
Autotour (f) motoring trip
Autounfall (m) motor accident
Autoverkehr (m) automobile traffic, car traffic, motor traffic
Autoverladung (bei Schiffen) (f) roll on - roll off, car-loading
Autoverleih (m) car hire (rental) service
Autovermietung (f) **an Selbstfahrer** (pl. m) self-drive car hire service
avisieren advise, inform, notify
Avocadobirne (f) avocado pear

B

Babysitter (m) baby-sitter
Babytragekorb (m) infant's carrying basket
Bachforelle (f) brook-trout
Backblech (n) cookie sheet
backen bake, fry
backen, in der Schale (f) bake in their jackets
Backhuhn (n) fried chicken
Backofen (m) oven
Backpflaume (f) prune
Backpulver (n) yeast powder
Bad (Wanne) (n) bath
Bad (n) **medizinisches** medicinal bath
Badeanlage (f) bathing facility
Badeanstalt (f) bathing establishment, swimming-pool
Badeanzug (m) bathing costume, bathing suit, bathing suit, swimsuit
Badearzt (m) spa doctor
Badebucht (f) cove for bathing
Badefreuden (pl. f) seaside pleasures
Badegast (m) bather, watering-place visitor
Badehaube (f) bathing cap
Badehose (f) bathing shorts, bathing trunks, slips, trunks
Badekur (f) course of treatment at a spa, cure at a spar
Bademantel (m) bathing gown, bathrobe
Badematte (f) bath mat
Bademeister (Heilbad) (m) bath attendant
Bademeister (m) swimming master
Bademütze (f) bathing cap
baden (i. Freien) bath
Baden (n) **verboten!** bathing prohibited
Badeort (m) bathing resort, spa, watering-place
Badeplatz (m) bathing place
Badesaison (f) bathing season
Badesteg (m) bathing pier
Badestrand (m) bathing beach
Badetasche (f) beach-bag
Badetuch (n) bath towel
Badewärter (m) beach-guard, life-guard
Badewanne (f) bathtub

Badezimmer (n) bathroom
Badezimmer (n), **gemeinsames** shared bathroom
Bäcker (m) baker
Bäderbehandlung (f) balneotherapy
Bäderwesen (n) balneology
Bahn- oder Busanschluß (m) surface connection
Bahn-Bus-Verkehr (m) surface transport
Bahn-Schiffsreise (f) rail-steamer journey
Bahnbus (m) railway bus
Bahnfahrt (f) railway journey, train journey
Bahnhof (m) railway station
Bahnhofsaufsicht (f) station superintendant
Bahnhofsbuchhandlung (f) railway bookstand
Bahnhofsgaststätte (f) station restaurant
Bahnhofshalle (f) station hall
Bahnhofshotel (n) station hotel
Bahnhofsmission (f) Traveller's Aid Office
Bahnhofsvorstand (m) stationmaster
Bahnhofsvorsteher (m) stationmaster
Bahninklusivreise (f) all-in journey by rail
Bahnnetz (n) railway network
Bahnpersonal (n) railroad staff, railway staff
Bahnpostamt (n) station post office
bahnpostlagernd poste restante railway station
Bahnreise (f) railway journey, train journey
Bahnschalter (m) rail-ticket office, ticket office
Bahnstation (f) railway station

Bahnsteig (m) platform
Bahnsteigkarte (f) platform ticket
Bahnsteigschaffner (m) ticket-collector
Bahnsteigsperre (f) ticket barrier
Bahnstrecke (f) railway line
Bahnübergang (m) grade crossing, railway level, level crossing
Bahnverbindung (f) rail connection
Baiser (n) meringue
Balkon (m) balcony
Balkonzimmer (n) room with balcony
Ballettaufführung (f) ballet performance
Ballsaal (m) ballroom
Banane (f) banana
Bananen (pl. f) **flambiert** flamed bananas
Band (Buch) (m) volume
Bandnudeln (pl. f) ribbon maccaroni
Bank (f) bank
Bankett (n) banquet
Bankettgeschäft (n) banquet business
Bankettinformation (f) function sheet
Bankettküche (f) banquet kitchen
Bankettleiter (m) banquet manager
Bankettoberkellner (m) banquet headwaiter
Bankfeiertag (m) bank holiday
Bankkonto (n) bank account
bankrott bankrupt
Bankrott (m) bankruptcy
bar cash
Bar (f) bar
bar bezahlen pay cash

Barauslage (f) out-of-pocket expense
Barbe (f) barbel
Bareinkauf (m) cash purchase
Bargeld (n) cash
Bargeldkasse (f) petty cash
Bargeldstrom (m) cash flow
Bargerät (n) bar utensil
Barhocker (m) stool
Barkasse (f) launch, motor launch
Barkellner (m) cocktail bar tender
Barliquidität (f) available cash
Barmann (m) barman
Barometer (m) barometer
Barsch (m) perch
Barscheck (m) open check
Bartheke (f) bar counter
Barverkauf (m) cash sale
Barwert (m) actual cash value
Barwert (m) cash value
Barzahlung (f) cash payment
Basilika (f) basilica
Basilikum (n) basil
Basis (f) basis
Bau (m) construction
Bau, im under construction
Bauch (m) stomach
Bauerngulasch (n) beef stew peasant style
Bauernhaus (n) farmhaus
Bauernhof (m) farm
Bauernschinken (m) farmer's ham
Bauernstube (f) farmhouse room
Baugenehmigung (f) building permit
Baummelone (f) pawpaw
Bauplatz (m) building lot, building site
Baustelle (f) construction site
Bauwerk (n), **historisches** historical building

Bauwert (m) building cost
Bayern Bavaria
beachten mind
beachten, nicht ignore
beanspruchen claim
beanstanden object to
Beanstandung (f) objection
beantragen propose, move
Bearbeitungsgebühr (f) charge for handling
beaufsichtigen supervise
beauftragen order, commission
Beauftragter (m) representative, agent
Bechamelsoße (f) bechamel sauce
Becher (m) mug
Bedarf (m) need
Bedarfshaltestelle (f) request stop
Bedarfsmeldung (f) purchase requisition
Bedarfsschätzung (f) estimate of demand
bedauern regret
Bedeutung (f) meaning
bedienen attend, serve, waiton
Bedienung (f) waitress, attendance
Bedienung (f) **inbegriffen** service included
Bedienungsgeld (n) service, service charge
Bedienungspersonal (n) service staff
Bedienungszuschlag (m) service charge, extra charge for service
bedingen condition
Bedingung (f) condition
Bedrohung, tätliche (f) assault
Bedürfnis (n) requirement, want
Beefsteak (n) beefsteak, steak
Beefsteak (n) **doppeltes** double-

23

sized steak
Beefsteak Tartar (n)   tartare steak
Beefsteak a la Meier (n)   beefsteak with fried egg
Beefsteak a la tartare (n)   beefsteak tartare style
Beefsteakpastete (f)   beef pie
beeinflussen   influence
beeinträchtigen   impair, interfere, disturb
Beeinträchtigung (f)   disturbance
beendigen   terminate
Beendigung (f)   termination
Beere (f)   berry
befähigen   qualify
befahrbar   passable, usable
Befahrbarkeit (f)   navigability, passability
befahren (Schiff)   navigate
befördern   forward
Beförderung (f)   transport, carriage, conveyance
Beförderung (f) **auf dem Luftweg** (m)   air carriage
Beförderungsbedingung (f)   condition of conveyance
Beförderungskosten (pl.)   transport charges
Beförderungsmittel (n)   conveyance, means of transportation
Beförderungspreis (m)   transport charge
befreien   relieve
befreit   exempt
befriedigen   satisfy
Befugnis (f)   authority
begeben, sich   go to
begießen, mit Fett (n)   baste
Begleitbrief (m)   couvering letter
begleiten   accompany
begleitende Kinder (pl. n)   accompanying children
begleitende Person (f)   accompanying person
Begleitung (f)   accompanying person
begrenzen   limit
Begrenzung (f)   limitation
Behälter (m)   container
behaglich   snug, cosy
Behaglichkeit (f)   cosiness
Behandlung (f)   treatment
behaupten   affirm, assert
Behauptung (f)   statement, affirmation, assertion
beherbergen   lodge, put up, accomodate
Beherbergungsabteilung (f)   rooms department
Beherbergungsbereich (m)   room division department
Beherbergungsbetrieb (m)   establishment of the hotel trade
Beherbergungskapazität (f)   accomodation capacity
Beherbergungsstatistik (f)   rooms statistic
Beherbergungsvertrag (m)   contract of accomodation
bei (Adresse)   care of (c/o)
Beifahrer (m)   assistant driver
Beifall (m)   applause
beifügen   annex, attach, enclose
Beifuß (m)   tarragon
Beigeschmack (m)   aftertaste, tang
Beilage (f)   side dish, trimmings
Beilagenwerbung (f)   insert advertising
Bein (n)   leg
Beinfleisch (n)   rib of beef boiled
Beisammensein (n)   gathering
beistehen   assist
beitreten   join, adopt

beiwohnen attend
Bekannter (m) acquaintance
Bekanntgabe (f) notice, notification
bekanntgeben notice, announce
Bekanntmachung (f) announcement
Bekanntschaft (f) acquaintance
Beköstigung (f) board
belästigen molest, annoy, disturb
Belästigung (f) molestation, nuisance, annoyance, disturbance
belasten charge, debit
Belastungsspitze (f) peak load
belaufen auf, sich amount to
belebt animated, busy
Beleg (m) voucher
Belegschaft (f) work force
belegt (Telefon) busy
Belegung (f) occupancy, reservation
Belegungsprozentsatz (m) percentage of occupancy
beleidigen insult, offend
Beleidigung (f) affront, insult
beleuchten illuminate
Beleuchtung (f) light
belichten (Foto) expose
Belichtungsmesser (m) exposure meter
Beliebtheitsgrad (m) popularity rate
belohnen reward, award
Belohnung (f) reward, award
bemängeln complain
benachbart adjacent
benachrichtigen inform, advise
Benachrichtigung (f) notification, advice
Benehmen (n) behavio(u)r, performance
benehmen, sich behave
benennen name

Benützer (m) user
Benzin (n) petrol, fuel, gasoline
Benzinkanister (m) petrol can, gasoline can
Benzinschein (m) petrol voucher, gasoline coupon
Benzintank (m) petrol tank, fuel tank
Benzinverbrauch (m) petrol consumption
beobachten observe
Beobachtung (f) observation
bequem comfortable
Bequemlichkeit (f) comfort
beraten advise
Berater (m) advisor, consultant
Beratungsdienst (m) advisory service
berechnen invoice, bill, calculate, charge
Berechnung (f) calculation
berechtigen justify
Berechtigung (f) justification, right
Bereich (m) range
Bereichsergebnis (n) departmental profit
Bereichsergebnis (n) **Speisen** (pl. f) **und Getränke** (pl. n) food an beverage profit
Bereichsergebnissumme (f) profit from operated departments
Bereichsgewinn (m) brutto departmental profit
bereisen perambulate
bereit ready
bereitstellen furnish
Berg (m) mountain
Berg- und Talfahrt (f) upward and downward journey
bergauf uphill
Bergausrüstung (f) climbing equipment
Bergbahn (f) mountain railway

Bergdorf (n) mountain village
Bergfahrt (f) upward journey
Bergführer (m) mountain guide
Berggasthof (m) mountain inn
Berggipfel (m) mountain peak, mountain top
Berghotel (n) mountain hotel, mountain lodge
Berghütte (f) mountain cabin, mountain hut
Bergpaß (m) mountain pass, defile
Bergrestaurant (n) mountain restaurant
Bergschuh (m) climbing boot
Bergsee (m) mountain lake
Bergstation (f) top terminal, unloading station
Bergsteigen (n) mountaineering, rock-climbing
Bergsteiger (m) mountain climber, mountaineer
Bergsteigerausrüstung (f) mountaineering equipment
Bergsteigerschule (f) mountaineering school
Bergstraße (f) mountain road
Bergtour (f) mountain tour
Bergwacht (f) mountain rescue service
Bergwanderung (f) mountain hike
Bergwiese (f) mountain meadow
Bericht (m) report
berichten report, advise
berichtigen adjust, correct
Berichtigung (f) adjustment
Berichtigungsbuchung (f) adjusting entry
Berichtswesen (n), **internes** internal reporting
Berliner Pfannkuchen (m) Berlin doughnut

Berner Platte (f) sauerkraut or string beans with meat and sausage
Bernstein (m) amber
Beruf (m) occupation, profession
Berufsausbildung (f) vocational training
Berufskrankheit (f) occupational illness
Besatzung (f) crew
beschädigen injure
beschäftigen employ, engage
beschäftigt busy
Beschäftigung (f) employment, engagement, occupation, volume
Beschäftigung (f), **saisonale** seasonal employment
Beschäftigungsgrad (m) operating rate, utilization of capacity, volume, activity level
Beschaffenheit (f) quality
Bescheidenheit (f) modesty
Bescheinigung (f) certificate
beschleunigen accelerate
beschließen decide
Beschließerin (f) matron
Beschluß (m) decision
Beschränkung (f) restriction
beschreiben describe
Beschreibung (f) description, specification
Beschwerde (f) complaint, grievance
Beschwerdebuch (n) complaints book
beschweren aggrieve
beschweren, sich complain
beseitigen remove
Besen (m) broom
besetzt full, occupied, taken
besetzt (Telefon) busy, engaged
besichtigen inspect, perambulate

Besichtigungsfahrt (f) sightseeing excursion
Besichtigungsreise (f) perambulation
Besitz (m), **ungestörter** quiet enjoyment
Besitzerin (f) landlady
Besitzgesellschaft (f) holding company
besonder(er, e, es, s) extra
besorgt anxious
Besprechung (f) conference
bestätigen acknowledge, affirm, confirm, reconfirm, verify
Bestätigung (f) acknowledg(e)ment, affirmation, confirmation, reconfirmation, verification
Bestandsaufnahme (f) inventory taking, stocktaking
Bestandsaufnahme (f), **körperliche** physical inventory
Bestandskontrolle (f) inventroy control
Bestandsmenge (f), **festgelegte** par stock
Bestandsüberwachung (f) stock control
Bestandsveränderung (f) change in stocks
Bestandsverzeichnis (n) inventory
Bestandteil (m) part
Bestattungsunternehmen (n) undertaker
bestechen bribe
Bestechung (f) bribe
Bestechungsgeld (n) bribe
Besteck (n) cutlery
bestehen aus consist of
Besteigung (f) ascent
Bestellaufnahme (f) ordertaking
bestellen order
bestellen, telefonisch book by telephone

Bestellformular (n) order form
Bestellhäufigkeit (f) ordering rate
Bestellkopie (f) order copy
Bestellkosten (pl.), **jährlich** annual ordering costs
Bestellmenge (f) order quantity
Bestellmenge (f), **Berechnung** (f) **der wirtschaftlichen** calculation of an economic order quantity
Bestellscheinblock (m) order pad
Bestellung (f) booking, order, requisition
Bestellung (f), **telefonische** order by telephone
Bestellungen, Anzahl (f) **der jährlichen** annual placing of orders
Bestellverfahren (n) ordering procedure, reorder system
besteuern tax
Besteuerung (f) taxation
bestimmen determine
bestimmt definite
Bestimmungsbahnhof (m) destination station
Bestimmungsflughafen (m) airport of destination
Bestimmungshafen (m) port of call
Bestimmungsland (n) country of destination
Bestimmungsort (m) place of destination, destination
Bestrahlung (f) heat therapy
bestreuen powder, sprinkle
Besuch (m) visit
besuchen visit
Besucher(m) visitor
Besucherbalkon (m) observation platform
Besucherkarte (f) visitors' card

Besuchervisum (n)   visitor visa
Besuchszeiten (pl. f)   visiting hours
beteiligen, sich   participate
Beteiligung (f)   participation
Betrag (m)   amount
Betrag (m), **aufgelaufen**   accumulated amount
betragen   amount
betreten   enter
Betreuung (f)   care
Betreuung (f), **persönliche**   individual care
Betrieb (m)   business, company, organization
betrieblicher Mittagstisch (m)   food service
Betriebsabteilungen (pl. f), **sonstige**   other operated departments
Betriebsanalyse (f)   operations analysis
Betriebsanalytiker (m)   operations analyst
Betriebsausgabe (f)   business expense
Betriebsberater (m)   management consultant, business consultant
Betriebsbesichtigung (f)   field trip
Betriebsergebnis (n)   operating profit, operating results, results from operations
Betriebsergebnisrechnung (f)   operating statement
Betriebserweiterung (f)   increase in capacity, capacity increase
Betriebsferien (pl.)   staff holiday
betriebsfertig   ready for use
Betriebsführung (f)   management, top management
Betriebsführung (f), **wissenschaftliche**   scientific management
Betriebsfunktion (f)   activity

Betriebsgewinn (m) operating profit
Betriebskapital (n)   capital, working capital
Betriebsklima (n)   working climate
Betriebskosten (pl.)   operating cost, operating expenses
Betriebsmaximum (n)   maximum capacity
Betriebsmittel (n)   working fund
Betriebsrat (m)   labor committee
Betriebsschluß (m)   closing hour
Betriebsstätte (f)   outlet
Bestriebssystem (n)   operating system
Betriebsverlust (m)   operating loss
Betriebsvermögen (n)   assets
Betriebszeit (f)   hours of service, operating months
Betriebszugehörigkeit (f)   company seniority
betrügen   betray
Betrug (m)   betrayal
Bett (n)   bed, berth, sleeping-berth
Bettcouch (f)   studio couch, bed-couch, divan
Bettüberzug (m)   bedspread
Bettvorleger (m)   bedside rug
Bettwäsche (f)   bed-linen
Bettzeug (n)   bedding
Beute (f)   quarry
Bevölkerung (f)   population
Bevölkerungsdichte (f)   population density
bevollmächtigen   authorize
Bevollmächtigter (m)   representative
bevorraten   keep in stock
bevorschussen   advance
bevorzugen   prefer
bevorzugt   favourite
Bewachung (f)   guard

bewegen move
beweglich movable
Bewegungsstudie (f) motion study
Beweis (m) proof
Bewerber (m) applicant
Bewerbung (f) application, employment application
Bewerbungsbogen (m) application form
bewerten evaluate, value
Bewertung (f) appraisal, evaluation
Bewilligung (f) grant
bewirten cater for
bewirten, festlich feast
Bewirtung (f) entertainment
Bewirtungsspesen (pl. f) entertainment expense
bewölkt cloudy
Bewohner (m) resident
bezahlen pay
Bezahlung (f) payment
bezeichnen describe
Bezeichnung (f) description
beziehen auf, sich refer
Beziehung (f) relation
Beziehungen (pl. f), **zwischenmenschliche** human relations
Bezirk (m) area, district
Bezugnahme (f) reference
bezugsfertig ready for occupancy
bezweifeln doubt
Bibliothek (f) library
Bidet (n) bidet
Bier (n) beer
Bier (Lager-) (n) lager
Bier (n) **vom Faß** (n) beer on tap, beer on draft, beer on draught
Bier (n), **deutsches helles (dunkles)** German light (dark) beer
Bier (n), **dunkles** dark beer, porter
Bier (n), **dunkles (schwächeres)** stout beer
Bier (n), **englisches** ale (pale ale)
Bier (n), **helles** light beer, pale ale
Bier (n), **offenes** beer on tap, beer on draft, beer on draught
Bierausschank (m) ale-house, beer-shop
Bierfest (n) beer festival
Biergarten (m) beer-garden
Bierkeller (m) beer-cellar
Bierkrug (in Form eines Mannes) (m) toby jug
Bierlokal (n) public house
Bierstube (f) beer saloon, taproom
bieten bid
Bilanz (f) balance, balance sheet
Bilanz (f), **konsolidierte** consolidated balance sheet
Bilanzanalyse (f) statement analysis
Bilanzprüfung (f) balance sheet audit
Bildprospekt (m) illustrated booklet
Bildschirm (m) screen
Bildungsaufenthalt (m) educational stay
Bildungsreise (f) educational tour
Bildungsurlaub (m) educational holiday
Billardzimmer (n) billiard-room
Billett (n) ticket
billig cheap, inexpensive, low-priced, reasonable
billigen approve, authorize
bindend obligatory
Binnenflugverkehr (m)

domestic air traffic
Binnenhafen (m)   inland harbour, river port
Binnenland (n)   interior
Binnenschiffahrt (f)   inland navigation
Binnentarif (m)   internal tariff
Binnenverkehr (m)   inland carriage
Birchermüsli (n)   Swiss porridge with fresh fruit
Birkhahn (m)   heath-cock, black-cock
Birkhenne (f)   heath-hen, moor-hen
Birkhuhn (n)   black grouse
Birne (f)   pear
bis heute   up-to-date
Biskotten (pl. f)   lady fingers
Biskottentorte (f)   lady finger cake
Biskuit (m) **mit Weinschaum** (m)   biscuit in wine sauce
Biskuitrolle (f)   sponge (Swiss) roll
Biskuittorte (f)   fancy-cake of biscuit
Bismarckhering (m)   marinated herring, soused herring
Bitte (f)   request
Bitte anschnallen!   fasten seat belts
Bitte nicht berühren!   please do not touch
Bitte nicht stören!   do not disturb
bitten   request
bitten um   ask for
bitter   bitter
Bläßhuhn (n)   water hen
Blätterteig (m)   puff-paste
Blätterteiggebäck (n)   puff pastry
Blätterteigpastetchen (n)   patty, puff-paste patty

Blätterteigpastete (f)   filled puff pastry, large patty, large puff-paste pie, vol-au-vent
Blätterteigpastete (f) **mit Geflügelfüllung**   large puff-paste pie stuffed with chicken and mushrooms
Blätterteigstengelchen (n)   puff-paste stick
Blankofahrschein (m)   blank ticket
Blatt (n)   folio, leaf
Blaupause (f)   blue print
Blauschimmelkäse (m)   Stilton (cheese)
bleiben, am Apparat (Telefon) (m)   hold on, hold the line
bleiben, auf dem laufenden   keep up to date
Blick (m)   look, view
Blick (m) **auf**   overlooking
blicken   look
Blickfang (m)   ey appeal
Blitz (m)   lightning
Blitzlichtbirne (f)   flash bulb
Blitzwürfel (m)   flash cube
Blumenhändler (m)   florist
Blumenkohl (m)   cauliflower
Blumenkohl (m) **gratiniert**   cauliflower browned
Blumenkohlcremesuppe (f)   cream of cauliflower
Blumenkohlsalat (m)   cauliflower salad
Blumenkohlsuppe (f)   cauliflower soup
Blumenladen (m)   flower shop
Blumenschale (f)   jardiniere
Blumenständer (m)   jardiniere
Blumenstand (m)   flower stand
Blumenstrauß (m)   bunch of flowers (bouquet)
blutig gebraten   rare, underdone
Blutübertragung (f)   blood transfusion

Blutvergiftung (f) blood poisoning
Blutwurst (f) black pudding
Bob (m) bob
Bobbahn (f) bob run
Bobschlitten (m) bobsled
Bobsport (m) bobsledding
Boccia-Bahn (f) boccie-court
Boden (m) ground
Bodenrenke (f) blue char
Bodensatz (m) sediment
Bodenseefelchen (n) felchen from Lake Constance
Bodenstewardeß (f) gound hostess
Bö (f) gust
Bogenschießen (n) archery
Bohne (f) bean
Bohne (f), **dicke** broad bean
Bohne (f), **grüne** flageolet, French bean, green bean, haricot bean, runner bean
Bohne (f), **rote** red bean
Bohne (f), **weiße** white bean
Bohneneintopf (m), **brasilianischer** Brazilian bean-stew
Bohnenkaffee (m), **gemahlener** ground coffee
Bohnenpüree (n) puree of beans
Bohnensalat (m), **grüner** French beans salad
Bohnensuppe (f) haricot soup, soup with white beans
Bohnensuppe (f), **weiße** white bean-soup
Bon (m) coupon
Bonität (f) ability to pay
Boom (m) boom
Boot (n) boat
Bootfahren (n) boating
Bootsanhänger (Auto) (m) boat trailer
Bootsdeck (n) boat deck
Bootsfahrt (f) boat-ride, boat trip, row
Bootshaus (n) boat-house
Bootssteg (m) landing-stage
Bootsverleih (m) boat-hire
Bootsvermietung (f) boat-hire
Bord (Schiff) (m) board
Bord (m), **an** on board
Bordausweis (m) boarding pass (card)
Bordbuch (n) log-book
Bordeauxwein (m) claret
Bordfest (n) festivity on board (ship)
Bordkarte (f) boarding pass (card)
Bordmechaniker (m) flight engineer
Bordpersonal (n) crew
Bordspiel (n) ship game, deck game
Bordzeitung (f) ship's newspaper
Botanischer Garten Botanical Garden
Botengang (m) errand
Botschaft (f) message
Botschaft (Diplomatie) (f) embassy
Bouillon (f) broth, clear soup, hot broth
Bouillon (f) **mit Ei** (n) beef broth with egg
Bouillon (f) **mit gebackenen Erbsen** (pl. f) soup with fried peas
Boutique (f) boutique
Bowle (f) claret-cup, wine soup, cold punch
Bowling (n) bowling
Bräuche (pl. m) manners
bräunen bask
Branchentelefonbuch (n) classified telephone directory
Brandschutzbestimmungen (pl. f) fire regulations

Brandung (f) surf
Brandungsreiten (n) surf-riding
brasilianischer Bohneneintopf (m) Brazilian bean-stew
Brasse (f) sea-bream
braten fry
Braten (m) joint, roast
braten, auf dem Rost (m) barbecue
braten, zu stark overcook
Bratenplatte (f) platter
Bratensoße (f) gravy
Brathähnchen (m) roast chicken
Brathühnchen (n) broiler
Brathuhn (n) roast chicken
Bratkartoffeln (pl. f) fried potatoes, saute potatoes
Bratkartoffeln (pl. f) **mit Zwiebeln** (pl. f) butterfried potatoes, with onions
Bratofen (m) oven
Bratpfanne (f) frying-pan, skillet
Bratwürstchen (n) fried sausage
Bratwürstchen (n), **mit Sauerkraut** grilled sausages with sauerkraut
Bratwurst (f) butterfried sausage, pan fried pork sausage, roast sausage
Brauch (m) custom, usage
brauchbar usable
brauchen require
Brauchtum (n) folklore
Brauerei (f) brewery
Braunschweiger Wurst (f) Brunswick sausage
Brause (f) pop
Brause (Dusche) (f) shower
Brauselimonade (f) fizzed lemonade
Brechbohne (f), **junge** string bean
Brechreiz (m) nausea

Brei (m) mash, pap
breiig pappy
Breite (f) width
Breitling (m) whitebait
Brennöl (n) kerosene
Bretzel (f) pretzel
Bridge (n) bridge
Briefkasten (m) letter-box, mailbox
Brieflocher (m) letter punch
Briefmarke (f) postal stamp, stamp
Briefmarkenautomat (m) stamp machine
Brieforder (m) letter file
Briefpapier (n) letter-paper, note-paper
Brieftasche (f) wallet
Briefträger (m) mailman (amerik.), postman
Briefumschlag (m) envelope
Briefversand (m) letter service
Briefwechsel (m) correspondence
Brise (f) breeze
Britischer Hotel und Gaststättenverband (m) British Hotels and Restaurants Association

Britischer Verband (m) **für Reise** (f) **und Urlaub** (m) British Travel and Holiday Association
brodeln lassen simmer
Brötchen (n) bun, roll
Brokkoli (pl.) sprouts
Brombeere (f) blackberry, brambleberry
Broschüre (f) booklet, brochure, pamphlet
Brot (n) bread
Brot (n), **geröstet mit heißem Käse** (m) Welsh rabbit (rarebit)
Brot (n) **und Butter** (f) bread

and butter
Brot (n), **altbackenes** stale bread
Brot (n), **belegtes** sandwich
Brot (n), **belegtes einfaches** open sandwich
Brot (n), **dunkles** brown bread
Brotkorb (m) bread-basket
Brotlaib (m) loaf of bread
Brotpudding (m), bread and butter pudding
Brotscheiben (pl. f) **hart geröstet** Melbatoast
Brotschnitte (f) **geröstet und garniert** canape
Brotzeit (f) elevenses, midmorning snack
Bruch (Geschirr) (m) breakage
Bruchlandung (f) crash landing
Bruder (m) brother
Brücke (f) bridge
Brückenzoll (m) bridge toll
brühen scald
Brunch (m) brunch
Brunnen (m) fountain, spring
Brunnenkresse (f) nasturtium
Brunnenkur (f) treatment at a spa
Brust (f) breast
Brust (f), **Bruststück (Küche)** (n) brisket
Bruststreifen (pl. m) **vom Huhn** (n) strips of chicken breast
brutto gross
Bruttoabteilungsgewinn (m), **Verpflegung** (f) food and beverage profit
Bruttobetrag (m) gross amount
Bruttobetriebsergebnis (n) gross operating profit
Bruttoeinkommen (n) gross income
Bruttogewicht (n) gross weight
Bruttogewinn (m) gross profit
Bruttolohn (m) gross pay

Bruttopreis (m) gross price
Bruttoumsatz (m) gross sales
Buch (n) book
buchen book, enter, make an entry reserve
Buchführung (f) accounting, audit, bookkeeping
Buchführungsfehler (m) bookkeeping error
Buchhändler (m) bookseller
Buchhalter (m) accountant, bookkeeper
Buchhaltung (f) accounting
Buchhaltungsabteilung (f) accounting department
Buchhaltungsleiter (m) chief accountant
Buchhandlung (f) bookshop
Buchinventur (f) book inventory, perpetual inventory
Buchprüfer (m) auditor
Bucht (f) bay
Buchung (f) booking, entry, bookkeeping entry
Buchungsabteilung (f) booking department
Buchungsbeleg (m) journal voucher
Buchungsgebühr (f) booking charge
Buchungsmaschine (f) accounting machine, bookkeeping machine
Buchungsnummer (f) reservation number
Buchungsposten (m) bookkeeping entry
Buchungstermin (m) date of booking
Buchverlust (m) book loss
Buchweizen (m) buckwheat
Buchwert (m) book value
Budget (n) budget
Budget (n) **der betrieblichen Aufwendungen** (pl. f) opera-

ting budget
Budgetkontrolle (f) budgetary control
Budgetkosten (pl.) estimated cost
Bücher (pl. n) **führen** keep books, maintain records
Büchsenfleisch (n) tinned meat
Büchsenöffner (m) tin opener
Bückling (m) bloater, kipper
Büffet (n) refreshment bar
Büffetier (m) bartender, barman
Büffetkellner (m) bartender
Büffetmädchen (n) barmaid
Büffetwagen (Eisenbahn) (m) buffet car
Bügel- und Reinigungsdienst (m) valet
Bügelbrett (n) ironing-board
bügelfrei drip-dry
Bügelservice (m) pressing service
Büglerei (f) ironing service, pressing service
Bühne (f) stage
Bühnenfestspiele (pl. n) theatre festival
Bündel (n) bunch
Bündner Fleisch (n) air-cured beef of the Grisons
Bürger (m) citizen
Bürgermeister (m) mayor
Bürgersteig (m) footpath, pavement, sidewalk
Büro (n) office
Büroangestellter (m) clerk, white collar worker
Büroarbeit (f) paper work
Büroausstattung (f) office equipment
Bürobedarf (m) stationery
Büromaterial (n) office supplies
Bürste (f) brush
Bug (m) bow

Bullauge (n) porthole
Bummel (m) stroll
Bummelzug (m) accomodation train, slow train
Bundesrepublik Deutschland (f) Federal Repubblic of Germany
Bungalow (m) bungalow
Bungalowdorf (n) bungalow village
Burg (f) castle, fortress, stronghold
Burgruine (f) castle ruins
Burgunderwein (m) Burgundy wine
Bus (m) bus, coach, motor coach
Busanhänger (m) bus trailer
Busbahnhof (m) bus and coach station, bus station
Busfahrer (m) bus driver, coach driver
Busfahrt (f) bus trip
Bushaltestelle (f) bus stop, coach stop
Buslinie (f) bus line, coach line
Busreise (f) bus trip
Busreisen (pl. f) bus travel, coach travel
Busschaffner (m) bus conductor, coach conductor
Busunternehmen (n) bus company
Busverbindung (f) bus connection, bus line, coach connection, coach line
Busvermietung (f) bus hire
Butter (f) butter
Butter (f), **braune** nut butter
Butter (f), **gebrannte** burnt butter
Butter (f), **in** cooked in butter
Butter (f), **zerlassene** melted butter

Butterbrot (n) buttered slice of bread
Buttermilch (f) buttermilk

C

Caerphilly-Käse (m) Caerphilly cheese
Cafe (n) cafe
campen camp
Camper (m) Camper
Camping (n) camping
Campingausrüstung (f) camping equipment
Campingausweis (m) camping permit
Campingbus (m) motor caravan
Campingplatz (m) camping-ground
Campingplatz (m), **bewachter** guarded camping-site
Campingplatz (m), **voll eingerichtet** camping-site, offering full facilities
Campingtourismus (m) camping
Campingtourist (m) camper
Canneloni (pl.) canneloni
Caravaner (m) trailtourist
Cayennepfeffer (m) Cayenne pepper
Champagner (m) champagne
Champignonomelett (n) omelet with mushrooms
Champignons (pl. m), **gebacken** fried button mushrooms
charakterisieren feature
Charterflug (m) charter flight
Chartermaschine (f) charter aircraft
chartern charter
Chateaubriand (n) Chataubriand
Chaudeau (n) sabayon
Checkliste (f) check list
Cheddarkäse (m) Cheddar cheese
Chef de rang (m) assistent head-waiter
Chefkoch (m) chef
Chefsekretärin (f) executive secretary
Chefsteward (m) chief steward
Chesterkäse (f) Cheshire cheese
Chinakohl (m) chinese cabbage
Chip (Elektronik) (m) chip
Cocktail (m) coktail
Cocktailempfang (m) cocktail reception
Cognacschwenker (m) brandy-glass
Computer (m) computer
Concierge (f, m) concierge
Container (m) container
Containerzug (m) freightliner train
Controller (m) comptroller, controller
Cordon bleu (n) cheese- and ham stuffed veal steak
Cornflakes (pl.) cornflakes
Couch (f) couch
Couchtisch (m) club table
Couvert (n) cover
Creme (Speise) (f) mousse
Creme (f), **bayrische** molded cream
Creme (f), **bayrische gestürzte** Bavarian cream
Cremeschnitte (f) cream slice
Cremespeise (f) mousse
Cremetörtchen (n) **mit Johannisbeergelee** (n) red currant-tartlets
Cremetorte (f) fancy-cake with cream
Cumberlandsoße (f) Cumberland sauce
Curling (n) curling

35

Curry (m)   curry
Currypulver (n)   curry powder

D

D-Zug (m)   express train
Dachgarage (f)   roof garage
Dachgarten (m)   roff-garden
Dachgesellschaft (f)   holding company
Dachkammer (f)   attic, garret
Dachwohnung (f)   penthouse
Dämmerung (f)   dawn
Damen(toilette) (f)   Ladies
Damenfriseur (m)   ladieś hairdresser
Damentoilette (f)   ladieś lavatory, ladieś room
Damenwahl (f)   ladies-choice
Damhirsch (m)   fallow-deer
Damm (m)   dike, embankment
Dampfbad (n)   Russian bath, vapour bath
Dampfbügeln (n)   steam-ironing
Dampfer (m)   steamer, steamship
Dampfkartoffeln (pl. f)   steamed potatoes
Dampfnudel (pl. f)   steamed noodles with vanilla-cream
darübergießen   pour over
Datenbank (f)   data bank
Datenbankanbieter (m)   host
Datenendstation (f)   terminal
Datenverarbeitung (f)   data processing
datieren   date
Dattel (f)   date
Dattelmuschel (f)   piddock
Datum (n)   date
Dauer (f)   duration
Dauerabonnement (n)   season ticket
Dauerauftrag (m)   standing order

Dauerausweis (m)   all-year round admission ticket
Dauergast (m)   permanent resident
Dauerkarte (f)   commutation ticket
Dauerlauf (m)   jogging
dauernd   permanent
Dauerwurst (f)   hard sausage
Daunendecke (f)   eider-down
debitieren   debit
Debitor (m)   account receivable
Deck (n)   deck
Deckel (m)   lid
Deckelkrug (m)   tankard
decken   secure
Deckoffizier (m)   warrant officer
Deckplatz (m)   place on deck
Decksteward (m)   deck steward
Deckungsbeitrag (m)   contribution margin
Deckungsbeitragsfaktor (m), vom Umsatz (m)   contribution margin ratio
Deckungsbeitragsrechnung (f)   cost-volume-profit-analysis
Defizit (n)   deficit, deficiency
Deflation (f)   deflation
Deich (m)   dike
Dekoration (f)   decorations
delegieren   delegate
Denkmal (n)   memorial, monument
Denkmalspflege (f)   preservation of monuments
Dependance (f)   annex
deponieren   deposit
Derby-Kaese (m)   Derby cheese
Dessert (n)   dessert, sweet dish
Dessertwein (m)   dessert wine
destillieren   distil
destilliertes Wasser (n)   distilled water
deutlich   distinctly
Deutsche Bundesbahn (DB) (f)

German Federal Railways
Deutsche Schlaf- und Speisewagengesellschaft (DSG) (f) Dining Car Company
Deutsche Zentrale (f) **für Fremdenverkehr** (m) Central Office of German Travel
Deutscher Camping Club (DCC) (m) German Camping Club
Deutscher Fremdenverkehrsverband (m) German Tourist Association
Deutscher Hotel- und Gaststättenverband (m) German Hotel and Catering Assiciation
Devise (Geld) (f) foreign currency, foreign exchange
Devisenbestimmungen (pl. f) currency regulations
Devisenbewirtschaftung (f) currency control, currency restrictions, exchange control
Devisenfreigrenze (f) currency allowance
Devisenkontrolle (f) currency control, exchange control, foreign currency control
Devisenkurs (m) rate of exchange
Devisenvorschriften (pl. f) currency regulations, exchange regulations
Devisenzuteilung (f) allocation of foreign exchange
Diät (f) diet
Diätkost (f) diet, dietary cooking, dietary foods
Diätküche (f) dietary cooking, diet kitchen
Diätkur (f) diet cure, dietic treatment
Diätnahrung (f) dietary foods
Diätplan (m) diet plan
Diagramm (n) chart
Diapositiv (n) diapositive

dicht dabei near at hand
Dickmilch (f) curds and whey
Diebstahl (m) pilferage, theft
Diebstahlversicherung (f) theft insurance
dienen serve
Dienst (m) duty, service
Dienstalter (n) length of service
Dienstalter (im Betrieb) (n) company seniority
Dienstanweisungs (f) working instructions
Dienstanweisungs-Handbuch (n) instruction manual
Dienstleistung (f) service
Dienstleistungen (pl. f), **sonstige** other catering operations
Dienstleistungsgewerbe (n) service trade
Dienstmädchen (n) maid
Dienstplan (m), **gestaffelter** staggering scheduling
Dienstprogramm (n) service program, utility program
Differenz (f) differnce
Differenzierung (f) diversification
diktieren dictate
Dill (m) dill
Diner (n) dinner
Diner (n) **mit Show** (f) dinner with floor show
Direkt-Kostenrechnung (f) direct costing
Direktflug (m) through flight
Direktionsvertreter (m) **während der Nacht** (f) night manager
Direktkosten (pl.) direct cost
Direktkostenrechnung (f) marginal costing
Direktor (m) manager
Direktor (m), **stellvertretender** executive assistant manager

37

Direktverbindung (f) through connection
Diskette (f) diskette
Diskont (m) discount
diskontieren discount
Diversifikation (f) diversification
Dobostorte (f) fancy-cake with caramel
Docht (m) wick
Dörrpflaume (f) prune
Dom (m) cathedral
donnern thunder
Doppellendenstück (n) double tenderloin
Doppelbett (n) double bed
Doppelte Buchführung (f) double-entry bookkeeping
Doppelzimmer (n) double room, twin-bedded room
Dorf (n) village
Dorfgasthaus (n) country inn, village inn, wayside inn
Dorfschenke (f) country pub, village pub
Dorsch (m) cod
Dosenbier (n) canned beer, tinned beer
Drachenfisch (m) dragon fish
Drahtseilbahn (f) aerial railway
Dreibettabteil (n) three-berth compartment
Dreibettkabine (f) three-berth room
Dreibettzimmer (n) triple room, three-bed room
dreifach triplicate
Dreimeilenzone (f) three-mile zone
Dreiminutenei (n) three-minute egg
dringend urgent
Drink (m) drink
Drogist (m) druggist
Druck- und Büromaterial (n) printing and stationery

drucken print
Drucker (m) printer
Drucksache (f) printed matter
dubiose Forderung (f) doubtful account
Düne (f) dune
Dünnbier (n) near beer
Düsenflugzeug (n) jet, jet plane
Düsenmaschine (f) jet
Düsentriebwerk (n) jet propulsion unit
Düsenverkehrsflugzeug (n) jet liner
Duft (m) odour
Dumping (n) dumping
Dunkelheit (f) darkness
dunstig hazy
durchdrehen mince
Durcheinander (n) mess
Durchfahrt (f) passage
durchführbar feasible
Durchführbarkeit (f) feasibility
Durchführbarkeitsstudie (f) feasibility study
Durchgang (m) pass
Durchgangsland (n) transit country
Durchgangsreisender (m) through passenger
Durchgangsstraße (f) thoroughfare
Durchgangsverkehr (m) through traffic, transit traffic
durchgebraten well-done
durchgehend geöffnet permenantly open
Durchreisender (m) chance guest, temporary hotel guest, transient guest
Durchreisevisum (n) transit visa
Durchschnitt (m) average
Durchschnitt (m), **gewogener** weighted avarage
Durchschnittsaufenthaltsdauer (f) average length of stay

Durchschnittsaufenthaltsdauer (f) pro Gast (m)   average length of guest stay
Durchschnittsbeschäftigtenzahl (f)   average working force
Durchschnittsbeherbergungsertrag (m)   average room rate
Durchschnittsbestand (m)   average value of the stock
Durchschnittsertrag (m) pro Gedeck (n)   average receipt per food cover
Durchschnittsinventarbestand (m)   average store room inventory
Durchschnittskosten (pl. f)   average cost
Durchschnittspreis (m)   average price
Durchschnittsspeisenertrag (m) pro Gedeck (n)   average food check
Durchschnittsumsatz (m) pro Gast (m)   average revenue per guest, per day
Durchschnittsverdienst (m)   average earnings (income)
Durchschnittsverhältnis (n)   average ratio
Durchschnittszimmerpreis (m)   average room rate
durchsehen   revise
durchseien   strain
durchsuchen   search
durchwandern   perambulate
Durchwanderung (f)   perambulation
Durst (m)   thirst
durstig   thirsty
Duschanlage (f)   showers
Dusche (f)   shower, shower-bath
Dusche (f), medizinische   douche
Duschkabine (f)   shower-bath cubicle
Duschnische (f)   shower stall

Duschraum (m)   shower-room
Dutzend (n)   dozen (doz.)

E

Eberfleisch (n)   brawn
Echtzeit (f)   real time
Eckplatz (m)   corner seat
Edamer Käse (m)   Dutch cheese, Edam cheese
Edelkastanie (f)   chestnut
Edelpilz (m)   mushroom
Ehefrau (f)   wife
Eheleute (pl.)   couple, sponses
Ehemann (m)   husband
Ehrenmal (n)   cenotaph
ehrlich   honest
Ei (n)   egg
Ei (hart und in Teig eingehüllt) (n)   Scotch egg
Ei (n), hartgekochtes   hard-boiled egg
Ei (n), verlorenes   poached egg
Ei (n), verlorenes auf Toast (m)   poached egg on toast
Ei (n), weichgekochtes   soft boiled egg
Eiche (f)   oak
Eidotter (m)   yolk
Eier gefüllt (pl. n)   stuffed eggs
Eier (pl. n) im Glas (n)   eggs in a glass
Eier (pl. n) im Näpfchen (n)   eggs in cocotte
Eier (pl. n) in Öl (n) gebacken   deep-fried eggs
Eier (pl. n) mit Speck (m)   bacon and eggs
Eierbecher (m)   egg-cup
Eierbrot (n)   egg sandwich
Eierfrucht (f)   egg-plant
Eiergerichte (pl. n)   egg-dishes
Eiersalat (m)   egg-salad

39

Eiersandwich (m) egg sandwich
Eierteig (m) **gebacken** Yorkshire pudding
eifrig zealous
Eigelb (n) egg yolk, yolk
Eigenkapital (n) entity capital, net worth
Eigentümer (m) owner
Eigentümergesellschaft (f) owning company
Eigentum (n) ownership, property
Eigenverbrauch (m) own consumption
Eignung (f) qualification
Eilauftrag (m) rush order
Eile (f) haste, rush
Eilgüterzug (m) fast freight train
Eimer (m) bucket
einarmiger Bandit (Spielautomat) (m) one-armed bandit
Einbahnstraße (f) one-way street
Einbaukosten (pl.) installation cost
Einbauschrank (m) built-in cupboard (wardrobe)
Einbettabteil (n) single-berth compartment
Einbettzimmer (n) single bedroom, single room
Einbrecher (m) burglar
einbringen yield
Einbruch (m) burglary
Einbruchsversicherung (f) burglary insurance
einbüßen lose
einfach plain, simple, single
Einfahrt (f) driveway, entrance
Einfahrt verboten! no entry
einfetten grease
Einflugschneise (f) air corridor
Einfluß (m) influence
einführen (Außenhandel) import
einführen introduce
Einführung (Amt) (f) induction

Einführung (f) introduction
Einführungsschulung (f) induction training, orientation training
Einführungswerbung (f) initial advertising
Einfuhrbeschränkung (f) import restriction
Einfuhrgenehmigung (f) import license
Einfuhrhandel (m) import trade
Einfuhrzoll (m) import duty
Eingabe (f) input
Eingabeaufforderung (f) prompt
Eingang (m) entrance, entry, input
Eingangsmeldung (f) receiving report
eingeboren native
eingedickt jellied
Eingemachtes (n) preserves
eingeschneit snow-bound, snowed up
eingleisig single track
einheimisch national, native
Einheimischer (m) native
Einheit (f) unit
einheitlich uniform
Einheitsklasse (f) standard class
Einheitspreis (m) flat price
einholen overtake
Einkäufer (m) buyer, purchasing agent
Einkauf (m), **zentraler** central buying
einkaufen buy, purchase, shopping
Einkaufsabteilung (f) purchasing department
Einkaufspolitik (f) purchasing policy
Einkaufsrichtlinien (pl. f) purchasing specifications
Einkaufsverfahren (n) purchasing procedure

Einkaufszentrum (n) shopping center
Einkommen (n) earnings, income, revenue
Einkommensteuer (f) income tax
Einkünfte (pl. f) income
Einkünfte (pl. f), **sonstige** other revenue
einladen invite
Einladung (f) invitation
Einladungsbrief (m) letter of invitation
Einlaß (m) admission
Einlaufsuppe (f) clear soup with beaten egg
einlösen cash
einmachen pot
Einmannbetrieb (m) one-man operation
einmischen interfere
Einnahme (pl. f) receipts
einordnen rank
einordnen, sich get in lane
Einreise (f) entry, entry into the country
Einreisebewilligung (f) entry permit
Einreisegenehmigung (f) entry permit
einreisen (in ein Land) enter a country
Einreisevisum (n) entry visa
einrichten organize
Einrichtung (f) equipment, facility, feature, organisization
Einrichtungsgegenstand (m) fixture
Einrichtungsgegenstände (pl. m) furniture and fixtures
Einrichtunsplanung (f) facilities planning
Eins-A-Hotel (n) high-class hotel
Einsatz (m) input
einschalten turn on
einschiffen embark

Einschiffung embarkation
einschließen include
einschließlich inclusive
einschließlich Bedienung (f) **und Abgaben** (pl. f) inclusive of service and taxes
Einschränkung (f) limitation, restriction
Einschreibebrief (f) registered letter
einschreiben register
Einspänner (m) black coffee with whipped cream
einstecken plug
Einsteigekarte (f) boarding pass (card)
einsteigen get in
Einsteigen! all aboard
Einstellung (f) attitude
Einstellung (f) **der Arbeitnehmer** (pl. m) **zum Betrieb** (m) employee attitude
Einstellungspolitik (f) hiring policy
Einstellungsverfahren (n) hiring procedure
einstufen classify
Einstufung (f) classification
einstweilig interim
eintauchen dip
einteilen part
Eintopfgericht (n) hodge-podge
einträglich advantageous, lucrative
eintragen enroll, enter, record, register
Eintragung (f) enrollment, entry, record, registration
Eintreibung (f) collection
eintreten enter, join
eintreten ohne anzuklopfen enter without knocking
Eintritt (m) entry
Eintritt (m) **frei!** admission free

Eintritt verboten! keep out, no entry
Eintrittskarte (f) admission card, admission ticket, ticket of admission
Eintopfsuppe (f) soup with egg dough drops
einverstanden sein agree with
Einwanderer (m) immigrant
Einwanderung (f) immigration
einweichen soak
einwilligen approve
Einwilligung (f) approval
Einwirkung (f) impact
Einwohner (m) inhabitant, resident
einzahlen deposit
Einzahlung (f) deposit
Einzelangaben (pl. f) partieulars
Einzelbad (n) private bath
Einzelflugpauschale (f) iclusive single fare
Einzelkabine (f) single cabin, single room
einzeln individual
Einzelpauschalreise (f) individual inclusive journey
Einzelreise (f) individual journey
Einzelreisender (m) individual traveller, single passenger, single tourist
Einzelrückfahrt (f) individual return
Einzelzimmer (n) single, single room
Einzimmerappartement (n) one-room flat
Einzug (m) collection
Eis (n) ice
Eis (n), **gemischtes** mixed ice, mixed ice-cream
Eis (n), **halbgefrorenes** parfait
Eisauflauf (m) ice-cream souffle
Eisbaiser (m) ice-cream meringue

Eisbecher (m) coupe, ice-cream cup, ice-cream sundae, sundae
Eisbecher (m) **mit heißer Schokoladensoße** (f) ice-cream cup with hot chocolate sauce
eisbedeckt ice-coated
Eisbein (n) pickled pork, pickled shank of pork, pickled pork trotters, salted pig's knuckle, salted pig's trotter
Eisdiele (f) ice-bar, ice-cream parlour, ice-parlour
Eisenbahn (f) railroad, railway
Eisenbahnendstation (f) railway terminus
Eisenbahnfähre (f) train ferry
Eisenbahnfahrkarte (f) rail ticket, railway ticket
Eisenbahnfahrplan (m) railroad schedule, railway timetable
Eisenbahngütertransport (m) rail transport
Eisenbahnknotenpunkt (m) railway junction
Eisenbahnnetz (n) railway system
Eisenbahntarif (m) railway rates
Eisenbahnübergang (m) railroad grade crossing
Eisenbahnverkehr (m) rail traffic, railway traffic
Eisenbahnwagen (m) railroad car, railway carriage, railway coach, waggon
eiserne Reserve (f) minimum stock
eisfrei free from ice, ice-free
eisgekühlt iced
Eishalle (f) skating-rink
Eishockey (n) ice-hockey
eisig icy
Eiskaffee (m) coffee ice-cream, ice-cream coffee
Eiskübel (m) bucket, ice-pail
Eiskunstlauf (m) figure skating

Eisläufer (m)   skater
Eislauf (m)   ice-skating, skating
eislaufen   skate
Eislaufen (n)   ice-skating, skating
Eismaschine (f)   ice machine
Eismeringe (f)   ice-cream meringue
Eisomelett (n)   baked Alaska
Eisschnellauf (m)   speed skating
Eisschnitte (f)   brick of ice-cream
Eisschokolade (f)   iced chocolate
Eisschrank (m)   ice-box
Eissegeln (n)   ice-yachting
Eisstadion (n)   ice stadium
Eistee (m)   iced tea
Eistorte (f)   ice-cream cake
Eistüte (f)   ice-cone
Eisverkäufer (m)   ice man
Eiswaffel (f)   ice-cream wafer
Eiswasser (n)   ice water
Eiswürfel (m)   ice-cube
Eiszapfen (m)   icicle
elegant   elegant, fashionable
Elektriker (m)   electrician
Elektronische Datenverarbeitung (EDV) (f)   Electronic Data Processing (EDP)
elektronische Datenverarbeitung (f) **einsetzen**   computerize
Elektrotherapie (f)   electrotherapy
Elimination (f)   elimination
eliminieren   eliminate
Embargo (n)   embargo
Empfänger (m)   addressee, recipient
Empfang (m)   reception
Empfangsabteilung (f)   front office department
Empfangsbestätigung (f)   receipt
Empfangsbüro (n)   reception office
Empfangschef (m)   front office manager
Empfangsdame (f)   receptionist, room clerk
Empfangshalle (f)   lobby, reception hall
Empfangsherr (m)   desk clark, receptionist, room clerk
Empfangspersonal (n)   front office staff
Empfangspult (n)   front desk, reception desk
Empfangssekretär (m)   reception-clerk
empfehlen   recommend
Empfehlung (f)   recommendation
Empfehlungsbrief (m)   letter of recommendation
empfindlich   queasy
Endbestand (Waren) (m)   closing inventory
endgültig   definite
Endhaltestelle (f)   terminal point
Endivie (f)   endive
Endiviensalat (m)   endive salad
Endstation (f)   terminal, terminal point, terminus
Endsumme (f)   total
Endtermin (m)   final day
Endwert (m)   accumulated amount
Energieversorgung (f)   power supply
eng   narrow
englischer Cocktail (m)   Gin and It
englischer Kuchen (m)   sultana (fruit) cake
Engpaß (m)   bottleneck
endgültig   final
Enkel (m)   grand child, grandson
Enkeltochter (f)   granddaughter
Entschluß (m)   decision
entschuldigen   excuse
Entdeckung (f)   discovery
Entdeckungsfahrt (f)   exploration
Ente (f)   duck
Ente (f), **junge**   duckling

43

Ente gebraten (f) roast duck
entfernen remove
entfernt distant, far, remote
Entfernung (f) distance
Entfernung (in Meilen) (f) milage
Entfernungsmesser (m) range finder
Entfernungstabelle (f) table of distances
entgegengesetzt adverse, opposite
entlassen dismiss
entlassen, fristlos fire
Entlassung (f) dismissal
Entlassungsinterview (n) exit-interview
entlasten relieve
Entlastungszug (m) relief train
entleihen borrow
entnehmen withdraw
entschädigen compensate
Entschädigung (f) compensation
entscheiden decide, determine, rule
Entscheidung (f) decision, determination
entschuldbar excusable
entschuldigen, sich apologize
Entschuldigung (f) apology, excuse
entspannen relax
Entspannungskur (f) relaxation cure
entsprechen match
entsteinen stone
entwenden pilfer
entwerten depreciate
Entwicklung (f) development
Entwicklungsland (n) country in development
Entwicklungsrichtung (f) tendency
entzündlich, leicht inflammable
erblicken view

Erbse (f) pea
Erbse (f), gelbe yellow pea
Erbse (f), grüne green pea
Erbsenpüree (n) puree of peas, pea mash
Erbsensuppe (f) pea soup
Erbsensuppe (f), grün cream of green pea soup
Erdbeere (f) strawberry
Erdbeereis (n) strawberry ice-cream
Erdgeschoß (n) ground-floor
Erdnuß (f) peanut
Erdnußbutter (f) peanut butter
erfolglos inefficient
Erfolgsplanung (f), langfristige long-range profit planning
erfordern require
Erfordernis (n) requirement
erforschen explore
erfrischend refreshing
erfrischt refreshed
Erfrischung (f) refreshment
Erfrischungshalle (f) soda fountain
Erfrischungskiosk (m) refreshment stall
Erfrischungsraum (m) refreshment bar, refreshment room
erfüllen fulfill, meet
Erfüllung (f) fulfillment
Erfüllungsort (m) place of delivery, place of performance
ergänzen amend
Ergänzung (f) supplement
Ergänzungsbehandlung (f) supplementary treatment
Ergebnis (n) result
erhalten (bewahren) maintain
Erhaltung (f) maintenance
Erhebung (f) survey
Erhebungsbogen (m) survey sheet
erhöhen increase, raise, rise, ad-

vance
Erhöhung (f) increase, rise
erholen relax, get well again, recover
erholsam refreshing, restful
Erholung (f) convalescence, recovery, recreation, relaxation
Erholungsanlage (f) recreational facility
Erholungsaufenthalt (m) rest-cure
Erholungsgebiet (n) recreational area
Erholungsheim (n) convalescent home, rest-home
Erholungskur (f) rest-cure
Erholungsmöglichkeit (f) recreational facility
Erholungsort (m) holiday resort
Erholungspark (m) recreational park
Erholungspause (f) rest pause
Erholungsprogramm (n) recreation program
Erholungsreise (f) convalescent trip
Erholungsurlaub (m) convalescent leave, holiday leave, recreational holiday
Erholungszeit (f) relaxation time
Erholungszentrum (n) recreation centre
erinnern remind
Erinnerung (f) reminder
Erinnerungswerbung (f) reminder advertising
erkennen recognize
Erkennen (n) recognition
erkennen, nicht ignore
Erklärung (f) assurance, declaration, statement
Erkrankung (f) illness
Erkundigung (f) enquiry
erlauben allow, permit
Erlaubnis (f) permission, permit

erleichtern facilitate
Erleichterung (f) facilitation, relief
ermäßigen reduce
Ermäßigung (f) reduction
Ermäßigung (f), **für Hausgäste** (pl. m) reduction for hotel guests
Ermessen (n) discretion
ermitteln ascertain
ermüden fatigue
ermüdet fatigued, weary
Ermüdung (f) fatigue
ernähren feed, nourish
Ernährung (f) nutrition
erneuern render a service, renew, renovate, revalidate
Erneuerung (f) renewal, renovation
Ernte (f) crop, harvest
Erntedankfest (n) harvest thanksgiving, Thanksgiving Day
Eröffnung (f) opening
Eröffnungsinventur (f) opening inventory
errichten erect
Ersatz (m) compensation, substitute
Ersatzbeschaffung (f) replacement
Ersatzteil (n) spare part
erscheinen appear
Erscheinen (n) appearance
Erscheinung (f) appearance
Erschöpfung (f) fatigue
ersetzen compensate, reimburse, replace, substitute
Erstaufführung (f) first performance
erste Hilfe (f) first aid
erste Kategorie (f) first class catagory
erste Klasse first class
erste Klasse (Vermerk auf Flugscheinen) (f) F (= First)

45

erste Wahl (f)   prime choice
Ersteklassetarif (m)   first class fares
erster Rang (Theater) (m)   dress-circle
erstklassig   first class, prime
Erträge (pl. m)   sales
Erträge (pl. m) **aus Vermietung** (f) **von Veranstaltungsräumen** (pl. m)   public room rentals
Erträge (pl. m), **sonstige**   other income
Ertrag (m)   income, revenue, yield
Ertragskonto (n)   income account
Ertragskraft (f)   profitability
erwachsen   adult
Erwachsener (m)   adult, grown-up
erwärmen   warm
erwarten   await, expect
erweitern   expand, extend
Erweiterung (f)   expansion, extension
erwerben   buy, purchase
Erwerbssteuer (f)   acquirer's tax
Erzeugnis (n)   product
erziehen   educate
Esel (m)   donkey
Espresso (m)   espresso coffee
Espressobar (f)   espresso bar
essen   eat
Essen (n)   meal
Essen (n) **a la carte** (f)   meals a la carte
Essen (n) **kostenlos ausgeben**   furnished meal without charge
Essenabonnement (n)   luncheon voucher arrangement, meal ticket arrangement
Essenbon (m)   lucheon voucher
Essengutschein (m)   lucheon voucher, meal ticket
Essensbon (m)   meal ticket

Essensgedeckeanzahl (f)   number of food covers
Essenszeit (f)   meal-time
Eßgeschirr (n)   crockery
Essig (m)   vinegar
Essig- und Ölständer (m)   cruet-stand
Essiggemüse (n)   mixed pickles
Essiggemüse (n) **scharf gewürzt**   piccalilli
Essiggurke (f)   gherkin, pickle
Essigsoße (f), **grüne**   green vinegar sauce
Essigsoße (zum Einlegen) (f)   pickle, vinaigrette
Eßlöffel (m)   table-spoon
Eßlokal (n)   eating-place
Eßzimmer (n)   dining-room
Estragon (m)   tarragon
Etage (f)   floor
Etagenbad (n)   public bath-room
Etagenbeschließerin (f)   floor housekeeper
Etagendiener (m)   floor houseman, valet
Etagengouvernante (f)   floor housekeeper
Etagenhausdame (f)   floor housekeeper
Etagenhausdiener (m)   floor houseman
Etagenkellner (m)   floor waiter, room service waiter
Etagenoberkellner (m)   room service headwaiter
Etagenpersonal (n)   floor staff
Etagenservice (m)   room service
Etikett (n)   label
Etikette (f)   tag
etikettieren   label
Exkursion (f)   outing, study trip
expandieren   expand
Expansion   expansion
Expedient (m)   shipping clerk
Export (m)   export

exportieren export
Express... express
extra extra
Extrakellner (m) extra waiter

F

Fachkenntnis (f) skill
Fachmesse (f) trade fair
Fachwerkhaus (n) half-timbered house
Fachwissen (n) job knowledge, knowhow
fade insipid, tasteless
Fadennudeln (pl. f) vermicelli
fähig capable
Fähigkeit (f) ability, capability, capacity, skill
Fähre (f) ferry, ferry-boat
Fährmann (m) ferryman
fällig due, payable
fällig werden fall due
Fäßchen (n) keg
Fahrbahn (f) carriageway, roadway
Fahrbahn (f), **einspurige** single file traffic
Fahrbahn (f), **zweispurige** dual carriageway
Fahrdamm (m) roadway
fahren (Auto) drive, go by car
Fahrgast (m) fare, passenger
Fahrgäste (pl. m) **aussteigen lassen** set down passengers
Fahrgeld (n) fare
Fahrgestell (Flugzeug) (n) landing-gear
Fahrkarte (f) ticket
Fahrkarte (f) **zum halben Preis** (m) half-fare ticket
Fahrkarte (f) **zum vollen Preis** (m) general-tariff ticket

Fahrkarte (f), **einfache** single ticket
Fahrkarte (f), **ermäßigte** cheap ticket, reduced-fare ticket
Fahrkartenausgabe (f) booking office
Fahrkartenautomat (m) automatic ticket machine, ticket machine
Fahrkartenschalter (m) booking office, ticket office, ticket office window
Fahrkilometer (pl. m) voyage distance
fahrlässig careless
Fahrlässigkeit (f) carelessness
Fahrplan (m) schedule, timetable
Fahrplan (Ankünfte-Abreisen) (m) arrivals and departures table
fahrplanmäßig regular, scheduled
fahrplanmäßig fahren run at regular times
Fahrpreis (m) fare
Fahrpreisermäßigung (f) fare reduction, reduced fare
Fahrpreisermäßigung (f) **für Reisegesellschaften** (p. f) reduced fares for tourist groups, fare reduction for tourist parties
Fahrrad (n) bicycle
Fahrradausflug (m) bicycle excursion
Fahrradständer (m) cycle-stand
Fahrradvermietung (f) bicycle hire
Fahrradweg (m) cycle path
Fahrrinne (f) navigation channel
Fahrschein (m) ticket
Fahrscheinheft (n) booklet of coupons (tickets)
Fahrscheinkontrolle (f) ticket inspection
Fahrspur (f) lane

47

Fahrstuhl (m)　elevator, lift
Fahrstuhlführer (m)　elevator boy, lift-boy
Fahrt (f)　journey, sailing, trip, voyage
Fahrt (f) **ins Blaue** (n)　mystery tour
Fahrt (f), **auf der**　en route
Fahrtkosten (pl.)　car fare
Fahrtroute (f)　itinerary
Fahrtunterbrechung (f)　break of journey, intermediate stop
Fahrverkehr (m)　vehicle traffic
Fahrzeit (f)　journey time, running time, travel time
Fahrzeug (n)　vehicle
fakultativ　optional
fallen, ins Auge (n)　eye catching
fallen lassen　drop
falsch　improper
Falschbuchung (f)　irregular entry
falscher Hase (m)　forcemeat roasted
Faltboot (n)　faltboat
Familienbad (n)　mixed bathing
Familienbetrieb (m)　family business, family run firm
Familieneinkommen (n)　family income
Familienferien (pl.)　family holiday, family vacation
Familienferienhotel (n)　family guesthouse
Familienferienort (m)　family holiday resort
Familienkarte (f)　family ticket
Familienname (m)　surname
Familienpaß (m)　joint passport
Familienpension (f)　family boarding house, residential hotel
Familienstand (m)　family status, marital status, personal status
Familientourismus (m)　family tourism
Familienzulage (f)　family allowance
Fang (m)　catch
fangen　catch
Fangobehandlung (f)　mud treatment
Fangopackung (f)　mud pack
Fangotherapie (f)　mud therapy
Farbabzug (Foto) (m)　colour print
Fasan (m)　pheasant
Fasan (m) **gebraten**　roast pheasant
Faschingsdienstag (m)　Shrove Tuesday
Faschingskrapfen (m)　carnival fritter
Faschingszeit (f)　carnival season
Faß (n)　barrel
Faßbier (n)　draught
Faßhahn (m)　tap
Fassung (f)　socket
fast roh　underdone
Fastenzeit (f)　Lent
Fastnacht (f)　Shrove Tuesday
Fastnachtsdienstag (m)　Mardi-gras
Fastnachtszeit (f)　Shrovetide
faul　lazy
faul (verdorben)　rotten
Fauna (f)　fauna
Fausthandschuh (m)　mitten
Federball (m)　shuttle cock
Federballspiel (n)　badminton
Federwild (n)　feathered game
Fehlbetrag (m)　deficit, deficiency, shortage
Fehlbuchung (f)　bookkeeping error
Fehlen (n)　absenteeism, miss
fehlend　missing
Fehler (m)　defect, error, fault
Fehler (pl. m) **aufdecken**　locate errors
fehlerhaft　defective, faulty
fehlleiten　misguide

Fehlstunden (pl. f) hours absent
feiern celebrate
Feiertag (m) holiday
Feiertag (m), **gesetzlicher** legal holiday, public holiday
Feiertagslohn (m) holiday pay
Feige (f) fig
fein fine
Feinkosthändler (m) provision dealer
Feinschmecker (m) gourmet
Feinschmeckeressen (n) gourmet's meal
Feinschmeckerrestaurant (n) gourmet restaurant
Felchen (m) white fish
Feldbett (n) camp cot
Feldflasche (f) water-bottle
Feldweg (m) country lane, field path
Felsen (m) rock
felsig rocky
Fenchel (m) fennel
Fenster (n) window
Fensterladen (m) window shade
Fensterplatz (m) window seat
Fensterputzer (m) window cleaner
Fensterscheibe (f) window pane, pane
Fenstertechnik (f) windowing technique
Ferien (pl.) **machen** take a holiday
Feriendorf (n) holiday village
Ferienfahrkarte (f) holiday ticket
Ferienflugpreis (m) excursion fare
Ferienführer (m) holiday guide
Feriengast (m) holiday guest
Feriengebiet (n) holiday region
Ferienhaus (n) cottage, holiday house
Ferienhotel (n) holiday hotel
Ferieninsel (f) holiday island

Ferienkurs (m) holiday course, summer school
Ferienlager (n) holiday camp
Ferienland (n) holiday country
Feriennetzkarte (f) guest pass
Feriennetzkarte (f) holiday runabout ticket, holiday seson ticket
Ferienordnung (f) vacation schedule
Ferienort (m) holiday resort
Ferienplakat (n) travel poster
Ferienprogramm (n) vacation program(me)
Ferienreise (f) holiday trip
Feriensonderzug (m) holiday train
Ferienstaffelung (f) staggered holidays
Ferientag (m) holiday
Ferienunterkunft (f) holiday flat, vacation apartment
Ferienverkehr (m) holiday traffic
Ferienwohnung (f) holiday flat, vacation apartment
Ferienzeit (f) holiday season
Ferkel (n) porkling
Fernbleiben (n) absenteeism
Fernblick (m) distant view
Ferndurchwahl (f) direct distance dialing
Fernfahrplan (m) long-distance time-table
Ferngespräch (n) long-distance call, trunk-call
Ferngespräch (n) **anmelden** place a long distance call
Fernglas (n) binoculars, telescope
Fernlaster (m) long-distance lorry
Fernschnellzug (m) limited express train, long-distance express
Fernschreiber (m) teleprinter, teletype

Fernschreibercode (m) teleprinter code
Fernschreibnetz (n) telex
Fernsehraum (m) television room
Fernsehapparat (m) television set
Fernsehen (n) television
Fernsehgerät (n) television set
Fernsehturm (m) television tower
Fernsprechamt (n) telephone exchange, trunk exchange
Fernsprechzelle (f) call-box, telephone booth, telephone box
Fernsprechzelle (f), **öffentliche** public call-room
Fernverkehr (m) long-distance traffic
Fernverkehrsstraße (f) arterial road, highway, trunk road
fertig ready
Fertigerzeugnis (n) finished good, finished product
Fertiggericht (n) ready-to-serve dish
Fertiggerichtsysteme (pl. n) convenience foods
fest fixed
Festausschuß (m) festival committee
Festbeleuchtung (f) festive illumination
festellen fix
Festessen (n) anniversary dinner, banquet
Festessen (n) gala dinner
festgelegt fixed
festgesetzt fixed
Festhalle (f) banqueting hall, festival hall
festlegen fix
Festmahl (n) feast
festnehmen arrest
Festpreis (m) fixed price

Festsaal (m) banqueting hall, banquet room, festival hall
Festspiele (pl. n) festival
feststellen ascertain
Festtag (m) anniversary
Festumzug (m) pageant
Festung (f) fortress, stronghold
Festvorstellung (f) gala performance
Festwertspeicher (m) read-only memory (rom)
Festwiese (f) fair ground
Festwoche (f) festival week
Festwochen (pl. f) festival
Festzelt (n) fair-ground tent
Festzug (m) festive procession
fett fat, fatty
Fett (n) shortening, suet
Fett, tierisches (n) animal fat
Fettgebackenes (n) fritters
fettlos without fat
Fettpapier (n) greaseproof paper
feucht damp, humid, moist
Feuchtigkeit (f) humidity, moisture
Feuer (n) fire
feuergefährlich inflammable
Feuerhaken (m) poker
Feuerleiter (f) fire escape
Feuerlöscher (m) fire-extinguisher
Feuermelder (m) fire-alarm
Feuerversicherung (f) fire insurance
Feuerwehr (f) fire-brigade, fire department
Feuerwerk (n) fire-works
Feuerzeug (n) cigarette lighter, lighter
Feuerzeugbenzin (n) lighter fuel
Fieber (n) fever, temperature
Figur (f) figure
Filet (n) fillet
Filet Wellington (n) roast fillet of beef in puff-paste

Filetbraten (m) **in Rahmsoße** (f) fillet of beef in cream-sauce
Filetgulasch (n) **in Sauerrahmsoße** (f) beef Stroganoff
Filetsteak (Chateaubriand) (n) Chateaubriand
Filetsteak (n) fillet-mignon
Filetstück (n), **kleines** mignonette
Filialbetrieb (m) chain
Filiale (f) branch office
Film (m) film
Film (Kino) (m) movie
filmen film
Filmfestspiele (pl. n) film festival
Filmprogramm (n) cinema program, movie program
Filmschauspieler (m) film actor
Filmtheater (n) movie theater
Filmvorführung (f) movie performance
Filmvorstellung (f) movie performance, movie show
Filterkaffee (m) filter coffee
filtern (Kaffee etc.) percolate
Filterzigarette (f) filter-tipped cigarette
Finanzanalyse (f) financial analysis
Finanzbuchhaltung (f) financial accounting
Finanzhilfe (f) financial aid
Finanzplan (m) budget
Finderlohn (m) finder's reward
Firmenbetreuung (f) firm service
Firmenwert (m), **ideeler** goodwill
Firn (m) firn
Firnschnee (m) neve
First-class-Hotel (n) first class hotel
Fisch (m) fish
Fisch (m) **gebraten mit Pommes frites** (pl.) fish and chips
Fisch (m) **in Öl** (n)

gebacken deep-fried fisch
Fisch (m), **marinierter** pickled fish
Fischbesteck (n) fish knife and fork
Fische (pl. m) **und Schalentiere** (pl. n) fishes and crustaceous animals
Fischeintopfgericht (n) pot-stew of fish
fischen fish
Fischen (n) fishing
Fischer (m) fisherman
Fischerboot (n) fishing-boat
Fischerdorf (n) fishing-village
Fischfilet (n) fillet of fish
Fischfrikadelle (f) fishcake
Fischhandlung (f) fishmonger
Fischmayonnaise (f) mayonnaise of fish
Fischrestaurant (n) fish and chip shop
Fischsalat (m) fish salad
Fischsuppe (f) fishsoup, French fish soup
Fizz (m) fizz
FKK nudism
Flagge (f) flag
Flageolet (n) flageolet
flambieren flame
flambiert flambe, flamed
Flannell-Tafel (f) flannel-board
Flasche (f) bottle
Flaschenbier (n) bottled beer
Flaschenöffner (m) bottle-opener
Flaschenwein (m) bottled wine
flaumig fluffy
Fleisch (n) meat
Fleisch (n), **durchwachsenes** marbled meat
Fleisch (n) **in Streifen** (pl. m) **schneiden und dörren** jerk
Fleisch (n) **vom Grill** (m) grilled meat
Fleisch (n) **vom Holzkohlengrill** (m)

charcoal broiled mixed grill, barbecued meat
Fleischallerlei (n) **gekocht** mixed boiled meat, assorted boiled meat
Fleischanhänger (m) meat tag
Fleischbrühe (f) beeftea, meat broth
Fleischbrühe (f) **mit Nudeleinlage** (f) broth with rice
Fleischbrühe (f) **mit Reiseinlage** (f) broth with rice
Fleischer (m) butcher
Fleischfondue (Rindfleisch) (n) beef fondue
fleischig meaty
Fleischkäse (m) meat-puding
Fleischklößchen (n) meat-ball
Fleischklöße (pl. m), **gebraten** rissole
Fleischknödel (m) meat dumpling, quenelle
Fleischpastete (f) meat pie
Fleischschnitte grilliert (f) slice of grilled (beef) meat
Fleischspeise (f) meat dish
Fleischtest (m) butcher test
Fleischzerlegungsbericht (m) butcher test
Flieger (m) aviator
Flitterwochen (pl. f) honeymoon
Floppydisk (f) floppy disk
Flora (f) flora
Floß (n) raft
Flosse (f) flipper
Flotte (f) fleet
Flügel (m) wing
Flügel (Musikinstrument) (m) grand piano
Flügelspitze (f) **vom huhn** (n) chicken winglet, chicken wing, winglet
flüssig liquid
Flüssigkeit (f) liquidity
Flug (m) air-journey, flight

Flug (m) **ohne Zwischenlandung** (f) non-stop flight
Flug (m), **planmäßiger** scheduled flight
Flug-Bus-Verbindung (f) bus-air service, coach-air service
Flug-Eisenbahn-Verkehr (m) air-rail transport
Flug-Schiffs-Reise (f) air-steamer voyage
Flugbuchung (f) air booking
Fluggast (m) air-passenger
Fluggastgebühr (f) airport service charge
Fluggastversicherung (f) aircraft passenger insurance
Fluggeschwindigkeit (f) flying speed
Fluggesellschaft (f) airline
Flughafen (m) aerodrome, airport
Flughafenbus (m) airport bus, shuttle
Flughafenempfangsgebäude (n) airport terminal building
Flughafenrestaurant (n) airport restaurant
Flughafensteuer (f) airport tax
Flughafenzollamt (n) airport customs office
Fluginformation (f) flight information
Flugkapitän (m) captain, flight captain
Flugkarte (f) airline ticket, airticket, plane ticket
Fluglinie (f) airline
Flugnetz (n) route network
Flugpauschale (f) all-in air fare, inclusive air fare
Flugpauschalreise (f) inclusive air journey
Flugplan (m) flight schedule, schedule, timetable
Flugplatz (m) aerodrome, air-

field
Flugplatzbahnhof (m)   town terminal
Flugplatzreservierung (f)   air reservation
Flugpreis (m)   airfare
Flugreise (f)   air-journey
Flugschein (m)   airline ticket, air-ticket, plane ticket
Flugschein (m)   pilot's licence
Flugschein (m), **offener**   open-air ticket
Flugscheinverkaufsstelle (f)   air-ticket issuing office
Flugscheinvermerk (m) **für Touristenklasse** (f)   y
Flugsicherheit (f)   flying safety
Flugsicherung (f)   air traffic control
Flugsteig (m)   gate, gateway
Flugstrecke (f)   air route
Flugtouristik (f)   air tourism, holiday air travel
Flugverbindung (f)   connecting flight
Flugverkehr (m)   air services
Flugzeit (f)   flight time, flying time
Flugzettel (m)   flyer
Flugzeug (n)   aircraft, airplane, plane
Flugzeug (n) **der Touristenklasse** (f)   air coach
Flugzeug (n) **besteigen**   board a plane
Flugzeug (n) **verlassen**   deplane
Flugzeug (n), **einmotoriges**   single-engined aircraft
Flugzeugabsturz (m)   plane crash
Flugzeugankunft (f)   arrival by air
Flugzeugbesatzung (f)   aircrew
Flugzeugentführung (f)   hijacking
Flugzeugführer (m)   aircraft pilot
Flugzeughalle (f)   hangar

Flugzeugladung (f)   plane load
Flugzeugmotor (m)   aircraft engine
Flugzeugrumpf (m)   fuselage
Flunder (f)   flounder, fluke
Fluß (m)   river
Fluß (m), **schiffbarer**   navigable river
Flußschiffahrt (f)   river traffic
Flußdampfer (m)   river steamer
Flußforelle (f)   river-trout, stream trout
Flußhotel (n)   riverside hotel
Flußkarte (f)   river map
Förderband (n)   conveyer belt
fördern   promote
förmlich   formal
Fogosch (Zander) (m)   perch-pike
Folgeerscheinung (f)   after-effect
Folio (n)   folio
Folklore (f)   folklore
Fonds (m)   funds
Fondue Bourgignonne (n)   fondue Bourgignonne
Food und Beverage-Manager (m)   food and beverage manager
Footballspiel (n)   football match
fordern   claim, demand
Forderung (f)   claim
Forderungen (pl. f)   accounts receivable
Forderungen (pl. f) **und Verbindlichkeiten** (pl. f)   receivables and payables
Forelle (f)   trout
Forelle (f) **blau**   blue boiled trout
Forelle (f) **in Butter gebraten**   butterfried trout
Forelle (f) **in Champagner** (m)   trout in champagne
Forellenfischen (n)   trout fishing
formal   formal
Formalität (f)   formality
Formel (f)   formular
Formular (m)   blank, form

53

formulieren form
forschen research
Forschung (f) research
Forschung (f) **und Entwicklung** (f) research and development
Forschungsabteilung (f) research department
Forsthaus (n) forester's house
Fortbildungsseminar (n) workshop
Foto (n) photo
Fotoausrüstung (f) photographic equipment
fotografieren take a photo
Fotografieren verboten! photographing not allowed
Fotosafari (f) photo safari
Foyer (n) foyer, lobby
Fracht (f) cargo, carriage, freight
Frachtbrief (m) consignment note
Frachtbuch (n) cargo book
Frachtflugzeug (n) airfreighter, cargo aircraft, freight aircraft
Frachtführer (m) carrier
Frachtgebühr (f) freightage
Frachtkosten (pl.) freight charges
Frachtrechnung (f) freight bill
Frachtschiff (n) freighter
Frachtsendung (f) cargo consignment
Frachttarif (m) goods tariff
Frack (m) tailcoat
Fräulein (n) miss
Frage (f) question
Fragebogen (m) questionary, questionnaire, survey sheet
Franchising (n) franchising
Frankfurter Würstchen (n) Frankfurter, Frankfurter sausage
Frankiermaschine (f) franking machine, postage meter
frankieren stamp
frankiert post-paid
franko post-paid

Frankreich France
frei disengaged, free vacant
frei Eisenbahn (f) free on rail (f. o. r.)
frei Kai (m) free on quai (f. o. q.)
frei Waggon (m) free on truck (f. o. t.)
frei an Bord (m) free on board (f.o.b.)
Freibad (n) bathing place, lido, open-air bath, open-air swimming-pool, outdoor bath
Freibetrag (m) allowance
Freibetrag (m) allowance
Freifahrtkarte (f) complimentary ticket
Freigepäck (n) free baggage allowance
freigestellt optional
freigiebig generous
Freigrenze (f) allowance
Freihafen (m) free port
Freihalten! keep clear
Freihandelszone (f) Free Trade Area
Freikarte (f) free ticket
Freikörperkultur (FKK) (f) nudism, naturism
Freiluftbühne (f) open-air stage, open-air theatre
Freilufttheater (n) open-air theatre
freimachen (räumen) vacate
Freisein (n) vacancy
Freistempler (m) franking machine
freiwillig gratuitous
Freizeit (f) off-time
Freizeitbeschäftigung (f) leisure time activity
Freizeit (f) leisure time, spare time
fremd alien
Fremdenbuch (n) visitors' block
Fremdenfeindlichkeit (f) xeno-

phobia
Fremdenführer (m)   guide
Fremdenführer (m)   German-speaking guide
Fremdenheim (n)   boarding-house, guest-house
Fremdenregister (n)   hotel register
Fremdenverkehrswirtschaft (f)   tourist economy
Fremdenverkehr (m)   tourism, toursit trade, tourist traffic
Fremdenverkehrsamt (n)   tourist-board, tourist office
Fremdenverkehrsbetrieb (m)   tourist trade establishment
Fremdenverkehrsbüro (n)   tourist office
Fremdenverkehrsförderung (f)   promotion of the tourist trade
Fremdenverkehrsforschung (f)   travel research
Fremdenverkehrsgebiet (n)   tourist region
Fremdenverkehrsindustrie (f)   hotel and tourist industry, touristic industry
Fremdenverkehrskampagne (f)   tourist campaign
Fremdenverkehrsland (n)   holiday country, tourist country
Fremdenverkehrsort (m)   tourit centre, tourist resort
Fremdenverkehrspolitik (f)   tourist policy
Fremdenverkehrsprospekt (m)   travel booklet
Fremdenverkehrssaison (f)   tourist season
Fremdenverkehrsstadt (f)   tourist town
Fremdenverkehrsstatistik (f)   tourist trade statistics, travel statistics
Fremdenverkehrsstreuung (f)

staggering of tourist traffic
Fremdenverkehrsträger (m)   tourist traffic institution
Fremdenverkehrsverband (m)   tourist association
Fremdenverkehrswerbung (f)   tourist advertising, tourist publicity
Fremdenverkehrswesen (n)   tourism
Fremdenverkehrszeitschrift (f)   tourist journal
Fremdenverkehrszentrale (f)   central office of tourism
Fremdenzimmer (n)   guest-room, spare room
Fremdenzimmer (pl. n)   rooms to let
Fremder (m)   stranger
Fremdkapital (n)   borrowed capital
Freude (f)   joy
freundlich   kind
Freundlichkeit (f)   kindness
Friedensstifter (m)   trouble-shooter
Friedhof (m)   cemetery, churchyard
friedlich   peaceful
Frikadelle (f)   beefburger, fricadelle, meat croquet
Frikassee (n)   fricassee
frisch   fresh
frisch gestrichen   wet paint
Frischling (m)   young wild boar
Frischwarenverzeichnis (n)   market list
Frischwasser (n)   fresh water
Friseur (m)   hairdresser
Frisiersalon (m)   hairdresser's saloon, barber shop
Frisiersalon (m)   **(für Damen)**   beauty palor
Frisiertisch (m)   dressing-table
Frist (f)   time limit

55

Frisur (f) hair-style
fröhlich jolly
Fröhlichkeit (f) gaiety
Fronleichnam Corpus Christi
Frosch (m) frog
Froschschenkel (m) frog-leg
Frost (m) frost
frostig chilly
Frostschutzmittel (n) anti-freezing mixture
Frottiertuch (n) Turkish towel
Frucht (f) fruit
Fruchtbrei (m) squash
Fruchteiscreme (f) fruit sundae
fruchtig fruity
Fruchtsaft (m) fruit juice, squash
Früchte (pl. f) fruit, fruits
Früchte (pl. f.), **eingemachte** preserves
Früchte (pl. f), **gehackt (zur Pastetenfüllung)** mincemeat
Früchtekorb (m) fruit-basket
früh early
Frühjahr (n) spring
Frühjahrsferien (pl.) spring holiday
Frühjahrsmesse (f) spring trade fair
Frühjahrsputz (m) spring cleaning
Frühkonzert (n) morning concert
Frühling (m) spring
Frühlingsgemüse (n) early vegetable
Frühstück (n) breakfast
Frühstück (n), **einfaches** continental breakfast
Frühstück (n), **englisches** English breakfast
Frühstück (n), **komplettes** complete breakfast
Frühstück (n), **zweites** elevenses, mid-morning snack
Frühstücksausgabestelle (f) pontry

Frühstücksfleisch (n) luncheon meat
Frühstückspause (f) mid-morning break
Frühstückspension (f) residential hotel
Frühstückstablett (n) breakfast tray
Frühstückszimmer (n) breakfast room, tea-room
frühzeitig in good time
Frühzug (m) morning train
führend leading
Führer (m), multilingual guide
Führerschaft (f) leadership
Führerschein (m) driver's license, driving license
Führerschein (m), **internationaler** international driving permit (IDP)
Führung (Reise) (f) guided visit
Führung (f) **übernehmen** take the lead
Führungsentscheidung (f) management decision
Führungsfähigkeit (m) leadership-ability
Führungskräfteentwicklung (f) management development
Führungskraft (f) executive
Führungskräfteausbildung (f) executive development
Führungsverantwortung (f) managerial responsibility
Führungszeugnis (n) certificate of conduct
Füllsel (n) forcemeat, stuffing
Füllung (f) forcemeat, stuffing
Fünfuhrtee (m) five-o'clock-tea
Fuhrlohn (m) cartage
Fuhrpark (m) fleet of trucks
Fundbüro (n) lost-property office
Fundgegenstand (m) found article
Funktaxi (n) radio taxi

Funktion (f) function
funktionieren operate
Fusion (f) merger
fusionieren merge
Fuß (m) **(Längenmaß= 0.3048 m)** foot
Fußballspiel (europ. Sport) (n) soccer
Fußgängerbrücke (f) footbridge
Fußgängertunnel (m) subway
Fußgängerübergang (m) peel
Fußwanderung (f) hike

G

Gabel (f) fork
gähnen yawn
Gänse (pl. f) geese
Gänsebraten (m) roast goose
Gänsebraten (m) **mit Sauerkraut** (n) roast goose with sauerkraut
Gänseklein (n) giblets of goose
Gänseleber (f) goose liver
Gänselebermoussee (n) gooseliver-mousse
Gänseleberpastete (f) gooseliver patty, gooseliver pie, pate de foie gras
gären (lassen) ferment
Gärtner (m) gardener
Gäste (pl. m) **bedienen** serve, attend, wait on
Gästeanzahl (f) guest count
Gästebuch (n) visitors' block
Gästefragebogen (m) guest questionnaire
Gästegeschenke (pl. n) guests' supplies
Gästehaus (n) guest-house
Gästeregistrierung (f) guest registration
Gästeverzeichnis (f) hotel register
Gästewäsche (f) guest laundry
Gästezahlung (f) guest count
Gästezimmer (n) guest-room, sitting-room, spare room
Galerie (f) gallery
Gallone (f) gallon
Gang (Essen) (m) course
Gang (m) passage
Gang (m), **erster** first course
Gangschaltung (f) gear-change
Gans (f) goose
ganz quite
ganzjährig geöffnet open all the year round
ganzjährig in Betrieb (m) operating all the year round
Ganzjahresetrieb (m) year-round service
Garage (f) garage, garage-parking lot
Garage (f), **verschließbare** lock-up garage
Garantie (f) guarantee, guaranty
garantieren guarantee
garantiert warranted
Garautomat (m) automatic cooker
Garderobe (f) checkroom, cloak-room, wardrobe
Garderobenfrau (f) checkroom girl, cloakroom attendant
Garderobenmarke (f) cloakroom ticket
Garküche (f) cook-shop
Garn (f) yarn
Garnele (f) prawn, shrimp
garnieren garnish
garniert garnished
Garnierung (f) dressing, garnishing
Gartencafe (n) open-air cafe
Gartenfest (n) garden party
Gartenlokal (n) open-air restaurant

Gartenrestaurant (n) open-air restaurant, tea garden
Gartenschau (f) horticulture show
Gartenstadt (f) garden city
Gas (n) **geben** accelerate
Gasfeuerzeug (n) gas lighter
Gashahn (m) gas tap
Gasherd (m) gas cooker, gas range
Gaspedal (n) accelerator
Gasse (f) lane
Gassenschenke (f) off-licence inn
Gast (m) guest, patron, pax
Gast (m) **zahlender** paying guest
Gastaufnahmevertrag (m) contract of accomodation
Gastfamilie (f) host family
gastfreundlich hospitable
Gastfreundschaft (f) hospitality
Gastgeber (m) host
Gastgeberin (f) hostess
Gastgewerbe (n) catering business, hotel and restaurant business
Gasthof (m) inn
Gasthaus (n) cafe, hotel, inn, pub
Gastland (n) host country
gastlich hostible
Gastronom (m) hotel-keeper, innkeeper
Gastronomie (f) gastronomy
Gastronomiebereich (m) food and beverage department
Gastspiel (n) guest performance
Gaststättenbesitzer (m) restaurant-keeper
Gastwirt (m) innkeeper, landlord, restaurant-keeper
Gastwirtschaft (f) inn, saloon
Gastzimmer (n) dining-room, parlour, spare-room
Gatte (m) husband

Gattung (f) kind
Gaumen (m) palate
gebacken baked
Gebäck (n) pastry, pastries
Gebäck (n), **kleines** cookie, cooky
Gebäude (n) building
Gebiet (n) area, territory, zone
Gebirge (n) mountains
Gebirgsklima (n) mountain climate
Gebirgswelt (f) mountains
gebraten roast, roasted, sauteed
Gebrauch (m) use
gebrauchen make use of
gebräuchlich customary
Gebrauchsanweisung (f) instruction for use
gebrauchsfertig ready-to-use
Gebrauchsgegenstand (m), **persönlicher** personal belonging
gebraucht used, second hand
Gebühr (f) fee
Gebühr (f) **erheben** levy a charge
gebührenpflichtig liable to charges
Geburt (f) birth
Geburtsdatum (n) date of birth
Geburtsname (m) maiden name
Geburtsort (m) birthplace, place of birth
Geburtsurkunde (f) birth certificate
Geschäftsbuchhaltung (f) financial accounting
gedämpft (kochen) steamed, stewed
Gedeck (n) cover
Gedeck (n), **trockenenes** cover charge
Gedeckpreis (m) cover charge
gedünstet braised, steamed
gefährden jeopardize
Gefährdung (f) hazard, jeopardy

gefährlich dangerous, risky
Gefälle (n) hill
Gefäß (n) jar
Gefahr (f) danger, jeopardy, risk
Gefahr (f) **laufen** run the risk
Geflügel (n) fowl, poultry
Geflügel (n) **kalt** cold fowl
Geflügelbrust (f) breast of chicken
Geflügelklein (n) giblets of chicken
Geflügelkleinsuppe (f) giblet soup
Geflügelkroketten (pl. f) croquettes of fowl
Geflügelleber (f) chicken liver
Geflügelpastete (f) **warm** chicken pie
Geflügelragout (n) ragout of chicken
Geflügelrahmragout (n) chicken a la king
Geflügelrahmsuppe (Mulligatawny) (f) curried chicken-cream soup
Geflügelreis (m) chicken rice
Geflügelsalat (m) chicken salad
Geflügelsuppe (f) soup with fowl
Geflügelsuppentopf (m) chicken noodle soup
gefräßig greedy
gefroren iced
Gefühl (n) emotion
gefüllt filled, stuffed
Gegend (f) region
Gegengift (n) antidote
gegenseitig mutual
Gegenstand (m) object
Gegenteil (n) opposite
gegenüber facing, opposite
Gegenverkehr (m) oncoming traffic, two-way traffic
Gegenwert (m) equivalent
gegrillt broiled, barbecued
gehackt chopped, fricasseed, has-

hed
Gehalt (n) pay, salary
Gehaltsscheck (m) pay check
gehaltvoll meaty
gehen go, walk
Gehen Sie gerade aus! go straight on
gehen, an Bord (m) go on bord
gehen, an Land (n) debark, go ashore
gehen, vor Anker (m) anchor
Gehilfe (m) assistant
Gehweg (m) footpath
gekocht cooked, plain boiled
Geländefahrt (f) cross-country drive
Gelbfilter (n) yellow filter
Geldabwertung (f) currency devaluation
Geldanlage (f) investment
Geldbedarf (m) need of money
Geldbeutel (m) purse
Geldkassette (f) cash box
Geldstrafe (f) fine, penalty
Geldstrafe (f) **auferlegen** impose a fine upon
Geldsystem (n) monetary system
Geldumlauf (m), **betrieblicher** cash flow
Geldwechsel (m) currency conversion, exchange of money
Geldwechselautomat (m) change-giving machine
Geldwertänderung (f) change in value of currency
Gelee (m) jelly
Gelegenheit (f) occasion
Gelegenheitsarbeiter (m) casual worker
Gelegenheitswerbung (f) opportunity advertising
geliert jellied
geltend machen assert
Geltungsdauer (f) validity
Gemäldegalerie (f) picture

gallery
Gemeinde (f) community
Gemeindesteuer (f) community tax
Gemeindekosten (pl.) overhead cost, overhead expenses
Gemeindekostenstelle (f) overhead department
gemeinsam joint
Gemeinschaft (f) community
gemeinschaftlich teamwork
Gemeinschaftsbadezimmer (n) communal bathroom
Gemeinschaftsküche (f) communal canteen, communal kitchen
Gemeinschaftsraum (m) recreation room
Gemeinschafts-verkaufsförderung (f) group business promotion
Gemeinschaftsverpflegung (f) communal feeding, communal provisions
Gemeinschaftswerbung (f) associate advertising, cooperative advertising, group advertising
gemälzt, nicht non-maltet
gemischt assorted, mixed
Gemischtwarenhandlung (f) general store
Gemse (f) chamois
Gemüse (n) vegetable
Gemüse (n) **in Essig eingelegt** pickles
Gemüse (n), **gemischtes** mixed vegetable
Gemüsecremesuppe (f) cream of vegetable
Gemüsegericht (n) vegetable dish
Gemüseplatte (f) vegetable plate
Gemüsesalat (m) vegetable salad
Gemüsesuppe (f) julienne, vegetable broth
Gemüsesuppe (f) **gekühlt** chilled vegetable soup, grits

Gemüsesuppe (f) **klar** clear soup with vegetables
Gemüsesuppe (**mit Fleisch**) (f), **dicke** pottage
Gemüsesuppe (**mit Hammelfleisch**) (f) Sotch broth
gemütlich cosy, snug
Gemütlichkeit (f) cosiness, leisureliness
genau exact
Genauigkeit (f) accuracy
genehmigen approve
Genehmigung (f) approval, permit
Generaldirektor (m) general manager
Generalüberholung (f) reconditioning
genießen enjoy
Genüsse (pl. m), **kulinarische** pleasures of the table
geöffnet open
Gepäck (n) baggage, luggage
Gepäck (n) **aufgeben** check-in baggage, register luggage
Gepäck (n), **Bestätigung für abhanden gekommenes** send luggage in advance prosperity irregularity report (PIR)
Gepäck (n), **sperriges** bulky baggage
Gepäckabfertigung (f) baggage registration counter, cheking of baggage, luggage office, luggage registration counter, registering of luggage, registration of luggage
Gepäckabholung (f) collection of luggage
Gepäckablage (f) baggage rack, luggage rack
Gepäckanhänger (**Auto**) (m) baggage trailer
Gepäckanhänger (m) baggage label, luggage label

60

Gepäckannahme (f) receipt of baggage to be deposited
Gepäckannahmeschalter (m) receipt of baggage to be deposited
Gepäckaufbewahrung (f) checkroom, left-luggage office
Gepäckaufbewahrungsschein (m) receipt for registered luggage
Gepäckaufgabestelle (f) baggage office, luggage office
Gepäckausgabe (f) handing out of baggage
Gepäckbahnsteig (m) baggage platform, luggage platform
Gepäckbeförderung (f) conveyance of luggage
Gepäckdienst (m) baggage service, luggage service
Gepäckgebühr (f) **je Stück** (n) charge per piece of baggage
Gepäckkontrolle (f) examination of luggage
Gepäcknetz (n) baggage rack, luggage rack
Gepäckraum (m) luggage compartment luggage room
Gepäckraum (Bahn) (m) baggage compartment
Gepäckraum (Flugzeug) (m) baggage hold
Gepäckraum (Schiff) (m) baggage room
Gepäckschalter (m) deposit counter
Gepäckschein (m) baggage check, consignment note, left-luggage ticket, luggage receipt, luggage-ticket
Gepäckschließfach (n) baggage locker, luggage locker, station locker
Gepäckträger (m) luggage porter, porter, redcap
Gepäcktransfer (m) luggage transfer
Gepäckversicherung (f) baggage insurance
Gepäckwagen (m) baggage car, luggage an
Gepäckzustellung (f) delivery of baggage
gepökelt pickled, salted
Gerät (n) appliance, implement, tool
Gerätschaften (pl. f) equipment
geräuchert smoked
geräumig roomy
Geräusch (n) noise
gerecht fair
Gericht (Essen) (n) dish, meal
Gericht (aus den feinsten Stücken Geflügel) (n) supreme
Gericht (n), **fleischloses** meatless dish
geringwertig low valued
gern essen relish
gern haben like
gerinnen curdle
geröstet toasted, roast
Gerste (f) barley
Gerstenmehlkuchen (dreieckig) (m) scone
Gerstenschleimsuppe (f) barley soup
Geruch (m) odour, smell fragrance
Gerücht (n) gossip, grapevine
gesalzen salted
Gesamtkosten (pl.) total cost
Gesamtplanung (f) master scheduling
Gesamtstreckenfahrpreis (m) through fare
Geschäft (n) business, concern, deal dealing, transaction
Geschäftsbrief (m) business letter
Geschäftsentwicklung (f) trend

61

of operations
geschäftsfähig capable of contracting
Geschäftsfreund (m) business friend
Geschäftsführer (m) manager
Geschäftsführung (f) management, top management
Geschäftsleben (n) business life
Geschäftsleitung (f) management
Geschäftsmann (m) businessman
Geschäftspolitik (f) business policy
Geschäftspolitik (f) policy
Geschäftsräume (pl. m) business premises
Geschäftsreise (f) business trip (tour)
Geschäftsrückgang (m) business recession
Geschäftsschluß (m) closing hour
Geschäftsstraße (f) shopping street
Geschäftsstelle (f) branch office
Geschäftsstellenleiter (m) branch manager
Geschäftsumfang (m) business volume
Geschäftsverbindung (f) business relation
Geschäftsverkehr (m) dealing, traffic
Geschäftsviertel (n) business district, downtown, shopping center
Geschäftsvorfall (m) transaction
Geschäftswagen (m) business car
Geschäftszeit (f) business hours, office hours
geschält peeled
Geschenk (n) gift, gratuity, present
Geschenkartikel (m) gift article

Geschenkartikel (pl. m) fancy-goods
Geschenkgutschein (m) gift token
Geschenkladen (m) gift shop
Geschirr (n) dishes
Geschirrspülmaschine (f) diswashing machine
Geschirrtuch (n) tea-cloth
geschlossen closed
Geschmack (m) flavour, taste
geschmacklos insipid, tasteless
Geschmacklosigkeit (f) tastelessness
Geschmackseigenschaft (f) attribute of taste
Geschmacksreichtum (m) tastefulness
geschmackvoll tasteful
geschmolzen melted
geschmort braised
Geschnetzeltes (n) shredded meat
geschützt sheltered, protected
Geschwätz (n) gossip
Geschwindigkeit (f) speed
Geschwindigkeitsbegrenzung (f) speed limit
Gesellschaft (f) association, society, company
Gesellschaft (f) **mit beschränkter Haftung (GmbH)** (f) limited liability company (Ltd.)
Gesellschaft (f), **geschlossene** private party
Gesellschaftsabend (m) social evening
Gesellschaftsfahrt (f) party outing, party trip
Gesellschaftsflug (m) party flight
Gesellschaftskleidung (f) formal dress, evening dress
Gesellschaftsraum (m) lounge, private room
Gesellschaftsreise (f) conducted

tour, escorted tour, guided tour, organized tour (f), party tour
Gesellschaftsreisen (pl. f) party travel
Gesellschaftsreiseverkehr (m) group travel
Gesellschaftsspiel (n) parlour game, party game
Gesellschaftszimmer (n) function room
gesetzlich lawful, legal, legitimate
gesetzmäßig legitimate
gespickt mit Speck (m) larded
Gesprächsstoff (m) topic
Gestalt (f) figure
gestatten let, permit
gestern yesterday
gesund healthy, wholesome
Gesundheit (f) health
Gesundheitsbestimmungen (pl. f) public health regulations
Gesundheitsvorschriften (pl. f) sanitary regulations
Gesundheitszeugnis (n) health certificate
Gesundheitszutand (m) health
Getränk (n) beverage, drink
Getränk (n), **mit Eis(würfeln)** (pl., m) (n) on the rocks
Getränk (n), **alkoholfreies** non-alcoholic beverage
Getränke (pl. n) **nicht inbegriffen** drinks extra
Getränke (pl. n) **und kalte Speisen** (pl. f) **im Zug** (m) drinks and snacks on board
Getränkeautomat (m) bellcaptain, drink dispenser
Getränkekarte (f) list of beverages
Getränkekellner (m) wine-butler
Getränkekontrolle (f) beverage control
Getränkesteuer (f) beverage-tax

Getreide (n) cereals
Getreideflocken (pl. f) cereals
Getriebe (Fahrzeug) (n) transmission
Getriebe (n), **automatisches** automatic transmission
getrocknet dried
getrüffelt truffled
gewähren allow, grant
Gewässerverschmutzung (f) pollution of the waters
Gewand (n) garment
Gewerbe (n) trade
Gewerkschaft (f) labo(u)r union, union
Gewicht (n) weight
Gewinn (m) gain, profit, surplus
Gewinn (m) **vor Abschreibung** (f) profit before depreciation
Gewinn (m) **vor Zinsen** (pl. m) **und Abschreibung** (f) profit before interest and depreciation
Gewinn (m), **entgangener** lost profit
Gewinn- und Verlustrechnung (f) general profit and loss statement, profit and loss statement
Gewinnaufschlag (m) markup
gewinnbringend profitable
Gewinneinflußfaktoren-Analyse (f) profit sensitivity study
gewinnen (erhalten) benefit, gain
Gewinnmultiplikator (m) profit multiplier
Gewinnschwelle (f) break-even point
Gewinnschwellen-Diagramm (n) break-even chart
Gewinnspanne (f) return on sales
Gewitter (n) eletric storm, thunderstorm
gewöhnen an accustom to, become used to

gewöhnlich ordinary
gewöhnt an accustomed
Gewohnheit (f) custom, habit
Gewürz (n) spice
Gewürzgurke (f) pickle, pickled gherkin
Gewürznelke (f) cloves
Gezeiten (pl.) tides
gezuckert sugared
Gipfel (Gebäck) (m) crescent
gierig greedy
gießen pour
giftig toxic(al)
Gin (m) gin
glänzend glossy
Gläschen (n) tot
Gläsergestell (n) rack
Glas (n) glass
Glasfaserski (m) glass fibre ski
Glasur (f) icing
Glaswaren (pl. f) glass-ware
glatt slippery
Glatteis (n) glazed frost
Glaubersalzquelle (f) sodium sulphate spring
gleich equal
gleichbedeutend equivalent
gleichkommend quasi
gleichmäßig equal
gleichwertig equivalent
Gleis (n) line, track
Gleise (pl. n) rails
Gletscher (m) glacier
Gletschereis (n) glacial ice
Gletschersee (m) glacial lake, glacier lake
Gletscherspalte (f) crevasse
Gletscherwanderung (f) glacier travel
Glied (m) member
Global-Versicherungspolice (f) insurance-general
Globetrotter (m) globetrotter
Glocke (f) bell
Glücksspiel (n) gambling, game of chance
Glühbirne (f) bulb, electric bulb
Glühwein (m) hot claret with cinnamon and clove, hot wine, mulled claret, mulled wine
gnädige Frau (f), **gnädiges Fräulein** (n) madam (umgangssprachl.: ma'am)
Go-kart-Sport (m) karting
Goldbarsch (m) dorado
Goldmakrele (f) blue fish, gilt head, golden mackerel
Golfausrüstung (f) golf equipment
Golfplatz (m) golf course, links
Golfspieler (m) golfer
Gondel (f) cable car, gondola
Gondelfahrt (f) gondola ride
Gorgonzola (m) Gorgonzola
Gottesdienst (m) divine service, service, mass
Gourmet (m) gourmet
Graben (m) moat
Grad (m) degree
Granatapfel (m) pomegranate
Grapefruit (f) grapefruit
Grapefruit (f) **eisgekühlt** chilled grapefruit
Grapefruitsaft (m) grapefruit juice
grafisch darstellen chart
Gatifikation (f) bonus, gratuity
garatiniert browned, gratinated
Gratiszimmer (n) complimentary room
Gremium (n) committee
Grenzbahnhof (m) frontier station
Grenze (f) **überschreiten** cross the frontier
Grenzertrag (m) marginal income
Grenzformalitäten (pl. f) frontier formalities
Grenzgebiet (n) border area, frontier area

Grenzkosten (pl.) marginal cost
Grenzkostenrechnung (f) marginal costing
Grenzstadt (f) border town, frontier town
Grenzübergang (m) border crossing, frontier crossing
Grenzübergangsstelle (f) border crossing point, frontier crossing point
Grenzübertritt (m) border crossing, frontier crossing
Grenzverkehr (m) border traffic
Grenzzone (f) border zone, frontier zone
Griechenland Greece
Grieß (m) semolina
Grießklößchen (pl. n) **gratiniert** baked semolina dumplings
Grießklößchensuppe (f) soup with semolina dumplings
Grießpudding (m) semolina pudding
Grießpudding (m) **kalt** cold semolina pudding
Grießstrudel (m) semolina pie
Grießsuppe (f) semolina soup
Griff (m) handle
Griff- und Bewegungsstudie (f) micromotion study
Grill (m) grill
Grill (m), **vom** grilled
Grillbar (f) grill-bar
Grillrestaurant (n) grill-room
Grillstube (f) grill-room
Grippe (f) influenza
Grog (m) grog, toddy
Grog (m) **mit Rum** (m) hot rum grog
Großabnehmer (m) outlet
großartig magnificent
Großsegel (n) main sail
Großeltern (pl.) grandparents
Großhandelsrabatt (m) wholesale discount
Großmast (m) main mast
Großmutter (f) grandmother
Großvater (m) grandfather
Großwildreservat (n) big-game reservation
großzügig generous
Grotte (f) grotto
gründen establish, from
Gründling (m) goby
Gündonnerstag (m) Maunday Thursday
Gründung (f) establishment, foundation
grüne Versicherungskarte (f) international motor insurance card
Grünfläche (f) open space
Grünkohl (m) green cabbage, kale
Grütze (f), **rote** red grits
Grund (Boden) (m) ground
Grund (m) cause, reason
Grundfahrpreis (m) basic fare
Grundgehalt (n) base salary
Grundlage (f) basis
Grundlagenforschung (f) basic research
Grundlohn (m) base pay
grundlos gratuitous
Grundpreis (m) basic price
Grundstück (n) plot of land
Grundstück (n), **bebautes** built-up property
Grundstücke (pl. n) **und Gebäude** (pl. n) land and buildings
Grundstücksmakler (m) estate agent
Grundzubereitung (f) pre-preparation
Gruppenbesichtigung (f) group visit
Gruppenfahrt (f) party outing, party trip

Gruppenleiter (m) group leader
Gruppenreise (f) group journey, party tour
Gruppenreisen (pl. f) party travel
Gruppentarif (m) party rate
Gruppenversicherung (f) group insurance
Gruß (m) greeting
Grußkarte (f) greetings card
Gruyerekäse (m) Gruyere chesse
gültig available, valid
gültig, wechselweise interavailable
Gültigkeit (f) availability, validity
Gültigkeitsdauer (f) availability, time of validity
Gürtel (m), **grüner** green belt
Güte (Qualität) (f) quality
Güteklasse (f) grade
Güter (pl. n) goods
Güterbahnhof (m) freight station, goods station
Güterkraftverkehr (m) road haulage
Güterverkehr (m) freight traffic, goods traffic
Güterwagen (m) freight car, goods waggon
Güterzug (m) freight train, goods train
Gütezeichen (n) quality label
Gugelhupf (m) plain circle cake, Vienna plum pudding
Gulasch (n) brown stew, goulash
Gulasch (n), **ungarisches** Hungarian goulash
Gulaschsuppe (f) goulash soup
Gummilinse (f) zoom lens
Gummistiefel (pl. m) gum boots, rubber boots
Gurke (f) cucumber
Gurke (f), **saure** pickled cucumber
Gurkensalat (m) cucumber salad

gut good, well
gut eingerichtet well-furnished
gutbürgerlich plain
gutbürgerlich (Küche) homely
gute Nacht (f) good night
guten Abend (m) good evening
guten Morgen (m) good morning
guten Tag (m) good afternoon
guter Glaube (m) good faith
Gutschein (m) coupon, give-away, voucher
Gutschein (m), **noch nicht eingelöster** matured coupon
gutschreiben credit
Gutschrift (f) credit
Gutschriftkarte (f) credit card
Gutschriftsanzeige (f) credit note
Gymnastik (f) gymnastics, setting-up exercises

H

Haarbürste (f) hairbrush
Haarklemme (f) hair-grip
Haarnadel (f) hairpin
Haarnadelkurve (f) hairpin bend
Haarnetz (n) hair-net
Haarschnitt (m) hair-cut
Haarspange (f) hair-slide
Haarwasser (n) hair lotion
Haarwild (n) furred game
Habensaldo (m) credit balance
Hackbeefsteak (n) Hamburger, Hamburger steak, hashed steak Russian style
Hackbraten (m) hashed meat, meat-loaf
Hackbrett (n) chopping board
hacken mince
Hackfleisch (n) ground meat, minced beef, minced meat

Hackfleisch (n) **mit braunen Bohnen** (pl. f) chili con carne
Hackfleischkotelett (n) **vom Kalb** (n) chopped veal cutlet
Hackmaschine (für Fleisch) (f) mincer, mincing machine
Hackmesser (n) chopping knife, chopper
Hühnchen (n) spring-chicken
Hähnchen (oder Suppenhuhn) (n) **und Lauch** (m) chock-a-leekie
Hängematte (f) hammock
Häschen (n) leveret
häßlich ugly
häufig frequent
Häufigkeit (f) frequency
Hafen (m) harbour, harbor, port
Hafen (m) **am offenen Wasser** (n) open-water port
Hafenanlagen (pl. f) docks, port installations
Hafenausfahrt (f) harbour mouth
Hafenbahnhof (m) harbour station, marine railway station
Hafeneinfahrt (f) entrance to a harbour, harbour mouth, port entrance
Hafengebühren (pl. f) harbour dues, keelage
Hafengeld (n) port dues
Hafenpolizei (f) harbour police
Hafenrundfahrt (f) circular tour of port
Hafenschlepper (m) harbour tug
Hafenviertel (n) dock area, dock quarter
Hafer (n) oat
Haferbrei (m) porridge
Haferflocken (pl. f) oats, oat flakes
Hafermehl (n) oatmeal
Haferschleim (m) gruel
Haferschleimsuppe (f) oatmeal cream soup

Haft (f) arrest
haftbar responsible
Haftpflicht (f) third-party liability
Haftpflichtdeckung (f) liability insurance coverage
haftpflichtig liable
Haftpflichtversicherung (f) liability insurance, third-party insurance
Haftung (f) responsibility, liability
Hagebutte (f) hip
Hagebuttentee (m) hip-tea
Hagelversicherung (f) hail insurance
Hahn (m) cock, rooster
Haifischflossen (pl. f) shark's fins
Haifischflossensuppe (f) shark's fins soup
Haken (m) hook
halb durch rare
halbe Flasche (f), **eine** half a bottle
halbe Portion (f), **eine** half a portion
halber Preis (m) half-fare
halbes Backhuhn (n), **ein** half a fried chicken
Halbfabrikate (pl. n) goods in process
Halbinsel (f) peninsula
halbjährlich semiannual
halbmonatlich semimonthly
Halbmondpastetchen gefüllt (n) stuffed half-moon patty
Halbpension (f) demi-pension half pension
halbtags half-day
Halbtagsausflug (m) half-day excursion
Hallenschwimmbad (n) indoor swimming-pool
Hallensport (m) indoor sport

67

Hallentennis (n) covered-court tennis
Halskette (f) necklace
Halt (m) halt
Halt (m), **planmäßiger** scheduled halt, scheduled stop
Halt - Vorfahrt (f) **beachten** halt at major road ahead
halten halt, stop
Haltestelle (f) stop
Halteverbot (n) no stopping, prohibition to stop
Halteverbot (n) **heute auf dieser Straßenseite** (f) no stopping this side today
Haltung (f) attitude
Hamburger (m) Hamburger, Hamburger steak
Hammel (m) mutton
Hammel-, Rindfleisch- und Kartoffeleintopf (m) Lancashire hot pot
Hammelkeule (f) leg of mutton
Hammelragout (n) mutton-stew
Hammelragout (n) **irische Art** (f) Irish stew
Hammelrippchen (n) mutton chop
Hammelrücken (m) saddle of mutton
Hammelspießchen (n) mutton on skewers
Hand (f) hand
handbetrieben hand-operated
Handblasebalg (m) hand bellows
Handbremse (f) hand brake
Handbuch (n) manual
Handel (m) bargain, deal, trade, traffic
Handeln bargain, deal, trade
Handelsbrauch (m) trade custom, usage of trade
Handelsschiff (n) merchant ship, trading vessel
Handelssperre (f) embargo

Handelsvertreter (m) traveller
Handelsware (f) merchandise
Handgepäck (n) hand luggage, portable luggage
handhaben handle
Handkoffer (m) suitcase
Handlung (f) action
Handlungsreisender (m) commercial travel(l)er
Handschuh (m) glove
Handserviette (f) hand-napkin
Handtasche (f) handbag
Handtuch (n) towel
Handtuchhalter (m) towel-rack
Handwerk (n) handicraft
Handwerker (m) craftsman
Hang (m) slope
Hangar (m) hangar
Hardware (f) hardware
Harpune (f) harpoon
hart hard
hart am Wind (m) **segeln** sail near to the wind
hartgekocht hard-boiled, hard-cooked
Hase (m) hare
Hase (m), **junge** leveret
Haselhuhn (n) hazel-hen
Haselhuhnragout (n) brown hazel-hen-stew
Haselnuß (f) hazelnut
Haselnußtorte (f) hazelnut tart
Hasenbraten (m) roast hare
Hasenpfeffer (m) jugged hare
Hasenrücken (m) saddle of hare
Hast (f) haste
Haube (f) hood
Hauptbahnhof (m) central station, main station
Hauptbuch (n) general ledger
Hauptbuchhalter (m) chief accountant
Hauptbüro (n) head office, main office
Hauptdeck (n) main deck

Haupteingang (m)   main entrance
Hauptfleischgang (m)   main joint, main meat course
Hauptgang (Speisen) (m)   main course, main joint, main meat course
Hauptgericht (n)   main course, main dish
Hauptjournal (n)   general journal
Hauptmahlzeit (f)   main meal
Hauptreiseverkehr (m)   peak tourist traffic
Hauptreisezeit (f)   peak tourist season
Hauptsaisonflugpreis (m)   peak season fare
Hauptschlüssel (m)   pass-key, master-key
Hauptspeise (f)   main dish
Hauptstadt (f)   capital, metropolis
Hauptstraße (f)   main road, main street
Hauptteil (m)   bulk
Hauptverkehrsstraße (f)   highway
Hauptverkehrszeit (f)   rush hours
Hauptversammlung (f)   annual meeting
Hauptverwaltung (f)   headquarter
Haus-zu-Haus-Gepäckbeförderung (f)   door-to-door pick up and delivery service
Hausdame (f)   executive housekeeper, housekeeper, matron
Hausdiener (m)   bellman, houseman, valet
Hauseigentümer (m)   landlord
Hausgast (m)   border, resident
hausgemacht   home-made
Haushaltsgüter (pl. n)   household goods
Haushaltspackung (f)   family size package
Haushaltsrechnung (f)   family budget
Hausmannskost (f)   plain fare
Hausmantel (m)   housecoat
Hausmeister (m)   janitor
Hausnummer (f)   house number
Hausordnung (f)   house rules, regulations of the house, rules of residents
Hausreinigung (f)   spring cleaning
Hausreinigungsabteilung (f)   housekeeping department
Hausschlüssel (m)   house key
Hausschuh (m)   slipper
Haustelefon (n)   house telephone
Haustier (n)   pet
Haustür (f)   front door
Hauszeitung (f)   house organ
Haut (f)   skin, peeling
Haxe (f)   knuckle
Hecht (m)   pickerel, pike
Hechtklößchen (pl. m)   pike dumplings
Heck (n)   stern
Hecke (f)   hedge
Hefe (f)   leaven, yeast
Hefeextrakt (m)   yeast extract
Hefeteigkuchen (m) **mit Früchten** (pl. f)   fruit savarin
Hefter (m)   folder
Heide (f)   heath, pagan
Heidelbeere (f)   bilberry
Heilanzeige (f)   indication
Heilbad (n)   health resort, spa
Heilbadekur (f)   balneation, course of treatment at a spa
Heilbäder (pl. n) **nehmen**   bathe
Heilbäderwesen (n)   balneation
Heilbutt (m)   halibut
Heilfaktor (m)   curative factor
Heilfaktor (m), **natürlicher**   natural curative factor
Heilgymnastik (f)   physiotherapy
Heilklima (n)   curative climate, wholesome climate

Heilkraft (f)   curative power
Heilmethode (f)   method of treatment
Heilmittel (n)   remedy
Heilmoor (n)   curative-mud
Heilpraktiker (m)   naturopath
Heilquelle (f)   medicinal spring, mineral spring, spa
Heilschlamm (m)   curative-mud
Heilstätte (f)   sanatorium
Heilung (f)   cure
Heilwasser (n)   medicinal mineral water
Heim (n)   hostel
Heimat (f)   home country
Heimatabend (m)   folkloristic evening
Heimatanschrift (f)   home address
Heimatfest (n)   local festival
Heimathafen (m)   home port, port of registry
Heimatstadt (f)   native town
Heimcomputer (m)   home computer
Heimkehr (f)   return home
Heimreise (f)   homeward journey, journey home, voyage home
heiß   hot
Heißluftbad (n)   hot-air bath
Heißwasser (n)   hot water
Heißwasserboiler (m)   water-heater
Heiterkeit (f)   gaiety
Heizöl (n)   fuel
Heizung (f)   heating
helfen   aid, assist, help
Helikopter (m)   helicopter
Helikopterflugplatz (m)   helicopterport
Heliotherapie (f)   sun-light treatment
Henne (f)   hen
herabsetzen   reduce

Herabsetzung (f)   reduction
herausfordern   challenge
Herausforderung (f)   challenge
herb   dry, tart
Herberge (f)   hostel
Herbst (m)   autumn, fall
Herbstferien (pl.)   autumn holiday, fall vacation
Herbstmesse (f)   autumn trade-fair
Herd (m)   range
Herd (m), **elektrische**   electric range
Hering geräuchert (m)   smoked herring
Heringssalat (m)   herring salad
Herkunft (f)   origin
Herrenfriseur (m)   barber, gentlemen's hairdresser, men's hairdresser
Herrennachthemd (n)   night shirt
Herrentoilette (f)   gentlemen's cloakroom, gentlemen's lavatory, men's lavatory
herstellen   produce
hervorheben   highlight
hervorragend   outstanding
Herz (n)   heart
herzhaft   hearty
herzlich   hearty
Herzoginnenkartoffeln (pl. f)   dutchess potatoes
Heu (n)   hay
Heuhaufen (m)   haystack
heute   today
Hilfe (f)   aid, help
Hilfe (f) **leisten**   assist
Hilfs- und Betriebsstoffe (pl. m)   operating supplies
Hilfsdienst (m)   auxiliary service
Hilfskoch (m)   assistent cook, junior cook
Hilfsquelle (f)   resource
Himbeere (f)   raspberry
Himbeereis (n)   raspberry ice

Himbeersaft (m) raspberry juice
Himmel (m) sky
Himmelfahrtstag (m) Ascension Day
Himmelsrichtung (f) quarter
Hin- und Rückfahrschein (m) roundabout ticket, return ticket
Hin- und Rückflug (m) outward and inward flight, outward and return flight
Hin- und Rückreise (f) outward and homeward voyage, outward and homeward journey
Hin- und Rückreisepreis (m) return fare
Hinfahrt (f) outward journey, outward voyage
Hinflug (f) outward flight, outward journey
hinreichend adequate
Hinreise (f) outward journey, outward voyage
Hintergrundmusik (f) background music
Hinterland (n) hinterland
Hinterlegung (f) deposit
Hinweis (m) reference
hinzufügen add
Hinzufügung (f) addition
Hirn (n) brains
Hirnsuppe (f) calf's brains soup
Hirsch (m) deer, stag, venison
Hirse (f) millet
hissen hoist
Hitze (f) heat
hitzig zealous
Hobelkäse (m) shaved cheese
Hoch (Wetter) (n) anticyclone
Hochbahn (f) overhead railway
Hochbetrieb (m) great bustle
Hochgarage (f) multi-storey garage
Hochgebirge (n) high mountains
Hochkonjunktur (f) boom
Hochplateau (n) high plateau

Hochsaison (f) height of the season, high season, peak season
hochseetüchtig ocean-going
Hochstraße (f) mountain road
Hochtourist (m) high altitude climber
Hochtouristik (f) mountaineering
Hochwasserversicherung (f) wave damage insurance
hochwertig high value
Hochzeit (f) wedding
Hochzeitsreise (f) honeymoon
hochziehen hoist
Höchstbesetzung (f) **mit Personal** (n) maximum manning
Höchstbestand (m) maximum inventory
Höchstgebot (n) highest bid
Höchstgeschwindigkeit (f) maximum speed, top speed
Höchstpreis (m) maximum price
höflich polite
Höflichkeit (f) courtesy
Höhe (f) height
Höhenbegrenzung (f) height restriction
Höhenklima (n) mountain climate
Höhenlage (f) high altitude
Höhenluft (f) mountain air
Höhenluftkurort (m) high altitude health resort
Höhenrestaurant (n) mountain restaurant
Höhensonne (f) ultra-violet lamp
Höhenunterschied (m) vertical drop
höhere Gewalt (f) act of God
Höhle (f) cave
Hörensagen (n) hearsay
Hörnchen (Gebäck) (n) half moons
Hörnchennudeln (pl. f) elbow

macaroni
Hof (m)   court, courtyard, yard
Hofzimmer (n)   back room
Hoheitsgewässer (pl. n)   territorial waters
Holding (f)   holding company
Holländische Sauce (f)   Dutch sauce
Holland   Holland
Holsteiner Schnitzel (n)   veal collop with fried egg
Holundertee (m)   elderberry-tea
Holz (n)   wood
Holzfeuer (n)   wood fire
Holzkohle (f)   charcoal
Holzkohlen-Grillgericht (n)   barbecue
Holzkohlenfeuer (n), **vom**   charcoal broiled
Holzzucker (m)   xylose
Honig (m)   honey
Honorar (n)   fee
Hopfen (m)   hop
Hopfensprossen (pl. f)   hop sprouts
Hoppel-poppel (n)   veal stew with scrambled eggs
Horizont (m)   skyline
Horsd'oeuvre (n)   horsd'oeuvre
Hospiz (n)   hospice
Hostess (f)   hostess
Hot dog (m)   hot dog
Hotel (n)   hotel
Hotel (n) **der gehobenen Mittelklasse** (f)   upper-bracket hotel
Hotel (n) **erster Klasse** (f)   first class hotel
Hotel (n) **für Durchreisende** (pl. m)   transient hotel
Hotel (n) **garni**   residential hotel, lodging-house
Hotel (n) **internationaler Klasse** (f)   hotel of international standard
Hotel (n), **erstklassiges**   high-class hotel
Hotel (n), **gutgeführtes**   hotel under good management
Hotel- und Gaststättenführer (m)   hotel and restaurant guide
Hotel- und Gaststättengewerbe (n)   hotel and catering trade
Hotelangestellter (m)   hotel employee
Hotelanzeiger (m)   hotel directory
Hotelbelegung (f)   hotel bookings, hotel occupancy, occupancy
Hotelbesitzer (m)   hotel owner
Hotelbetrieb (m)   hotel operation
Hotelbetriebsführung (f)   operational management
Hotelbett (n)   hotel bed
Hotelbettenüberschuß (m)   hotel bedrooms surplus
Hotelboy (m)   hotel bellboy, boy
Hotelbüro (n)   hotel office
Hoteldiener (m)   bellman, porter
Hoteldirektion (f)   hotel management
Hoteldirektor (m)   hotel manager, resident manager
Hoteleigenschaft (f)   hotelhood
Hoteleinstufung (f)   classification of hotels
Hotelempfangshalle (f)   hotel lobby
Hotelfach (n)   hotel business
Hotelfachschule (f)   hotel training school, school of hotel management
Hotelfriseur (m)   hairdresser at the hotel
Hotelführer (m)   hotel guide
Hotelführung (f)   hotel-keeping
Hotelgast (m)   hotel guest
Hotelgebäude (n)   hotel building
Hotelgelände (n)   hotel site

Hot — hup

Hotelgröße (f) hotel size
Hotelgrundstück (n) hotel site
Hotelgutschein (m) hotel voucher
Hotelhalle (f) entrance hall, hotel entrance hall, hotel foyer, hotel vestibule, lobby, lounge
Hotelier (m) hotel-keeper
Hotelkapazität (f) hotel capacity
Hotelkette (f) hotel chain
Hotelklassifizierung (f) classification of hotels
Hotelkosten (pl.) hotel expenses
Hotelleitung (f) hotel management
Hotelerie (f) hotel and catering trade, hotel industry, hotel trade
Hotelwesen (n) hotel trade
Hotelmanagement (n), **praktisches** operational management
Hotelnachweis (m) hotel broker
Hotelordnung (f) hotel rules and regulations
Hotelpage (m) bellboy, bellhop, hotel pageboy
Hotelpension (f) private hotel
Hotelpersonal (n) hotel staff
Hotelportier (m) hall porter
Hotelrechnung (f) hotel bill
Hotelreservierung (f) hotel booking
Hotelrestaurant (n) hotel dining-room
Hotelstammgast (m) regular hotel guest
Hoteltelegrafenschlüssel (m), **internationaler** international hotel code
Hotelunterbringung (f) hotel accomodation
Hotelunterkunft (f) hotel accomodation
Hotelverband (m) hotel association
Hotelvertrag (m) hotel contract
Hotelwesen (n) hotel-keeping, innkeeping
Hotelzettel (Gepäck) (m) hotel label
Hotelzimmer (n) hotel room
Hubschrauber (m) helicopter
Hubschrauberflugplatz (m) helicopterport
Hubschrauberlandeplatz (m) airstop
Huckepackverkehr (m) road-rail service
hübsch handsome
Hüfte (f) hip
Hügel (m) hill
Hühnchen (n) baby chicken, hen-chicken, pullet
Hühnerbrust (f) chicken breast
Hühnerkeule (f) chicken leg
Hülsenfrucht (f) legume
Hülsenfrüchte (pl. f) pulse
Hütte (f) hut
Hütte (f), **bewirtschaftete** serviced hut
Hüttenkäse (m) cottage cheese
Hüttenzelt (n) umbrella tent
Huhn (n) chicken
Huhn (n) **in Aspik** (n) chicken in jelly
Huhn (n) **in Tomatensauce** (f) **mit Pilzen** (pl. m) **und Eiern** (pl. n) chicken stew
Hummer (m) lobster
Hummercocktail (m) lobster cocktail
Hummermayonnaise (f) lobster mayonnaise
Hund (m) dog
Hunde (pl. m) **sind an der Leine** (f) **zu halten** dogs must be kept on the lead
Hunger (m) hunger
Hupe (f) horn
hupen honk, hoot

Hupen verboten! no honking, no hooting
Husten (m) cough
Hutkoffer (m) hatbox
Hutzucker (m) loaf sugar

I

Indentifizierung (f) indentification
Imbiß (m) luncheonette, snack
Imbißbar (in Restaurants) (f) lunch-counter
Imbißpaket (n) box meal, food pack, lunch packet
Imbißstube (f) cafe, luncheonette, snack-bar, snack-counter, tea-shop
Immobilien (pl. f) immovables
Impfbestimmung (f) inoculation requirements
impfen vaccinate
Impfung (f) inoculation, vaccination
Impfzeugnis (n) certificate of vaccination
Import (m) import
importieren import
Index (m) index
Indien India
indisches Geflügelgericht (n) chicken curry
individuell individual
Industrieausstellung (f) industrial fair
Industriegebiet (n) industrial area
Industriemesse (f) industry fair
Information (f) information
Information (f) **und Betreuung** (f) reception and information office
Informationsbüro (n) information bureau, inquiry office
Informationsdienst (m) information service
Informationsquelle (f) source of information
Informationsreise (f) information trip
informieren brief, inform
Ingenieur (m) engineer
Ingwer (m) ginger
Ingwerbier (n) ginger beer
Ingwerkuchen (m) pepper cake
Ingwerlimonade (f) ginger ale
Ingwerpudding (m) ginger pudding
Inhaber (m) holder, keeper
Inhalation (f) inhalation
Inhalationsapparat (m) inhaler
Inhalationskur (f) inhalation therapy
Inkasso (n) collection
inkognito incognito
inländisch domestic
Inlandpostgebühren (pl. f) inland postage rates
Inlandsflug (m) domestic flight
Inlandsgast (m) national tourist
Inlandsstrecke (f) domestic route
Inneneinrichtung (f) interior equipment
Innenhof (m) inner courtyard
Innenkabine (f) inside room
Innenrevision (f) administrative audit
Innenstadt (f) city, town centre
Innere (n) interior
Innereien (pl. f) offals
Insekt (n) insect
Insel (f) island, isle
Inserat (n) advertisement (Abk.: ad)
Installateur (m) plumber
instandhalten maintain
Instandhaltung (f) maintenance
Instandhaltung (f) **und Repara-**

tur (f) maintenance and repair
Instandhaltungsauftrag (m) maintenance work order
instandsetzen repair
Instandsetzung (f) reconditioning
instruieren brief, instruct
Intercity-Zug (m) Inter-City train
Internationale Fachausstellung (f) **für das Hotel- und Gaststättengewerbe** (n) International Exhibition of the Hotel and Catering Trade
Internationale Vereinigung (f) **der Fremdenverkehrszentralen** (pl. f) International Union of Touristic Centers
Internationale Zivil-Luftfahrt-Organisation (f) International Civil Aviation Organization (ICAO)
Internationaler Automobilverband (m) International Automobile Federation
Internationaler Hotelverband (m) International Hotel Association (IHA)
Internationaler Luftverkehrsverband (m) International Air Transport Association (IATA)
Internationaler Verband (m) **der Reisebüros** (pl. n) Federation of Travel Agencies (FIAV)
Internationaler Verband (m) **der Jugendherbergen** (pl. f) Intenational Youth Hostel Federation (IYHF)
Internationales Impfzeugnis (n) International Vaccination Certificate
Interpreter (Datenverarbeitung) (m) interpreter
Interzonenverkehr (m) interzonal traffic
Interzonenzug (m) interzonal train
Inventar (n) inventory
Inventarstück (n) fixture
Inventur (f) taking of inventory
Inventur (f) **machen** take inventory
Inventur (f), **permanente** perpetual inventory
Inventurabweichung (f) inventory variation
Inventurberichtigung (f) inventory adjustment
Inventurbewertung (f) inventory pricing
investieren invest
Investitionen (pl. f) investment
Investitionsrechnung (f) capital expenditure budgeting
inzwischen meanwhile
Irische See (f) **und Ärmelkanal** (m) narrow seas
Irland Ireland
irreführend misleading
irren mistake, err
Irrtümer (pl. m) **und Änderungen** (pl. f) **vorbehalten** errors and alterations excepted
Irrtum (m) error, mistake
Island Iceland
Israel Israel
Ist (n) actual
Ist-Bestand (m) actual stock
Ist-Kosten (pl.) actual costs
Ist-Kostenrechnung (f) actual cost system
Ist-Wareneinsatz (m) **Getränke** (pl. n) actual beverage cost
Ist-Wareneinsatz (m) **Speisen** (pl. f) actual food cost
italienischer Salat (m) Italian Salad

75

J

Jacht (f)   cabin cruiser, yacht
Jachthafen (m)   marina
Jacke (f)   jacket, jerkin
jährlich   annual, per annum, yearly
Jagd (f)   hunt, hunting, shooting
Jagdaufseher (m)   gamekeeper
Jagdgebiet (n)   hunting ground
Jagdhütte (f)   hunting box, shooting box, shooting lodge
Jagdreise (f)   shooting trip
Jagdreservat (n)   game reserve
Jagdrevier (n)   hunting ground, shoot
Jagdsaison (f)   hunting season, open season, shooting season
Jagdschein (m)   gamelicense, shooting licence
Jagdzeit (f)   open season, shooting season
jagen   hunt, shoot
Jahr (n), **im**   per annum
Jahresabschluß (m)   annual financial statement, year-end closing
Jahresbedarf (m)   annual usage
Jahrestag (m)   anniversary
Jahrestemperatur (f), **mittlere**   mean annual temperature
Jahresurlaub (m)   annual holiday (vacation)
Jahresverbrauch (m)   annual usage
Jahresverdienst (m)   annual earnings
Jahresversammlung (f)   annual meeting
Jahreszeit (f)   season
Jahreszeitsalat (m)   season's salad
Jahrmarkt (m)   fun-fair
Jakobsmuschel (f)   scallop St. Jacques

Jalousien (pl. f)   Persian blinds
Jamaikapfeffer (m)   pimento
Japan   Japan
Jodquelle (f)   iodine spring
Joggen (n)   jogging
Joghurt (m, n)   yoghourt
Johannisbeere (f), **rote**   red currant
Johannisbeere (f)   currant
johlen   maffick
Jolle (f)   dinghy, sailing dinghy
Joule (n)   joule
Journal (n)   journal
Journalbuchung (f)   journal entry
Jubiläumsgeschenk (n)   anniversary present
jüdische Veranstaltung (f)   kosher function, kosher party
Jugend (f)   youth
Jugendfahrpreis (m)   youth fare
Jugendgruppenreise (f)   youth group journey
Jugendherberge (f)   youth hostel
Jugendherbergsausweis (m)   Youth Hostel Association Membership Card
Jugendklub (m)   youth club
jugendlich   juvenile
Jugendlicher (m)   youth
Jugendreise (f)   youth travel
Jugoslawien   Yugoslavia
Jumbo Jet (m)   jumbo jet
jung   young
Jungfernbraten (m)   fillet of pork roasted
Junggeselle (m)   bachelor
Jungkellner (m)   waiter apprentice
Jungkoch (m)   junior cook
Jungschwein (n)   baby pig
Juwelen (pl. f)   jewellery, jewelery
Juwelier (m)   jeweller, jeweler

K

Kabarett (n) cabaret
Kabel (n) cable, line cord
Kabeljau (m) hake
kabeln cable
Kabine (f) cabin
Kabine (Seilbahn) (f) cable car
Kabinengepäck (n) cabin luggage
Kabinenkoffer (m) trunk
Kabinenseilbahn (f) cabin cable railway
Känguruhschwanzsuppe (f) kangoroo tail soup
Kännchen (n) jug, pannikin
Käse (m) cheese
Käse (m), geriebener grated cheese
Käseauflauf (m) cheese souffle
Käsebrot (n) cheese sandwich
Käsefondue (n) cheese fondue
Käsekuchen (m) cheese cake, cheese pie
Käsekuchen (m), süßer sweet cheese cake
Käseplatte (f) selection of cheese
Käseschnitte (f) toasted cheese
Käseschnitte (f) geröstet Welsh rabbit (rarebit)
Käsetörtchen (n) cheese tartlet
Käufer (m) buyer
Käufermarkt (m) buyer's market
Kaffee (m) coffee
Kaffee (m) koffeinfrei coffee without caffeine
Kaffee (m) mit Sahne (f) coffee with cream
Kaffee (m) mit einem Schuß (m) Branntwein (m) lace-coffee
Kaffee (m) türkisch Turkish coffee
Kaffee(filter)maschine (f) percolator
Kaffeecremetorte (f) fany-cakee
with coffee cream
Kaffeekanne (f) coffee-pot
Kaffeemühle (f) coffee-mill
Kaffeepause (f) coffee break
Kaffeetasse (f) coffee cup
Kahn (m) boat
Kahnfahrt (f) boat-ride, boat trip
Kai (m) quay, wharf
Kai (m) am on the quay
Kaianlagen (pl. f) quayage
Kaigebühren (pl. f) quay dues
Kaigeld (n) quayage
Kaiserschmarrn (m) pancake, Emperor style
Kajak (n) kayak
Kajüte (f) cabin
Kakao (m) cocoa
Kakifrucht (f) kaki
Kakipflaume (f) persimmon
Kalb (n) calf, veal
Kalbfleisch (n) veal
Kalbfleisch (n) geschnetzelt chipped veal
Kalbfleisch (n) kalt in Thunfischsoße (f) veal with tuna
Kalbfleisch (n), eingemachtes stewed veal
Kalbfleischröllchen (pl. n) veal birds, veal olives
Kalbfleischwürstchen (n) small veal sausage
Kalbshaxe (f) calf's knuckle, knuckle of veal
Kalbshaxenscheibe (f) sliced knuckle of veal
Kalbsbraten (m) roast loin of veal, roast of veal
Kalbsbries (n) sweetbreads
Kalbsbries (n) gebacken calf's sweetbread baked
Kalbsbrust (f) calf's breast
Kalbsbrust (f) gefüllt stuffed breast of veal, roast stuffed breast of veal
Kalbsbrustknorpel (m) calf's

77

gristle
Kalbsfilet (n)   fillet of veal
Kalbsfricandeau (n)   fricandeau of veal
Kalbsfrikassee (n)   fricassee of veal
Kalbsfüße (pl. m)   calf's feet
Kalbsgoulasch (n) **mit Klößen** (pl. m)   stew of veal with dumplings
Kalbsherz (n)   calf's heart
Kalbshirn (n)   calf's brain
Kalbshirn (n) **gebacken**   calf's brains fried
Kalbskarreebraten (m)   rib roast of veal
Kalbskeule (f)   leg of veal
Kalbskopf (m)   calf's head
Kalbskopf (m) **gebacken**   calf's head fried
Kalbskopf (m) **in Essigsoße** (f)   calf's head vinaigrette
Kalbskopf en tortue (m)   calf's head with turtle sauce
Kalbskotelett (n)   veal chop, veal cutlet
Kalbskotelett (n) **natur**   plain veal cutlet
Kalbsleber (f)   calf's liver, liver of veal
Kalbsleber (f) **gebacken**   calf's liver fried
Kalbsleber (f) **geröstet**   calf's liver roasted
Kalbsleber geschnetzelt (f)   shredded calf's liver
Kalbsleberscheiben (pl. f)   sliced calf's liver
Kalbsleberspießchen (pl. m)   calf's liver on skewers
Kalbslunge (f)   calf's lights
Kalbsmedaillon (n)   medaillon of veal
Kalbsnieren (pl. f)   kidney of veal
Kalbsnierenbraten (m)   roast loin of veal with kidney
Kalbsnierensteak (n)   kidney steak
Kalbsnüßchen (n)   small veal steak
Kalbsnuß (f)   kernel of veal
Kalbsragout (n)   brown veal stew, veal stew
Kalbsröllchen (pl. n) **am Spieß** (m)   rolled veal on skewers
Kalbsroulade (f)   rolled veal steak, veal roll
Kalbsrücken (m)   saddle of veal
Kalbsschlegel (m)   leg of veal
Kalbsschnitzel (n)   veal collop, veal scallop
Kalbsschnitzel (n) **gefüllt**   cheese- and ham stuffed veal steak, stuffed veal collop
Kalbsschnitzel (n) **paniert**   breaded veal steak
Kalbsschnitzelchen (pl. n) **gespickt**   larded veal collops
Kalbsschulter (f)   shoulder of veal
Kalbssteak (n)   veal steak
Kalbszunge (f)   calf's tongue
Kalkulation (f)   calculation
kalkulieren   calculate
Kalorientabelle (f)   table of calorific values
kalt   cold
kalte Speisen (pl. f)   cold dishes
kaltes Bueffet (n)   cold buffet
Kamera (f)   camera
Kamille (f)   camomile
Kamillentee (m)   camomile tea
Kamin (m)   chimney, fireplace, fire-side
Kaminecke (f)   inglenook
Kamm (m)   comb
Kammuschel (f)   scallop
Kaninchen (n)   rabbit
Kanne (f)   pitcher
Kantine (mit großem Warenangebot) (f)   commissare store

Kanu (n)   canoe
Kanzel (Flugzeug) (f)   cockpit
Kapaun (m)   capon
Kapazität (f)   capacity
Kapazitätsausnutzung (f)   utilization of capacity
Kapazitätsausweitung (f)   capacity increase, increase in capacity
Kapazitätskosten (pl.)   capacity cost
Kapelle (Musik) (f)   band
Kapelle (Kirche) (f)   chapel
Kapellmeister (m)   bandleader
Kaper (f)   caper
Kapernsauce (f)   caper sauce
Kapital (n)   capital, funds
Kapitalbedarf (m)   capital demand, capital requirements
Kapitalumschlag (m)   capital turnover
Kapuzinerkresse (f)   nasturtium
Karaffe (f)   carafe, decanter
Karamelpudding (m)   caramel custard, caramel pudding, cup custard, custard pudding
Karawanenreise (f)   trekking
Karfiolsuppe (f)   cauliflower soup
Karfreitag (m)   Good-Friday
Karnevalszeit (f)   carnival season, Shrovetide
Karotte (f)   carrot
Karpfen (m)   carp
Karriere (f)   career
Karte (f)   map
Kartei (f)   file
Karteikarte (f)   file card
Kartenspiel (n)   game of cards
Kartenspiel (Gemeinsame Kasse) (n)   kitty
Kartenverkauf (m)   sale of tickets
Kartoffel (f)   potato
Kartoffel (f), süße   sweet potato
Kartoffelbrei (m)   creamed potatoes, mashed potatoes, potato-mash

Kartoffelchips (pl. m)   potato chips
Kartoffelknödel (m)   potato dumpling
Kartoffelkörbchen (n)   potato basket, potato nest
Kartoffelkroketten (pl. f)   croquettes potatoes, potato-croquettes
Kartoffeln (pl. f) **geröstet**   broiled potatoes
Kartoffeln (pl. f) **in der Schale** (f)   potatoes in their jackets
Kartoffeln (pl. f), **gebacken**   baked potatoes
Kartoffeln (pl. f), **neue**   new potatoes
Kartoffelpuffer (m)   potato pancake
Kartoffelsalat (m)   potato salad
Kartoffelscheiben (pl. f) **gebacken**   potato crips
Kartoffelstäbchen (pl. n) **gebacken**   French fried potatoes
Kartoffelstampfer (m)   potato masher
Kartoffelsuppe (f)   potato soup, soup with potatoes
Karussel (n)   merry-go-round, roundabout
Kasse (Kino etc.) (f)   box office
Kasse (f), **kleine**   petty cash
Kasseler Rippenspeer (m, n)   smoked pork ribs, roast smoked spare rib of pork
Kassenbestand (m)   cash balance
Kassenfehlbestand (m)   cash short
Kassenprüfung (f)   cash audit
kassieren   cash
Kassierer (m)   cashier
Kastanienpüree (n)   chestnut-vermicelli
Kategorie (f)   category

79

Kater (Katzenjammer) (m) hangover
Katerfrühstück (n) hangover breakfast
Kathedrale (f) cathedral
Katzenjammer (m) hangover
kauen chew
Kauf (m) purchase
Kauf (m), **vorteilhaftester** best buy
kaufen buy
Kaufentschluß (m) buying decision
Kaufgewohnheiten (pl. f) buying habits
Kaufkraft (f) buying power
Kaufvertrag (m) agreement of purchase and sale, contract of sale
Kaviar (m) caviar
Kaviarbrötchen (n) caviar sandwich
Kedgeree (Reisgericht mit Fisch, Eiern, Zwiebeln) (n) kedgeree
Kefir (m) kefir
Kegel (m) ninepin, skittle
Kegelbahn (f) bowling-alley, skittle-alley
kegeln bowl, play ninepins, play skittles
Kegeln (n) bowling
Kehrrichteimer (m) dustbin
kehrtmachen turn back
Keilkissen (n) bolster
Keilriemen (m) wedge strap
Kein Eintritt! no admittance, no entry
Keine Durchfahrt (f)! no through road
Keks (n), **dünner** cracker
Keller (m) cellar
Kellerbar (f) dive bar, underground bar
Kellergeschoß (n) basement
Kellerlokal (n) beer-cellar,

underground restaurant
Keller (m) waiter
Kellnerin (f) waitress
Kellnerlehrling (m) waiter apprentice
Kenntnis (f), **Kenntnisse** (pl. f) knowledge
Kennzahl (f) index figure
Kennzeichen (pl. n), **besondere** distinguishing marks
kennzeichnen feature
Kennzeichen (n) mark
Kennziffer (f) key number, ratio
Keramik (f) pottery
Kerbel (m) chervil
Kern (m) kernel, stone
Kerosin (n) kerosene
Kerzenabend (m) evening by candlelight
Kerzenlicht (n) candle light
Kerzenständer (m) candlestick
Kessel (m) kettle
Kessel (m), **elektrischer** electric kettle
Ketchup (n) catchup, ketchup
Kette (f) chain
Keule (Fleisch) (f) leg
Keule (f) haunch
Kibitzeier (pl. n) plover's eggs
Kichererbse (f) chick-pea
Kiebitz (m) lapwing, pewit, plover
Kiesstrand (m) pebbly beach
Kilometer (m) kilometre
Kinderausweis (m) child's travel document
Kinderbecken (n) children's pool
Kinderbetreuung (f) child care
Kinderbett (n) child's bed, cot, crib
Kinderbrei (m) pap
Kinderermäßigung (f) reduction for children
Kinderfahrkarte (f) child's ticket

Kindermädchen (n) nursemaid
Kinderspeisesaal (m) children's dining-room
Kinderspielplatz (m) children's playground
Kinderspielzimmer (n) children's playroom
Kinderzimmer (n) nursery
Kino (n) movie theater
Kinokarte (f) cinema ticket, movie ticket
Kinoprogramm (n) cinema program, movie program
Kinosaal (m) movie room
Kiosk (m) news stand
Kirchenkonzert (n) church concert
Kirchensteuer (f) church tax
Kirchturm (m) steeple
Kirchweih (f) local fair
Kirsche (f) cherry
Kirschkuchen (m) cherry cake
Kirschlikör (m) cherry brandy
Kirschtorte (f) cherry tart
Kiste (n) cushion
Kissenbezug (m) pillow-case, pillow-slip
Kissen (f) case
Kitsch (m) trash
klären clear
Klage (Gericht) (f) action
Klage (f) complaint
klagen (Gericht) sue
klagen complaint
Klappbett (n) fold-away bed, folding bed
Klappsitz (m) folding seat, tip-up seat
Klapptisch (m) fold-away table, folding table, pull-down table
Klasse (f) category
Klassifikation (f) grading
klassifizieren classify, grading
Klassifizierung (f) classification
Klausel (f) clause

Klavier (n) piano
Klebstoff (m) glue
Kleid (n) dress, gown
Kleiderablage (f) hall stand
Kleiderbügel (m) clothes-hanger, coat-hanger, hanger
Kleiderbürste (f) clothes-brush
Kleiderschrank (m) wardrobe
Kleiderständer (m) coat-rack
Kleidung (f) clothing
Kleinanzeige (f) want ad
Kleinbus (m) microbus, minibus
kleiner Teller (Brot) (m) bread-plate
kleingehackt minced
Kleingeld (n) change, coppers
Kleintaxi (n) minicab
Klempner (m) plumber
Kletterausrüstung (f) climbing equipment
Klettern (n) mountain-climbing
Klettersport (m) mountain-climbing
Klettertour (f) climbing tour
Klima (n) climate
Klima (n), **gemäßigtes** moderate climate
Klima (n), **mildes** mild climate
Klima (n), **rauhes** severe climate
Klimaanlage (f) air conditioning
Klimakurort (m) climatic health resort
Klimastation (f) climatological station
Klingel (f) bell
Klingelknopf (m) button
Klinik (f) clinic
Klipper (m) clipper
Klimaverhältnisse (pl. n) climatic conditions
Klößchen (n) small dumpling
klopfen knock
Klopfen (n) knock
Kloß (m) dumpling
Kloster (n) monastery

Klub (m) club
Klubabend (m) club evening
Klubhaus (n) clubhouse
Klumpen (m) lump
Knackwurst (f) plain sausage
Kneipe (f) pub, saloon-bar
Kneipenbummel (m) pub crawl
Kneippanlagen (pl. f) facilities for hydropathic treatment
Kneippkur (f) hydropathic treatment
Knoblauch (m) garlic
Knoblauchsoße (f) garlic sauce
Knochen (m) bone
Knöchel (m) ankle
Knödel (m) dumpling
Knödelsuppe (f) soup with dumpling
Knollensellerie (m) celeriac
Knoten (m) knot
Knurrfisch (m) gurnet
Knurrhahn (m) gurnard
knusprig crisp
Koch (m) cook
kochen boil, cook
Kochen (n) cooking
Kochen (n) **in Folie** (f) paper bag cooking
Kochgelegenheit (f) cooking-facilities
Kochgeschirr (n) cooking utensils, mess-tin
Kochkessel (m) kettle
Kochkunst (f) cooking, cuisine
Kochnische (f) kitchenette
Kochschrank (m) kitchenette
Kochstelle (f) cooking stove
Kochtopf cooking-pot, saucepan
Kodenummer (f) code number
Königinsuppe (f) cream of chicken
Königsberger Klopse (pl. m) meat-balls in white caper sauce
köstlich delicious, lovely
Koffer (m) case

Kofferanhänger (m) baggage label, luggage label
Kofferaufkleber (m) suitcase label
Kofferradio (n) portable radio
Kofferraum (Auto) (m) boot, trunk
Kohl (m) cabbage
Kohlfisch (m) whiting
Kohlrabi (m) kohlrabi
Kohlroulade (f) rolled stuffed cabbage leave
Kohlsprossen (pl. f) broccoli, sprouts
Koje (Schiff) (f) berth, bunk
Kokosnuß (f) coconut
Kolonialwarengeschäft (n) grocery store
Kolonie (f) colony
Kombiwagen (m) estate car, station wagon
Komfort (m), **moderner** luxurious fittings
Kommode (f) chest of drawers
Kommunikationssystem (n), **internes** internal communicating system
Kompetenz (f) authority
Kompott (n) preserved fruit, stewed fruit
Kompott (n) preserved fruit, stewed fruit
Kondensmilch (f) condensed milk
Konditor (m) confectioner
Konditorei (f) sweet shop
Konfekt (n) confections
Konferenz (f) conference, meeting
Konferenzraum (m) conference room
Konfitüre (f) jam, preserves
Konfitüre (f) preserve
Konfitürenomelett (n) jam-omelett

Kongreß (m) congress
Kongreßberatung (f) congress information service
Konkurrent (m) competitor
Konkurrenz (f) competition
Konkurrenz (f), **scharfe** keen competition
konkurrieren compete
Konkurs (m) bankruptcy
Konserven (pl. f) preserves, tinned food
Konservenbüchse (f) can, tin
Konsulat (n) consulate
Konsum (m) consumption
Konsument (m) consumer
konsumieren consume
Kontengliederung (f) account classification
Kontenplan (m) chart of accounts, classification of accounts
Kontenrahmen (m) **für Hotels** (pl. n) und **Verkehrsbetriebe** (pl. m) **(USA)** uniform system of accounts
Kontenstand (m) account balance
kontieren classify
Kontierung (f) account distribution
Kontingent (n) quota
Konto (n) **ausgleichen** settle an account
Konto (n) **saldieren** balance an account
Kontoabschluß (m) closing of an account
Kontoauszug (m) abstract account
Kontokorrent (n) account current (A/C), current account
Kontroll-Liste (f) check list
Kontrolle (f) control
Kontrolle (f) **durch Planung** (f) budgetary control

Kontrolle (f), **eingebaute** built-in check
Kontrolle (f), **genaue** close control
Kontrolle (f), **interne** internal control
Kontrolle (f), **scharfe** close control
Kontrolleur (m) ticket inspector
kontrollieren control
Kontrollspanne (f) span of control
Kontrollturm (m) control tower
konvertieren convert
Konzernbilanz (f) consolidated balance sheet
Konzerngesellschaft (f) affiliated company, allied company
Konzertpavillon (m) bandstand
Konzertsaal (m) concert-hall
Konzession (f) franchise, licence
Kooperation (f) cooperation
Kopf (m) head
Kopfkissen (n) pillow
Kopfsalat (m) cabbage lettuce, lettuce
Kopfschmerz (m) headache
Kopilot (m) co-pilot
Kopplungsverkauf (m) combination sale, tie-in sale
Korinthe (f) currant
Kork (m) cork
Korkenzieher (m) bottle screw, corkscrew
Korkgeschmack (m) corky taste
Korrespondenzqualität (f) letter quality
Korridor (m) corridor
kosher (rein nach jüdischen Speisegesetzen) kosher
Kosmetik (f) beauty culture
Kosmetikartikel (pl. m) cosmetics
Kosmetikerin (f) beautician
Kosmetiksalon (m) beauty

parlour
Kost (f) und **Logis** (n)   board and lodging
Kost (f), **abwechslungsreiche**   varied diet
Kost (f), **leichte**   light food
Kost (f), **vegetarische**   vegetarian diet
Kosten (pl.)   charges, cost, expenses, fee
Kosten (pl.) **der verkauften Erzeugnisse** (pl. n)   cost of goods sold
Kosten (pl.) **kontrollieren**   keep track of cost
Kosten (pl.) **pro Bestellung** (f)   cost per order
Kosten (pl.), **beeinflußbare**   controllable cost
Kosten (pl.), **direkt zurechenbare (variable)**   direct cost
Kosten (pl.), **fixe**   fixed cost
Kosten (pl.), **geplante**   budgeted cost
Kosten (pl.), **geschätzte**   estimated cost
Kosten (pl.), **halbveränderliche**   semivariable cost
Kosten (pl.), **kalkulatorische**   imputed cost
Kosten (pl.), **proportionale**   variable cost
Kosten (pl.), **variable**   variable cost
Kosten (pl.), **veränderliche**   variable cost
Kostenanalyse (f)   cost analysis
Kostenaufschlüsselung (f)   allocation
Kosteneinsparung (f)   cost saving
Kostenerhöhung (f)   cost increase
Kostenfluß (m)   flow of cost
Kostenkontrolle (f)   cost control
kostenlos   complimentary, gratuitous

Kostenrechnung (f)   cost accounting
Kostensenkung (f)   cost reduction, decrease in costs
Kostenstelle (f)   cost centre
Kostenträgerrechnung (f)   cost accounting
Kostenumlage (f)   allocation
Kostenvergleich (m)   cost comparison
Kostenzuwachs (m)   cost increase
Kostüm (n)   suit
Kostümball (m)   fancy-dress ball
Kotelett (n)   cutlet, rib steak
Kotelett (ohne Knochen) (n)   chop
Krabbe (f)   crab, prawn, shrimp
Krabben (pl. f)   hard-shell crabs
Krabbencocktail (m)   prawn cocktail
Krabbenfleisch (n)   crabmeat
Kräuter (pl. n), **feingehackte**   fines herbes
Kräuteromelett (n)   omelet with fine herbs
Kräuterbutter (f)   butter with fine herbs
Kräuteressig (m)   aromatic vinegar
Kräuterkäse (m)   green cheese
Kräutertee (m)   infusion of herbs
Kraftbrühe (f)   clear soup
Kraftfahrer (m)   motorist
Kraftfahrzeug (n)   motor vehicle
Kraftfahrzeugbenutzer (m)   motor vihicle user
Kraftfahrzeugversicherung (f)   motor insurance, motor vehicle insurance
Kraftstrom (m)   electric power, power current
Kragen (m)   collar
krank   ill
Kranken- und Unfallversicherung (f)   health an accident

insurance
Krankengymnast (m) physiotherapist
Krankengymnastik (f) physiotherapy, remedial gymnastics
Krankenhaus (n) hospital
Krankenhauskostenversicherung (f) hospitalization insurance
Krankenhauskostenzuschuß (m) hospital benefits
Krankenschwester (f) nurse
Krankenurlaub (m) sick leave
Krankenversicherung (f) health insurance, sickness insurance
Krankenwagen (m) ambulance, motor ambulance
Krankheit (f) illness
Krankheit (f), **ansteckende** contagious desease
Krankheitsrate (f) illness frequency rate
Krapfen (m) doughnut, fritter
Kraut (n) herb
Krautfleisch (n) boiled pork with pickled cabbage
Krautsalat (m) cabbage salad, cole slaw
Krawall (m) affray
Kreativität (f) creativeness
Krebs (m) crawfish, crayfish
Krebsrahmsuppe (f) bisque of crayfish, crayfish cream soup
Krebsschwanzsalat (m) crayfish salad
Krebssuppe (f) crayfish soup
Kredit (m) credit
Kreditaufnahme (f) borrowing
Kreditgrenze (f) credit limit
kreditieren credit
Kreditkarte (f) credit card
Kreditkauf (m) credit purchase
Kreditoren (pl. m) accounts payable
Kreditüberwachung (f) credit control

Kreisverkehr (m) roundabout, traffic circle
Kresse (f) cress, water-cress
Kreuzfahrt (f) cruise, crisscross journey, zigzag cruise
Krickente (f) teal
Kricketspiel (n) chriket match
kritischer Weg (Netzplantechnik) (m) critical path
Kroketten (pl. f) croquettes
Krug (m) jar, jug, mug, pitcher
Krustentiere (pl. n) crustaceans
Kuchen (m) cake
Küche (f) cuisine, kitchen
Küche (f), **gutbürgerliche** plain cooking
Küchenbenutzung (f) kitchen privileges
Küchenbrigade (f) kitchen brigade
Küchenbuffet (n) kitchen cupboard, kitchen dresser
Küchenchef (m) chef, executive chef
Küchenchef (m), **stellvertretender** sous-chef
Kücheneinrichtung (f), **maschinelle** mechanical kitchen equipment
Küchengerät (n) kitchen utensil
Küchengeruch (m) kitchen smell
Küchenherd (m) kitchen range
Küchenhilfe (f) cook's assistant, kitchen help, pantry girl
Küchenjunge (m) kitchen-boy
Küchenkraut (n) pot-herb
Küchenmädchen (n) kitchenmaid
Küchenpersonal (n) kitchen personnel, kitchen staff
Küchenplanung (f) kitchen layout planning
Küchlein (n) fritters
Kücken (n) poussin, young chikken
kühl chilly, cool, fresh

kühlen chill
Kühler (Auto) (m)   radiator
Kühlhaus (n)   cold storage
Kühlhauslagerung (f)   cold storage
Kühlschrank (m)   fridge, refrigerator
Kühltasche (f)   insulated picnic bag
Kühlwagen (m)   refrigerator car
Kühlwasser (n)   cooling-water
Kühlwasser (n) **nachfüllen**   top up the radiator
Kümmel (m)   careaway-seed
kündigen   give notice, withdraw, terminate
Kündigung (f)   resignation, termination
Kündigungsquote (f)   quit rate
Kündigungsrate (f)   labor turnover
Künstler (m)   artist
Kürbis (m)   pumpkin
Kürzung (f)   reduction
Küste (f)   coast, seaside, shore
Küstengebiet (n)   coastal area
Küstenkreuzfahrt (f)   coastal cruise
Küstenschiffahrt (f)   coastal shipping
Küstenstraße   coastal road
kulinarische Genüsse (pl. m)   culinary delights
Kulturzentrum (n)   cultural centre
Kummer (m)   grief
kumuliert zum Datum (n)   month-do-date
Kunde (m)   customer, patron
Kundenbewirtung (f)   entertaining customers
Kundengruppe (f)   type of customers
Kundenkreis (m)   type of customers

Kunstfliegen (n)   aerobatics
Kunstgalerie (f)   art gallery
Kunsthändler (m)   art-dealer
Kunsthonig (m)   artificial honey
Kunstmuseum (n)   art museum
Kunstreise (f)   art historical journey
Kunstsammlung (f)   art collection
Kunstschatz (m)   art treasure
Kunstzentrum (n)   art centre
Kur (f)   course of treatment, treatment
Kur (f), **zusätzliche**   supplementary course of treatment, supplementary cure
Kurarzt (m)   spa doctor
Kuraufenthalt (m)   stay at a spa
Kurbehandlung (f)   cure, spa treatment
Kurbetrieb (m), **ganzjähriger**   spa open all the year round
Kureinrichtungen (pl. f)   therapeutical facilities
Kurhaus (n)   spa house
Kurkonzert (n)   spa concert
Kurmittel (n)   treatment
Kurorchester (n)   spa orchestra
Kurort (m)   health resort
Kurort (m)   spa
Kurpark (m)   spa park
Kurpatient (m)   health resort patient
Kurpfuscher (m)   quack doctor
Kurs (m)   course, rate of exchange
Kursbuch (n)   railway guide, timetable
Kursdifferenz (f)   foreign exchange adjustment
Kursgewinn (m)   exchange profit
Kursmaschine (f)   scheduled plane
Kursnotierung (f)   quotation
Kursverlust   exchange loss
Kurswagen (m)   through-carriage

Kurtaxe (f)   tax de sejour, visitors' tax
Kurve (f)   bend
Kurve (f), **scharfe**   sharp bend
Kurzarbeiter (m)   part-timer
kurzfristig   short term
Kurzparker (m)   short-term parker
Kurzparkzone (f)   zoned street, limited parking zone
Kurzstreckenflug (m)   short-distance flight
Kurzwarenladen (m)   haberdasher
Kutteln (pl.)   tripe
Kutteln (pl. f), **gedämpfte**   pot-stew of tripes
Kutteln (pl.) **in Weißwein** (m) **gekocht**   tripe a la mode de Caen
Kuttelnsuppe (f)   tripes soup

L

Lachs (n)   salmon
Lachsforelle (f)   salmon-trout
Ladefähigkeit (f)   pay-load capacity
Ladeluke (f)   loading hatch
laden   take shippings
Ladentisch (m)   counter
Laderaum (m)   hold
Ladeschein (m)   carrier's receipt
Ladung (f)   cargo
ländlich   rural
Länge (f)   length
Lärm (m)   noise
Lärmbekämpfung (f)   noise control
lärmend feiern   maffick
Lage (f)   locality, position
Lage (f), **in der**   capable
Lage (f), **in ruhiger**   quietly located
Lager (n)   camp
Lager (Waren) (n)   stock, store, storeroom
Lager (n), **allgemeines**   general store
Lager- und Bestellkosten (f)   acquisition cost
Lageranforderung (f)   requisition, storeroom requisition
Lagerbestand (m)   stock, stock on hand
Lagerfachkarte (f)   bin card, inventory card
Lagerhalter (m)   storekeeper
Lagerhaltungskosten (pl.)   holding costs
Lagerhaus (n)   warehouse
Lagerkontrollbuch (n)   storeroom inventory control record
Lagerkosten (pl.)   storage cost
Lagermindestbestand (m)   minimum stock
lagern   keep in stock, store
lagern im Kühlhaus (n)   coldstore
Lagerort (m)   location of goods
Lagerraum (m)   storage space
Lagersollbestand (m)   storeroom-book inventory
Lagerumschlag (m)   inventory turnover
Lagerumschlagsgeschwindigkeit (f)   storeroom inventory turnover
Lagerung (f)   storage
Lagerverwalter (m) **für Lebensmittel** (pl. n)   food storekeeper
Lagune (f)   lagoon
Laie (m)   layman
Laken (n)   sheet
Lamm (n)   lamb, yeanling
Lammbraten (m)   roast lamb
Lammbrust (f)   lamb breast
Lammkeule (f)   leg of lamb
Lammkotelett (n)   lamb cutlet

Lammragout (n)   lamb stew
Lammschulter (f)   lamb shoulder
Lampe (f)   lamp
Lancashirekäse (m)   Lancashire (cheese)
Land (n)   country
Land (n), **an**   ashore
Land (n), **ans**   on shore
Landaufenthalt (m)   stay in the country
Landausflug (m)   outing in the country, shore excursion
Landbezirk (m)   rural district
Landebahn (f)   landing-runway, runway
Landegeschwindigkeit (f)   landing speed
landen in   land at
Landeplatz (m)   landing-field, landing-strip
Landesgrenze (f)   frontier
Landesspezialität (f)   local speciality
Landessprache (f)   national language
landesüblich   conventional, in accordance with local customs
Landeswährung (f)   national currency
Landfriedensbruch (m)   affray
Landgasthof (m)   country inn
Landhaus (n)   cottage, country house
Landkarte (f)   map
Landluft (f)   country air
Landschaft (f)   landscape, scenery
Landschaft (f), **natürliche**   nature
landschaftlich schön   scenic
Landschaftsschutz (m)   protection of places of natural beauty
Landschinken (m)   country ham
Landseite (f), **zur**   facing inland
Landspitze (f)   naze
Landstraße (f)   country road

Landstreicher (m)   tramp, tramper
Landung (f)   landing
Landungsbrücke (f)   gangway, jetty, landing-pier, landing-stage
Landungssteg (m)   jetty
Landwein (m)   local wine
lang   long
langfristig   in the long run, long-range, long-term
Langlauf (m)   jogging
Langlauf (Ski) (m)   cross-country skiing, langlauf
Langsam fahren!   drive slowly, reduce speed now
Langstreckendienst (m)   long-distance service
Langstreckenflug (m)   long-distance flight
Langstreckenflugzeug (n)   long-range plane
Languste (f)   rock lobster, spiny lobster
Lappen (m)   rag
lassen   let
Lastenaufzug (m)   freight elevator, goods elevator
Last(kraft)wagen (m)   lorry, truck
Lastwagenanhänger (m)   truck trailer
Lateinamerika   Latin America
Laterne (f)   lantern
Laubengang (m)   arcade
Laubenpromenade (f)   mall
Lauch (m)   leek
Lauchgemüse (n)   leeks
Lauchsuppe (f)   leek soup
Laufbahn (f)   career
Laufgang (m)   walkway
Laufkundschaft (f)   occasional customers
Laufzeit (f)   duration
Laune (f)   fancy
lauwarm   lukewarm
lawinengefährdet   exposed to

avalanches
lawinensicher safe from avalanches
Leasing (n) leasing
Lebensart (f) manners, way of living
Lebensgewohnheit (f) living habit
Lebenshaltungskosten (pl.) cost of living
Lebenslauf (m) curriculum vitae
Lebensmittel (pl. n) provisions
Lebensmittelhändler (m) grocer
Lebensmittelinventarkontrollbuch (n) food inventory control record
Lebensmittellagerraum (m) food store
Lebensmittelvergiftung (f) food-poisoning
Lebensstandard (m) living standard, standard of living
Lebensversicherung (f) life insurance
Leber (f) liver
Leberkäse (m) leberkaese
Leberknödel (m) liver dumpling
Leberknödelsuppe (f) hot broth with liver dumplings, soup with liver dumpling
Leberpüreesuppe (f) liver puree soup
Leberreissuppe (f) soup with liver rice
Leberwurst (f) liver sausage, leberwurst
Leberwurst (f) **mit Sauerkraut** (n) liver sausage with sauerkraut
lebhaft animated
Lebkuchen (m) ginger bread
lecken leak
ledig single, unmarried
leer empty
Leerlaufzeit (f) idle time

leerstehend unoccupied
Legitimation (f) legitimation
Lehnstuhl (m) arm-chair, easy chair
Lehrfilm (m) training film
Lehrling (m) apprentice
Lehrmethode (f) teaching method, training method
Lehrvertrag (m) contract of apprenticeship, indenture of apprenticeship
Lehrzeit (f) apprenticeship
Leicesterkäse (m) Leicester
leicht mild
leicht erreichbar easy to get to
Leichtathletik (f) athletics
leihen borrow, lend
Leihgebühr (f) lending-fee
Leihwagen (m) hired car
Leihwagendienst (m) car hire (rental) service
Leinkuchen (m) linseed-cake
Leinsamen (m) linseed
Leipziger Allerlei (n) Leipzig hodge-podge
leisten, sich afford
Leistung (f) efficiency, pace, performance, productivity
Leistung (f) **pro Arbeitsstunde** (f) man hour output
Leistungsbericht (m) efficiency report, productivity report
Leistungsbeurteilung (f) merit rating
Leistungsbewertung (f) performance appraisal
Leistungseinheit (f) production standard
leistungsfähig efficient
Leistungsfähigkeit (f) efficiency
Leistungsfähigkeit (f), **betriebliche** operating efficiency
Leistungsgrad (m) performance
Leistungskontrolle (f) performance control

89

Leistungsmaßstab (m) performance standard, production standard, standard of performance
Leistungsmessung (f) measurement of performance
Leistungsstandard (m) standard of performance
Leistungsvermögen (n) capacity
leiten manage
leitender Angestellter (m) executive
Leiter (m) manager
Leiter (m) **der Beherbergungsabteilung** (f) rooms division manager
Leiter (m) **der Wareneinsatzkontrolle (Speisen)** (f) food cost controller
Leiter (m) **der Wareneinsatzkontrolle (Speisen u. Getränke)** (f) food and beverage controller
Leiter (m) **des Rechnungswesens** (n) auditor
Leiter (m), **technischer** engineer
Leiterin (f) **der Hausdamenabteilung** (f) executive housekeeper
Leiterin (f) **der Reservierungsabteilung** (f) reservation supervisor
Leitkarte (f) guide
Leitung (f) control
Leitungsentscheidung (f) administrative decision
Lende (f) loin
Lendenschnitte (f) fillet-mignon, fillet of beef, tenderloin steak
Lendenstück (n) loin
Lendenstück (n), **zartes** tenderloin
Lerche (f) lark
Lernender (m) learner
Leseraum (m) reading-room
Lesespeicher (m) read-only memory
Lesezimmer (n) reading-room
Leuchtreklame (f) electric sign advertising
Leuchtturm (m) lighthouse
Licht (n) light
Lichtbildervortrag (m) lecture with slides
Lichteffekt (m) lighting effect
Lichthupe (f) flashing signal
Lichtschalter (m) switch
lieblich lovely
Lieblingsgericht (n) favourite dish
Lieferant (m) supplier
Lieferbedingungen (pl. f) terms of delivery
Lieferer (m) supplier
liefern deliver, supply
Lieferschein (m) delivery note, delivery slip
Liefertermin (m) delivery date
Lieferung (f) delivery, supply
Lieferzeit (f) delivery time, time of delivery
Liege (f) couch
Liegegeld (n) quay dues
Liegehalle (f) open-air veranda
Liegekur (f) open-air rest cure, rest-cure
liegen, in der Sonne (f) basket
Liegeplatz (m) couchette
Liegeplatzgebühr (f) couchette charge
Liegestuhl (m) deck-chair
Liegetag (m) layday
Liegeterrasse (f) rest-cure terrace
Liegewiese (f) gardens, rest-cure lawn, sun-bathing lawn
Lift (m) elevator, lift
Liftboy (m) elevator boy, lift-boy
Likör (m) liqueur
Limit (n) limit
Limonade (f) lemonade

Limone (f) lime
Limonensaft (m) lime juice
Lindenblütentee (m) lime tea
Linie (f) line
Linienbus (m) scheduled bus, town bus
Linienfluggesellschaft (f) scheduled airline
Linienflugzeug (n) airliner, liner
Linienfunktion (f) line function
Linienmaschine (f) scheduled plane
Linienschiff (n) liner
Linienstelle (f) line position
Linienverkehr (m) regular traffic
Links fahren! keep left
Linksverkehr (m) left-hand traffic
Linnen (n) linen
Linse (Gemüse) (f) lentil
Linsensuppe (f) lentil soup
Linzenzinhaber (m) licensee
Linzer Torte (f) fancy-cake with Linz nut, trellis cake
Lippenstift (m) lipstick
Liptauer Käse (m) **garniert** Liptauer garnished
Liquidität (f) liquidity
Liquiditätsgrad (m) degree of liquidity
Liste (f) list
Listenpreis (m) list price
livriert liveried
Lizensgeber (m) licensor
Lockenwickler (m) curler
locker fluffy
Löffel (m) spoon
Löhne (pl. m) **für Aushilfen** (pl.f) extra wages
Löhne (pl. m) **und Gehälter** (pl. n) salary and wages
Logan-Beere (f) **(Brombeerenart)** loganberry
Loge (f) **(Theater)** box
Logiergast (m) temporary guest

Logierhaus (n) lodging-house
Logierzimmer (n) guest-room
Logis (n) lodging
Lohn (m) pay, wage
Lohn- und Gehaltsstruktur (f) wage and salary structure
Lohn- und Leistungskontrollsystem (n) payroll and performance control system
Lohnanreiz (m) wage incentive
Lohnaufwand (m) payroll
Lohnbuchhalter (m) paymaster
Lohnbüro (n) payroll department
Lohnerhöhung (f) increase of wages, wage increase
Lohnkostenkontrolle (f) payroll control
Lohnliste (f) payroll
Lohnnachzahlung (f) back pay
Lohnscheck (m) pay check
Lohnsteuer (f) **und Sozialleistungen (Personal)** (pl. f) payroll taxes and employee relations
Lohntarif (m) wage scale
Lohnvorauszahlung (f) advance wage payment, advance pay off
Lohnvorschuß (m) wage advance, advance wage payment
lokal local
Lokal (n) tavern
Lokalkolorit (n) local colour
Lokomotivführer (m) engine driver
Lorbeer (m) laurel
Lorbeerblatt (n) bay leaf
loswerden get rid of
Lose-Blatt-Buchführung (f) loose-leaf card record
Losgröße (f) lot size
Losgröße (f), **optimale** optimal lot size
Lothringer Specktorte (f) hot bacon tart
Lotse (m) pilot
lotsen pilot

91

Lotsendienst (m) guide service
Lotsengebühr (f) pilotage
Lücke (f) gap
Lüftung (f) ventilation
Luft (f), reine ozon
Luftbad (n) air-bath
Luftdruck (m) atmospheric pressure
Luftfahrt (f) aviation
Luftfahrtausstellung (f) air display
Luftfahrtgesellschaft (f) airline
Luftfahrtgesellschaft (f), **angeschlossene** associated airline
Luftfilter (m) air filter
Luftfracht (f) air cargo, airfreight
Luftfrachtbüro (n) cargo office air
Luftfrachtkosten (pl.) air-freight charges
Luftfrachtraum (m) air-fleight space
Luftfrachtspedition (f) air-freight service
Luftheizung (f) hot-air heating
luftig airy
Luftkarte (f) aviation chart
Luftkissen (n) aircushion
Luftkissenboot (n) hovercraft
Luftkorridor (m) air corridor
luftkrank airsick
Luftkrankheit (f) airsickness
Luftkurort (m) air resort, climatic health resort
Luftloch (n) air pocket
Luftmatratze (f) airmattress
Luftpost (f) airmail
Luftpostkuvert (n) airmail envelope
Luftpostpaket (n) air parcel
Luftpostpapier (n) airmail stationary
Luftpumpe (f) air pump
Luftraum (m) air space

Luftreisedienst (m) air-passenger service
Lufttaxi (n) airtaxi
Lufttemperatur (f) air-temperature
Luftverkehr (m) air traffic
Luftverkehrsgesellschaft (f) air transport company
Luftverschmutzung (f) pollution
Luftzug (m) draught
Luke (f) hatch
Lunchpaket (n) box meal, lunch packet, packed lunch
Lunge (f) lights, lungs
lustig jolly
Luxus (m) de luxe, fancy, luxury
Luxusbus (m) luxury bus
Luxusdampfer (m) luxury liner
Luxusgüter (pl. n) luxury goods
Luxushotel (n) luxury hotel
Luxusjacht (f) luxury yacht
Luxuskabine (f) luxury cabin
Luxusreise (f) luxury trip
Luxusrestaurant (n) luxury restaurant

M

Madeira (Wein) (m) Madeira
Madeirasoße (f) Madeira sauce
Mädchenname (m) maiden name
mähen mow
Mängelanzeige (f) notice of defects
männlich male
Magenbitter (m) bitters
Magenfahrplan (Luftfahrt) (m) catering arrangements
Magenstärkung (f) pick-me-up
mager lean, meagre

Magermilch (f)   skim (med) milk
Magerspeck (m)   lean bacon
Mahlzeit (f)   meal
Mahlzeit (f), **gemeinsame**   table d'hote meal
Mahlzeit (f), **reichliche**   substantial meal
Mahlzeiten (pl. f) **an Bord** (m)   meals on board (a) ship
Mahlzeitengutschein (m)   luncheon voucher
Mahnbrief (m)   dunning letter
mahnen   remind
Mahnung (f)   dunning, reminder
Maibaum (m)   Maypole
Maifisch (m)   shad
Maikräuter (pl. n)   woodruff
Mais (m)   corn, Indian corn, maize, sweetcorn
Maisbrei (m)   hominy
Maisbrot (amerik.) (n)   pone
Maisflocken (pl. f)   cornflakes
Maisgrütze (f)   Italian corn-pudding
Maiskolben (m)   corn-cob
Maiskuchen (m), **amerikanischer**   johnny-cake
Maismehl (n)   corn flour
Maisstärkemehl (n)   maizena
Majoran (m)   marjoram
Makkaroni (pl.)   macaroni
Makrele (f)   mackerel
Makrone (f)   macaroon
Malerarbeiten (pl. f) **und Dekoration** (f)   painting and decorating
malerisch   picturesque, scenic
Malteser (m)   Maltese
Malve (f)   mallow
Malz (n)   malt
Management (n), **mittleres**   middle management
Managementgebühren (pl. f)   management fees
Managementtraining (n)   management training
Manager (m)   manager
Managerkrankheit (f)   managerial desease
Mandarine (f)   mandarine, tangerine
Mandel (f)   almond
Mandelgebäck (n)   almond pastry
Mandelkuchen (m)   almond cake
Mandelpudding (m)   almond pudding
Mandelschnitte (f)   almond bar
Mandeltorte (f)   almond tart, fancy-cake with almonds
Mangel (m)   defect, deficiency, fault, lack, want
mangelhaft   defective, faulty
mangeln   lack
mangels   in default of
Mangold (m)   chard, spinach beets, Swiss chard
Mangopflaume (f)   mango
Maniküre (f)   manicure
Manko (n)   shortage
Mansarde (f)   attic, mansard
Mantel (m)   overcoat
Manteltarifvertrag (m)   overall labor agreement
manuell   manual
Margarine (f)   margarine
Marillenknödel (pl. m)   apricot dumplings
Marinade (f)   marinade, souse
mariniert   marinated
Mark (n)   marrow
Markbein (n)   marrow-bone
Marke (f)   brand, mark
Markenname (m)   brand
Marketing (n)   marketing
Marketing Manager (m)   marketing manager
Markise (f)   awning, window awning
Markklößchen (pl. m)   marrow dumplings

93

Markknochen (m) marrow-bone
Markstein (m) milestone
Markt (m) market
Markt (m), **freier** open market
Marktanalyse (f) market analysis
Marktanteil (m) market couverage
Marktforschung (f) market-research
Markthalle (f) market-hall
Marktliste (f) market list
Marktplatz (m) market-place
Marktpreis (m) market price
Marktsättigung (f) market saturation
Marktstudie (f) market study
Marktuntersuchung (f) field survey
Marktwirtschaft (f), **freie** free enterprise system
Marmelade (f) jam
Marmeladenbrötchen (n) jam roll
Martini Sweet Cocktail ähnlich (m) Gin and It
Martini dry Cocktail (ähnlich) (m) Gin and French
Marzipan (n) marchpane
Maschine (Flugzeug) (f) plane
maschinell mechanical
maschinelle Kücheneinrichtung (f) mechanical kitchen equipment
Maschinen (pl. f) **und Ausrüstungen** (pl. f) machinery and equipment
Maskenball (m) fancy-dress ball, masked ball
Maß (n) measure
Massage (f) massage
Masse (f) bulk
Massenkauf (m) bulk purchase
Massentourismus (m) large-scale tourism
Massenverkehrsmittel (n) large-scale public transport
Massenversammlung (f) rally
Masseur (m) masseur
Masseuse (f) masseuse
Maßnahme (f) measure
Maßstab (m) yardstick
Mast (m) mast
Masthähnchen (n) spring-chicken
Masthuhn (n) fattened chicken
Mastschwein (n) porker
Materialkosten (pl.) material cost
Matineevorstellung (f) morning performance
Matjeshering (m) red herring, salt(ed) herring
Matratze (f) mattress
Matritze (f) stencil
Matrixdrucker (m) matrix printer
Matrose (m) sailor
matt dim
Mauer (f) wall
Maulbeere (f) mulberry
Maulesel (m) mule
Maultier (n) mule
Maurer (m) mason
Maut (f) toll
Mayonnaise (f) mayonnaise
Mayonnaiseeier (pl. n) eggs in mayonnaise
Mayonnaisesalat (m) mayonnaise salad
Mayonnaisesoße (f) mayonnaise sauce
Mechaniker (m) mechanic
mechanisch mechanical
mechanisieren mechanize
Medikament (n) remedy
Meer (n) sea
Meeraal (m) conger-eel
Meeräsche (f) mullet
Meerbarbe (f) mullet
Meerbarsch (m) sea-perch, white bass

Meerbutt (m)   brill
Meerdrachen (m)   dragon fish
Meeresfrüchte (pl. f)   sea-food
Meereskrebs (m)   marine cray fish
Meerrettich (m)   horse-radish
Meerrettichsoße (f)   horse-radish sauce
Meerfisch (m)   salt-water fish, sea-fish
Meerwasser (n)   sea-water
Meerwasserkur (f)   seawater cure, thalassotherapy
Mehl (n)   flour
Mehlspeise (f)   farinaceous dish
Mehrbenutzersystem (n)   multi-user system
Mehrbetrag (m)   agio, overage, surplus
Mehrgepäck (n)   excess baggage
Mehrheitsnachlaß (m)   group discount
Mehrwertsteuer (f)   added value tax
Mehrzweckraum (m)   multi-purpose room
Meilenstein (m)   milestone
Meilenzahl (f)   milage
Meinungsuntersuchung (f)   opinion survey
Meldeamt (n)   registration office
Meldebuch (n)   hotel register
melden bei der Polizei (f), **sich**   register with the police
Meldepflicht (f), **polizeiliche obligation to register with the police**
meldepflichtig   notifiable
Meldeschein (m)   registration form
Meldeschluß (Luftfahrt) (m)   check in time, latest check-in time
Meldezeit (f)   reporting time
Melone (f)   melon

Melone (f) **geeist**   chilled melon
Menge (f)   quantity
Menge (f), **kleine**   dash
mengen   mingle
Mengenprämie (f)   quantity bonus
Mengenrabatt (m)   quantity discount volume discount
Mengenstandard (m)   quantity standard
Mengenvorgabe (f)   quantity standard
Menü (n)   menu
Menü (n) **für Autofahrer** (pl. m)   menu for motorists
Menü (n) **und Preis** (m) **fest**   table-d'hote
Menü (n) **zu festen Preisen** (pl. m)   menu at fixed prices
Menüplanung (f)   menu planning
Merkblatt (n)   leaflet
Merkmal (n)   feature
Messe (f)   fair
Messe-Informationsstelle (f)   fair information office
Messegelände (n)   exhibition grounds, fair ground
Messeleitung (f)   fair authorities
Messer (n)   knife
Metropole (f)   metropolis
Mettwurst (f)   smoked sausage
Metzger (m)   butcher
Metzgerei (f)   butcher's shop
Meuniere Soße (f)   meuniere sauce
Miesmuschel (f)   scallop (mussel)
mietbar   rentable
Miete (f)   hire, rent
Mieteinnahmen (pl. f)   rental
mieten   hire, lease, rent
Mieter (m)   leaseholder, lessee, tenant, lodger
Mietertrag (m)   rental revenue

Mietflugzeug (n)　airtaxi
Mietkaufvertrag (m)　hire purchase agreement
Mietvertrag (m)　lease
Mietwagen (m)　hired car
mietweise　on lease
Mietwohngrundstück (n)　apartment house property
Mikrocomputer (m)　micro computer
Milch (f)　milk
Milch (f), **heiße**　hot milk
Milch (f), **pasteurisierte**　pasteurized milk
Milchbar (f)　milk bar
Milchbrötchen (n)　milk-roll
Milchgelee (n)　junket
Milchhändler (m)　milkman
Milchkännchen (n)　milk-jug
Milchkaffee (m)　coffee with hot milk, white coffee
Milchlamm (n)　baby lamb
Milchmixgetränk (n)　milk shake
Milchreis (m)　milk-rice, rice pudding
Milchspeise (f)　milk-dish
mild　mild
minderjährig　under age
Minderjähriger (m)　infant
Minderjährigkeit (f)　age of minority
minderwertig　inferior
Mindestaufenthalt (m)　minimum stay
Mindestbesetzung (Personal) (f)　minimum manning
Mindestbestand (m)　minimum inventory
Mindestgebot (n)　lowest bid
Mindestlohn (m)　minimum wage
Mindestteilnehmerzahl (f)　minimum number of participants
Mineralbad (n)　mineral bath

Mineralie (f)　mineral
Mineralquelle (f)　mineral spring, spa
Mineralwasser (n)　mineral water, table water
Mineralwasser (halbe Flasche) (n)　split
Minestrone (f)　minestrone
Minicomputer (m)　mini computer
Minigolf (n)　miniature golf
Minigolfplatz (m)　miniature golf course
Minus (n)　shortage
Minzensoße (f)　mint sauce
Mirabelle (f)　mirabelle plum, yellow plum
mischen　merge, mix
mischen, sich　mingle
Mischgericht (n)　mixture (of food)
Mischkosten (pl.)　semivariable cost
Mischung (f)　mix
Mispel (f)　medlars
Mißbrauch (m)　abuse, misuse
mißbrauchen　abuse, misuse
Mißhandlung (f)　ill-treatment
mißlingen　fail
mißtrauen　distrust
Mißtrauen (n)　distrust
Mißverhalten (n)　misconduct
Mißverständnis (n)　misunderstanding
Mißwirtschaft (f)　mismanagement
Mitarbeit (f)　cooperation
Mitarbeiter-Beurteilungsskala (f)　employee rating scale
Mitarbeiterbefragung (f)　employees opinion survey
Mitbesitzer (m)　joint owner
Miteigentümer (m)　joint proprietor
Mitglied (n)　member

Mitgliederbeitrag (m) membership fee
Mitgliedsaufnahme (f) affiliation
Mitgliedschaft (f) membership
Mitgliedskarte (f) membership card
Mitreisegepäck (n) accompanied luggage
Mitreisender (m) fellow-passenger
Mittag (m) noon
Mittagessen (n) lunch(eon)
Mittagsgeschäft (n) lunch business
Mittagspause (f) lunch break, lunch hour
Mittagsrestaurant (n) luncheon-bar, lunch-room
Mittagsschlaf (m) siesta
Mittagszeit (f) lunch-hour
mitteilen inform
Mitteilung (f) note, communication
mittel medium
Mittel (pl. n) funds, means
Mittel (pl. n), **flüssig** liquid assets, cash
mittelfristig medium term
Mittelmeer (n) Mediterranean
mittelmeerisch Mediterranean
Mittelrippenstück (Rind) (n) piece of the ribs of beef
Mittelstation (f) mid station
Mittelstreckenflug (m) medium-range flight
Mitternacht (f) midnight
Mixed Grill (m) mixed grill
Mobiliar (n) furniture
Mode (f) fancy, fashion
modernisieren modernize
Modernisierungsplan (m) improvement budget
Modeschau (f) fashion show
Modewaren (pl. f) fancy-goods
Modewettbewerb (m) fashion contest
Modezeitschrift (f) fashion magazine
modifizieren modify
Modifizierung (f) modification
modisch fashionable
möblieren furnish
möblierte Wohnung (f) furnished apartment
möbliertes Appartement (n) furnished self contained flat
möbliertes Haus (n) furnished house
mögen like
Möglichkeit (f) facility
Möwe (f) sea-gull
Möwenei (n) mew eggs
Mohnbeugel (n) poppy-seed bun
Mokka (m) demi-tasse
Mole (f) jetty, pier, mole
Molkerei (f) dairy
Monatsabschluß (m) monthly closing
Monatskarte (f) monthly season ticket
Monatsprogramm (n) monthly programme
Monatsverbrauch (m) monthly consumption
Mond (m) moon
Mondschein-Bootsfahrt (f) moonlight boat-trip
Moorbad (n) mud bath
Moorbehandlung (f) mud treatment
Moorschnepfe (f) snipe
Moors (n) moss
Moral (f) morale
moralisch moral
Morast (m) quagmire
Morchel (f) morel
morgen tomorrow
Morgen (m) orient
Morgenrock (m) dressing gown,

robe
Moschee (f) mosque
Moselwein (m) Moselle wine
Moskitonetz (n) mosquito net
Motel (n) motel, motor hotel, tourist court
motivieren motivate
Motorboot (n) motor boat, motor launch
Motorenlärm (m) engine noise
Motorrad (n) motor-cycle
Motorroller (m) motor scooter, scooter
Motorschiff (n) motor vessel (MV), motorship (MS)
Motorschlitten (m) motor sleigh, snowmobile
müde tired, weary
Müll (m) rubbish
Müllbeseitigung (f) rubbish removal
Müllschlucker (m) waste-disposer
München Munich
mündig of age
mündlich oral, verbal
Münze (f) coin
mürbe well-cooked
Mürbekuchen (getaucht in Sirup, Sherry etc.) (m) trifle
Mürbeteigkuchen (m) shortcake
Muffins (engl. Teegebäck) (pl.) muffin
Mulligatawny (f) curried chickencream soup
Mulligatawny-Suppe (Geflügelrahmsuppe mit Curry) (f) mulligatawny soup
multilateral multi-lateral
Multimomentaufnahme (f) work sampling study
Multiplikator (m) multiplier
multiplizieren multiply
Mundwasser (n) mouth wash
Muschel (f) mussel, clam

Muschelsuppe (f) clam broth, clam chowder, mussel soup
Muscheltiere (pl. n) sea-shells
Museum (n) museum
Musical (n) musical
Musik (f) **und Unterhaltung** (f) music and entertainment
Musikabend (m) evening concert, musical evening
Musikbox (f) juke-box
Musiker (m) musician
Muskatblatt (n) mace
Muskatblüte (f) mace
Muskatellerwein (m) muscatel (wine)
Muskatnuß (f) nutmeg
Muße (f) leisure
Muster (n) draft, pattern
musterhaft exemplary
Muttergesellschaft (f) parent company
Muttersprache (f) native language

N

nach Ankunft (f) upon arrival
nach Verladung (f) when shipped
Nach- und Vorsaison (f) off-peak season
Nachbarland (n) neighbouring country
Nachbarschaft (f) neighbourhood
Nachbehandlung (f) after-treatment
nachbestellen reorder
Nachbestellung (f) reorder
Nachfaßverfahren (n) follow-up system
Nachfrage (f) demand, inquiry
Nachfrage, jährliche (f) annual

demand
Nachfragepreis (m) bid price
Nachkur (f) after-treatment, rest after treatment
Nachlaß (Rabatt) (m) discount
nachlösen take a supplementary ticket
Nachmittag (m) afternoon
nachmittags p. m.
Nachmittagstee (m) afternoon tea
Nachmittagstee (m) **und Abendessen** (n) **kombiniert** high tea
Nachnahme (f) cash on delivery (c. o. d.)
nachprüfen review
Nachricht (f) communication, message
Nachsaison (f) after-season, low season
Nachsaisonermäßigung (f) after-season reduction
nachsenden redirect
Nachspeise (f) dessert, sweets
Nacht- und Sonntagsdienst (m) night and sunday duty
Nachtarbeit (f) nightwork
Nachtbar (f) night club
Nachteil (m) disadvantage
Nachtfahrt (f) night trip
Nachtflug (m) night flight
Nachthemd (n) nightdress
Nachtisch (m) dessert, sweets
Nachtklub (m) cabaret, night club
Nachtleben (n) night life
Nachtlokal (n) night club
Nachtpiste (f) night run
Nachtportier (m) night concierge
Nachtrag (m) annex
Nachtreinigungspersonal (n) night-cleaner
Nachtruhe (f) night rest
Nachtschicht (f) lobster shift, night shift

Nachtschichtvergütung (f) night shift bonus
Nachtschnellzug (m) overnight express
Nachttarif (m) night rate
Nachttelefonistin (f) night-telephone operator
Nachttisch (m) bedside-table
Nachttopf (m) chamber-pot
Nachtverkehr (m) night service, night traffic
Nachtwächter (m) night-watchman
Nachtzug (m) night train
Nachweis (m) proof
Nachzahlung (f) late payment, post payment, subsequent payment
nächste (Entfernung) nearest
Nähe (f) vicinity
Nähe (f), **in der** near at hand
Nähzeug (n) sewing kit
Nässe (f) wetness
nahe near, near at hand
Nahrung (f) food, nourishment
Nahrung (f) **aufnehmen** ingest
Nahrungsaufnahme (f) ingestion
Nahrungsmittel (n) food, nourishment
Nahrungsmittelverfälschung (f) adulteration of food
Nahschnellverkehrszug (m) fast lokal train
Nahverkehr (m) local traffic, short-distance traffic
Name (m) name
namens on behalf of
Napfkuchen (m) pound-cake
naß humid, moist, wet
national national
Nationalfeiertag (m) national holiday
Nationalität (f) nationality
Nationalitätszeichen (n) nationality sign

Nationalpark (m) national park
Nationaltracht (f) national costume
Natron (n), **kohlensaures** bicarbonate, natron
Natur (f) nature
Naturalleistung (f) payment in kind
Naturheilbehandlung (f) nature cure
Naturheilkundiger (m) naturopath
Naturheilmethode (f) naturopathy
Naturheilverfahren (n) naturopathy
Naturschätze (pl. m) natural resources
Naturschnitzel (n) plain veal steak
Naturschönheit (f) beauty spot
Naturschutz (m) nature conservation, wildlife conservation
Naturschutzgebiet (n) nature reserve
Nautik (f) navigation
Navelorange (f) navel orange
Navigation (f) navigation
Navigationskarte (f) navigation guide
Navigationskunde (f) navigation
Nebel (m) fog, mist
nebelfrei free from fog
Nebenausgaben (pl. f) extras
Nebenbetriebe (pl. m) other operated departments
nebeneinander liegende Zimmer (pl. n) adjoining rooms
Nebengebäude (n) annex, penthouse
Nebengebühr (f) extra
Nebenkosten (pl.) additional charge, extra cost, incidental charges
Nebenstelle (f) branch office

Nebenstraße (f) by-road, by-street
Nebenstrecke (f) branch line
neblig foggy, misty
Neffe (m) nephew
Negativ (n) negative
nehmen, an Bord take shipping
nennen name
nett kind
Nettobeherbergungsertrag (m) net rooms revenue
Nettobetrag (m) net amount
Nettoumsatz (m) net sales
Nettoverdienst (m) net earnings
Nettoverkaufserlöse (pl. m) net sales
Nettozimmereinkünfte (pl. f) net rooms revenue
Netzplantechnik (CPM-Methode) (f) Critical Path Method
Neuheit (f) novelty
Neuinvestition (f) additional investment
Neujahrskreuzfahrt (f) New Year cruise
Neujahrstag (m) New Year's Day
Neuklassifizierung (f) reclassification
Neunauge (n) lamprey
Neuschnee (m) new fallen snow
Nicht berühren! don't touch
nicht erfüllen fail
nicht haben lack
Nicht hinauslehnen! do not lean out
nicht mögen dislike
Nicht öffnen! do not open
Nichte (f) niece
Nichterfüllung (f) nonfulfillment, failure of performance
Nichtlieferung (f) nondelivery
Nichtraucher (m) non-smoker
Nichtraucherabteil (n) non-smoker compartment

Nichtschwimmer (m) non-swimmer
Nichtschwimmerbecken (n) non-swimmers' pool
Nichtzutreffendes (n) **streichen** delete what is not applicable
Niederlassung (f) establishment
Niederschlag (m) precipitation, rainfall
Niere (f) kindney
Nierstückbraten (m) roast sirloin of beef
nippen sip
Niveau (n) level
Non-Stop-Flug (m) non-stop flight
Nordsalm (m) Scandinavian salmon
Nordwind (m) north wind
Normalarbeitszeit (f) regular time
Normalleistung (f) normal performance
Normung (f) standardization
Not (f) distress
Notadresse (f) emergency address
Notausgang (m) emergency exit
Notbremse (f) communication cord, emergency brake
Notbremse (f) **ziehen** pull the emergency brake
Notfall (m) emergency
notieren note, quote
Notiz (f) memorandum, note
Notlage (f) distress
Notlage (f), **finanzielle** financial distress
Notlandung (f) emergency landing, forced landing
Notleine (f) communication cord
Notrutsche (f) emergency chute
Notsitz (m) folding seat, tip-up seat
Notstand (m) distress

Nudel (f) noodle
Nudelbrett (n) pastry board
Nudelholz (n) rolling pin
Nudeln (pl. f), **grüne** green noodles
Nudeln (pl. f), **hausgemachte** home-made noodles
Nudelsuppe (f) noodle soup
nüchtern sober
null zero
null und nichtig null and void
Nullkontrolle (f) zero balancing
Nummer (Telefon) (f) line
Nummer (f), **fortlaufende** consecutive number
Nummernschild (n) number plate
Nuß (f) kernel, nut
Nußbeugel (n) nut bun
Nußbutter (f) browned butter, nut butter
Nußeis (n) nut ice
Nußpudding (m) nut pudding
Nußtorte (f) fancy-cake with nuts, nut tart
Nutzen (m) benefit
Nutzenschwelle (f) break-even point
Nutzlast (f) pay load

O

Oase (f) oasis
obdachlos homeless
Oberbett (n) upper berth
Oberdeck (n) upper deck
Oberkellner (m) head waiter, maitre
Objektiv (n) lens
obligatorisch mandatory
Observatorium (n) observatory
Obst (n), **gemischtes** mixed fruit
Obst- und Gemüsehändler (m)

greengrocer
Obstgelee (n) fruit jelly
Obsthändler (m) fruiterer
Obstkuchen (m) fruit cake, fruit pie, flan
Obstsalat (m) fresh fruit cup, fruit salad
Obstschüssel (f) fruit bowl
Obsttörtchen (n) tartlet
Obsttorte (f) fruit flan, fruit tart
Ochse (m) ox
Ochsenbraten (m) roast beef
Ochsenfleischschnitte (f) **gebraten** steak
Ochsengaumen (m) ox-palate
Ochsenmaulsalat (m) ox-muzzle salad, pickled beef's muzzle, salad of ox-palate
Ochsenrippenstück (n) prime rib of beef, rib of beef
Ochsenschwanz (m) oxtail
Ochsenschwanzragout (n) oxtail stew
Ochsenschwanzsuppe (f) oxtail soup
Ochsenschwanzsuppe (f), **gebunden** thick oxtailsoup
Ochsenschwanzsuppe (f) **klar** clear oxtail soup
Ochsenzunge (f) ox-tongue
Ochsenzunge (f) **gebraten** braised ox-tongue
öffentliche Anlagen (pl. f) public gardens
öffentliche Bekanntmachungen (pl. f) public notices
öffentliche Fernsprechzelle (f) public call-room
öffentliche Toilette (f) comfort-station, public convenience, public lavatory
Öffentlichkeit (f) publicity
Öffentlichkeitsarbeit (f) public relations
öffnen open

ökonomisch economical
Öl (n) oil
Ölheizung (f) oil heating
Ölsardinen (pl. f) sardines
Ölstand (m) oil level
Ölwechsel (m) oil-changing
Ölzentralheizung (f) oil-fired central heating
örtlich local
Örtlichkeit (f) locality
österreichische Bundesbahn (f) Austrian Federal Railways
ofengebacken oven-baked
Ofenheizung (f) stove heating
offen open
offenstehend (Forderung) outstanding
offerieren offer
Offerte (f) offer
offiziell official
ohne without
ohne Berechnung (f) free of charge
Ohrenschützer (pl. m) ear-warmers
Olive (f) olive
Olive (f), **große grüne** queen olive
Olive (f), **reife** ripe olive
Olive (f) **gefüllt** stuffed olive
Olivenöl (n) olive oil
Olympiastadt (f) Olympic city
Olympische Spiele (pl. n) Olympic Games
Omelett (n) omelet
Omelett (n) **Souffle** puff omelet
Omelett (n) **mit Rum** (m) flaming rum-omelet
Omelett (n), **einfaches** plain omelet
Omnibus (m) bus, coach, motor coach, omnisbus
Onkel (m) uncle
Oper (f) opera

Operational Management (n) operational management
Operations Analysis (f) operations analysis
Operations Analyst (m) operations analyst
Operettentheater (n) operetta house
Opernball (m) Opera Ball
Opernhaus (n) opera house
optisch optical
Orange (f) orange
Orangeade (f) orangeade
Orangeat (n) candied orange peel
Orangeneis (n) orange ice-cream
Orangenlimonade (f), **natürliche** orangeade
Orangenmarmelade (f) marmelade
Orchester (n) orchestra
Orchesterplatz (m) bandstand
ordentlich orderly, tidy
Ordnung (f) order, regulation
ordnungsgemäß orderly
Organigramm (n) organization chart
Organisation (f) organization
Organisationsplan (m) organization chart
Organisator (m) organizer
organisieren organize
Orient (m) orient
Orientierungstafel (f) orientation plan
Ort (m) town, village
Ortschaft (f), **geschlossene** built-up area
Ortsgebrauch (m) local custom
Ortsgespräch (n) local call
Ortstafel (f) place-name sign
Ortstaxe (f) local tax
ortsüblich in accordance with local customs
Ortsverkehr (m) local carriage, local traffic
Ortswerbestempel (m) local advertisement postmark
Ortszeit (f) local time
Osten (m) east
Osterferien (pl.) Easter holidays
Osterfest (n) Easter
Ostern (n) Easter
Ostwind (m) east wind
Ouvertüre (f) overture
Ozean (m) ocean
Ozeandampfer (m) ocean liner, transatlantic liner
Ozeanflug (m) transatlantic flight
Ozeanreise (f) transoceanic voyage
Ozon (m) ozon
Ozonbad (n) ozonic bath
ozonhaltig ozoniferous
ozonisch ozonic

P

Pacht (f) leasehold, rent
pachtbar rentable
Pachtbesitz (m) leasehold
Pachteinnahmen (pl. f) rental
pachten lease, rent
Pachtvertrag (m) lease, leasing contract
pachtweise on lease
packen pack
Packpapier (n) kraft paper, wrapping paper
Packung (f) pack, package
Packwagen (m) luggage van
Paddel (n) paddle
Paddelboot (n) canoe, paddlingboat
paddeln paddle
Pächter (m) leaseholder, lessee, tenant

Page (m) hotel bellboy, page-boy
Paket (n) package, parcel
Paketkarte (f) dispatch note
Paketpost (f) parcel post
Palatschinken (m) rolled pancake, stuffed pancakes, thin pancakes filled with jam
Palette (f) range
Palmenmark (n) hearts of palm
Palmsonntag (m) Palm Sunday
Pampelmuse (f) grapefruit
Pampelmusensaft (m) grapefruit juice
paniert bread-crumbed
Pannenhilfe (f) breakdown service
Panorama (n) panorama
Papierkorb (m) waste-paper basket
Papierserviette (f) paper napkin
Papierwaren (pl. f) paper supplies
pappig pappy
Pappschnee (m) sticky snow
Paprika (m) paprika
Paprika gefüllt (pl. f) stuffed green (sweet) peppers
Paprikahühnchen (n) stewed chicken in paprika (cream) sauce
Paprikaschnitzel (n) braised veal cutlet in paprika sauce, veal steak Hungaria style
Paranuß (f) Brazil nut
Paravent (m) folding screen
Pariser Kartoffeln (pl. f) fried potato balls
Parka (m) parka
Parkdauer (f) **bis zu** waiting limited to
Parken (n) **gebührenfrei** free parking
Parken (n) **verboten!** waiting prohibited
Parkett (Sitz) (n) stall

Parkgelegenheit (f) parking facilities
Parkhochhaus (n) multi-storey car park
Parkmöglichkeit (f) parking facilities
Parkplatz (m) car park, garage-parking lot, parking lot, parking place
Parkplatz (m), **bewachter** guarded car park
Parkscheibe (f) parking disk
Parkuhr (f) parking meter
Parkverbot (n) no waiting, prohibition to park
Parkwächter (m) parking attendant
Parmesankäse (m) Parmesan cheese
Paß (Ausweis) (m) passport
Paß (Berg) (m) pass
Paßabfertigung (f) passport inspection
Passagenpreis (m) passenger fare
Passagevertrag (m) contract of passage
Passagier (m) passenger, pax
Passagierdampfer (m) liner, passenger steamer
Passagierflugzeug (n) passenger plane
Passagiergepäck (n) passenger's luggage
Passagierschiff (n) passenger ship
Passant (m) chance guest, temporary hotel guest, trasient (guest)
Passantenhotel (n) transient hotel
passend machen match
Paßhöhe (f) altitude of a pass
Passierschein (m) permit
passive Zahlungsbilanz (f) ad-

verse balance of payments
Passivkonto (n)   liability account
Paßkontrolle (f)   passport inspection
Paßstelle (f)   passport office
Paßvorschriften (pl. f)   passport regulations
Pastetchen (n)   patty
Pastetchen (n) **mit gehackten Früchten** (pl. f) **gefüllt**   mince-pie
Pastete (f)   pate, pie
Pastetenkruste (f)   pie-crust
Pasteurisierung (f)   pasteurization
Patissier (m)   pastry cook
pauschal   flat
Pauschalarrangement (n)   iclusive arrangement, inclusive terms
Pauschalbetrag (m)   flat sum, lump sum
Pauschale (f)   inclusive price, lump sum
Pauschalgebühr (f)   inclusive charge
Pauschalpreis (m)   inclusive fare, inclusive price
Pauschalpreis (pl. m) **für Selbstfahrer** (pl. m)   inclusive rates for self-drive car hire
Pauschalpreisferien (pl.)   all-in holiday, inclusive holiday
Pauschalreise (f)   all-expense trip, all-in journey, inclusive journey, inclusive trip, package tour
Pellkartoffeln (pl. f)   baked potatoes
Pellkartoffeln (pl. f), **gebacken**   potatoes baked in their jacketts
Pelzgeschäft (n)   furrier
Pelzmantel (m)   fur coat
Pemmikan (Dörrfleisch) (n)   pem(m)ican

Pendelverkehr (m)   shuttle service
Pension (Übernachtung) (f)   boarding-house, guest-house
Pension (Rente) (f)   retirement
Pension (f) **gehen, in**   retire
Pensionsgast (m)   border, resident
Pensionsplan (m)   pension scheme
Pensionspreis (m)   board, price for board and lodging
per Adresse   care of (c/o)
per Anhalter (m) **reisen**   hitchhike
Perkolator (m)   percolator
perlend   sparkling
Perlhuhn (n)   guinea-fowl
Perlwein (m)   prickling wine
Perlzwiebel (f)   pickled onion
persönlich   individually
persönliche Gebrauchsgegenstände (pl. m)   articles for daily use, personal belongings
Personal (n)   personnel
Personalabteilung (f)   personnel department
Personalanforderung (f)   personnel requisition
Personalaufwand (m), **übriger**   payroll taxes and employee relations
Personalbeschreibung (f)   personal data
Personalbudget (n)   manpower budget
Personalchef (m)   personnel manager
Personalcomputer (m)   personal computer
Personalgemeinkosten (pl.)   payroll taxes and employee relations
Personalhöchststand (m)   maximum manning

105

Personalkostenkontrolle (f)   payroll control
Personalmindestbestand (m)   minimum manning
Personalpförtner (m)   time keeper
Personalplanungsleitfaden (m)   manning table
Personalumschlag (m)   labor turnover
Personalverpflegung (f)   employees meals
personell übersetzt   overstaffed
Personenfähre (f)   passenger ferry
Personentransport (m)   passenger carriage
Personenverkehr (m)   passenger carriage, passenger traffic
Personenwagen (m)   passenger car
Personenzug (m)   passenger train
Petersfisch (m)   John Dory (fish)
Petersilie (f)   parsley
Petersilienkartoffeln (pl.f)   parsley potatoes
Petersiliensoße (f)   parsley sauce
Petroleum (n)   kerosene
Pfad (m)   trail
pfänden   attach, pawn
Pfännchen (n)   pannikin
Pfanne (f)   pan
Pfannenstiel (m)   panhandle
Pfannkuchen (m)   pancake
Pfannkuchensuppe (f)   pancake soup
Pfau (m)   peacock
Pfeffer (m)   pepper
Pfeffer (Fleischgericht) (m)   jugged meat
Pfeffer (m), **grüner**   green pepper
Pfeffergefäß (n)   pepper-box
Pfefferkorn (n)   pepper-corn
Pfefferkuchen (m)   ginger bread
Pfefferminze (f)   peppermint
Pfefferminztee (m)   mint tea
Pfeffermühle (f)   pepper mill
Pfefferschote (f)   pepper
Pfefferschote (f), **rote**   red pepper
Pfefferschoten-Mischgericht (n)   French pepper-stew
Pfeffersteak (n)   pepper-steak
Pfefferstreuer (m)   peppe-castor, pepper-pot
pfeifen   wistle
Pferdedroschke (f)   hackney-cab
Pferderennen (n)   horse-race
Pferdeschlitten (m)   horse sleigh
Pferdesport (m)   equestrian sport
Pferdeverleih (m)   hacking
Pferdewagen (m)   horse drawn vehicle
Pfifferling (m)   chanterelle
Pfingsten (n)   Pentecost, Whitsunday
Pfingstferien (pl.)   Whitsun holidays
Pfirsich (m)   peach
Pfirsich Melba (m)   peach Melba
Pfirsichreis (n)   peaches ice-cream
Pflanzenfett (n)   shortening
Pflanzenöl (n)   plant oil
Pflanzenwelt (f)   flora
Pflaume (f)   plum, prune
pflaumen- od. rosinenreich   plummy
Pflaumenkuchen (m)   plum flan
Pflicht (f)   duty
pflichttreu   loyal
Pflichttreue (f)   loyality
Pförtner (m)   commissionaire, door-keeper
Pfund (engl.: ca. 450 g) (n)   pound
Phantasie (f)   fancy
Pichelsteiner Fleisch (n)   mixed meat-stew with vegetables
Pickles (pl.)   pickles

Picknick (n) picnic
Picknicktasche (f) picnic bag
pikant spicy
Pilgermuscheln (pl. f) cockles
Pilgerreise (f) pilgrimage
Pilot (m) aircraft pilot, pilot
Pilz (allgemein) (m) fungus
Pilz (m), **eßbarer** mushroom
Pilzcremesuppe (f) cream of mushroom
Pilze (pl.) **auf Toast** (m) mushrooms on toast
Pilzschnitte (f) mushrooms on toast
Pilzsoße (f) mushroom sauce
Pilzsuppe (f) mushroom soup, soup with mushrooms
Pint (Holmaß: ca. $^1/_2$ Liter) (m) pint
Piste (f) runway, ski run, slope
Pistenpflege (f) ski run maintenance, slope grooming
Pizza (f) open vegetable pie, pizza
Plätzchen (n) buiscuit
Plaid (n) plaid
Plakat (n) poster
Plakatwerbung (f) poster advertising
Plan (n) blue print, forecast, plan
Planbestand (m) target inventory
Plane (f) awning
planen schedule
Plankostenrechnung (f) standard-cost system
planmäßig on schedule, scheduled
Planschbecken (n) paddling-pool
planschen paddle, splash
Planung (f) planning
Planung (f) **der Speisekarte** (f) menu planning
Planungsforschung (f) operations research

Planziel (n) target
Plastikbeutel (m) plastic bag
Platte (f) plate, platter, serving dish
Plattenlaufwerk (n) hard disk
Platz (Sitz) (m) seat
Platz (Ort) (m) square
Platz (m), **besetzter** taken seat
Platzanweiser (m) attendant, usher
Platzanweiserin (f) usherette
Platzanzahl (f), **begrenzte** limited number of seats
Platzbelegung (f), **elektronische** teleregister
Platzbestellung (f) booking of seats, seat reservation
Platzkarte (f) reserved seat ticket, ticket for reserved seat
Platzkarten (pl. f) **erforderlich** seats should be reserved in advance
Platzkartengebühr (f) seat reservation fee
Platzmiete (f) tennis court fee
Platzregen (m) downpour
Platzreservierung (f) seat reservation
Platzzuteilung (f) allocation of seats
Plinsen (pl. f) buckwheat pancakes
Plötze (f) roach
Plumpudding (engl. Weihnachtskuchen) (m) plum pudding
Pockenschutzimpfung (f) variolization
Pökelfleisch (n) corned beef, pickled pork
Pökelrindfleisch (n) salted beef
Pökelzunge (f) red beef tongue
Pokerspiel (n) poker
polieren polish
Politesse (f) meter maid, traffic warden

107

Politik (f) policy
Politik (f) **der offenen Tür** (f) open-door policy
Polizei (f) police
Polizeipräsidium (n) policeheadquarters
Polizeirevier (n) police station
Polizist (m) constable, policeman
Pommes frites (pl.) chips, French fried potatoes, chipped potatoes
Popkonzert (n) pop concert
Popmusik (f) pop
Porree (m) leek
Porrigde (n) porridge
Portal (n) porch
Porterhousesteak (n), **kleines T-bone steak**
Portier (m) bellcaptain, concierge
Portion (f) portion
Portionsgröße (f) portion size
Portionsgrößenkontrolle (f) portion control
Portionskostenfaktor (m) portion cost factor
Porto (n) postage
Portogebühr (f) postal rate
Portwein (m) port
Porzellan (n) china, porcelain
Porzellan- und Glaswaren (pl. f) china and glassware
Position (f) position
Positionslicht (n) navigation light
Post (f) mail
Postamt (n) post office
Postanweisung (f) postal money order, postal order
Postanweisung (f), **internationale** international money order
Postbezirk (m) postal district
Postbus (m) post-office bus
Posten (m) item
Poster (n) poster

Postfach (n) pigeon hole, post-office box
postfertig ready for mail
Postflug (m) mail flight
Postflugzeug (n) mail plane
Postkarte (f) postcard
postlagernd general delivery, poste restante
Postleitzahl (f) postal zone number, zip code
Postliste (f) mailing list
Postscheck (m) giro
Postscheckamt (n) postal giro office
Postscheckkonto (n) postal check account
Postsparkonto (n) postal savings account
Poststempel (m) postmark
Postwurfsendung (f) unaddressed mailing
Postzustellung (f) postal delivery
Poularde (f) pullet
prächtig magnificent
Prämiensystem (n) incentive system
Praktikant (m) trainee
Pralinen (pl. f) chocolates
Preis (m) rate
Preis (m) **anheben** jack price
Preis (m) **drücken** cut price
Preis (m) **einschließlich sämtlicher Kosten** (pl.) FAS price
Preis (m) **erhöhen** raise price
Preis (m) **je Tag** (m) **und Person** (f) price per day and person
Preis (m) **pro Einheit** (f) unit price
Preis (m) **senken** cut price
Preis (m), **angemessener** reasonable price
Preis (m), **ermäßigter** reduced rates
Preis (m), **freier** open price
Preis (m), **kontrollierter** admini-

stered price
Preisänderung (f)   prices subject to alteration
Preisangabe (f)   quotation, quotation of prices
Preisangebot (n) **machen**   quote
Preisanpassung (f)   adjustment of prices
Preisbeschränkung (f)   rate restriction
Preisdruck (m)   dumping
Preise (pl. m) **auf Anfrage** (f)   prices on request, rates on application
Preise (pl. m) **einschließlich Bedienungsgeld** (n) **und Mehrwertsteuer** (f)   prices include service charge and added-value tax
Preise (pl. m) **ohne Gewähr** (f)   prices without guarantee
Preise schließen die folgenden Leistungen (pl. f) **ein**   prices include the following services
Preiselbeere (f)   cranberry, red bilberry
Preiserhöhung (f)   advance in price, price increase
Preisermäßigung (f)   price cut
Preisfestsetzung (f)   pricing
preisgeben   give up
Preisgefüge (n)   price structure
Preiskalkulation (f)   price estimate
Preisklasse (f)   price category
Preiskontrolle (f)   rate restriction
Preislage (f), **mittlere**   medium priced
Preisliste (f)   price list
Preisnachlaß (m)   price allowance, rebate
Preisniveau (n)   level of prices
Preisnotierung (f)   quotation
Preisobergrenze (f)   price ceiling
Preispolitik (f)   price policy

Preisschild (n)   price tag
Preisschwankung (f)   fluctuation of price
Preissenkung (f)   mark down, reduction of the rates
Preissteigerung (f)   advance in price
Preisunterbietung (f)   dumping
Presseerklärung (f)   press release
Presseinformation (f)   press release
Pressemitteilung (f)   hand out
Presskopf (m)   head cheese, pressed hog's head
Priorität (f)   precedence, priority
Prise (f)   dash, pinch
Privatbadestrand (m)   private bathing-beach
Privatbesitz (m)   private property
Privatgrundstück (n)   private property
Privathaus (n)   private house
Privatjacht (f)   private yacht
Privatkonto (n)   drawing account
Privatquartier (n)   private room
Privatwagen (m)   private car
Privatzimmer (n)   private room
pro Tag (m)   per day
Probe (Muster) (f)   pattern
Probe (f), **auf**   on trial
Probelauf (m)   trial run
probieren   try
Problemlöser (m)   trouble-shooter
Produkt (n)   product
Produktionsmenge (f)   output
Produktionsplanung (f)   production planning
Produktionssteuerung (f)   production control
Produktivität (f)   productivity
Prognose (f)   forecast
Prognosefaktor (m)   forecast factor
Prognosekostenrechnung (f)   esti-

mating-cost system
Programm (n)   package, program (amerik.), programme (brit.)
Programmänderung (f)   change in the programme
Programmiersprache (f)   programming language
Promenade (f)   promenade
Promenadendeck (n)   promenade deck
Propangas (n)   propan gas
Propellerflugzeug (n)   airscrew-driven aeroplane
Prosit!   cheerio, cheers, to your health
Prospekt (m)   booklet, brochure, folder, leaflet, prospectus
Prost!   bottoms up
Protokoll (n)   minutes
Proviant (m)   provisions
Proviantkorb (m)   luncheon-basket
Provision (f)   commission
Provision (f) **gewähren**   grant a commission
Provisionskonto (n)   commission account
Prozeß (m)   action
prüfen   audit, examine, inspect, test
Prüfliste (f)   check list
Prüfung (f)   test
Prüfung (f) **an Ort** (m) **und Stelle** (f)   spot check
Prünelle (f)   prunelle
Pub (n)   pub
Public Relations (pl. f)   public relations
Publikation (f)   publication
Publizität (f)   publicity
Pudding (m)   pudding
Puder (m)   powder
Puderzucker (m)   icing sugar
Pufferzeit (f) **(Netzplan)**   buffer time

Puffmais (m)   pop-corn
Pullmanwagen (m)   Pullman (car)
Pult (n)   desk
Pulver (n)   powder
Pulverschnee (m)   powder snow
Pumpernickel (m)   Westphalian rye-bread
Punsch (m)   punch
Puppe (f)   doll
pur   neat
Puter (m)   turkey
PX (Warenhaus für amerik. Armeeangehörige) (n)   PX (post exchange)

Q

Quacksalber (m)   quack doctor
Qualifikation (f)   qualification
qualifizieren   qualify
qualifiziert   qualified
Qualität (f)   quality
Qualitätsbewertung (f)   quality evaluation
Qualitätskennzeichnung (f)   grade labelling
Qualitätskontrolle (f)   quality control
Qualitätskontrolleur (m)   quality checker
Qualitätsprüfung (f) **der Speisen** (pl. f)   food test
Qualitätsstandard (m)   quality standard
Qualitätsüberprüfungsprogramm (n)   quality assurance program
Qualle (f)   jellyfish
Quantität (f)   quantity
Quarantäne (f)   quarantine
Quark (m)   curd cheese
Quarkknödel (m)   white cheese dumpling

Quarktaschen (pl. f) pastry envelopes filled with white chese
Quart (1.136 l) (n) quart
Quarter (amerik. Münze) (m) quarter
Quartier (n) lodging, quarters
Quartiergeber (m) landlord
Quartiermeister (m) quartermaster
quasi quasi
Quelle (f) fountain, spring
Quellpavillon (m) pump room
Quellwasser (n) spring water
Querulant (m) trouble maker
Quitte (f) quince
quittieren receipt
Quittung (f) receipt
Quote (f) quota
Quotient (m) quotient
quotieren quote

R

Rabatt (m) allowance, discount, rebate
Rad (Fahrrad) (n) bike
Raddampfer (m) paddle-steamer, side-wheeler
Radfahrweg (m) cycle track
Radieschen (n) radish
Radio (n) radio, wireless
Radio (n) **in allen Zimmern** (pl. n) radio sets in every room
Radioübertragung (f) transmission
Radlermaß (f) shandy
Radonquelle (f) radon spring
Radtourist (m) cycling tourist
Räucheraal (m) smoked eel
Räucherhering (m) kippered herring
Räucherhering (m) **gebraten** fried kipper
Räucherlachs (m) smoked salmon
Räucherschinken (m) gammon, smoked ham
räumen clear, vacate
Räumung (f) clearance
Ragout (n) fricassee, hash, ragout, stew
Ragout (n), **weißes** white stew
Rahm (m) cream, sweet cream
Rahm (m), **saurer** sour cream
Rahmkäse (m) cream chesse
Rahmkäsetorte (f) cream cheese tart
Rahmsoße (f) cream sauce
Rahmschnitzel (n) creamed veal collop, veal steak in sour cream
Rahmsuppe (f) cream soup
Rallye (f) rallye
Rampe (f) ramp
Ramschverkauf (m) jumble sale
Rand (m) edge
Rang (m) rank
Rang, zweiter (im Theater) (m) amphie
rangieren shunt, rank
ranzig rancid
Rapunzelsalat (m) lamb's lettuce-salad
Rasen (m) **nicht betreten!** keep off the grass
Rasierapparat (m), **elektrischer** electric razor
Rasierwasser (n) **(n. d. Rasur)** after-shave lotion
Rastplatz (m) lay-by
Raststätte (f) road-house
Rat (m) advice
Rate (f) instalment, rate
Ratgeber (m) guide
Rathaus (n) city hall, town hall
rationalisieren economize, rationalize
Rationalisierung (f) economizing, rationalization

Rationalisierungsfachmann (m) efficiency expert
Ratschlag (m) advice
Raucher (m) smoker
Raucherabteil (n) smoker
Rauchfleisch (n) smoked beef, smoked meat
Rauchfleisch (n) **mit Kraut** (n) smoked pork with pickled cabbage
Rauchsalon (m) smoke room
rauh rugged
Rauigote-Soße (f) rauigote sauce
Raum (m) **für Säuglingsbetreuung** (f) babies' room
Raumkosten (pl.), **sonstige** utilities
Reaktion (f), **gefühlsmäßige** emotional reaction
Rebhuhn (n) partridge
Rebhuhnpastete (f) partridge pie
Rebstock (m) vine
Rechenmaschine (f) calculating machine, calculator
Rechentabelle (f) ready reckoner
rechnen calculate
rechnen mit relevanten Kosten (pl.) relevant costing
Rechnung (f) bill, calculation, invoice
Rechnung (f) **stellen, in** bill
Rechnung (f) **vorlegen** present a bill
Rechnungsbetrag (m) invoice amount
Recht (n) right
rechtfertigen justify
Rechtfertigung (f) justification
rechtlich lawful
rechtmäßig lawful, legitimate, rightful
Rechtmäßigkeit (f) rightfulness
Rechts fahren! keep right
Rechtsabbiegen verboten (n) no right turn

Rechtsanspruch (m) legal claim
Rechtsanwalt (m) lawyer
Rechtsanwaltsgebühren (pl. f) legal fees and expenses
Rechtsform (f) legal form
rechtsgültig legal
Rechtshilfe (f) legal aid
Rechtsschutzversicherung (f) legal aid insurance
Rechtsverkehr (m) right-hand traffic
rechtswidrig illegal
Reeder (m) ship owner
Reederei (f) shipping company
Regel (f) regulation, rule
regeln control, rule
Regeltarif (m) general tariff
Regelzug (m) scheduled train
Regen (m) rainfall
Regenbogenforelle (f) rainbow trout
regendicht rainproof
Regenmantel (m) mackintosh, raincoat
Regenschauer (m) shower of rain
Regenversicherung (f) rain insurance
Regenzeit (f) rainy season
Registratur (f) filing cabinet
regnerisch pluvial, rainy
Reh (n) deer, roebuck, venison
Rehbock (m) venison
Rehbraten (m) roast venison
Rehkeule (f) haunch of venison
Rehragout (n) stew of venison
Rehrücken (m) saddle of venison
Rehrücken (m) **flambiert** flamed saddle of venison
Rehschlegel (m) leg of venison
Reibeisen (n) grater
Reibekuchen (m) potato-fritters
reiben grate
reichlich ample

reif mature, ripe
Reifen (m)   tyre
Reifendruck (m)   tyre pressure
Reifenwechsel (m)   changing a wheel
Reihe (f)   queue
rein   clean (sauber), neat (ordentlich)
Reineclaude (f)   greengage
Reingewicht (n)   net weight
Reingewinn (m)   net income, net profit
reinigen   clean, cleanse
reinigen, chemisch   dry-clean
Reinigung (f)   cleaning
Reinigung (f) **der Veranstaltungsräume** (pl. m)   public space and kitchen cleaning
Reinigung (f)**, chemische**   dry cleaning
Reinigungsabteilung (f)   stewarding department
Reinigungskraft (f)   parlour-maid
Reinigungsmittel (n)   cleaning supply
Reinigungspersonal (n)   cleaning personnel, housemen
Reinverlust (m)   net loss
Reis (m)   rice
Reis (m)**, gekochter**   boiled rice
Reis (m)**, roher**   paddy
Reisauflauf (m)   souffle of rice
Reise (f)   journey, tour, travel, trip, voyage
Reiseagent (m)   tourist agent
Reiseagentur (f)   tourist agency
Reiseandenken (n)   travel souvenir
Reiseanmeldung (f)   final holiday registration
Reiseapotheke (f)   portable medicine-case, tourist's medicine-case
Reiseatlas (m)   tourist atlas
Reiseauskunft (f)   travel information
Reisebedingungen (pl. f)**, allgemeine**   general travel conditions
Reisebeginn (m)   start
Reisebegleiter (m)   travel companion
Reisebeilage (f)   travel supplement
Reisebetreuung (f)   travel service
Reisebüro (n)   tourist agency, travel agency
Reisebüroverband (m)   association of travel agencies, International Federation of Travel Agencies
Reisebus (m)   tourist bus
Reisedauer (f)   duration of a journey
Reisedichte (f)   passenger density
Reiseetappe (f)   stage of journey
Reiseführer (m)   guide, guidebook, itinerary
Reisegebiet (n)   touring area, tourist area, tourist region
Reisegepäck (n) **verschlepptes**   wrongly routed luggage
Reisegepäck (n)**, fehlendes**   lost luggage
Reisegeschwindigkeit (f)   cruising speed
Reisegesellschaft (f)   tourist party
Reisegutschein (m)   travel voucher
Reiseintensität (f)   volume of tourist traffic
Reisekasse (f)   travelling funds
Reisekosten (pl.)   travelling expenses
Reisekostenrückvergütung (f)   reimbursement of travel expenses
Reisekostenvergütung (f)   travel allowance

Reisekreditbrief (m) traveller's letter of credit
Reiseleiter (m) courier, tour conductor, tour manager, travel supervisor
Reiseleiter (m), **sprachkundiger** linguist-courier
Reiseleiterin (f) tour manager
Reiseleitung (f) courier's office, tour management
Reisemarkt (m) tourist market, travel market
Reisemitbringsel (n) holiday gift
Reisemittler (m) tourist agent
reisen travel
Reisen (n) travel
Reisen (pl. f) **abwickeln** operate
reisen ins Ausland (n) go abroad
reisen mit dem Zug (m) travel by train
Reisender (m) tourist, traveller, voyager
Reisender (Verkäufer) (m) salesman
Reisepapiere (pl. n) travel documents
Reisepaß (m) passport
Reiseplakat (n) touristic poster, travel poster
Reiseplan (m) itinerary
Reiseprogramm (n) travel program(me)
Reiseprospekt (m) travel booklet
Reiseproviant (m) packed lunch, travelling provisions
Reiseroute (f) itinerary, touring itinerary
Reiseroute (f) **festlegen** fix the route of a journey
Reiseruf (m) S.O.S. message
Reisescheck (m) traveller's cheque (check)
Reisespesen (pl.) travel expenses, travelling charges
Reisespesen-Tagessatz (m) per diem allowance
Reisespesenabrechnung (f) travel expense report
Reisespesenvorschuß (m) travel advance
Reisestrecke (f) touring itinerary
Reisetag (m) travelling day
Reisetasche (f) bag, travelling bag
Reiseunfallversicherung (f) travel accident insurance
Reiseunterbrechung (f) stopover
Reiseveranstalter (m) tour operator, travel organizer
Reiseverkehr (m) tourist traffic, travel
Reiseverlauf (m) course of a journey, touring itinerary
Reiseversicherung (f) travel insurance
Reisevorbereitungen (pl. f) travel preparations
Reisewegänderung (f) change of route
Reisewelle (f) travel boom
Reisewetterversicherung (f) tourist weather insurance
Reisezahlungsverkehr (m) payments of travellers
Reisezeit (f) tourist season, travel time
Reiseziel (n) destination
Reisezug (m) passenger train
Reisfleisch (n) meat rice, steamed rice with chopped pork (beef)
Reisgericht (n) **in Form** (f) rice pie, rice timbale
Reisgericht (n) **mit Erbsen** (pl. f) rice of peas
Reisgericht (n) **mit Reibkäse** (m) rice dish with grated cheese
Reissuppe (f) rice soup
Reißverschluß (m) zip
Reitbahn (f) riding-ring

Reitgelände (n)   riding-ground
Reitgelegenheit (f)   riding-facilities
Reitklub (m)   riding-club
Reitkurs (m)   riding-course
Reitpferde (pl. n) **zu vermieten**   horses for hire
Reitschule (f)   riding-school
Reitstall (m)   riding-stable
Reitweg (m)   bridle-path, riding-track
Reiz (m)   zest
Reklamation (f)   complaint
Reklame (f)   advertising
reklamieren   complain, reclaim
Rekonvaleszenz (f)   convalescence
Reling (f)   rail
Ren (n)   reindeer
Rendite (f)   yield
Rennboot (n)   racing boat
rennen   race
Rennen (n)   race
Rennstrecke (f)   race course, trail
Rentabilität (f)   profitability
Rentabilitätsstudie (f)   feasibility study
Rentier (n)   reindeer
Reparaturauftrag (m)   maintenance work order, repair order
Reparaturdienst (m)   service station
Reparaturen (pl. f) **und Instandhaltung** (f)   repairs and maintainance
Reparaturkosten (pl.)   repair cost
Reparaturwerkstätte (f)   garage, repair shop
reparieren   fix, repair
repariert   fixed
Repräsentationswerbung (f)   prestige advertising
Reservat (n)   national park, nature reserve, reservation
Reservations- und Beschwerdebuch (m) **im Restaurant** (n)   log-book
Reserve (f)   reserve, resource
Reservebett (n)   spare bed
reservieren   reserve
Reservierung (f)   reservation
Reservierungsdame (f)   reservation clerk
Reservierungskosten (pl.)   reservation charges, reservation expenses
Rest (m)   remainder, residue
Restaurantbesetzung (f)   sitting
Restaurantdeck (n)   restaurant deck
Restaurantdirektor (m)   restaurant manager
Restaurateur (m)   restaurant-keeper
Restbetrag (m)   balance, residue
Restzahlung (f)   final payment, payment of balance
Resultat (n)   result
Rettich (m)   black radish, radish
Rettungsboot (n)   life-boat
Rettungsexpedition (f)   rescue expedition
Rettungsgürtel (m)   life-belt
Rettungsmannschaft (f)   rescue party
Rettungsstation (n)   life-guard station, life-saving station
Rettungswagen (m)   ambulance, motor ambulance
revidieren   revise
Rezept (Küche) (n)   recipe
Rezeption (f)   reception desk, office
Rhabarber (m)   pie-plant (amerik.), rhubarb (brit.)
Rheinsalm (m)   Rhine salmon
Rheinwein (m)   hock, Rhine wine
richtig   correct
Richtlinie (f)   regulation
Richtlinien (pl. f)   business policy

Richtung (f)   direction
Richtungspfeil (m)   direction arrow
riechen   smell
Riesenslalom (m)   giant slalom
Rind (Fleisch) (n)   beef
Rind(vieh) (n)   cattle
Rinde (f)   peeling
Rinderbrust (f)   brisket of beef
Rinderschmorbraten (m)   potted beef, stewed beef
Rinderschwanzstück (n) **geschmort**   braised aitchbone
Rindfleisch (n)   beef
Rindfleisch (n) **in Essig** (m) **und Öl** (n)   cold beef in vinegar
Rindfleisch (n), **gekocht**   boiled beef
Rindfleischsalat (m)   salad of boiled beef
Rindsbraten (m)   joint of beef
Rindsfilet (n)   fillet of beef, tenderloin
Rindsfilet (n) **im Blätterteig** (m)   tenderloin of beef 'Wellington'
Rindsgulasch (n)   beef stew
Rindslendenbraten (m)   roast fillet of beef
Rindsmagen (m) **in Milch** (f) **und Wasser** (n)   tripe and onions
Rindsragout (n)   brown beef stew
Rindsrostbraten (m)   top cut roast
Rindsroulade (f)   rolled braised beef, beef olive
Rindszunge geräuchert (f)   smoked beef tongue
Ringbahn (f)   belt line, circle railway
Ringstraße (f)   belt highway, circular road, ring road
Rippchen (n)   rib
Rippenspeer (m)   spare-rib
Risiko (n)   hazard, risk

risikoreich   risky
Risikoübernahme (f), **volle**   full coverage
riskieren   risk
Roastbeef   roast sirloin
Roastbeef (n), **englisches**   roast beef (English style)
Rochen (m)   skate
Rodelbahn (f)   toboggan run, toboggan slide
Rodelhang (m)   coasting slide, toboggan run, toboggan slide
Rodellift (m)   sledge tow, toboggan tow
rodeln   toboggan
Rodeln (n)   luging, tobogganing
Rodelsport (m)   luging, tobogganging
Röhre (f)   tube
Röntgenaufnahme (f)   X-ray photo
Röstbrot (n)   grilled bread
Röstbrotschnitte (f)   toast
Röstbrotwürfelchen (pl. n)   fried slippets
Rösti (pl.)   hash brown potatoes
Rogen (m)   roe
Roggen (m)   rye
Roggenbrot (n)   rye-bread
roh   raw
Rohertrag (m)   gross profit on sales, raw yield
Rohgewinn (m)   gross profit, margin
Rohkost (f)   vegetarian food
Rohkostplatte (f)   salad plate
Rohmaterial (n)   raw material
Rohrpost (f)   tube post
Rohschinken (m)   raw ham
Rollbahn (f)   runway
Rollbraten (m)   rolled beef
Roller (m)   scooter
Rollfilm (m)   roll film
Rollgeld (n)   cartage, wheelage
Rollmops (m)   collared herring,

rolled herring, rollmop herring
Rollschinken (m) rolled ham
Rollschuhbahn (f) skating-rink
Rollstuhl (m) bath chair, wheelchair
Rolltreppe (f) escalator
Roquefort-Käse (m) Roquefort
Rose (f) rose
Rosenkohl (m) Brussels sprouts
rosig gebraten medium done
Rosine (f) raisin
Rosinenpudding (m) baked sultana pudding
Rosmarin (m) rosemary
Rost (m) grill
Rostbraten (m) boned rips of beef, roast beef
rot red
Rotbarbe (f) red mullet
Rotbrasse (f) sea-bream
Rote Beete (f) beet-root
Rote Beete-Salat (m) beet-root salad
rote Grütze (f) red grits
rote Rübe (f) red beet
rotieren rotate
Rotkohl (m) red cabbage
Rotwein (m) red wine
Rotzunge (f) dab, lemon-sole
Roulade (f) collared beef
Routinearbeit (f) routine work
Ruder (n) oar
Ruderboot (m) rowboat, rowing-boat
rudern row
Rudersee (m) boating-lake
Rübe (f), **rote** red beet
Rübe (f), **weiße** swede, turnip
Rückantwortkarte (f) reply postcard
Rücken (Fleisch) (m) saddle
Rückenschmerzen (pl. m) backache
Rückenstück (n) saddle
Rückenstück (n) **vom Lamm** (n) baron of lamb
Rückenwind (m) tail-wind
Rückerstattung (f) refund, reimbursement, repayment
Rückfahrkarte (f) return ticket, roundabout ticket
Rückfahrt (f) return journey, return trip
Rückflug (m) return flight
Rückgabe (f) return
Rückgang (m) decline
Rückinformation (f) feed-back
Rückkehr (f) return
Rücklage (f) reserve
Rückreise (f) return journey, return trip, return voyage
Rückreiseverkehr (m) homeward tourist traffic
rückständig in arrears
Rückstellung (f) **für Betriebsmittel** (pl. n) equipment, reserve for operating equipment
Rückstellung (f) **für Ersatz** (m) **von Geschirr** (n), **Steingut** (n), **Glaswaren** (pl. f) **und Wäsche** (f) provision for replacement of china, crockery, glassware, and linen
Rückstellung (f) **für zweifelhafte Forderungen** (pl. f) allowance for doubtful accounts
Rücktrittsfrist (f) escape period
Rücktrittsrecht (n) right of rescission
Rückvergütung (f) quantity discount, reimbursement
rückwärtiges Zimmer (n) back room
rückzahlbar repayable
Rückzahlung (f) repayment
Rühreier (pl. n) scrambled eggs
Ruf (m) reputation
Ruhebank (f) park bench
Ruheraum (m) rest room
Ruhestand (m) retirement

117

Ruhezeiten (pl. f) hours of rest
Ruhezone (f) zone of rest
ruhig quiet
Ruine (f) ruin
Rum (m) rum
Rumbaba (m) rhum-baba
Rummelplatz (m) amusement park, fun-fair
Rumpsteak (n) rumpsteak
Rumpsteak (n) **am Rost** (m) rumpsteak grilled
rund round
Rundblick (m) panorama
Runde (f) round
Rundfahrt (f) circular tour, trip
Rundflug (m) excursion flight, sight-seeing flight
Rundfunk (m) radio, wireless
Rundfunk (m) broadcast
Rundfunkwerbung (f) broadcast advertising
Rundgang (m) tour round, walk round
Rundreise (f) circle trip, circular tour, circular trip, round trip
Rundreisefahrschein (m) circle trip ticket
Rundschreiben (n) circular
Rundsicht (f) panorama
Rundzelt (n) bell tent
russische Eier (pl. n) eggs Russian style, mayonnaise eggs, Russian eggs
russische rote Rübensuppe (f) Russian beetroot soup
rutschig slippery

S

Sachertorte (f) chocolate cake Sacher style, fancy-cake with chocolate
Sachkenntnis (f) knowhow

Sachkonto (n) ledger account
Sackgasse (f) blind alley, cul-de-sac
Säuberung (f) cleaning
säumig tardy
Safari (f) safari, trekking
Safran (m) saffron
Safranreis (m) risotto with saffron, saffron-risotto
Saft (m) juice, sap
Saftgulasch (n) beef stew in juice
saftig juicy
Sahne (f) cream, sweet cream
Sahnebaiser (m) meringue
Saibling (m) char
Saison (f) season
Saison (f), **tote** off-season
Saison (f), **vorherige** previous season
Saisonaufschlag (m) seasonal price increase
Saisonbetrieb (m) seaonal establishment, seasonal service
Saisoneröffnung (f) opening of the season
Saisongeschäft (n) seasonal business
Saisonhotel (n) seasonal hotel
Saisonhotellerie (f) seasonal hotel trade
Saisonschwankung (f) seasonal fluctuation, sesonal variation
Saisonspitze (f) seasonal peak
Saisonzuschlag (m) seasonal surcharge
Sakko (m) jacket
Salami (f) salami
Salat (m) salad
Salat (m), **gemischter** mixed salad, tossed salad
Salat (m), **grüner** green salad
Salatsoße (f) dressing, salad dressing
Salatsoße (f), **französisch**

French dressing
Salatschüssel (f) salad bowl
Salbei (m) sage
saldieren balance
Saldo (m) balance
Saldovortrag (m) balance carried forward
Salm (m) salmon
Salm (m), **pochierter** boiled salmon
Salmmayonnaise (f) salmon mayonnaise
Salmmittelstück (n) salmon cut, salmon cutlet
Salon-Schlafwagen (m) Pullman(car)
Salonwagen (m) saloon carriage
Salz (n) salt
Salzbretzel (f) pretzel
Salzburger Norckerl (n) Salzburg sweet dumpling
salzen salt
Salzfäßchen (n) salt-cellar
Salzgurke (f) salted cucumber
Salzkartoffeln (pl. f) boiled potatoes, plain boiled potatoes
Salzmandeln (pl. f) salted almonds
Salzstreuer (m) salt-cellar
Samenkorn (n) kernel
Sammeleinkauf (m) group buying
Sammelfahrschein (m) party ticket
Sammelfahrt (f) party outing
Sammelgarage (f) large-capacity garage, multi-car garage
Sammeljournal (n) general journal
Sammelkonto (n) collection account
sammeln collect, compile
Sammeln (n) rally
Sammelpaß (m) collective passport, group passport
Sammelpunkt (m) meeting-place
Sammelstelle (f) meeting-place, place of assembly
Sammelvisum (n) group visa
Sammlung (f) collection
Sanatorium (n) sanatorium
Sandbad (n) sand-bath
Sandbank (f) sandbank
Sandburgenwettbewerb (m) sand-castle competition
Sanddüne (f) sand-dune
Sandkuchen (m) Madeira cake
Sandsteinfelsen (m) sandstone rock
Sandstrand (m) sandy beach
Sandwich (m) sandwich
sanieren reorganize
sanitäre Anlagen (pl. f) sanitary facilities
Sardelle (f) anchovy
Sardellenbutter (f) anchovy-butter
Sardellenbuttersoße (f) anchovy butter sauce
Sardellensoße (f) anchovy sauce
Sardellenstäbchen (pl. n) anchovy straws
Sardine (f), **große** pilchard
Sardinen (pl. f) **in Öl** (n) sardines in oil
sauber neat, tidy
Sauce Hollandaise Hollandaise sauce
Sauce Bearnaise (f) Bearnaise sauce
Sauciere (f) sauce-boat
sauer acid, sour
Sauerampfer (m) sorrel
Sauerbraten (m) braised beef marinated, German pot roast, sauerbraten
Sauerkraut (n) pickled cabbage, sauerkraut

119

Sauerkrautplatte (f) sauerkraut with smoked meat, ham and sausage
Sauerstoffbad (n) oxygen bath
Sauerteig (m) leaven
saufen guzzle, tope
Säuglingsbetreuung (f) baby care
Saum (m) hem
Sauna (f) sauna
Sauterne (m) Sauterne
Schabkäse (m), **heißer** hot Swiss cheese-mush
Schablone (f) template
Schachtel (f) box
schaden damage, injure
Schaden (m) damage, disadvantage, loss
Schadenersatz (m) compensation for damages, damages
Schadenersatz (m) **leisten** pay damages
Schadenersatzanspruch (m) claim for damages
Schadenersatzklage (f) action for damages
Schadenshaftung (f) liability for damages
Schadensanzeige (f) notice of claim
Schadensfall (m) event of loss
Schadensfeststellung (f) ascertainment of damage
Schadensregulierung (f) loss settlement
schadhaft defective
schädigen aggrieve, damage
schälen peel
schätzen esteem, estimate, rate
Schätzung (f) estimate
Schätzung (f), **grobe** rough estimate
schäumen foam
schäumend sparkling
Schaffner (m) conductor, guard

Schafskäse (m) sheep's cheese, eve cheese
Schale (f) peel, peeling
Schalentier (n) shellfish
schalldicht soundproof
Schallplatte (f) record, grammophone record
Schalotte (f) scallion, shallot
Schalter (z. B. Bank-) (m) window
Schalterbeamter (m) booking clerk, ticket clerk
Schalterhalle (f) booking hall
Schalterstunden (pl. f) **der Bank** (f) banking hours
Schalthebel (m) gear lever
Schaltjahr (n) leap year
Schalttafel (f) patchboard
Schampus (m) fizz
Schankerlaubnis (f) **und Gewerbeaufsicht** (f) licenses and inspections
Schankkellner (m) barman, bartender, tapster
Schankkellnerin (f) barmaid
Schankstube (f) taproom
Schanktisch (m) bar
Schankwirt (m) saloonkeeper
Schankwirt (m) tavern-keeper, publican
scharf (gewürzt) deviled, highly seasoned, hot, spicy
Schatten (m) shadow
schattig shady
schauen look
Schaufensterbummel (m) window-shopping
Schaukasten (m) display case
Schaum (m) foam
Schaumbad (n) bubble-bath
Schaumgefrorenes (n) sponge ice-cream
Schaumlöffel (m) skimmer
Schaumwein (m) sparkling hock

Schauplatz (m)   site
Schauspieler (m)   actor
Schauspielerin (f)   actress
Schauspielhaus (n)   playhouse
Scheck (m)   cheque
Scheck (durch die Bank bestätigt) (m)   certified check
Scheckbuch (n)   checkbook, cheque book
Scheckheft (n)   cheque book
Scheckkarte (f)   bank card, credit card
Scheibe (f)   slice
Scheibenwischer (m)   windshield wiper
Scheinwerfer (m)   headlight
Schellfisch (m)   haddock
Schema (n)   table
Schenke (f)   bar, saloon-bar
Schenkung (f)   gift
Scherbett (m)   sherbet
Scherz (m)   joke
Scheuerlappen (m)   scouring cloth
Scheuertuch (n)   floor cloth
Schicht (f)   layer, shift
Schicht (f), **unterbrochene**   split shift
Schichttorte (f)   layer-cake
Schiebedach (n)   sliding roof
Schieber (Kinderlöffel) (m)   pusher
Schienenweg (m)   railway line
schießen   shoot
Schiff (n)   ship, vessel
Schiff (n) **besteigen**   board a ship
Schiff (n), **auf dem**   on board (a) ship
Schiff (n), **beladenes**   fullship
Schiff-Eisenbahn-Umladeplatz (m)   rail and water terminal
Schiffahrt (f)   navigation
Schiffahrtsgesellschaft (f)   liner company

Schiffahrtskunde (f)   navigation
Schiffahrtsverkehr (m)   waterborne traffic
schiffbar   navigable
Schiffbarkeit (f)   navigability
schiffen   navigate
Schiffer (m)   seaman
Schiffsanlegestelle (f)   wharf
Schiffsanschluß (m)   steamship connection
Schiffsarzt (m)   ship's doctor
Schiffsbau (m)   shipbuilding
Schiffskapitän (m)   captain, sea-captain
Schiffskarte (f)   steamer ticket
Schiffskellner (m)   steward
Schiffskoch (m)   ship's cook
Schiffsladung (f)   cargo
Schiffsmiete (f)   charter money
Schiffsraum (m)   shipping space
Schiffsreise (f)   cruise, voyage
Schiffsrumpf (m)   hull
Schiffsschraube (f)   screw
Schiffstonnage (f)   tonnage
Schiffsverbindung (f)   steamer service
Schildkröte (f)   turtle
Schildkrötensuppe (f)   real turtle soup
Schildkrötensuppe (f) **klar**   clear turtle soup
Schildkrötensuppe (f), **echte**   real turtle soup
Schildkrötensuppe (f), **falsche**   mock turtle soup, clear mock turtle soup
Schinken (m)   ham
Schinken (m) **im Brotteig** (m)   baked ham in bread crust
Schinken (m), **gekochter**   boiled ham
Schinken (m), **gepökelter**   ham cured
Schinken (m), **geräucherter**   ham smoked

121

Schinken (m), **roher** ham raw
Schinkenknödelsuppe (f) soup with ham dumplings
Schinkenomelett (n) ham omelet, omelet with ham
Schirm (m) umbrella
Schlägerei (f) affray
Schlafabteil (n) sleeper section, sleeping-compartment
schlafend asleep
Schlafgelegenheit (f) sleeping accomodation
Schlafkur (f) hypnotherapy, sleeping-cure
Schlafplatz (m) sleeping-berth
Schlafraum (m) dormitory
Schlafsaal (m) dormitory
Schlafsack (m) sleeping-bag
Schlafstelle (f) night's lodging, overnight accomodation
Schlafwagen (m) sleper
Schlafwagen (m), **mit Speisewageneinrichtung** (f) hotel car
Schlafwagenkarte (f) sleeping-car ticket
Schlafwagenschaffner (m) sleeping-car attendant
Schlafwagenzuschlag (m) sleeping-car charge
Schlafzimmer (n) bedroom
Schlagbaum (m) turnpike
schlagen knock
Schlaglicht (m) highlight
Schlagloch (n) road-hole
Schlagsahne (f) whipped cream
Schlagteig (m) batter
Schlammbad (n) mud bath
Schlammpackung (f) mud pack
Schlange (f) queue
Schlange (f) **stehen** queue up
Schlauchboot (n) pneumatic boat, rubber dinghy
Schleichhandel (m) black market
Schleie (f) tench
schlemmen revel

Schlepper (Schiff) (m) tugboat
Schlepplift (m) rope tow, T-bar tow
Schlesisches Himmelreich (n) boiled smoked bacon Silesian style
Schleudergefahr (f) slippery when wet
schleudern skid
Schleuse (f) lock, sluice
schlichten adjust
Schlichtung (f) adjustment
Schließfach (n) lock box, locker, safe deposit box
Schlitten (m) luge, sled, toboggan
Schlittenfahrt (f) sleigh-ride
Schilttenlift (m) sledge tow, toboggan tow
schlittschuhlaufen skate
Schloß (Tür) (n) lock
Schloß (Gebäude) (n) castle
Schloßruine (f) castle ruins
Schlückchen (n) tot
Schlüpfer (m) knickers
schlürfen quaff, sip
Schlüssel (m) key
Schlüsselarbeitskräfte (pl. f) key personnel
Schlüsselposition (f) key position
Schlüsselzahl (f) code number
Schlußabrechnung (f) final account
Schlußsaldo (m) balance carried forward
Schlußlicht (n) tail-light
schmackhaft savoury, tasty
Schmackhaftigkeit (f) tastiness
schmal narrow
Schmalfilm (m) narrow film
Schmalz (n) dripping, lard
schmausen feast
schmecken lassen, sich relish
schmelzen thaw

Schmelzkäse (m) cheese spread, cream cheese
Schmelzkartoffeln (pl. f) butter-fried potatoes
schmerzstillend anodyne
Schmorbraten (m) braised beef, pot roast
schmoren casserole
schmücken decorate
schmuggeln smuggle
schmutzig dirty
Schmuck (m) jewellery, jewelery
Schnaps (m) hard liquor
Schnäpschen (n) pick-me-up
Schnappschuß (m) snapshot
Schneeball (m) snowball
schneebedeckt snow-covered
Schneebericht (m) snow report
Schneebesen (m) (egg)beater, whisk
Schneebrille (f) snow-goggles
Schneefall (m) snow-fall
Schneefeld (n) snowfield
schneegeräumt snow-cleared
Schneehuhn (n) ptarmigan
Schneeketten (pl. f) snow-chains, tyre chains
Schneelage (f) snow conditions
Schneemann (m) snow man
Schneematsch (m) slush
Schneepflug (m) snow-plough, snowplow (amerik.)
Schneeräumung (f) snow-clearing
schneereich snowy
Schneesaison (f) snowy season
Schneeschmelze (f) snow break
Schneesturm (m) snowstorm
Schneeverhältnisse (pl. n) snow conditions
Schneewehe (f) snowdrift
schneiden cut
Schneider (m) tailor
schnell quick

schnell... express
Schnellbus (m) express coach, high-speed bus
Schnelldampfer (m) fast steamer
Schnellgaststätte (f) quick lunch restaurant, quick service restaurant
Schnellhefter (m) letter file
Schnellimbißstube (f) self-service snack bar
Schnellstraße (f) express road, high-speed road
Schnelltriebwagen (m) express railcar
Schnellverkehr (m) express traffic
Schnellzug (m) express train, fast train
Schnepfe (f) partridge, wood cock
Schnepfen (pl. f) **gegrillt** grilled snipes
Schnitt (m) cut
Schnitte (f) slice
Schnittlauch (m) chives
Schnittstelle (f) interface
Schnitzel (n) collop, escalope, scallop (of meat)
Schnorchel (m) snorkel
Schnupftabak (m) snuff
schön beautiful, lovely, picturesque
Schönheitskur (f) cosmetic therapy
Schönheitssalon (m) beauty parlour
Schönheitswettbewerb (m) beauty contest
Schöpflöffel (m) ladle, soup-ladle
Schokolade (f) chocolate
Schokoladebaiser (n) chocolate-meringue
Schokoladeeis (n) chocolate ice-cream

123

Schokoladenauflauf (m) souffle of chocolate
Schokoladenpudding (m) chocolate pudding
Schokoladentorte (f) chocolate cake
Scholle (Fisch) (f) plaice
Schonfaktor (m) sedative factor
Schonkost (f) mild diet
Schonzeit (f) closed season
Schopfbraten (m) shin of pork, spare-rib
Schoppenwein (m) carafe wine, wine by the glass
Schorle (f) shandy, wine with sodawater
Schottenrock (m) kilt
Schrank (m) cupboard, wardrobe
Schranke (f) barrier
Schrankkoffer (m) wardrobe trunk
schrecklich awful
Schreibabteil (n) secretarial compartment
Schreibbüro (n) letter service
Schreibmappe (f) writing case
Schreibmarke (f) corsor
Schreibmaschine (f) typewriter
Schreibpapier (n) note-paper, writing paper
Schreibtisch (m) desk
Schreibzeug (n) writing kit
schriftlich written
Schritt (m) pace
Schritt (m) **fahren!** slow down
schrumpfen shrink
Schublade (f) drawer
Schürze (f) apron
Schüssel (f) bowl, dish
schütteln shake
schützen secure
Schützenfest (n) shooting-match

Schuhanzieher (m) shoehorn
schuhputzen clean the shoes, shine the shoes
Schuhputzer (m) bootblack, boots (Hotel), shoeblack
Schuhputzlappen (m) shoe-shining cloth
Schulausflug (m) educational tour, school outing
Schuld (f) debt, liability, obligation
Schulden (pl.) debts
Schulden (pl. f) **machen** incur debts
schuldig sein owe
Schulferien (pl.) school holidays
Schulter (f) shoulder
Schulter gefüllt (f) stuffed shoulder
Schulungshotel (n) training hotel
Schund (m) trash
Schuppen (m) shed
Schuß (m) **Branntwein** (m) **in Getränken** (pl. n) lace
Schutzhütte (f) refuge
Schutzimpfung (f) protective inoculation, protective vaccination
Schwägerin (f) sister-in-law
Schwager (m) brother in law
Schwalbennestersuppe (f) birds nest soup
Schwamm (m) sponge
schwanken fluctuate
Schwankung (f) fluctuation
Schwanz (m) tail
Schwartenmagen (m) pork galantine
Schwarzarbeit (f) illicit work
Schwarzbrot (n) brown bread
schwarze Bohne (f) black bean
schwarze Johannisbeere (f) black currant
schwarzer Kaffee (m) black coffee

schwarzes Brett (n)   bill-board,
   bulletin board
Schwarzmarkt (m)   black market
Schwarzwurzel (f)   salsify
Schwebebahn (f)   suspension
   railway
schweben   hover
Schwefelquelle (f)   sulphur
   spring
Schwein (n)   pig
Schweinebraten (m)   roast joint
   of pork, roast pork
Schweinefleisch (n)   pork
Schweinekotelett (n) gebacken
   fried pork cutlet
Schweinekotelett (n) gegrillt
   grilled pork chop
Schweineschlegel (m)   leg of
   pork
Schweineschnitzel (n) gegrillt
   grilled pork cutlet
Schweinesülze (f)   jelly of pork
Schweinsbrust (f)   breast of
   pork
Schweinsfüße (pl. m)   pettitoes,
   pig's trotters
Schweinsgulasch (n)   stew of
   pork Hungarian style
Schweinshaxe (f)   pork knuckles
Schweinskarree (n)   rib of pork
Schweinskopf (m)   pig's head
Schweinskopfsülze (f)   brawn
Schweinskotelett (n)   pork chop,
   cutlet
Schweinskotelett (n) gebacken
   breaded pork cutlet
Schweinsnieren (pl. f)   pork
   kidneys
Schweinsohren geräuchert (pl. n)
   smoked pig's ears
Schweinsrippchen (n) mit Sauerkraut (n)   smoked rib of pork
   with sauerkraut
Schweinsschulter (f)   shoulder
   of pork

Schweinswürstchen (n) in gebakkenem Eierteig (m)   toad-in-
   the-hole
Schweiß (m)   sweat
Schweizer Käse (m)   Swiss
   cheese
Schwelle (f)   threshold
schwenken   wave
Schwenkkartoffeln (pl. f)   saute
   potatoes, roast potatoes
schwer (Wein)   full bodied
Schwerpunkt (m)   center
Schwertfisch (m)   swordfish
Schwestergesellschaft (f)   affiliated company
Schwiegereltern (pl.)   parents-in-
   law
Schwiegermutter (f)   mother-in-
   law
Schwiegersohn (m)   son-in-law
Schwiegertochter (f)   daughter
   in law
Schwiegervater (m)   father-in-
   law
Schwimmatratze (f)   beach
   mattress
Schwimmbad (n)   swimming-
   bath, swimming-pool
schwimmen   float, swim
Schwimmen (n)   natation, swim-
   ming
Schwimmendes Hotel   floating
   hotel
Schwimmer (m)   swimmer
Schwimmhalle (f)   swimming-
   hall
Schwimmlehrer (m)   swimming
   instructor
Schwimmluftmatratze (f)   inflatable beach mattress
Schwimmunterricht (m)   swimming lessons
Schwimmweste (f)   life-jacket,
   life vest
Schwimmweste (f), aufblasbare

Mae West
Schwitzbad (n) hot-air bath, sudatory bath, vapor bath
schwitzen sweat
schwül sultry
Schwund (m) shrinkage
Schwundverlust (m) shrinkage
See (f) sea
See (f), **an der** on the sea
See (f), **auf hoher** on high seas, in the open sea
See (f), **hohe** high seas pl
See (f), **zur** on the sea
See (m) lake
See-Luft-Reise (f) sea-air voyage
Seebad (n) sea bath, seaside resort
Seebadekur (f) marinotherapy
Seebarbe (f) mullet
Seebarsch (m) bass, snook
Seebrasse (f) bream
Seeforelle (f) lake trout
Seefracht (f) cargo
Seehafen (m) seaport
Seehecht (m) coal fish, hake, silver hake
Seeheilbad (n) sea bath, seaside health resort
Seehotel (n) sea-front hotel, seaside hotel
Seekarte (f) nautical chart
Seeklima (n) sea-climate
seekrank seasick
Seekrankheit (f) nausea, seasickness
Seemann (m) seaman
Seemeile (1.852 km) (f) nautical mile, knot
Seereise (f) cruise, voyage
Seereisender (m) voyager
Seeroute (f) sea route
Seesack (m) sea bag
Seeschiffahrt (f) maritime shipping

Seestern (m) starfish
Seeteufel (m) angler, frog fish
Seetiere (pl. n) sea-food
Seetourismus (m) sea tourism
Seetourist (m) sea tourist
Seetouristik (f) sea tourism
Seewasser-Badebecken (n) seawater bathing pool
Seeweg (m) sea route
Seezunge (f) sole
Seezungenröllchen (pl. n) rolled fillets of sole
Seezungenstreifen (pl. m) strips of sole fillets
Segel (n) sail
Segelboot (n) sailing-boat, yacht
segelfliegen glide
Segelfliegen (n) gliding
Segelflugsport (m) gliding
Segelflugzeug (n) glider, sailing-plane
Segeljolle (f) yawl
segeln glide, sail
Segelregatta (f) yacht-race
Segelsaison (f) yachting-season
Segelschule (f) yachting-school
Segelsport (m) yachting
Segeltuch (n) canvas
sehenswert remarkable, worth seeing
Sehenswürdigkeit (f) place of interest, sight
Sehenswürdigkeiten (pl. f) beauty spots, sights
Sehenswürdigkeiten (pl. f) **besuchen** sight-seeing
Sehenswürdigkeiten (pl. f) **eines Ortes** (m) **zeigen** lionize
Seidenpapier (n) tissue paper
Seilbahn (f) cable railway, rope railway
Seilschwebebahn (f) aerial ropeway
Sekt (m) champagne, sparkling hock

selbständig self employed, free lance
Selbstbedienung (f) self-service
Selbstbedienungsladen (m) self-service store, supermarket
Selbstbedienungsrestaurant (n) cafeteria, self-service cafeteria, self-service restaurant
Selbstfahrer (m) owner-driver
Selbstkostenpreis (m) cost-price
Sellerie (m) celery
Selleriesalat (m) celery salad
Selterswasser (n) soda-water
Semmel (f) roll
Semmelknödel (m) white bread dumpling
senden forward, send
Sendung (f) transmission
Senf (m) mustard
Senf (m), **englischer** English mustard
Senffrüchte (pl. f) pickled fruit
Senfglas (n) mustard pot
Senfgurke (f) gherkin in piccalilly
Senfobst (n) pickled fruit
Senfsoße (f) mustard sauce
senkrecht perpendicular
seriös respectable
Serpentinenstraße (f) switch-back road, winding road
Service (m) service
Service (m) **an Bord** (m) service on board
Service-Office (n) office
servieren serve, service
Serviererin (f) waitress
Servierleistung (f) service
Serviette (f) napkin, table napkin
Sessel (m) arm-chair, easy chair, seat

Sessellift (m) chairlift
Setzerei (pl. n) fried eggs
setzen, auf eine Warteliste (f) put on a waiting list
Shake (m) shake
Sherry (m) sherry
Show (f) show
Shuffleboard (Bordspiel) (n) shuffle-board
sicher safe
Sicherheit (f) safety
Sicherheitsbestand (m) buffer stock
Sicherheitsbindung (f) safety binding
Sicherheitsgürtel (m) seat belt
Sicherheitsgurt (m) seat belt
Sicherheitsvorkehrungen (pl. f) **treffen** take security precautions
sichern secure
Sicherung (f) fuse
Sicht (f) visibility
Sichtvermerk (m) visa
Sieb (n) sieve
sieben (Sieb) sift
sieden, leicht simmer
Silberfelchen (m) silver trout
Silvesterdiner (n) New Year's dinner
Silvesterfeier (f) New Year's Eve celebration
Silvesterreise (f) New Year cruise
Sirup (m) molasses, syrup, treacle
Sitte (f) custom
Sitten (pl. f) manners
Sittenwidrigkeit (f) immorality
sittlich moral
Sitz (m) seat
Sitzbad (n) hip-bath
Sitzplatzkapazität (f) seating-capacity
Sitzung (f) conference,

127

meeting
Sitzungsraum (m) conference room
Sitzungssaal (m) conference hall
Skala (f) scale
Skateboard (n) skateboard
Ski (m) ski
Skifahren ski
Skiausrüstung (f) ski equipment
Skibindung (f) ski binding
Skibob (m) skibob
Skidorf (n) skiing village
Skifahren (n) skiing
Skifahrer (m) skier
Skiferien (pl.) skiing holidays
Skiführer (m) ski guide
Skigelände (n) ski grounds
Skigymnastik (f) skiing exercises
Skihang (m) ski slope
Skihose (f) ski trousers
Skihotel (n) ski hotel
Skihütte (f) ski hut, ski lodge
Skikleidung (f) ski wear
Skiklub (m) skiing club
Skiläufer (m) skier
Skilanglauf (m) cross-country running on skis, langlauf
Skilauf (m) skiing
Skilehrer (m) ski-coach, skiing instructor
Skiort (m) ski center, ski resort
Skipaß (m) ski-lift season ticket
Skireise (f) skiing trip
Skirennen (n) ski race
Skischlepplift (m) ski tow
Skischule (f) ski school
Skisport (m) skiing
Skispringen (n) ski-jumping
Skistiefel (m) skiboot
Skistock (m) ski pole, ski stick
Skitagespaß (m) ski-lift day ticket
Skitour (f) ski tour
Skitourist (m) ski tourist
Skiträger (m) ski carrier
Skiunterricht (m) skiing instruction, skiing lessons
Skiurlaub (m) skiing holidays
Skiverleih (m) ski hire, ski rental
Skiwachs (n) ski wax
Skiwanderung (f) hike on skis
Skiwochenende (n) skiing weekend
Skizentrum (n) ski center
Skonto (n) **abzüglich** less discount
Skonto-Erträge (pl. m) discounts earned
Skontoverlust (m) lost discount
Smoking (m) dinner-jacket, tuxedos
Snackbar (f) cafeteria, snackbar
Soda (n) soda
Soda-Himbeer (n) raspberry syrup with soda water
Sodawasser (n) **mit Speiseeis** (n) ice-soda
sofort instant
Sofortkaffe (m) instant coffee
Software (f) software
Sojabohne (f) soy bean
Solbad (Kurort) (n) salt-water resort, salt-water bath
Sole (f) salt water
Solebad (n) brine bath
Soll (n) debit, target
Soll-Wareneinsatz (m) **Speisen** (pl. f) potential food cost
Sollbestand (m) target inventory, target stock
Sollkosten (pl.) estimated cost
Sollsaldo (m) debit balance
Solquelle (f) salt spring
Sommelier (m) wine-butler

Sommeraufenthalt (m) summer resort
Sommerbad (n) open-air swimming-pool
Sommerendivie (f) romaine
Sommerfahrplan (m) summer timetable
Sommerferien (pl.) sumer holidays, summer vacation
Sommerferiendorf (n) summer holiday village
Sommerfest (n) summer party
Sommerfrische (f) summer health resort, summer holiday resort
Sommergast (m) summer visitor
Sommerhaus (n) holiday house
Sommerkohl (m) savoy cabbage
Sommerkurort (m) summer health resort
Sommermesse (f) summer fair
Sommerreiseverkehr (m) summer tourist traffic
Sommersaison (f) summer season
Sommersitz (m) summer residence
Sommerspiele (pl. n) summer festival
Sommerzeit (f) daylight-saving time, summer time
Sonderaufwendungen (pl. f) extra cost
Sonderbus (m) special bus
Sonderflug (m) extra flight, non-scheduled flight
Sonderflugzeug (n) special plane
Sonderkontingent (n) special quota
Sonderkosten (pl.) extra cost
Sonderpreis (m) special rate
Sonderprospekt (m) special brochure, special folder
Sonderschicht (f) extra shift

Sondertarif (m) special rate
Sondertour (f) extra tour
Sonderurlaub (m) special leave
Sondervergütung (f) bonus
Sonderzug (m) extra train, relief train
Sonn- und Feiertagsvergütung (f) extra pay for sunday and holiday work
Sonnenaufgang (m) sunrise
Sonnenbad (n) sunbath
Sonnenbad nehmen (n) sunbathe
Sonnenbestrahlung (f) solar radiation
Sonnenblende (f) window screen
Sonnenbrand (m) sunburn
Sonnenbrille (f) sun glasses
Sonnendeck (n) sun deck
Sonneneinstrahlung (f) insolation
Sonnenkur (f) heliotherapy, sun treatment
Sonnenschirm (m) parasol, sunshade, sun umbrella
Sonnenstich (m) sunstroke
Sonnenstrahlung (f) solar radiation
Sonnenterrasse (f) summer terrace, sunterrace
Sonnenuntergang (m) sunset
sonnig sunny
Sonntagsausflug (m) Sunday excursion
Sonntagsfahrkarte (f) Sunday excursion ticket
Sonntagsrückfahrtkarte (f) weekend return ticket
sonstige sundry
Sorbett (m) sherbet
sorgen für take care of
sorgen, sich worry
sorgfältig careful
Sorgfalt (f) care

Sorte (f)   brand, kind
sortieren   assort
Sortiment (n)   product mix, sales mix
Soße (f)   sauce
Soße (f), **pikant**   piquant sauce
Soße (f), **milde**   veloute sauce
Soße (f), **pikante fertige**   Yorkshire relish
Sozialleistungen (pl. f)   fringe benefits
Sozialtourismus (m)   social tourism
Sozialversicherung (f)   social insurance
spät   late
Spätbuchung (f)   late booking
Spätsaison (f)   after-season
Spätzle (pl.)   dough dumplings, tiny flour dumplings
Spaghetti (pl.) **mit Hackfleischsoße** (f)   spaghetti with minced meat-sauce
Spaghetti (pl.) **mit Tomatensoße** (f)   spaghetti with tomato sauce
Spalte (f)   column
Spanferkel (n)   suckling pig
spanischer Fischeintopf (m)   Spanish fish stew
spanischer Suppentopf (m)   Spanish meat-pot
spanisches Reisgericht (n) **mit Fisch** (m) **und Fleisch** (n)   Spanish rice dish with fish and meat
Spanne (f)   margin
Spannung (f)   voltage
sparen   economize
Spargel (m)   asparagus
Spargelcremesuppe (f)   cream of asparagus
Spargelsalat   asparagus salad
Spargelspitzen (pl. f)   asparagus tips

Spargelsuppe (f)   asparagus soup
sparsam   thrifty
Spaß (m)   fun, joke
spazierengehen   walk
Spazierfahrt (f)   pleasure drive
Spaziergang (m)   ramble, walk
Spazierweg (m)   walk
Speck (m)   bacon
Speckstreifen (m) **zum Spikken** (n)   lardon
Spediteur (m)   forwarding agent, carrier
Spedition (f)   forwarding agency
Speicher (m) **mit wahlfreiem Zugriff** (m)   random access memory (RAM)
speichern   store
Speise (f)   dish, food, meal
Speise- und Weinkarte (f)   menu and wine list
Speiseartikel (m), **standardisierter**   standardized menu item
Speiseeis (n)   ice (brit.), ice-cream
Speisekammer (f)   larder, pantry
Speisekarte (f)   bill of fare, menu
Speisekarte (f) **für Kinder** (pl. n)   children's menu
Speisekürbis (m)   pumpkin, vegetable marrow
Speiselokal (n)   eating-place
speisen   dine, eat, feed
Speisen (pl. f), **frisch gemachte**   dishes prepared to order
Speisen (pl. f), **warme**   hot dishes
Speisenaufzug (m)   service lift
Speisenertrag (m)   food revenue
Speisenertrag (m), **durchschnittlicher pro Gast** (m)   food average check
Speisefolge (f)   menu
Speiserest (m)   left-over

Speisesaal (m) dining-saloon
Speisewagen (m) diner, dining-car, restaurant-car
Speisezimmer (n) dining-room
Sperre (f) barrier
sperren block
Sperrfrist (f) blocked period
Sperrgebiet (n) prohibited area
Sperrgut (n) bulky goods (freight)
Sperrsitz (m) stall
Sperrstunde (f) closing time
Spesen (pl.) charge
Spesenkonto (n) expense account
Spesenkontrolle (f) control of expenses
Spezialarrangement (f) special arangement
Spezialität (f) **des Hauses** (n) speciality of the house
Spezialitätenwochen (pl. f) food festival
Spezialpreis (m) **für Familien** (pl. n) family rate
Spezialslalom (m) special slalom
Spezifikation (f) specification
spezifizieren itemize, specify
Spicknadel (f) larding-needle, larding-pin
Spiegel (m) looking-glass, mirror
Spiegeleier (pl. n) fried eggs, shirred eggs
Spiegeleier (pl. n) **mit Schinken** (m) ham and eggs
Spiel (Golf) (n) **eröffnen** tee off
Spielautomat (m) one-armed bandit, slot machine
Spielbank (f) gaming casino, gaming table
spielen gamble
Spieler (m) gambler, player
Spielfilm (m) feature
Spielkasino (n) gaming casino
Spielmarke (f) chip

Spielplatz (m) playground
Spielschuld (f) gambling debt
Spieltisch (m) gaming table
Spielwiese (f) playing-field
Spielzeug (n) toy
Spielzimmer (n) games room, nursery, playroom
Spieß (m) skewer
Spieß (m), **gebraten am** on the spit
Spießchen (n) skewer
Spießchen (n), **am** en brochette
Spinat (m) spinach
Spirituose (f) liquor
Spirituosen (pl. f) spirits
Spirituosengeschäft (n) liquor shop
Spirituskocher (m) spirit stove
Spitzenbelastungszeit (f) peak hour
Spitzengehalt (n) top salary
Spitzenverkehr (m) peak hour traffic
Spitzenwein (m) vintage wine
Sportanlagen (pl. f) sports facilities
Sportartikel (m) sporting good
Sportausrüstung (f) sports equipment
Sportdeck (n) game deck
Sportflugzeug (n) sporting plane
Sporthalle (f) gym, sports hall
Sporthotel (n) sports hotel
Sportkleidung (f) sports clothes, sportswear
Sportler (m) sportsman
Sportplatz (m) athletic ground, sports field
Sportsegler (m) yachtsman
Sportveranstaltung (f) athletics meeting, sporting event
Sportwagen (Auto) (m) sports car
Sprache (f) language

131

spracheigentümlich idiomatic
Sprecher (m) announcer, speaker
Springbrunnen (m) fountain
Spritzer (m) dash
Spritzer (m) **Soda** (n) dash of soda
Sprotte (f) sprat
Sprudelbad (n) effervescent bath
Sprungbrett (n) spring-board, take-off board
Sprungschanze (f) ski jump
Sprungturm (m) diving-tower, high-diving tower
spülen rinse, wash up
Spüler (m) dishwasher
Spülküche (f) stewarding department
Spülküchenleiter (m) steward
Spülmaschine (f) dish washer
Spülmaschine (f) **für Gläser** (pl. n) glass-washing machine
Spur (f) trail
Squash (n) squash
Staat (m) country
Staatsangehöriger (m) citizen, national
Staatsangehörigkeit (f) nationality
Staatsbürgerschaft (f) citizenship
Staatsgrenze (f) state frontier
Staatswald (m) state forest
Stab-Linien-Organisation (f) line and staff organization
Stabsfunktion (f) staff function
Stabsstelle (f) staff position
Stabsverantwortung (f) staff responsibility
Stachelbeere (f) gooseberry
Stadion (n) stadium
Stadt (f) city, town
Stadtautobahn (f) urban freeway

Stadtbahn (f) city railway
Stadtbezirk (m) municipal district
Stadtbüro (n) ticket office, town office
Stadtgebiet (n) city zone, urban area
Stadtkoffer (m) overnight bag
Stadtmauer (f) town wall
Stadtmotel (n) motor inn
Stadtmuseum (n) municipal museum
Stadtplan (m) map of the town, street plan, town plan
Stadtrundfahrt (f) city sightseeing tour, sight-seeing tour
Stadtrundflug (m) aerial city tour, city sightseeing flight
Stadtschnellstraße (f) urban express road
Stadttheater (n) municipal theater
Stadtverkehr (m) urban traffic
Stadtviertel (n) quarter
Stadtzentrum (n) town centre
städtisch municipal, urban
ständig permanent
staffeln scale
Stahlfach (n) safe deposit box
Stammgast (m) regular customer
Stammkunde (m) patron
Stammlokal (n) favourite pub
Stammtisch (m) table reserved for regular customers
Stand (m) status
Standard (m) standard
standardisieren standardize
Standardisierung (f) standardization
Standtort (m) location
Stange (f), **von der** off the peg
Stangenbohne (f) string bean
Stangensellerie (m) celery sticks

Stangenspargel (m)   asparagus sticks
stark   hearty, strong
Start (m)   start, take-off
Startbahn (f)   runway
Station (f)   stop
stationär   stationary
Stationsoberkellner (m)   captain (waiter)
Statistik (f)   statistic
statistisch   statistical
Stativ (n)   tripod
stattfinden   take place
Status (m)   status
Staub (m)   dust
staubsaugen   hoover
Staubsauger (m)   hoover, vacuum cleaner
Staubtuch (n)   duster
Staubzucker (m)   icing sugar
Staudamm (m)   barrage, dam
Stausee (m)   reservoir
Steak (n)   steak
Steak- und Nierenpastete warm (f)   steak and kidney pie
Steckdose (f)   outlet, socket, wall plug, wall socket
Steckdose (f) **für Elektrorasierer** (pl. m)   razor point, shaver point
stecken   plug
Stecker (m)   connector
Steg (m)   plank
Stehbierhalle (f)   public bar
stehen, auf der Warteliste (f)   stand-by
stehen, im Wettbewerb (m)   compete
stehlen   pilfer
Stehplatz (m)   standing-place
steigern   intensify
Steigerung (f)   advance
Steigung (f)   grade, gradient, hill
steil   steep
steil hochziehen   zoom

Steilflug (m)   zoom
Steilhang (m)   steep slope
Steilküste (f)   bluff, steep coast
Stein (m)   stone
Steinbutt (m)   turbot
Steingarten (m)   rock garden
Steinhuhn (n)   rock partridge
Steinpilz (m)   boletus, cep
Steinschlag (m)   falling stones
Stelle (f), **freie**   opening
Stelle (f), **offene**   vacancy
Stelle (f), **produktionsunabhängige**   nonproduction group
Stellenangebot (n)   offer of employment
Stellenbeschreibung (f)   job description
Stellenbesetzungsplan (m)   staffing schedule
Stellenbezeichnung (f)   job title
Stellengruppe (f)   job category
Stelleninhaber (m)   job holder
Stellung (f)   position
Stellvertreter (m)   substitute
Stellvertretung (f)   representation
Stempel (m)   stamp
stempeln   stamp
Steppdecke (f)   quilt
Sterlet (m)   sturgeon
Sternfahrt (f)   rallye
Sternwarte (f)   observatory
Steuer (Abgabe) (f)   tax
Steuer (n)   helm
Steuermann (m)   helmsman, navigator
Steuermannsmaat (m)   quartermaster
steuern   control, pilot, steer
Steuerruder (n)   rudder
Steuerungs- und Überwachungssystem (n)   control system
Steuervorauszahlung (f)   prepaid taxes
Steward (m)   steward
Stewardeß (f)   air hostess,

stewardess
Stichprobenprüfung (f) random test
Stiefel (m) boot
Stierkämpfer bull-fighter
Stierkampf (m) bull-fight
Stiftung (f) foundation
still quiet
stillschweigend implied
stillstehend idle
Stimmung (f) mood
Stimmungsmusik (f) mood music
Stint (m) smelt
Stockfisch (m) dried cod, salt cod, salted codfish
Stockung (f) stoppage
Stockwerk (n) floor
Stör (m) sturgeon
stören disturb
Störung (f) annoyance, disturbance, interference, nuisance
Stoffgeschäft (n) draper's
stopfen darn
stornieren cancel
Stornierungsgebühr (f) cancellation fee
Storno (m) cancellation
Stoßarbeit (f) peak load
stoßen push
Stoßverkehr (m) peak hour traffic, rush hour traffic
Stoßzeit (f) peak hour, peak period, rush hours
Strafstoß (Sport) (m) penalty
Strahlen (pl. m), **ultraviolette** ultraviolet rays
Strand (m) beach, sea-shore, shore
Strandbad (n) lido
Strandfest (n) seaside gala
Strandgut (n) wreck
Strandhotel (n) beach hotel, seaside hotel
Strandkorb (m) beach-chair

Strandpromenade boardwalk
Strandschirm (m) beach-umbrella
Strandschuhe (pl. m) beach shoes
Strandwärter (m) beach attendant
Straße (f), **breite** avenue
Straße (f), **gebührenpflichtige** toll road
Straße (f), **gesperrte** road closed
Straße (f), **schneegeräumte** road cleared of snow
Straße (f), **zweibahnige (zweispurige)** two-lane road
Straßenanzug (m) business suit, lounge suit
Straßenatlas (m) road atlas
Straßenbahn (f) streetcar, tram, tramway
Straßenbahnhaltestelle (f) tram-stop
Straßenbahnkarte (f) tram-ticket
Straßenbahnlinie (f) streetcar line, tram-line
Straßenbahnwagen (m) tramcar
Straßenbau (m) road construction
Straßenbauarbeiten (pl. f) road works
Straßenbaustelle (f) road site
Straßenbenutzungsgebühr (f) toll
Straßenbiegung (f) turning
Straßencafe (n) open-air cafe, sidewalk cafe
Straßeneinmündung (f) T-junction
Straßengabel (f) bifurcation
Straßengabelung (f) road fork
Straßengraben (m) road ditch
Straßenhändler (m) street hawker
Straßenkarte (f) road map
Straßenkleidung (f) outdoor

134

dress
Straßenkreuzung (f)   intersection, crossing, cross-roads, junction, road junction
Straßenlaterne (f)   street-lamp
Straßennetz (n)   road network
Straßenschild (n)   street sign
Straßenschuhe (pl. m)   oxfords, walking shoes
Straßentransportunternehmen (n)   highway carrier
Straßentunnel (m)   road tunnel
Straßenverengung (f)   road narrows
Straßenverkehr (m)   road traffic
Straßenzoll (m)   toll
Straßenzustand (m)   road conditions
Straßenzustandsbericht (m)   road report
Strategie (f)   strategy
Strauch (m)   shrub
Strauß (m)   bunch
Strecke (f)   course, distance, line, stretch
Stecke (f), **zurückgelegte** distance travelled
Strecken (pl. f), **auf kurzen** on short routes
Streckenänderung (f)   change of route
Streckenführung (f)   routing
Streckenkarte (f)   route map
Streckennetz (n)   airways system, route network
Streckennetz (n), **interkontinentales** intercontinental network
streichen cancel
Streichholz (n)   match
Streichholzkartoffeln (pl. n) shoestring potatoes
Streichholzschachtel (f)   matchbox
Streichung (f)   cancellation
Streik (m)   strike

streiken strike
Streit (m)   argument, quarrel
streiten argue, quarrel
Streithahn (m)   trouble maker
streng geheim top secret
Strichliste (f)   tally
stricken knit
Strickhemd (n)   jersey shirt
Strickjacke (f)   jersey dress
Strickleiter (f)   rope-ladder
strohgedeckt thatched
Strohhalm (m)   straw
Strohkartoffeln (pl. f)   potato straws, straw potatoes
Strom (m)   electric power
Strom- und Heizungskosten (pl.) heat, light and power expenses
Strom-, Gas- und Wasserkosten (pl.)   heat, light and water expenses
Stromtarif (m)   electric rate schedule
Stromverbrauch (m)   electric power consumption, power consumption
Strudel (Speise) (m)   strudel
Struktur (f)   structure
Studentenfahrt (f)   student travel, student trip
Studentenreiseverkehr (m)   student travel
Studienreise (f)   educational trip, study trip
Studienurlaub (m)   educational holiday
Stück (n)   part, piece
Stück Kuchen (n)   piece of cake
Stückgutfracht (f)   package freight
stürmisch rough, tempestuous
Stuhl (m)   chair
stumpf blunt
Stunde (f), **angemessene** reasonable hour
stunden defer

135

Stundenlohnsatz (m) hourly rate
suchen search
Sucher (Foto) (m) view-finder
Südbalkon (m) balcony facing south
Süden (m) gehen, nach facing south
Südterrasse (f) terrace facing south
Südzimmer (n) room facing south
Sülze (f) aspic, jelly
süß sweet
süßen sweeten
Süßigkeiten (pl. f) candy, sweets
Süßkartoffel (f) sweet potato
Süßmost (m) sweet cider
Süßspeise (f) dessert, sweet dish
Süßwasserfisch (m) fresh-water fish, sweet water fish
Süßwasserkrebs (m) fresh water crayfish
Süßwasserschwimmbad (n) fresh-water swimming pool
Süßwein (m) dessert wine, sweet wine
Suite (f) suite
Sultanine (f) sultana
Sultaninenpudding (m) spotted dick
summieren add up, sum up
Sumpf (m) swamp
Supermarkt (m) supermarket
Suppe (f) klar mit Eierstich (m) clear soup royal
Suppe (f) soup
Suppe (f), dicke bisque, chowder, potage
Suppe (f), legierte thick soup
Suppeneinlage (f) garnish
Suppenfleisch (n) mit Meerettich (m) boiled meat with horse-radish
Suppenhuhn (n) boiled chicken

Suppenschüssel (f) soup-tureen, tureen
Suppenteller (m) soup-plate
Suppentopf (m) mit Fleischeinlage (f) boiled beef in broth, pot of broth with boiled meat
Suppentopf (m) mit Geflügeleinlage (f) chicken in broth
Surfbrett (n) surf board
Symbol (n) symbol
System (n) system
Szegediner Gulasch (n) Hungarian pork stew, stewed pork and sauerkraut in paprika sauce

T

T-bone steak (n) T-bone steak
Tabak (m) tobacco
Tabakladen (m) tobacconist's shop
Tabakspfeife (f) tobacco pipe
Tabaksteuer (f) tobacco tax
Tabelle (f) chart, table
Tabellenkalkulation (f) worksheet calculation
Tablett (n) tray
Tablett (amerik. drehbares) (n) lazy Susan
täglich daily, per day
Tätigkeit (f) activity, function, job
Tätigkeitsbericht (m) activity report
Tätigkeitsbeschreibung (f) job-breakdown, job description
Tätigkeitsbezeichnung (f) job title
Tätigkeitsgebiet (n) field of activity
Tätigkeitsmerkmal (n) job attribute
Tafel (f) table

Tafel-Tischmesser (n) table-knife
Tafelsalz (n) table-salt
Tafelspitz (m) boiled round of beef
Tafelwasser (n) table-water
Tagesanbruch (m) dawn, daybreak
Tagesausflug (m) day excursion, whole-day tour
Tagesfahrt (f) day excursion
Tagesflug (m) day flight
Tagesgericht (n) ready-to-serve dish, table d'hote meal
Tageskarte (f) day ticket, today's bill of fare, today's menu
Tageskassenbericht (m) daily cash report
Tageskurs (m) current rate
Tageslichtfilm (m) daylight colour film
Tagesordnung (f) agenda
Tagesplatte (f) the days dish
Tagesprogramm (n) today's program
Tagesraum (m) day-room, sitting-room
Tagesrestaurant (n) day restaurant
Tagesrückfahrkarte (f) day turn ticket
Tagesspezialität (f) today's special dish, today's speciality
Tagessuppe (f) the days soup
Tagestour (f) day excursion
Tageszeit (f) time of day
Tagwerk (n) man-day
Takelung (f) rigging
Tal (n) valley
Talfahrt (f) downward journey
Talsperre (f) barrage, dam
Talstation (Bergbahn) (f) base terminal, loading station
tanken refuel, take in petrol

Tankstelle (f) filling-station, petrol station, service station
Tankwart (m) filling-station attendant, garage assistant, service-station attandant
Tante (f) aunt
Tanz (m) dancing
Tanz (m) **im Freien** (n) open-air dance
Tanzabend (m) dancing-party, evening dance
Tanzbar (f) dance bar
Tanzdiner (n) dinner dance
Tanzfläche (f) dancing-floor
Tanzkapelle (f) dance band
Tanzkasino (n) spa ballroom
Tanzlokal (n) dance hall
Tanzorchester (n) dance band
Tanzsaal (m) ballroom, dance hall
Tanztee (m) afternoon dance, tea-dance
Tanzvorführung (f) dancing show
Tapiocasuppe (f) soup with tapioca
Tarif (m) tariff
Tarif (m), **ermäßigter** reduced rates
Tariflohn (m) wages according to agreement
Tarifsenkung (f) reduction of the rates
Tarifvertrag (m) collective agreement, labor contract, union agreement
Tarifvorschrift (f) tariff provision
Tartarensoße (f) tartare sauce
Tasche (f) bag
Taschendieb (m) pickpocket
Taschenfahrplan (m) pocket train schedule
Taschengeld (n) pocket money
Taschenlampe (f) electric torch,

137

flash light, pocket-lamp
Taschenmesser (n)   penknife
Taschenrechner (m)   calculator
Taschentuch (n)   handkerchief
Tasse (f)   cup
Tastatur (f)   keyboard
Taste (f)   key
Tastenfeld (n)   keyboard
Tastenknopf (m)   key button
Tat (f)   action, fact
Tatar (n)   minced raw beef
Tatsache (f)   fact
tatsächlich   actual
Taube (f)   pigeon, squab
Tauchbecken (n)   diving-pool
tauchen   dive
Taucherausrüstung (f)   diving equipment
Taucherclub (m)   diving club
tauen   thaw
Tauen (n)   thaw
tauglich   capable
Tauglichkeit (f)   capability, qualification
Tausch (m)   exchange
tauschen   change, exchange, swap
Tauwetter (n)   thaw
Taxi (n)   cab, taxi
Taxichauffeur (m)   taxi-driver
Taxifahrer (m)   taxi-driver
Taxistand (m)   cab stand, taxi-rank
Team (n)   team
Techniker (m)   technician
technischer Leiter (m)   chief engineer
Tee (m)   tea
Tee (m) **mit Milch** (f)   tea with milk
Tee (m) **mit Zitrone** (f)   tea with lemon
Tee (m) **vor dem Aufstehen** (n)   early morning tea
TEE-Zug (m)   TEE-train (Trans-Europe-Express)
Teebüchse (f)   tea-caddy
Teegebäck (n)   scones, tea cakes
Teegebäck (engl.) (n)   pikelet
Teegeschirr (n)   tea-things
Teegesellschaft (f)   tea-party
Teehaus (n)   tea-house
Teekanne (f)   tea-pot
Teekessel (m)   tea-kettle
Teelöffel (m)   tea-spoon
Teemaschine (f)   tea-urn
Teerestaurant (n)   tea-shop
Teeservice (m)   tea set
Teestube (f)   tea-room
Teestunde (f)   tea-time
Teetasse (f)   teacup
Teewärmer (m)   tea-cosy
Teewagen (m)   tea-cart, tea-trolley
Teich (m)   pond
Teig (m)   dough, paste
Teigdecke (f)   pie-crust
Teiggraupen (pl. f)   grape-nuts
Teigtaschen (pl. f)   pastry envelopes, stuffed fritters
Teigwaren (pl. f)   farinaceous food
Teigwaren (pl. f) **mit geriebenem Käse** (m)   noodle dish with grated cheese
Teigwaren-Vorgericht (n)   farinaceous sidedish
Teil (m)   part, portion
teilen   part
teilhaben   participate
Teilhaber (m)   associate, participant
Teilmassage (f)   partial massage
Teilnahme (f)   participation
Teilnahmebedingung (f)   condition of participation
teilnehmen   attend, participate
teilnehmen an   take part in
Teilnehmer (m)   participant
Teilnehmerliste (f)   list of partici-

pants
Teilnehmerzahl (f) number of participants
Teilstornierung (f) partial cancellation
Teilstrecke (f) stage
Teilung (f) division
Teilverpflegung (f) partial board
teilweise partial
Teilzahlung (f) instalment, partial payment, part-payment
Teilzeitarbeiter (m) part-timer
Telefon (n) telephone
Telefonbuch (n) telephone directory
Telefonhörer (m) telephone-receiver
telefonisch bestellen reserve by telephone
telefonische Telegrammaufgabe (f) telegram by telephone
Telefonistin (f) operator, telephone operator
Telefonleitung (f) line
Telefonvermittlung (f) telephone exchange, trunk exchange
Telefonverzeichnis (n) telephone directory
Telefonzelle (f) call-box, telephone booth, telephone box
Telefonzentrale (f) switchboard
Telegrafenamt (m) telegraph office
telegrafieren cable, wire
telegrafisch telegraphic
telegrafische Anweisung (f) telegraphic money-order
Telegramm (n) cable, telegram, wire
Telegrammadresse (f) telegraphic address
Telegrammformular (n) telegram form
Telegrammkosten (pl.) telegram charges

Telekommunikation (f) telecommunication
Teleobjektiv (n) telephoto lens
Telex (n) telex
Teller (m) dish, plate
Tellerwäscher (m) dishwasher
Temperatur (f) temperature
Tempo (n) pace, speed
Tendenz (f) tendency, trend
Tendenz (f), **steigende** uptrend
Tennis (n) tennis
Tennisball (m) tennis ball
Tennisklub (m) tennis club
Tennisplatz (m) tennis court
Tennisschläger (m) racket, tennis racket
Tennisschuhe (pl. m) plimsolls, tennis shoes
Tennisspiel (n) tennis game
Tennisturnier (n) tennis tournament
Teppich (m) carpet
Termin (m), **letzter** deadline
termingerecht in due time
Terminierung (f) timing
Terminkalender (m) calender of cases
Terrainkur (f) terrain treatment
Terrassenrestaurant (n) terrance restaurant
teuer expensive
Textverarbeitung (f) word processing
Theaterabend (m) evening performance
Theaterbesucher (m) playgoer
Theaterkarte (f) theatre ticket
Theatersaison (f) theatrical season
Theatervorstellung (f) theatrical performance
Theke (f) bar, counter
therapeutisch therapeutical
Thermalbad (n) thermal baths

Thermalbadehaus (n) hydropathic establishment
Thermalbecken (n) thermalwater pool
Thermalhallenbad (n) thermal indoor swimming-pool
Thermalwasser (n) thermal water
Thermosflasche (f) thermos flask
Thermotherapie (f) thermotherapy
Thunfisch (m) tuna fish, tunny
Thymian (m) thyme
Tief (n) depression
Tiefe (f) depth
Tiefgarage (f) underground garage
tiefgefroren deep-frozen
tiefgekühlt quick frozen
Tiefkühlerzeugnis (n) frozen good
Tiegel (m) casserole, pot, saucepan
Tiergarten (m) zoo
Tierwelt (f) fauna
tilgen amoritze
Tilgung (f) extinction
Tilsiter Käse (m) tilsit cheese
Tintenfisch (m) cuttle-fish, squid
Tisch (m) table
Tisch (m) **decken** lay the table, set the table
Tisch (m) **reservieren** reserve a table, book a table
Tischdecke (f) table-cloth, table-cover
Tischedecke (f), **kleine** tea-cloth
Tischgeschirr (n) table-ware
Tischgespräch (n) table-talk
Tischkarte (f) place-card
Tischlampe (f) table-lamp
Tischmesser (m) table-knife
Tischnummer (f) table number

Tischplatte (f) table-top
Tischreservierung (f) table reservation
Tischtennis (n) ping-pong, table-tennis
Tischtennishalle (f) ping-pong room, tabletennis room
Tischtuch (n) table-cloth
Tischwein (m) dinner wine, table wine
Tischzeiten (pl. f) meal-times
Tischzeug (n) table-linen
Toast (m) grilled bread, toast
Toaster (m) toaster
Toastmeister (m) toastmaster
Toaströster (m) toaster
Toboggan (m) toboggan
Tochter (f) daughter
Tochtergesellschaft (f) allied company, subsidiary company
Törtchen (n) tartlet
Toilette (f) lavatory, rest room, toilet, washroom, water-closed, W.C.
Toilette (f), **öffentliche** public convenience, public lavatory
Toilettenpapier (n) toilet-paper
Toilettenseife (f) toilet soap
Toilettentisch (m) dressing-table
Tollwutimpfung (f) antirabic vaccination
Tollwutimpfzeugnis (n) certificate of antirabic vaccination
Tomate (f) tomato
Tomaten (pl. f) **gefüllt** stuffed tomatoes
Tomatencremesuppe (f) cream of tomato
Tomatenketchzp (n) tomato ketchup
Tomatensaft (m) tomato juice
Tomatensalat (m) tomato salad
Tomatensoße (f) tomato sauce
Tomatensouce (spanisch) (f) creole sauce

Tomatensuppe (f) soup with tomatoes
Tomatensuppe (f) tomato-soup
Tonic, Tonicwasser (n) tonic, tonic water
Topf (m) jar, pan, pot
Topfenstrudel (m) sweet curds pie
Tor (Sport) (n) goal
Tor (n) gate
Torte (f) fancy-cake, tart
Torwart (Sport) (m) goalkeeper, keeper
Tour (f) excursion, tour
Tourenkarte (f) touristic map
Tourismus (m) tourism
Tourist(in) (m, f) tourist, tripper
Touristenabteil (n) compartment for ramblers
Touristenausweis (m) tourist card
Touristenflugpreis (m) tourist fare
Touristengebiet (n) tourist region
Touristenhotel (n) tourist hotel
Touristenkarte (f) tourist card
Touristenklasse (f) economy class, tourist class
Touristenverkehr (m) tourism, touristic traffic
Touristenvisum (n) tourist visa
Touristik (f) tourism
touristisch touristic
toxisch toxic(al)
Trachtenfest (n) pageant, show of national costumes
Trachtenumzug (m) procession in national costumes
Tragflächenboot (n) hydrofoil
Trainer (m) coach
trainieren coach, practise, train
Training (n) training
Trainingsanzug (m) training suit

Tramp (m) tramp
trampen tramp
Trampschiff (n) tramp
tranchieren carve
Transfer (m) transfer
Transit (m) transit
Transitgut (n) transit goods
Transitreise (f) transit journey
Transitreisender (m) transit passenger
Transitverkehr (m) transit traffic
Transitvisum (n) transit visa
Transport (m) carriage, transport, transportation
Transportgefahr (f) risk of conveyance
Transportgewerbe (f) transportation
Transporthaftung (f) liability of the carrier
transportierbar transportable
transportieren transport
Transportkosten (pl.) transportation cost
Transportschäden (pl. m) damages in transit
Transporttarif (m) carriage rates
Transportunternehmen (n) carrier, transport company, motor carrier, transport contractor
Transportversicherung (f) transport insurance
Transportvertrag (m) contract of carriage
Tratsch (m) gossip
Traube (f) grape
Traube (f), **weiße** white grape
Traube (f), **blaue** black grape
Traubenkur (f) grape cure
Traubensaft (m) grape juice
treffen meet
Treffpunkt (m) meeting-place, place of assembly

141

Treibstoff (m) fuel
Trekking (n) trekking
Trend (m) trend
trennen disconnect, separate
Treppe (f) stairs
Treppenhaus (n) staircase
Tretblasebalg (m) foot pump inflator
treu loyal
Treue (f) loyality
Tribüne (f) grand-stand
Trichter (m) funnel
Triebwagen (m) railcar
Triebwagenzug (m) multiple-unit train
trinkbar drinkable
Trinkei (n) fresh egg
trinken drink, tope
Trinken (n) potation
Trinker (m) alcoholic, dipsomaniac
Trinkgeld (n) gratuity, tip
Trinkgeld (n) **geben** tip
Trinkhalle (f) pump room
Trinkhalm (m) straw
Trinkkännchen (n) pannikin
Trinkkur (f) pump-room cure
Trinkkur (f) **machen** drink the waters
Trinkspruch (m) toast
Trinkspruch (m) **ausbringen** propose a toast
Trinkwasser (n) drinking water
trocken dry
Trockenfleisch (n) air-dried meat, dried meat
Trockengestell (n) rack
Trockenraum (m) drying-room
trocknen drain, dry
Tronk (m) service charge
Trabrennen (n) trotting race
Tropen (pl.) tropics
Tropfen (m) drop
Tropfsteinhöhle (f) limestone cave

tropisch tropical
Trüffel (f) truffle
Trüsche (f) burbot
Trunkenheit (f) drunkenness
Truthahn (m) turkey
Truthahn (m) **gebraten** roast turkey
Tuch (n) cloth
Tür (f) door
Tür (f) **bitte schließen!** please close the door
Türanhänger (m) **für die Frühstücksbestellung** (f) breakfast key
Türkisches Bad (n) Turkish bath
Türklinke (f) door handle
Türsteher (m) usher
Tunke (f) sauce
Turbinendampfschiff (n) turbo-steamship, TSS
Turbinenschiff (n) turbo-ship, TS
Turm (m) tower
Turnhalle (f) gym, gymnasium
Turnschuhe (pl. m) gym shoes, sneakers
Typenrad (n) daisywheel
Typenraddrucker (m) daisywheel
typisch typical

U

U-Bahn (f) subway, tube, underground
übel qualmish
Übelkeit (f) nausea
üben practise
über via
Überstunden (pl. f) overtime
überbacken au gratin, gratinated

Übe   **Übe**

Überbevorratung (f) overstocking
überblicken survey
überbringen deliver
überfällig overdue, past due
Überfahrt (f) crossing
Überfahrtsdauer (f) crossing time
überfordern overcharge
überfüllt crowded, overcrowded
Übergangszeit (f) transition period
übergar overdone
übergeben hand, pass, pass over
übergeben, sich vomit
übergehen pass, pass over
Übergepäck (n) baggage in excess, excess baggage
Übergepäckzuschlag (m) excess baggage fare
überhöht excessive
überholen overtake
Überholverbot (n) no overtaking, prohibition to overtake
Überkapazität (f) excess capacity, overcapacity
überladen overload
überlagern overlap
Überlandverkehr (m) interurban traffic, overland transportation
überlappen overlap
Überlauf (m) overflow
überlaufen overcrowded, touristed
Übernachtung (f) night's lodging, overnight stay
Übernachtungsgast (m) chance guest
Übernachtungshotel (n) transient hotel
Übernachtungsmöglichkeit (f) overnight accomodation
Übernachtungspreis (m) overnight charge

Übernachtungspreis (m) **für Durchreisende** (pl. m) transient rate
Übernachtungsvertrag (m) contract of accommodation
Übernahme (f) assumption
Überpreis (m) excessive charge, excessive price
Überproduktion (f) overproduction
überprüfen review, verify
Überprüfung (f) review
Überprüfung (f) **der Hotels** (pl. n) checking of the hotels
Überraschungsinventur (f) spot check
Überraschungsomelette (f) baked Alaska
überschätzen overestimate
Überschätzung (f) overestimate
überschlagen, sich turn upside down
Überschlagsrechnung (f) rough calculation
Überschrift (f) heading
Überschuß (m) balance, overage, surplus
Übersee, in od. nach oversea(s)
Überseefahrt (f) transoceanic voyage
Überseeflugzeug (n) clipper
Überseetransport (m) oversea(s) shipment
übersehen (nicht beachten) ignore
übersetzen translate
übersetzen (Fähre) ferry over
Übersetzer (m) interpreter
Übersetzung (f) translation
Übersicht (f) statement
übersteigen surpass
Überstundenanforderung (f) request for overtime
Übertrag (m) amount carried over, transfer

143

übertragbar transferable
übertragen assign, delegate, transfer
Übertragung (f) posting
übertreffen surpass
übertreiben exaggerate
übertreten violate
übertrieben excessive
überwachen control
überwältigen overwhelm
überweisen remit
Überweisung (f) money transfer, remittance
überwinden overwhelm
überzahlen overpay
überziehen overdraw
Überzieher (m) overcoat
überzuckert iced
üblich customary, usual
Übung (f) exercise
Übungsgelände (n) training ground
Übungshang (m) practice slope
Ufer (n) shore
Uferstraße (f) coastal road, embankment
Uhr (f) clock
Uhrzeigersinn, entgegen dem (m) anticlockwise
Ultraschall (m) ultrasonics, ultrasound
Umberfisch (m) umber
umbuchen change reservations
Umbuchung (f) adjusting entry
Umgebung (f) surroundings
Umgehungsstraße (f) by-pass, diversion
umgruppieren rearrange
umherreisen itinerate, perigrinate
Umherreisen (n) itineracy
umkehren turn round
Umkehrpunkt (m) point of turnaround
Umkleidekabine (f) bathing cabin
Umkleideraum (m) changing room
Umkreis (m) **von, im** within the radius of
Umladungsgebühr (f) reloading charge
Umlauf (m) circulation
Umlaufvermögen (n) current assets, working capital
Umleitung (f) detour, diversion
Umorganisation (f) reorganization
umorganisieren reorganize
umrechnen convert, translate
Umrechnung (f) translation
Umrechnungskurs (m) rate of exchange
Umrechnungstabelle (f) conversion table
umreißen outline
Umriß (m) outline
Umsatz (m) revenue, sales, turnover
Umsatz (m) **bei Speisen** (pl. f) food revenue
Umsatzbereich (m) operated departments
Umsatzmix (m) sales mix
Umsatzprognose (f) sales forecast
Umsatzprovision (f) sales commission
Umsatzsteuer (f) turnover tax
Umsatzzusammensetzung (f) sales mix
Umschlag (m) turnover
Umschlaghafen (m) port of transsshipment
Umschlagplatz (m) transshipment point
Umschlagsgeschwindigkeit (f) rate of turnover
umschulen re-educate
Umschulung (f) re-education,

retraining
Umsteigebahnhof (m) connecting station
Umsteigekarte (f) transfer, transfer ticket
Umsteigen (n) change of carriage
Umsteigepunkt (m) connecting point
umwandeln convert
Umweg (m) detour, roundabout way
Umwelt (f) environment
Umzug (m) procession
Umzugskosten (pl.) moving expense
Unternehmung (f) business
unabhängig independent
unangemessen inadequate
unangenehm disageeable
unauffindbarer Gegenstand (m) article not to be found
Unaufmerksamkeit (f) inattention
unbefugt unauthorized
unbekannt unknown
unbequem uncomfortable
unberechtigt unauthorized
unbesetzt vacant
unbewohnt unoccupied
unbezahlt unpaid
undatiert undated
undeutlich dim
undurchführbar impracticable
uneinbringliche Forderung (f) bad dept
unentgeltlich free, gratuitous
unerfahren inexperienced
unerkannt incognito
unerläßlich indispensable
unerlaubt unauthorized
unerschwinglich unattainable
unfähig incapable
Unfall (m) accident
Unfallmeldung (f) notice of accident
Unfallquelle (f) accident hazard
Unfallrisiko (n) accident risk
Unfallschutzkarte (f) medical identification card
Unfallstation (f) casualty department, first-aid post
Unfallverhütungsvorschrift (f) safety regulation
Unfallversicherung (f) accident insurance
unfreundlich unfriendly
Unfug (m) nuisance
ungelernte Arbeitskräfte (pl. f) unskilled manpower
ungemütlich uncomfortable
Ungenauigkeit (f) inaccuracy
ungesetzlich illegal, lawless
ungestört peaceful, undisturbed
ungesund insanitary
Ungeziefer (n) vermin
Unglücksfall (m) accident
ungültig invalid, void
Uniform (f) uniform
unklar misty
unkonvertierbar inconvertible
unmittelbar direct
unproduktiv idle
Unrecht (n) wrong
unreif unripe
unrichtig incorrect
unsauber unclean
unschmackhaft tasteless
unsittlich immoral
Unsittlichkeit (f) immorality
untätig idle
Unterbett (n) lower berth
unterbieten undercut
unterbrechen interrupt
Unterbrechung (f) interruption
unterbringen accomodate, lodge
Unterbringung (f) accomodation
Unterdeck (n) lower deck
Unterführung (f) underpass

Untergebener (m) subordinate
Unterhalt (m) maintenance
unterhalten maintain
unterhaltend amusing
Unterhaltung (f) entertainment
Unterhaltungsabend (m) evening entertainment
Unterhose (f) drawers, underpants
Unterkunft (f) accomodation, lodging, shelter
Unterlage (f) hand out, proof
Unterlagen (pl. f) records
unterlassen fail
Untermiete (f) subletting
Untermieter (m) sublessee, subtenant
unternehmen undertake
Unternehmen (n) company, concern, establishment
Unternehmensberater (m) management consultant
Unternehmensforschung (f) operations research
Unternehmer (m) employer
Unternehmer (m), **gastgewerblicher** entrepreneur of the hotel and catering trade
unterordnen subordinate
Unterpacht (f) subletting
Unterpächter (m) sublessee, subtenant
untersagen prohibit
Untersatz (m) table-mat
Unterschenkel (m) leg
Unterschied (m) differnce
unterschreiten undercut
Unterschrift (f) signature
Untersetzer (m) mat, saucer
unterstellt sein report to
unterstützen relieve, support
Unterstützung (f) support
untersuchen analyze, examine, test
Untersuchung (f) analysis, inquiry, research, survey, test
Untersuchung (f), **quantitative** quantitative analysis
Untertasse (f) saucer
unterteilen subdivide
Unterteilung (f) breakdown, subdivison
untervermieten sublet
Untervermieter (m) sublessor
Untervermietung (f) sublease
Untervermietungsrecht (n) right of sublease
unterverpachten sublet
Unterverpächter (m) sublessor
Untervertrag (m) subcontract
Unterwäsche (f) underwear
Unterwasserausrüstung (f) underwater equipment
Unterwassergymnastik (f) underwater exercises
Unterwassermassage (f) underwater massage
Unterwassersport (m) aqua-lunging, scuba diving
unterwegs en route, in transit
Unterwegsaufenthalt (m) stop en route
unerweisen instruct
Unterweisung (f) instruction
Unterweisung (f), **betriebliche** job instruction training
unterzeichnen sign
unübersichtliche Kurve (f) blind bend
unveräußerlich inalienable
unverbindlich without obligation
unverdünnt neat
unvereinbar incompatible
unverheiratet unmarried
unverträglich uncompatible
unverzüglich instant, without delay
Unwetter (n) tempest
unwirksam ineffective

unwirtschaftlich inefficient
unwohl qualmish, queasy
Unze (28, 350 g) (f) ounce, o. z.
unzerbrechlich unbreakable
unzufrieden querulous
unzulässig inadequate, inadmissible
Urlaub (m) holidays, leave, vacation
Urlaub (m), **bezahlter** paid holiday
Urlaub (m), **gesetzlicher** legal holiday
Urlauber (m) holiday-maker, vacationer
Urlauberzug (m) leave-train
Urlaubseinteilung (f) vacation schedule
Urlaubsgeld (n) holiday pay, vacation pay
Urlaubsort (m) holiday centre, holiday place
Urlaubsplan (m) leave schedule
Urlaubsreise (f) holiday trip
Urlaubsreisender (m) holiday-maker
Urlaubsverkehr (m) holiday traffic
Urlaubsversicherung (f) holiday insurance
Urlaubswetter (n) holiday weather
Urlaubszeit (f) holiday season
Ursprung (m) origin
Ursprungsland (n) country of origin
urteilen determine, reason
Urwald (m) virgin forest

V

Vakanz (f) vacancy
Vakanzliste (f) list of vacant rooms
Vanille (f) vanilla
Vanilleauflauf (m) souffle of vanilla
Vanilleeis (n) vanilla ice, vanilla ice-cream
Vanillepudding (m) blancmange
Vanillesoße (f) custard sauce
variabel variable
Vase (f) vase
Vegetarier (m) vegetarian
Vegetarierrestaurant (n) vegetarian restaurant
vegetarisch vegetarian
Ventil (n) valve
Ventilator (m) fan, ventilator
Venusmuschel (f) clam
Verabredung (f) appointment
veränderlich variable
verändern alter, vary
Veränderung (f) alteration, variancee
Verandadeck (n) veranda deck
veranlassen cause
Veranstalter (m) organizer
Veranstaltung (f) banquet, event
Veranstaltung (f), **gesellschaftliche** social activity
Veranstaltungsgeschäft (n) banquet business
Veranstaltungsinformation (f) event order
Veranstaltungsleiter (m) banquet manager
Veranstaltungsraum (m) banquet room, function room
verantwortlich machen hold accountable
verantwortlich liable, responsible
Verantwortung (f) liability, responsibility
verauslagen disburse
Verband (m) **der Wirtschaftsdirektoren** (pl. m) Food an

beverage Manager Association (FBMA)
Verbandskasten (m)　first-aid kit
Verbandszeug (n)　dressings, first aid kit
verbessern　amend, correct, improve, revise
verbieten　prohibit
verbinden (vereinigen)　associate
verbinden (Medizin)　bandage
verbinden (verpflichten)　oblige
Verbindlichkeit (f)　liability, obligation
Verbindlichkeiten (pl. f)　accounts payable
Verbindlichkeiten (pl. f), **sonstige kurzfristige**　other current liabilities
Verbindung (f)　connection, service
Verbrauch (m)　consumption
verbrauchen　consume
Verbraucher (m)　consumer, user
Verbrauchsgüter (pl. n)　nondurable goods
verbreiten durch Rundfunk (m)　broadcast
verdanken　owe
verdauen　digest
Verdauung (f)　digestion
Verdauungsstörung (f)　indigestion
Verderb (m)　waste
Verderb (von Waren) (m)　spoilage
verderben　spoil, waste
verderblich, leicht　perishable
verdienen　earn
Verdienst (m)　earnings
Verdienst (n)　merit
Verdienstausfall (m)　loss of earnings
Verdienstspanne (f)　profit margin

verdrehen　distort
verdünnen　dilute
Verein (m)　association, club
vereinbaren　agree upon, agree with, arrange, contract
Vereinbarung (f)　agreement, arrangement, contract
vereinheitlichen　standardize
Vereinheitlichung (f)　standardization
vereinigen　join
vereinigen, sich　associate
Vereinsmitgliedschaft (f)　club membership
Verfälschung (f)　adulteration
Verfahren (n)　procedure
Verfahrensforschung (f)　operations research
Verfalldatum (n)　date of expiry
verfallen　expire, out of date, waste
Verfalltag (m)　expiration date
verfault　rotten
verfehlen　miss
verfolgen　follow up
Verfrachtung (f)　shipment
verfügbar　available, liquid
Verfügbarkeit (f)　availability
verfügen über　dispose of
Verfügung (f)　disposal
vergehen　pass
Vergnügen (n)　pleasure
Vergnügungsdampfer (m)　pleasure boat
Vergnügungsfahrt (f)　cruise, pleasure drive
Vergnügungslokal (n)　place of entertainment
Vergnügungspark (m)　amusement park
Vergnügungsreise (f)　pleasure trip
Vergnügungssteuer (f)　entertainment tax
Vergnügungszentrum (n)

entertainment centre
Vergrößerung (f) enlargement
Vergünstigung (f) preference
Vergünstigungen (pl. f) reduced rates
vergüten compensate
Vergütung (f) compensation
Verhältnis (n) ratio
verhaften arrest
Verhaftung (f) arrest
Verhalten (n) behavior
verhalten, sich behave
verhandeln negotiate
Verhandlung (f) negotiation, transaction
verheiratet married
verhindern prevent
Verhinderung (f) prevention
verhüten prevent
verirren, sich get lost
Verjüngungskur (f) rejuvenation cure
Verkäufer (m) salesman
Verkäufermarkt (m) seller's market
Verkauf (m) sale
Verkauf (m), **persönlicher** personal selling
verkaufen market, sell
Verkaufsabteilung (f) sales department
Verkaufsanalyse (f) sales analysis
Verkaufsargument (n) sales argument
Verkaufsargument (n) **an das Gefühl** (n) **appelierend** emotional sales argument
Verkaufsautomat (m) penny-in-the-slot, vending machine
Verkaufserlöse (pl. m) sales
Verkaufsförderung (f) promotion, sales promotion
Verkaufsförderung (durch Ausstellung) (f) visual merchandising
Verkaufsgrundsätze (pl. m) merchandising policy
Verkaufsleiter (m) marketing manager, sales manager
Verkaufsort (m) point of sale
Verkaufspreis (m) sales price, selling price
Verkaufspreise (pl. m) **für Speisen** (pl. f) **und Getränke** (pl. n) food and beverage prices
Verkaufsrepräsentant (m) sales representative
Verkaufsvertreter (m) sales representative
Verkehr (m) traffic
Verkehr (m), **entgegenkommender** oncoming traffic
Verkehr (m), **täglicher** daily service
verkehren operate
Verkehrsader (f) traffic artery
Verkehrsampel (f) traffic light
Verkehrsamt (n) local tourist office, tourist information office
Verkehrsaufkommen (n) quantity of available traffic
Verkehrsdelikt (n) motoring offence
Verkehrsdichte (f) traffic density
Verkehrseinschränkung (f) traffic restriction
Verkehrsflugzeug (n) airliner, liner
Verkehrsfluß (m) traffic flow
Verkehrsgewerbe (n) transportation industry, carriers
Verkehrsinsel (f) refuge, street island
Verkehrsknotenpunkt (m) junction
Verkehrsmaschine (f) airliner
Verkehrsmittel (n) vehicle

149

Verkehrsmittel (pl. n), **öffentliche** public transport
Verkehrsmittelwerbung (f) transportation advertising
Verkehrsordnung (f) traffic regulation
Verkehrsplanung (f) transport planning
Verkehrspolitik (f) transport policy
Verkehrspolizei (f) traffic police
Verkehrspolizist (m) pointsman
Verkehrsregelung (f) traffic regulation
Verkehrssicherheit (f) road safety, traffic safety
Verkehrsspitze (f) peak days
Verkehrsstau (m) area congestion
Verkehrsstauung (f) traffic congestion
Verkehrsstockung (f) traffic block, traffic hold-up, traffic jam
Verkehrsüberwachung (f) traffic control
Verkehrsunfall (m) traffic accident
Verkehrsverbindung (f) communication
Verkehrsverbot (n) prohibition of entry of vehicles
Verkehrsverein (m) local tourist association
Verkehrswirtschaft (f) free economy
Verkehrszeichen (n) road sign
verkehrt wrong
verkehrt täglich daily service, operates daily
Verkehrsteilnehmer (m) road user
verklagen sue
verknüpfen knit
Verladebahnsteig (m) loading platform
Verladegebühr (f) loading charges
Verladekosten (pl.) shipping charges
Verladestelle loading point
Verladung (f) embarkation
verlängern extend, prolong, renew
Verlängerung (f) extension, prolongation, renewal
Verlängerungsschnur (f) extension cord
Verlängerungstag (m) additional day
Verlängerungswoche (f) additional week, extra week
verlangen demand, require
Verlangen (n), **auf** on demand
verlangen nach ask for
verlassen quit
verlassen auf, sich depend on, rely on
Verleih (m) hire service, rental service
verleihen lend
Verleihgebühr (f) hire charge
verletzen harm, hurt, violate
Verletzung (f) harm, hurt
verlieren lose
verlieren, an Wert (m) deteriorate
Verlobung (f) engagement
Verlust (m) damage, deficit, loss, net loss
Verlust (m) **erleiden** sustain a loss
Verlust (m) **und Beschädigung** (f) **von Gasteigentum** (n) loss and damage of guest property
Verlustanzeige (f) notification of a loss
Verlustzeit (f) lost time
vermehren increase
Vermehrung (f) increase

vermeiden avoid
Vermeiden (n) avoidance
Vermerk (m) memorandum
vermerken note
vermieten lease, let, rent
Vermieter (m) hirer, landlord, lessor
Vermietung (f) leasing, let, letting, renting
Vermietungen (pl. f) building rentals
vermindern impair, reduce
vermindern, sich shrink
Verminderung (f) decline
vermischen mix
vermischt miscellanious
vermissen miss
vermißt missing
Vermittlungsgebühr (f) commission
Vermögenswert (m) asset
vernachlässigen neglect
Vernunft (f) reason
veröffentlichen bring out, publish
Veröffentlichung (f) publication
verpachten let, rent
verpacken pack, package
Verpackung (f) pack, packaging
Verpächter (m) lessor
Verpflegung (f) board, catering, food, food supply
Verpflegungsbereich (m) food and beverage department
Verpflegungskapazität (f) food supply capacity
verpflichten engage, obligate, oblige
verpflichtend obligatory
verpflichtet bound, indebted, obliged
Verpflichtung (f) engagement, obligation
Verrechnungskonten (pl. n) **innerhalb der Hotels** (pl. n) inter-hotel-accounts
Verrechnungskonto (n) clearing account
verreisen go away on holiday
Verrichtung (f) job, performance
versäumen neglect
Versäumnis (n) default
versagen fail
versammeln, sich meet
Versammlung (f) meeting
Versandanzeige (f) advice of dispatch (shipment)
versandfertig ready for shipment
Versandkosten (pl.) shipping cost, transportation cost
Versandort (m) place of dispatch
verschieben postpone
Verschiebung (f) postponement
verschiedenartig miscellanious, various
verschiedene sundry
Verschiedenheit (f) variety
verschlafen oversleep oneself, sleep late
verschlechtern, sich deteriorate
verschließen (luftdicht) air-seal
verschlingen gulp
Verschluß (m) shutter
verschmelzen merge
verschneiden dilute
Verschneidung (f) adulteration
verschneit snow-covered, snowed up
Verschönerung (f) beautification
verschuldet indebted
Verschwiegenheit (f) discretion
verschwommen hazy
versenden ship
Versendung (f) shipment
versengen sear
Versetzung (f) transfer
versichern insure

151

versichern (behaupten, bestätigen) affirm
versichern (erklären) assure
Versicherung (f) insurance
Versicherung (Behauptung, Bestätigung) (f) affirmation
Versicherung (Erklärung) (f) assurance
Versicherungsbeitrag (m) insurance charge, insurance contribution
Versicherungsgesellschaft (f) insurance company
Versicherungsschutz (m) insurance protection
versorgen cater for, supply
verspäten delay
verspätet late
verspätete Ankunft (f) eines Fluggastes (m) late passenger arrival
Verspätung (f) delay
versprechen promise
Versprechen (n) promise
verstaatlichen nationalize
verstärken intensify
Verstärker (m) amplifier
verstehen understand
verstellbar adjustable
versteuert tax paid
versuchen try
vertagen postpone, put off
Vertagung (f) postponement
vertauschen swap
verteilen distribute
Verteilung (f) distribution, division
Vertrag (m) agreement, contract
Vertrag (m) gegenseitiger mutual agreement
vertragen agree with
vertraglich contractual
vertraglich gebunden bound by contract

Vertragsbedingung (f) term
Vertragsbestimmung (f) clause, term
Vertragsbruch (m) breach of contract
Vertragsbüro (n) appointed office
Vertragsgaststätte (f) appointed restaurant, authorized restaurant
Vertragshaftung (f) liability under the contract
Vertragshaus (n) authorized establishment
Vertragshotel (n) appointed hotel, authorized hotel
Vertragsstrafe (f) penalty
vertrauenswürdig trustworthy
Vertrauenswürdigkeit (f) trustworthiness
vertraulich confidential
vertretbar justifiable
vertreten represent
Vertreter (m) agent, representative, salesman
Vertreterbesuch (m) call
Vertretung (f) agency, representation
Vertrieb (m) distribution
Vertriebsleiter (m) marketing manager
verunglücken meet with an accident
verursachen cause
vervollkommnen improve
verwalten administer, manage
Verwaltung (f) adminitration
Verwaltungsgebühren (pl. f) administrative fees
Verwaltungskosten (pl.) administrative expense
Verwaltungskosten (pl.), allgemeine general administrative expenses
verwandeln in ein Hotel (n) hotelize

verwandt related
Verwandte(r) (f, m) relation, relative
Verwandtenbesuch (m) visit of relatives
Verwandter (m), **nächster** next of kin
Verwarnung (f) warning, ticket
verwerten make use of
Verwirrung (f) mess
Verzehr (m) consumption
verzeichnen list
Verzeichnis (f) list, index, register, schedule, statement
Verzeichnis (n) **der Sollportionsgrößen** (pl. f) portion chart
verzerren distort
Verzicht (m) quitclaim
verzichten give up, quit quitclaim, renounce
verzieren decorate
verzögern delay
Verzögerung (f) delay, retardation
verzollen clear, declare
verzollt duty paid
Verzollung (f) clearance
Verzollung (f) **einer Schiffsladung** clearing
Verzug (m) default
Vieh (n) cattle
vielbesucht much-frequented
vielfach multiple
Vielfalt (f) variety
Vielfraß (m) glutton, gourmand
vielseitig multi-lateral
vielsprachig polyglot
Viertel (n) quarter
vierteljährlich quarterly
Vierteljahr (n) quarter
Vierzehntage (pl.) fortnight
Vinnaigrettesoße (f) vinnaigrette(sauce)
Vip very important person, vip
Visagebühr (f) visa charge

Visum (n) visa
Visumsantrag (m) application for a visa
Vizepräsident (m) vice-president
Vogel (m) bird
Vögel (pl. f) **am Spieß** (m) **mit Polenta** (f) birds on skewer with corn pie
Volksfest (n) public festival
Volkskunst (f) folk art
Volkslied (n) folk song
Volkstanz (m) folk dance
Volkstracht (f) national costume
voll bezahlt paid-up
voll eingezahlt paid-up
voll im Geschmack (m) full-flavoured
Vollauslastung (f) sell out
Vollbad (n) full bath
vollbelegte Tage (pl. m) sell out days
Vollhaftung (f) full liability
volljährig full of age, of age
Volljährigkeit (f) age of majority, full age, lawful age
vollklimatisiert fully airconditioned
Vollkornbrot (n) whole(meal)bread
Vollmacht (f) authority
Vollmassage (f) full massage
Vollmond (m) full moon
Vollpension (f) board and lodging, board and residence, board residence, full board, full board and lodging, full pension
Vollpreisfahrkarte (f) normal-fare ticket
vollziehen fulfill
Vollziehung (f) fulfillment
Volumen (n) volume
von Bord (m) **gehen** leave the

153

ship
Vor- und Nachsaison (f) off-peak season
Vor- und Nachsaisonfahrpreis (m) off-peak fare
Voranmeldung (f) advance reservation
Voranschlag (m) budget, estimate
voranschlagen estimate
voraus, im in advance
vorausbezahlt prepaid
vorausplanen budget, forecast
Vorausplanung (f) budget
Vorausschau (f) forecast
voraussehen expect
voraussetzen assume
Voraussetzung (f) assumption
Vorauszahlung (f) advance payment, payment in advance, prepayment
Vorbehalt (m) reservation
vorbereiten prepare
Vorbereitung (f) preparation
vorbestellen book, reserve
Vorbestellung (f) advance booking
Vorbestellung (f) **von Plätzen** (pl. m) reservation of seats in advance
vorbeugend preventive
Vorbeugung (f) prevention
vorbildlich exemplary
Vorbildung (f) education
Vordeck (n) fore deck
Vorderdeck (n) forecastle
Vordersitz (m) front seat
Vorderzimmer (n) front-room
Voreröffnungsmanagement (n) pre-opening management
Vorfahre (m) ancestor
Vorfahren (pl. m) ancestry
Vorfahrt (f) right-of-way
Vorfahrt (f) **beachten!** give way
Vorfahrtsstraße (f) major road, priority road
Vorfinanzierung (f) advance financing, finance in advance
Vorführung (f) performance, show
Vorgabe (f) standard, target
Vorgebirge (n) promontory
Vorgericht (n) appetizer, side dish
Vorgericht (n), **pikantes** savoury
Vorgesetztenschulung (f) supervisory training
Vorgesetzter (m) superior, supervisor
Vorgesetzter (m), **direkter** immediate supervisor
Vorhalle (f) vestibule
Vorhalle (f), **überdachte** porch
vorhanden on hand
Vorhang (m) curtain
vorherrschend predominant
Vorjahr (n) previous year
Vorkalkulation (f) cost estimate
vorkochen pre-cook
vorkühlen pre-cool
vorläufig interim, provisional, temporary, tentative
Vorlage (f) draft
vorlegen produce
Vorleger (m) rug
Vorliebe (f) preference
Vormittag (m) forenoon
vormittags (bei Zeitangabe) a.m.
Vorname (m) Christian name
vornehm distinguished
Vorortzug (m) suburban train
Vorräte (pl. m) stock on hand
Vorrätebewertung (f) inventory pricing
vorrätig on hand
Vorrang (m) precedence, priority
Vorrat (m) stock
Vorratsraum (m) storeroom

Vorrecht (n)   franchise, precedence
Vorrichtung (f)   appliance
Vorsaison (f)   low season, preseason
Vorschau (f)   preview
vorschießen   advance
Vorschlag (m)   proposal, suggestion
vorschlagen   suggest
Vorschrift (f)   rule
Vorschub (m) **leisten**   promote
Vorschuß (m)   advance
Vorsicht Zug (m)!   beware of trains
Vorsicht!   caution, take care
vorsichtig   cautious
Vorspeise (f)   appetizer, cocktail savory, horsd'oeuvre, side dish
Vorspeisen (pl. f) **kalt**   cold side dishes
Vorstand (m)   executive board
vorstellen   introduce
Vorstellung (f)   introduction
Vorstellung (f), **geschlossene**   private performance
Vorteil (m)   advantage, benefit, gain
vorteilhaft   advantageous
vorteilhafter Kauf (m)   bargain
Vortrag (m)   lecture
vortragen (Buchhaltung) (m)   carry forward
Vortragsreise (f)   lecture tour
vorübergehend   temporary
Vorverkauf (m)   advance booking
Vorverkaufsstelle (f)   (advance) booking office
Vorvertrag (m)   preliminary agreement
vorwärmen   preheat
Vorwahlnummer (f)   area code
vorweg   in advance
vorwegnehmen   anticipate
vorzeitig   in advance

vorziehen   prefer
Vorzug (m)   preference, priority
Vorzugsbehandlung (f)   preferential treatment
Vorzugsfrachtrate (Luftverkehr) (f)   commodity rate
Vorzugspreis (m)   special price

W

W.C.   water-closet, W.C.
Waage (f)   scale
wach   awake
wach liegen   lie awake
Wachmacher (m)   eye opener
Wacholder (m)   juniper
Wachs (n)   wax
Wachsbohne (f)   kidney bean, wax bean
Wachsei (n)   wax-egg
wachsen (größer werden)   grow
wachsen (Wachs)   wax
Wachstum (n)   growth
Wachstumsrate (f)   growth rate
Wachtel (f)   quail
Wächter (m)   watchman
wählen (Telefon)   dial
Währung (f)   currency, monetary system
Währung (f), **harte**   hard currency
Währung (f), **konvertierbare**   convertable currency, free currency
Wärme (f)   warmth
wärmen   warm
Wärmflasche (f)   hot-water bottle
Wäsche (f)   laundry
Wäschebeschließerin (f)   linen keeper, linen room attendant
Wäscherei (f)   laundry
Wäschereileiter (m)   laundry

155

manager
Wäschesack (m)   laundry bag
Wäscheschacht (m)   laundry-chute
Wäscheschrank (m)   linen-closet
Wäscheverleih (m)   linen hire
Waffel (f)   wafer, waffle
Waffelkartoffeln (pl. f)   fried potato wafers
Wagen (m)   carriage
Wagen (Auto) (m)   car, motor-car
Wagenheber (m)   jack
Wagenpflege (f)   motor-car service
Wagentür (f)   carriage door
Waggonfracht (f)   carload freight
Waggonfrachtrate (f)   carload rate
Waggonladung (f)   carload
Wagnis (n)   risk
Wahl (f)   preference
wahlfrei   optional
wahrnehmen   notice
Wald (m)   forest, wood
Walderdbeere (f)   wild strawberry
Waldhahn (m)   wood grouse
Waldhuhn (n)   wood grouse
Waldmeister (m)   woodruff
waldreich   well-wooded
Waldspaziergang (m)   walk in the woods
Waldweg (m)   forest path
Wallfahrtskirche (f)   pilgrimage church
Wallfahrtsort (m)   place of pilgrimage
Walnuß (f)   walnut
Walzer (m)   waltz
Wandelhalle (f)   pump room
Wanderer (m)   hiker, rambler, tramper
Wanderfahrt (f)   walking tour
Wanderfahrer (m)   hikers' guide,

rambler's guide
Wandergebiet (n)   hiking region
wandern   hike, peregrinate, ramble, tramp, walk
Wandern (n)   hiking, peregrination, rambling, tramping, walking
Wanderschau (f)   touring exhibition
Wandersport (m)   hiking, rambling
Wandertourismus (m)   hiking, rambling
Wanderung (f)   peregrination, ramble, walking tour
Wanderverein (m)   rambling association
Wandkarte (f)   wall map
Wandschirm (m)   folding screen
Wanne (f)   tub
Wannenbad (n)   tub-bath
Ware (f)   commodity, goods, merchandise
Ware (f), **schwimmende**   goods afloat
Waren (pl. f)   goods
Waren (pl. f) **mit hoher Umschlagsgeschwindigkeit** (f) fast moving goods
Waren (pl. f) **unter Zollverschluß** (m)   goods in bond
Waren (pl. f), **verderbliche** perishable goods
Warenanfangsbestand (m) opening inventory
Warenannahme (f)   receiving department
Warenannehmer (m)   receiving clerk
Warenausgabe (f)   issuing
Wareneingangsbuch (n)   receiving record, receiving report
Wareneinsatz (m)   cost of sales
Wareneinsatz (m) **bei Speisen** (pl. f)   food cost, cost of food

sold
Wareneinsatz (m) **bei Getränken** (pl. n) cost of beverage sold
Wareneinsatz (m) **bei Speisen** (pl. f) cost of food sold
Wareneinsatzkontrollbüro (n) food control
Wareneinsatzkontrolle (f) **(Speisen)** food control
Wareneinsatzkosten (pl.) **(Speisen und Getränke)** food and beverage cost
Warenhaus (n) department store
Warenvorrat (m) goods in hand
warm warm
Warmwasser (n) hot water
Warnschild (n) warning sign
Warnung (f) warning
Warteliste (f) waiting list
warten wait
Wartestellung (f) stand-by position
Warteraum (m) waiting room
Wartesaal (m) waiting-room
Warteschlange (f) waiting line
Wartezeit (f) waiting period
Wartezeiten (pl. f) delays, waits
Wartung (f) maintenance, servicing
Wasch- und Toilettenanlagen (pl. f) washing and lavatory facilities
waschbar washable
Waschbecken (n) wash-basin
waschecht washable
Waschküche (umgangsspr. für dichter Nebel) (f) pea soup
Waschlappen (m) face cloth
Waschmaschine (f) washing-machine
Waschpulver (n) washing powder
Waschraum (m) lavatory, rest room
Waschtisch (m) washstand
Waschwanne (f) washing tub
Wasser (n) water
Wasser (n), **fließendes** running water
Wasser (n), **lauwarmes** tepid water
Wasserball (n) water-polo
wasserdicht waterproof
Wasserfall (m) waterfall
Wasserfliegen (n) water gliding
Wasserflugzeug (n) hydroplane, seaplane
Wasserglas (n) tumbler
Wasserhahn (m) tap, water-tap
Wasserhuhn (n) coot, water hen
Wasserkur (f) water cure
Wasserleitung (f) water pipes
Wassermelone (f) water-melon
Wassersegelflugzeug (n) sea glider
Wasserski (m) water-ski
Wasserspiele (pl. n) ornamental fountains
Wassersport (m) aquatic sports, water sports
Wasserstand (m) water level
Wasserstelle (f) watering-place
Wassertemperatur (f) water temperature
Wasserverunreinigung (f) water pollution
Wasserwelle (f) water wave
Watte (f) cotton wool
Wechsel (m) change
Wechselbad (n) contrast bath
Wechselgeld (n) change
Wechselgeld behalten! keep the change
Wechselkurs (m) exchange rate
Wechselkursschwankungen (pl. f) fluctuation of the exchanging rate

wechseln   change, exchange, rotate
Wechselschicht (f)   rotating shift
wechselseitig   mutual
Wechselstrom (m)   alternating current
Wechselstube (f)   exchange office, foreign exchange office
Weckdienst (m)   waking service
wecken   call, wake up
Wecker (m)   alarm-clock
weggeben   give-away
wegräumen   clear away
Wegweiser (m)   guidepost, signpost
Wegzeit (f)   travel time
weiblich   female
weich   soft
Weichkäse (m)   cream cheese
Weichtier (n)   mollusk
Weide (f)   pasture
Weideland (n)   pasturage
Weigerung (f)   refusal
Weiher (m)   fishpond
Weihnachten (n)   Christmas, yule X-mas
Weihnachtsferien (pl.)   Christmas holidays, Christmas vacation
Weihnachtsgratifikation (f)   Christmas bonus
Weihnachtsmann (m)   Santa Clause
Weihnachtspudding (m)   Christmas pudding
Weihnachtszeit (f)   Christmas period
Wein (m)   wine
Wein (m), **abgelagerter**   mature wine
Wein (m), **alter**   old wine
Wein (m), **gespritzter**   spritzer
Wein (m), **hellroter**   rose wine
Wein (m), **junge**   new wine
Wein (m), **leichter**   light wine

Wein (m), **naturreiner**   vintage wine
Wein (m), **offener**   open wine, wine by the glass, wine in a carafe
Wein (m), **roter offener**   red wine from the cask
Wein (m), **schwerer**   heavy wine
Wein (m), **süßer**   sweet wine
Wein (m), **trockener**   dry wine
Weinbau (m)   wine growing
Weinberg (m)   vinyard
Weinbergschnecke (f)   edible snail, snail
Weinblume (f)   wine bouquet
Weinbrand (m)   brandy
Weinbrandglas (n)   brandy-glass
Weinfest (n)   wine festival
Weinflasche (f)   wine bottle
Weingegend (f)   wine district
Weinglas (n)   wine-glas
Weingut (n)   vinyard
Weinhändler (m)   wine-merchant
Weinhandlung (f)   wine shop
Weinkarte (f)   wine-list
Weinkeller (m)   cellar
Weinkeller (m)   wine-cellar
Weinkellner (m)   wine-butler
Weinkraut (n)   cabbage in wine, pickled cabbage
Weinkühler (m)   ice-pail, wine cooler
Weinlese (f)   vintage
Weinlesefest (n)   vintage festival
Weinlokal (n)   wine-cellar
Weinprobe (f)   wine-test
Weinprobiergläschen (n)   taster
Weinrebe (f)   vine
Weinschenke (f)   wine-house
Weinstube (f)   wine-tavern
Weißbier (n)   white beer
Weißbohnengericht (n)   stew of white beans
Weißbrot (n)   white bread
Weißkohl (m)   white cabbage

Weißkraut (n)   white cabbage
Weißling (m)   whiting
Weißwein (m)   white wine
Weißwurst (f)   white sausage, weisswurst
Weißzeug (n)   linen
Weißwein (m) **offen**   white wine from the cask
weit   far
weiterfahren   set off again
Weiterfahrt (f)   continuation of ones journey
Weiterflug (m)   onward air journey
weiterreichen   pass
Weizenbrot (n)   wheaten bread
Weizengrießbrei (m)   cream of wheat
Weizenmehlkuchen (dreieckig) (m)   scone
Welle (Technik) (f)   shaft
Welle (Wasser) (f)   wave
Wellenbrecher (m)   breakwater
Wellenreiter (n)   aqua-planing
wellig   wavy
Wels (m)   sheat-fish
Weltausstellung (f)   international exhibition, world exhibition, World Fair
Weltenbummler (m)   globetrotter
Weltruf (m)   world-wide fame
Weltverband (m) **der Reisebüros** (pl. n)   World Association of Travel Agencies
Weltzeit (f)   Greenwich mean time
wenden   turn round
Wenden (n) **verboten!**   no u-turn
weniger   less
Wenslaydale-Käse (m)   Wenslaydale
Werbeabteilung (f)   publicity department
Werbeagentur (f)   advertising agency

Werbebrief (m)   advertising letter, sales letter
Werbebudget (n)   advertising budget
Werbeetat (m)   advertising budget
Werbefahrt (f)   advertising tour
Werbefeldzug (m)   advertising campaign, publicity campaign
Werbegeschenk (n)   advertising gift, give-away
Werbeidee (f)   advertising idea
Werbekampagne (f)   advertising campaign, campaign
Werbematerial (n)   sales literature
Werbemittel (pl. n)   advertising media
werben   advertise, promote
Werbeplakat (n)   poster
Werbeplan (m)   advertising program
Werberundschreiben (n)   advertising circular
Werbung (f)   advertising, promotion
Werbung (f) **durch Zugaben** (pl. f)   free gift advertising
Werbung (f), **gezielte**   angled publicity
Werbung (f), **indirekte**   indirect advertising
Werbung (f), **lokale**   local advertising
werfen, über Bord (m)   throw over board
Werft (f)   wharf
Werkstätte (f)   workshop
Werkzeug (n)   implement, tool
Wermut(wein) (m)   vermo(u)th
Wert (m)   value
Wert (m) **des Durchschnittsbestandes** (m)   average stock value
Wertabnahme (f)   deflation

159

Wertangabe (f)   declaration of value
wertlos   worthless
Wertmesser (m)   standard
Wertsachen (pl. f)   valuables
Weste (f)   waistcoat
Westeuropäische Zeit (WEZ) (f)   Western European time
Wettangeln (n)   angling competition
Wettbewerb (m)   competition
Wettbewerber (m)   competitor
Wettbewerbsbeschränkung (f)   restraint of trade
Wettbewerbsmarkt (m)   competitive market
Wetteramt (n)   meteorological office, weather bureau
Wetterbericht (m)   weather forecast
Wetterdienst (m)   meteorological services
wetterfest   weatherproof
Wetterkarte (f)   weather chart
Wettervorhersage (f)   weather forecast
Wetterwarte (f)   weather station
Whisky (m)   whisky, whiskey
widrig   adverse
wie   like
Wiederbeschaffung (f)   replacement
Wiederbeschaffungkosten (pl.)   replacement cost
Wiederbeschaffungswert (m)   replacement cost
Wiedereinreisevisum (n)   re-entry visa
wiedereinschiffen, sich   re-embark
wiedereinstellen   rehire
wiedererkennen   recognize
Wiedererkennen (n)   recognition
Wiedereröffnung (f)   re-opening
wiederherstellen   restore

Wiederherstellung (f)   restoration
wiederholen   repeat
Wiederholung (f)   repeat
Wiederholungsauftrag (m)   repeat order
Wiederholungsgeschäft (n)   repeat business
Wiedersehen (n)!, **auf**   good bye
Wiederverkäufer (m)   reseller
wiederverwenden   re-use
Wiederverwendung (f)   re-use
Wiedervorlagemappe (f)   follow-up file
Wiedervorlageverfahren (n)   follow-up system
wiegen   weigh
Wien   Vienna
Wiener Rostbraten (m)   rumpsteak with fried onions, steak Vienna style, Vienna steak with fried onions
Wiener Schnitzel (n)   fried slice of veal Vienna style, Viennese schnitzel
Wiener Würstchen (pl. n)   Wieners
Wiese (f)   meadow
wild   rugged, wild
Wild (n)   quarry
Wildbret (n)   game
Wildente (f)   pintail, wild duck
Wildfleisch (n)   game
Wildfleischragout (n)   jugged game
Wildgans (f)   wild goose
Wildkaninchen (n)   wild rabbit
Wildnis (f)   wilderness
Wildpastete (f)   cold game pie
Wildschwein (n)   wild boar
Wildschweinfilet (n) **gegrillt**   grilled fillet of wild boar
Wildschweinkeule (f)   wild boar haunch
Wildschweinrücken (m)   wild boar saddle

Wildschweinskopf (m) **gefüllt** head of wild boar, stuffed boar's head
willkommen welcome
Winchesterplattenlaufwerk (n) winchester hard disk
Windbeutel (m) cream puff, small cream puff
windgeschützt protected against the wind
windig airy, windy
Windjacke (f) windcheater
Windschutzscheibe (f) windsreen, wind-shield
Windstärke (f) wind force
Windstoß (m) gust
Windsurfen (n) windsurfing
Windtorte (f) meringue cake
winken wave
Winteraufenthaltsort (m) winter stay
Winterendivie (f) escarole
Winterfahrplan (m) winter timetable
Winterferiendorf (n) winter holiday village
Winterflugplan (m) winter timetable
Winterfreuden (pl. f) joys of winter
Winterfrische (f) winter holiday resort
Wintergarten (m) winter garden
Winterkur (f) winter cure
Winterkurort (m) winter health resort
winterlich wintry
Winterreifen (m) winter tyre
Winterreiseverkehr (m) winter tourist traffic
Wintersaison (f) winter season
Wintersport (m) winter sports
Wintersportarrangement (n) inclusive winter sport terms
Wintersportausrüstung (f) winter sports equipment
Wintersporteinrichtungen (pl. f) winter sports facilities
Wintersportort (m) winter sports centre, winter sports resort
Wintersportreise (f) winter sports trip
Wintersportsaison (f) winter sports season
Wintersportveranstaltung (f) winter sports event
Wintersportzug (m) snow train
Wintertourismus (m) winter tourism
Winzer (m) wine grower
Winzerfest (n) vintagers' festival
Wirbelsturm (m) tornado
wirksam effective, valid
Wirksamkeit (f) effectiveness
Wirkung (f) impact
Wirsingkohl (m) savoy cabbage
Wirt (m) publican, saloonkeeper
Wirtin (f) landlady
wirtschaftlich economical
Wirtschaftlichkeit (f) operating efficiency, profitability
Wirtschaftlichkeitsanalyse (f) economic analysis
Wirtschaftsabteilung (f) food and beverage department
Wirtschaftsanalyse (f) operations analysis
Wirtschaftsanalytiker (m) operations analyst
Wirtschaftsdirektion (f) food and beverage management
Wirtschaftsdirektor (m) food and beverage manager
Wirtschaftsgut (n) asset
Wirtschaftssystem (n) economic system
Wirtshaus (n) public house, tavern

wischen wipe
Wissen (n) knowledge
Wissen (n), praktisches knowhow
wissentlich knowingly
Wochenendausflug (m) week-end excursion
Wochenende (n) week-end
Wochenendfahrt (f) week-end outing, week-end trip
Wochenendpesion (f) week-end guest-house
Wochenendreiseverkehr (m) week-end tourist traffic
Wochenendspezialpreis (m) special weekend price
Wochenendtourismus (m) week-end tourism
Wochenmarkt (m) weekly market
Wochenrechnung (f) weekly bill
Wochenschau (f) newsreel
Wochentag (m) week-day
Wodka (m) vodka
wöchentlich weekly
Wörterbuch (n) dictionary
wörtlich verbal
wohl well
wohnen dwell, live, reside
Wohngebiet (n) residential area
wohnhaft resident
Wohnhaus (n) dwelling house
Wohnort (m) place of residence, residence
Wohnraum (m) living-room
Wohnschlafraum (m) bed-sitter, bed-sitting room
Wohnsitz (m) domicile, residence
Wohnsitz (m) haben reside
Wohnsitz (m), ständiger permanent residence
Wohnung (f) apartment, flat
Wohnungsbau (m) housebuilding

Wohnungsgeldzuschuß (m) housing allowance
Wohnwagen (m) caravan, trailer
Wohnwagenanhänger (m) caravan trailer
Wohnwagenfahrer (m) trailerite
Wohnwagentourist (m) caravaner
Wohnzimmer (n) living-room, sitting-room
Wolke (f) cloud
wolkig cloudy
Wolldecke (f) blanket, wool blanket
wollen want
Wrack (n) wreck
wünschen want
Würfelzucker (m) lump sugar
Würstchen (n) sausage
Würze (f) zest
würzen (Speisen) season
würzig spicy, well-seasoned
Wurst (f) sausage
Wurstaufschnitt (m) slices of sausage
Wurstplatte (f) assorted sausage

Z

zäh tough
zählen count
Zahl (f) figure
zahlbar payable
zahlen pay
Zahlkarte (w) money order
Zahlmeister (m) paymaster, purser
Zahlung (f) payment
Zahlung (f) der Gebühren (pl. f), gegen on payment of the fees
Zahlung (f) nach Wunsch (m) pay as you go

Zahlung (f), **einmalige** gratuity
Zahlungsbedingungen (pl. f) payment terms, terms of payment
Zahlungsbilanz (f) balance of payments
Zahlungsfähigkeit (f) ability to pay
Zahlungsgewohnheit (f) paying habit
Zahlungsmodus (m) mode of payment
Zahlungsort (m) place of payment
zahlungsunfähig bankrupt, insolvent
Zahlungsunfähigkeit (f) bankruptcy
Zahlungsverweigerung (f) refusal to pay
Zahlungsverzug (m) delay of payment
Zahlungsweise (f) mode of payment
Zahnarzt (m) dentist
Zahnbürste (f) tooth brush
Zahnpaste (f) tooth-paste
Zahnstocher (m) tooth-pick
Zander (m) pike-perch
zanken quarrel
Zapfenstreich (m) tat-too
zart tender
Zebrastreifen (m) zebra crossing
zechen quaff
Zecherei (f) potation
Zechprellerei (f) bilking, hotel fraud
Zeichen (n) mark, symbol
Zeichenerklärung (f) legend, signs and symbols
zeigen exhibit, show
Zeit (f) time
Zeit (f) **totschlagen** kill time
Zeit (f) **vertreiben** kill time
Zeit (f), **angemessene** reasonable time
Zeit (f), **verkehrsarme** off-peak period
Zeit- und **Bewegungsstudie** (f) time and motion study
Zeitansage (f) time signal
Zeitaufnahme (f) time exposure
zeitgemäß up-to-date
Zeitkarte (f) commutation ticket, season ticket
Zeitnahme (f) timing
Zeitplan (m) schedule
Zeitschrift (f) journal, magazine, periodical
Zeitschriftenkiosk (m) bookstall, news stall
Zeitung (f) newspaper
Zeitungsbeilage (f) insert
Zeitungsstand (m) news stand
Zeitungswerbung (f) newspaper advertising
Zeitvorgabe (f) time allowance
zeitweilig temporary
Zeitzeichen (n) time signal
Zelluloid (n) xylonite
Zelt (n) tent
Zelt- und **Wohnwagenwesen** (n) camping and caravaning
zelten camp, pitch a tent
Zelthering (m) tent-peg
Zeltlager (n) tent camp
Zeltplatz (m) camping-ground
Zeltstadt (f) tented city
Zeltvordach (n) tent awning
Zentrale (f) head office, home office, main office
Zentraleinheit (f) central processing unit (CPU)
Zentralheizung (f) central heating
Zentralverwaltungswirtschaft (f) government controlled economy
Zentrum (n) center
zerklüftet rugged
zerlassen melted

163

zerschneiden carve
zerteilen part
Zervelat(wurst) (f) saveloy
Zeugnis (n) certificate
Zichorie (Salat) (f) chicory
Zicklein (n) kid-goat, yeanling
Ziege (f) goat
Ziegenkäse (m) goat cheese
ziehen pull
ziehen: aus dem Wasser (n) **gezogen** plain boiled
Ziel (n) goal, objective
Ziel (Sport) (n) tee
Zielbahnhof (m) destination station
Zielflughafen (m) destination airport
Zielland (n) country of destination
Zielort (m) destination, point of turnaround
Zielsetzung (f) objective
ziemlich quite
Ziffer (f) figure
Zigarette (f) cigarette
Zigarettenverkäufer (m) tobacconist
Zigarillo (m) whiff
Zigarre (f) cigar
Zigeuner (m) gibsy
Zigeunergulasch (n) beef stew gipsy style
Zimmer (n) room
Zimmer (n) **im voraus bestellen** book a room in advance
Zimmer (n) **mit Bad** (n) **oder Dusche** (f) room with private bath or shower
Zimmer (n) **mit Frühstück** (n) bed and breakfast, CP (continental plan)
Zimmer (n) **mit Halbpension** (f) Modified American Plan (MAP)
Zimmer (n) **mit Meereshlick** (m) room with a view of the sea

Zimmer (n) **mit zwei Betten** (pl. n) double-bedded room
Zimmer (n) **ohne Berechnung** (f) complimentary room
Zimmer (n) **zur Straße** (f) room facing the street
Zimmer (pl. n) **frei** rooms vacant
Zimmer (pl. n) **mit Vollpension** (f) AP (American Plan)
Zimmer (pl. n) **zu vermieten** rooms to let
Zimmer (pl. n), **belegte und freie** rooms occupied and vacant
Zimmer (pl. n), **ineinandergehende** connecting rooms
Zimmerdecke (f) ceiling
Zimmerflucht (f) suite
Zimmerfrühstückskarte (f) door knob menu
Zimmerkellner (m) room service waiter
Zimmerlautstärke (f) room volume
Zimmermädchen (n) chambermaid, maid
Zimmernachweis (m) accomodation service
Zimmernummer (f) room number
Zimmerpreis (m) room charge, room rate
Zimmerpreis (m) **mit Frühstück** (n) charge for bed and breakfast
Zimmerpreis (m) **ohne Pension** (f) European plan
Zimmerreservierung (f) hotel reservation
Zimmertelefon (n) room telephone
Zimmervermittlung (f) accomodation service
Zimt (m) cinnamon
Zink (n) zinc
Zins (m), **Zinsen** (pl.) interest

Zins (m) **auf Anlagevermögen** (n) interest on investments
Zinsfuß (m) rate of interest
Zinssatz (m) interest charge, rate of interest
Zitadelle (f) citadel
Zitherspieler (m) zitherist
Zitronat (n) candied lemon peel
Zitrone (f) lemon
Zitronenbaiserpudding (m) lemon meringue pie
Zitroneneis (n) lemon-ice
Zitronenlimonade (f) lemon squash
Zitronenpresse (f) lemon-squeezer
Zitronensaft (m) lemon juice
Zitronenschale (f) lemon rind
Zivilflughafen (m) commercial airport
Zoll (m) customs, duty
Zoll- und Paßabfertigung (f) passport and customs examination
Zollabfertigung (f) customs clearance, customs clearing
Zollabfertigungsgebühren (pl. f) clearance charges
Zollabfertigungshalle (f) customs examination hall
Zollbeamter (m) customs officer
Zollbehörde (f) customs authorities
Zolldurchlaßschein (m) transire
Zollerhöhung (f) increase of customs
Zollerklärung (f) customs declaration
Zollerstattung (f) duty drawback
zollfrei duty-free
Zollfreiheit (f) exemption from duty

Zollgebiet (n) customs territory
Zollhinterziehung (f) evasion of customs
Zollkontrolle (f) customs inspection
Zollnummer (Auto) (f) customs number
zollpflichtig dutiable, liable to customs, liable to duty
zollpflichtig, nicht non-dutiable
Zolltarif (m) customs tariff, tariff
Zollverschluß (m), **unter** in bond
Zollvorschriften (pl. f) customs regulations
Zollwert (m) customs assessment value
Zone (f) range, zone
Zoo (m) zoo
zoologischer Garten (m) zoological garden
zoomen zoom
Zoomobjektiv (n) zoom lens
zu (allzu) too
zu (Richtung) to
zu verkaufen for sale
zu vermieten for hire
Zubehör (n) fixture
Zubehörteile (pl. n) accessory parts
zubereiten prepare
zubereitet am Tisch (m) prepared at (guest's) table
zubereitet in Butter (f) buttered, prepared with butter
Zubereitung (f) preparation
zubilligen award
Zubilligung (f) award
Zubringerbus (m) airport bus
Zubringerdienst (Bus) (m) bus service
Zubringerflugzeug (n) feeder-service aircraft
Zubringerstraße (f) feedway

165

Zubringerverkehr (m) road transport connection
Zubuchung (f) additional reservation
Zuchtforelle (f) farm trout
Zucker (m) sugar
Zuckerbäcker (m) pastry cook
Zuckerdose (f) sugar-basin
Zuckererbse (f) sugar pea
Zuckerglasur (f), **mit** iced
Zuckerguß (m) icing
Zuckermelone (f) cantoloupe
Zuckerschale (f) sugar-bowl
Zuckerzange (f) sugar-tongs
Zündholz (n) match
Zündholzkartoffeln (pl. f) matchstick potatoes
Zündholzschachtel (f) matchbox
Zufahrtstraße (f) approach road
Zufall (m) windfall
Zufall (m), **unabwendbarer** circumstances beyond control
Zufallsstichprobenuntersuchung (f) random sampling
zufrieden content
zufriedenstellend satisfactory
Zuführung (f) **und Ersatz** (m) **von Anlagevermögen** (n) additions and replacements
Zug (m) train
Zug (m) **mit Schiffsanschluß** (m) boat train
Zug (m) **versäumen** miss the train
Zug (m), **durchgehender** through train
Zug besteigen board train
Zug-Schiffs-Reise (f) **kombiniert** rail and steamship travel
Zugabe (f) addition, free gift
Zugabewerbung (f) free gift advertising
Zugang (m) access, pass

Zuganschluß (m) rear of the train
Zugauskunft (f) railway inquiry office
Zugbegleiter (m) conductor, guard, train conductor
Zugbrücke (f) drawbridge
Zugnummer (f) train number
Zugschaffner (m) guard, railway guard
Zugsekretärin (f) secretary rail
Zugspitze (f) head of a train
Zugteil (m) train set
Zugtelefon (n) telephone on the train
Zugverbindung (f) rail connection
Zugverspätung (f) delay of a train
Zugwagen (m) motor lorry, truck
Zugzeiten (pl. f) train timings
Zugzusammensetzung (f) train formation
zulässig allowable
Zulage (f) extra pay
Zulassung (f) admission, motor vehicle licence
Zulieferindustrie (f) supplying industry
Zum Wohl! cheers
zum halben Preis (m) half price
Zuname (m) surname
Zunge (f) tongue
zur Schau (f) **stellen** display
zurückbehalten retain
zurückerstatten refund, reimburse, repay
zurückgeben return
zurückgehen (Flut) neap
zurückkommen return
zurückrechnen reckon back
zurücktreten renounce, retire
zurückverfolgen trace

zurückvergüten reimburse
zurückweisen refuse
zurückzahlen refund, repay
zusätzlich additional, extra
Zusage (f) confirmation
zusammenfassen sum up
Zusammenfassung (f) recapitulation, summary
zusammenstellen compile, reconcile
Zusammenstoß (m) collision
Zusatz (m) addition, admixture
Zusatzbett (n) extra bed
Zusatzfahrkarte (f) supplementary ticket
Zusatzgeschäft (n) additional business
Zusatzkosten (pl.) additional cost
Zusatzzoll (m) additional duty
Zuschlag (m) extra, supplement, supplementary charge, supplementary fare, additional charge
Zuschlagssatz (m) rate of mark up
Zusteigemöglichkeit (f) picking-up point
Zustelldienst (m) delivery service
Zustimmung (f) agreement, approval
Zustrom (m) rush
Zutat (f) ingredient
zuteilen allocate, allot
Zuteilung (f) allocation, allotment
Zutritt (m) access, admission
Zutritt (m) **verboten!** off limits
zuverlässig reliable
Zuverlässigkeit (f) reliability
zuviel berechnen overcharge
zuweisen allocate
Zuweisung (f) allocation
zwanglos informal, unconventional
zweckmäßig advisable
Zweibettabteil (n) double-berth compartment, two-berth compartment
Zweibettkabine (f) two-berth room
Zweibettzimmer (n) double room, room with two beds
Zweifel (m) doubt
zweigleisige Strecke (f) double-track line
Zweigstelle (f) branch office
zweijährlich bi-annual
zweimonatlich bi-monthly
zweistöckig double deck
zweite Klasse (f) second class
zweiter Gang (m) second course
zweiter Rang (Theater) (m) upper circle
zweiwöchentlich bi-weekly
Zwergkürbis (m) summer-squash
Zwetschge (f) damson, plum, prune
Zwetschgenknödel (m) plum dumpling
Zwieback (m) rusk
Zwiebel (f) onion
Zwiebel (f), **kleine** spring onion
Zwiebelfleisch (n) beef stew with onions
Zwiebelmus (n) onion mash
Zwiebelrostbraten (m) braised filet of beef with onions, sirloin steak with onions
Zwiebelsoße (f) onion sauce
Zwielicht (n) twilight
zwingend mandatory
Zwischenaufenthalt (m) intermediate stop
Zwischendeck (n) between-decks, steerage

Zwischenergebnis (n) intermediate result
Zwischenfinanzierung (f) temporary financing
Zwischengericht (n) entree
Zwischenhafen (m) intermediate port
Zwischenlandung (f) stop en route, stopover
Zwischenrechnung (f) interim bill, interim invoice
Zwischenrippenstück (n) sirloin
Zwischenrippenstück (n) **mit Filet** (n) porterhouse steak
Zwischenrippenstück (n) **mit grünem Pfeffer** (m) sirloin steak with green pepper
Zwischensaison (f) intermediate season
Zwischenstation (f) intermediate station
Zwischenstecker (m) adaptor
Zwischenstock (m) mezzanine
Zwischensumme (f) subtotal
Zwischenübernachtung (f) overnight stay en route

Ländernamen und Nationalitätskennzeichen für Automobile

Names of countries and nationality signs for cars

Aden Aden ADN
Ägypten Egypt ET
Äthiopien Ethiopia ETH
Albanien Albania AL
Algerien Algeria DZ
Andorra Andorra AND
Argentinien Argentina RA
Australien Australia AUS
Belgien Belgium B
Birma Burma BUR
Bolivien Bolivia RB
Botswana Betchuanaland BP
Brasilien Brasilia BR
Bulgarien Bulgaria BG
Burundi Burundi RU
Ceylon Ceylon CL
Chile Chile RCH
China (Volksrepublik) China TI
Costa Rica Costa Rica CR
Dänemark Denmark DK
Dahome Dahomey DY
Deutschland Germany D
Dominikanische Republik Dominican Republic DOM
Ecuador Ecuador EC
Elfenbeinküste Ivory Coast CI
Finnland Finland SF
Frankreich France F
Gambia Gambia WAG
Ghana Ghana GH
Gibraltar Gibraltar GBZ
Griechenland Greece GR
Großbritannien Great Britain GB
Guatemala Guatemala GCA
Haiti Haiti RH
Hongkong Hong Kong HK
Indien India IND
Indonesien Indonesia RI
Irak Iraq IRQ
Iran (Persien) Iran IR
Irland Ireland (Eire) IRL
Island Iceland IS
Israel Israel IL
Italien Italy I
Japan Japan J
Jordanien Jordan JOR
Jugoslawien Yugoslavia YU
Kambodscha Cambodia K
Kamerun Cameroons TC
Kanada Canada CDN
Kenia Kenya EAK
Kolumbien Colombia CO
Kongo (Brazzaville) Congo RCB
Kongo (Lepoldville) Congo CGO
Kuba Cuba C
Laos Laos LAO
Libanon Lebanon RL
Liechtenstein Liechtenstein FL
Luxemburg Luxemb(o)urg L
Malawi Malawi RNY
Malaysia Malaysia RMM
Mali Mali RM
Marokko Marocco MA
Mexiko Mexico MEX
Monaco Monaco MC
Neufundland Newfoundland NF
Neuseeland New Zealand NZ
Nicaragua Nicaragua NIC
Niederlande Netherlands NL
Niger Niger NIG
Nigeria Nigeria WAN
Norwegen Norway N
Österreich Austria A

169

Pakistan Pakistan PAK
Panama Panama PA
Paraguay Paraguay PY
Peru Peru PE
Philippinen Philippines PI
Polen Poland PL
Portugal Portugal P
Ruanda Ruanda RWA
Rumänien Romania R
Sambia Zambia RNR
San Marino San Marino RSM
Schweden Sweden S
Schweiz Switzerland CH
Senegal Senegal SN
Sierra Leone Sierra Leone WAL
Singapur Singapore SGP
Somalia Somalia SP
Sowjetunion Soviet Union SU
Spanien Spain E
Südafrika South Africa ZA
Südrhodesien Southern Rhodesia RSR
Swasiland Swaziland SD
Syrien Syria SYR
Taiwan (Formosa) RC
Tansania Tanzania EAT
Thailand (Siam) Thailand T
Tschechoslowakei Czechoslovakia CS
Türkei Turkey TR
Tunesien Tunesia TN
USA USA USA
Uganda Uganda EAU
Ungarn Hungary H
Uruguay Uruguay U
Vatikanstadt Vatican City V
Venezuela Venezuela YU
Vietnam Vietnam VN
Zentralafrikanische Republik Central African Republic RCA.
Zypern Cyprus CY

Teil II
Englisch — Deutsch

Part II
English — German

A

abc-airline-guide Verzeichnis (n) der Flughäfen (pl. m) und Luftverkehrsgesellschaften (pl. f) im Linienverkehr
abc-flight (advanced booking charter) ABC-Flug (m) (verbilligte Flüge)
ability Fähigkeit (f)
ability to pay Zahlungsfähigkeit (f), Bonität (f)
ability to work Arbeitsfähigkeit (f)
abolition Abschaffung (f)
abroad im Ausland (n)
absence rate Abwesenheitsrate (f)
absentee Abwesende (m)
absenteeism Abwesenheit (f), Fernbleiben (n), Fehlen (n)
abstract Auszug (m)
abstract account Kontoauszug (m)
abuse Mißbrauch (m), mißbrauchen
accelerate Gas (n) geben, beschleunigen
accelerator Gaspedal (n)
accept annehmen, akzeptieren, abnehmen
acceptance Annahme (f), Akzept (n), Abnahme (f)
access Zugang (m), Zutritt (m)
access road (Autobahn-) Einfahrt (f)
accessory parts Zubehörteile (pl. n)
accident Unfall (m), Unglücksfall (m)
accident hazard Unfallquelle (f), Unfallrisiko (n)
accident insurance Unfallversicherung (f)
accommodate unterbringen, beherbergen
accommodation Unterbringung (f), Unterkunft (f)
accommodation capacity Beherbergungskapazität (f)
accommodation service Zimmervermittlung (f), Zimmernachweis (m)
accommodation train Bummelzug (m)
accompanied luggage Mitreisegepäck (n)
accompany begleiten
accompanying children begleitende Kinder (pl. n)
accompanying person begleitende Person (f), Begleitung (f)
account balance Kontenstand (m)
account classification Kontengliederung
account current (A/C) Kontokorrent (n)
account distribution Kontierung (f)
accountant Buchhalter (m)
accounting Buchhaltung (f), Buchführung (f)
accounting department Buchhaltungsabteilung (f)
accounting machine Buchhaltungsmaschine (f), Buchungsmaschine (f)
accounting period Abrechnungszeitraum (m)
accounts payable Kreditoren (pl. m), Verbindlichkeiten (pl. f)
accounts receivable Debitoren (pl. m), Forderungen (pl. f)
acid sauer
acknowledge anerkennen, bestätigen
acknowledg(e)ment Anerken-

nung (f), Bestätigung (f)
acquaintance Bekannter (m), Bekanntschaft (f)
acquirer's tax Erwerbssteuer (f)
acquisition cost Lager- und Bestellkosten
act of God höhere Gewalt (f)
action Tat (f), Handlung (f), Klage (f), Prozeß (m)
action for damages Schadenersatzklage (f)
activity Tätigkeit (f), Betriebsfunktion (f)
activity level Beschäftigungsgrad (m)
activity report Tätigkeitsbericht (m)
actor Schauspieler (m)
actress Schauspielerin (f)
actual tatsächlich, Ist (n)
actual beverage cost Ist-Wareneinsatz (m) Getränke (pl. n)
actual cash value Barwert (m)
actual costs Ist-Kosten (pl.)
actual cost system Ist-Kostenrechnung (f)
actual food cost Ist-Wareneinsatz (m) -Speisen (pl. f)
actual stock Ist-Bestand (m)
accrued liability antizipative Schuld (f)
accumulate auflaufen, ansammeln
accumulated amount Endwert (m), aufgelaufener Betrag (m)
accuracy Genauigkeit (f)
accusation Anklage (f), Anschuldigung (f)
accustom to gewöhnen an
accustmed gewöhnt an
adaptor Zwischenstecker (m)
add hinzufügen
add up summieren
added value tax Mehrwertsteuer (f)
addition Hinzufügung (f), Zugabe (f), Zusatz (m)
additions and replacements Zuführung (f) und Ersatz (m) von Anlagevermögen (n)
additional zusätzlich
additional business Zusatzgeschäft (n)
additional charge Zuschlag (m), Aufschlag (m), Nebenkosten (pl.)
additional charge for single room Einzelzimmerzuschlag (m)
additional cost Zusatzkosten (pl.)
additional day Verlängerungstag (m)
additional duty Zusatzzoll (m)
additional investment Neuinvestition (f)
additional reservation Zubuchung (f)
additional week Verlängerungswoche (f)
address Adresse (f), adressieren
address book Adreßbuch (n)
addressee Empfänger (m)
addressing machine Adressiermaschine (f)
adequacy Angemessenheit (f)
adequate angemessen, hinreichend
adjacent angrenzend, benachbart
adjoining anschließend an
adjoining rooms nebeneinander liegende Zimmer (pl. n)
adjust berichtigen, schlichten
adjustable verstellbar
adjusting entry Berichtigungsbuchung (f), Umbuchung (f)
adjustment Berichtigung (f),

173

Schlichtung (f)
adjustment of prices Preisanpassung (f)
administer verwalten
administered price kontrollierter Preis (m)
administration Verwaltung (f)
administrative decision Leitungsentscheidung (f)
administrative audit Innenrevision (f)
administrative expense Verwaltungskosten (pl.)
administrative fees Verwaltungsgebühren (pl. f)
administrative general expenses allgemeine Verwaltungskosten (pl.)
admission Zulassung (f), Zutritt (m), Einlaß (m)
admission card Ausweis (m), Eintrittskarte (f)
admission free Eintritt (m) frei!
admission ticket Eintrittskarte (f)
admixture Zusatz (m)
adopt annehmen, beitreten
adult Erwachsener (m), erwachsen
adulteration Verfälschung (f), Verschneidung (f)
adulteration of food Verfälschung (f) von Nahrungsmitteln (pl. n)
advance vorschießen, bevorschussen, erhöhen, Vorschuß (m), Steigerung
advance booking Vorbestellung (f), Vorverkauf (m)
advance booking office (Karten-)Vorverkaufsstelle (f)
advance financing Vorfinanzierung (f)
advance in price Preissteigerung (f), Preiserhöhung (f)

advance payment Vorauszahlung (f)
advance pay off Lohnvorauszahlung (f)
advance reservation Voranmeldung (f)
advance wage payment Lohnvorschuß (m), Lohnvorauszahlung (f)
advantage Vorteil (m)
advantageous vorteilhaft, einträglich
adverse entgegengesetzt widrig
adverse balance of payments passive Zahlungsbilanz (f)
advertise anzeigen, werben
advertisement, ad Annonce (f), Inserat (n)
advertisement column Anzeigenspalte (f)
advertising Werbung (f), Reklame (f)
advertising abroad Auslandswerbung (f)
advertising agency Werbeagentur (f)
adverting budget Werbebudget (n), Werbeetat (m)
advertising campaign Werbefeldzug (m), Werbekampagne (f)
advertising circular Werberundschreiben (n)
advertising gift Werbegeschenk (n)
advertising idea Werbeidee (f)
advertising letter Werbebrief (m)
advertising media Werbemittel (pl. n)
advertising program Werbeplan (m)

174

advertising rate Anzeigentarif (m)
advertising tour Werbefahrt (f)
advice Rat (m), Ratschlag (m), Benachrichtigung (f)
advice of dispatch Versandanzeige (f)
advisable zweckmäßig
advise beraten, avisieren, berichten, benachrichtigen
advisor Berater (m)
advisory service Beratungsdienst (m)
aerial Antenne (f)
aerial city tour Stadtrundflug (m)
aerial railway Drahtseilbahn (f)
aerial ropeway Seilschwebebahn (f)
aerobatics Kunstfliegen (n)
aerodrome Flugplatz (m), Flughafen (m)
affiliated company Schwestergesellschaft (f), Konzerngesellschaft (f)
affiliation Mitgliedsaufnahme (f), Angliederung (f)
affinity group Affinitätsgruppe (Reisegruppe mit bestimmtem Reisezweck)
affirm behaupten, bestätigen, versichern
affirmation Behauptung (f), Bestätigung (f), Versicherung (f)
afford sich leisten
affray Krawall (m), Schlägerei (f), Landfriedensbruch (m)
affront Beleidigung (f)
Africa Afrika
after-deck Achterdeck (n)
after-effect Folgeerscheinung (f)
afternoon Nachmittag (m)
afternoon dance Tanztee (m)
afternoon tea Nachmittagstee (m)
after-season Nachsaison (f), Spätsaison (f)
after-season reduction Nachsaisonermäßigung (f)
after-shave lotion Rasierwasser (n) nach der Rasur (f)
aftertaste Beigeschmack (m)
after-treatment Nachkur (f), Nachbehandlung (f)
age Alter (n)
age group Altersgruppe (f)
age limit Altersgrenze (f)
age of majority Volljährigkeit (f)
age of minority Minderjährigkeit (f)
agency Vertretung (f), Agentur (f)
agency commission Agenturprovision (f)
agency representative Agenturvertreter (m)
agenda Tagesordnung (f)
agent Beauftragter (m), Vertreter
aggrieve beschweren, schädigen
agio Aufgeld (n), Aufschlag (m), Mehrbetrag (m), Agio (n)
agree upon vereinbaren
agree with einverstanden sein, vereinbaren, vertragen
agreeable angenehm
agreement Zustimmung (f), Abkommen (n), Vereinbarung (f), Vertrag
agreement of purchase and sale Kaufvertrag (m)
aid helfen; Hilfe (f)
air-bath Luftbad (n)
air booking Buchung (f) eines Fluges (m)
air bus terminal Air-Terminal (m)
air cargo Luftfracht (f)

175

air carriage Beförderung auf dem Luftweg (m)
air charter Charterfluggesellschaft (f)
air coach Passagierflugzeug (n) der Touristenklasse
air-conditioned mit Klimaanlage (f)
air-conditioning Klimaanlage (f)
air corridor Luftkorridor (m), Einflugschneise (f)
aircraft Flugzeug (n)
aircraft departure time Abflugzeit (f)
aircraft passenger insurance Fluggastversicherung (f)
aircraft pilot Pilot (m), Flugzeugführer (m)
aircrew Flugzeugbesatzung (f)
air-cured beef of the Grisons Bündnerfleisch (n)
aircushion Luftkissen (n)
air display Luftfahrtausstellung (f)
air-dried meat Trockenfleisch (n)
aircraft engine Flugzeugmotor (m)
airfare Flugpreis (m)
airfield Flugplatz (m)
air filter Luftfilter (m)
air-freight Luftfracht (f)
air-freight charges Luftfrachtkosten (pl.)
air-freight space Luftfrachtraum (m)
airfreighter Frachtflugzeug (n)
air hostess Stewardeß (f)
air-journey Flug (m), Flugreise (f)
airline Fluggesellschaft (f), Fluglinie (f), Luftfahrtgesellschaft (f)

airline desk Abfertigungsschalter (m)
airliner Verkehrsflugzeug (n), Verkehrsmaschine (f), Linienflugzeug (n)
airline ticket Flugkarte (f), Flugschein (m)
airmail Luftpost (f)
airmail envelope Luftpostkuvert (n)
airmail stationery Luftpostpapier (n)
airmattress Luftmatratze (f)
air parcel Luftpostpaket (n)
air-passenger Fluggast (m)
air-passenger service Luftreisedienst (m)
airplane Flugzeug (n)
air pocket Luftloch (n)
air pollution Luftverschmutzung (f)
airport Flughafen (m)
airport bus Flughafenbus (m), Zubringerbus (m)
airport customs office Flughafenzollamt (n)
airport of destination Bestimmungsflughafen (m)
airport of dispatch Abfertigungsflughafen (m)
airport restaurant Flughafenrestaurant (n)
airport service charge Fluggastgebühr (f)
airport tax Flughafensteuer (f)
airport terminal building Flughafenempfangsgebäude (n)
air pump Luftpumpe (f)
air-rail transport Flug-Eisenbahn-Verkehr (m)
air reservation Flugplatzreservierung (m)
air resort Luftkurort (m)
air route Flugstrecke (f)
airscrew-driven aeroplane Pro-

pellerflugzeug (n)
air-seal luftdicht verschließen
air services Flugverkehr (m)
airsick luftkrank
airsickness Luftkrankheit (f)
air space Luftraum (m)
air-steamer voyage Flug- und Schiffs-Reise
air-stop Hubschrauberlandeplatz (m)
air taxi Mietflugzeug (n), Lufttaxi (n)
air-temperature Lufttemperatur (f)
air-ticket Flugkarte (f), Flugschein (m)
air-ticket issuing office Flugscheinverkaufsstelle (f)
air-tourism Flugtouristik (f)
air traffic Luftverkehr (m)
air traffic control Flugsicherung (f)
air transport company Luftverkehrsgesellschaft (f)
airways system Streckennetz (n)
airy luftig, windig
à la carte à la carte
alarm bell Alarmglocke (f)
alarm-clock Wecker (m)
alcohol Alkohol (m)
alcoholic alkoholisch, Alkoholiker (m)
alcoholic drink alkoholisches Getränk (n)
ale (pale ale) englisches Bier (n)
ale-house Bierausschank (m)
alien Ausländer (m), fremd
alight aussteigen
all aboard einsteigen!
all additional costs will be borne by the traveller sämtliche Mehrkosten (pl.) gehen zu Lasten des Reisenden

allergic allergisch
all-expense trip Pauschalreise (f)
allied company Tochtergesellschaft (f), Konzerngesellschaft (f)
all-in air fare Flugpauschale (f)
all included alles inbegriffen
all-in holiday Pauschalpreisferien (pl.)
all-in journey Pauschalreise (f)
all-in journey by rail Bahninklusivreise (f)
allocate zuteilen, zuweisen
allocation Zuteilung (f), Zuweisung (f), Kostenumlage (f), Kostenaufschlüsselung (f)
allocation of foreign exchange Devisenzuteilung (f)
allocation of seats Platzzuteilung (f)
allot zuteilen
allotment Zuteilung (f), Kontingent
allow erlauben, gewähren
allowable zulässig
allowance Rabatt (m), Abzug (m), Nachlaß (m), Freibetrag (m), Freigrenze (f)
allowance for doubtful accounts Rückstellung (f) für zweifelhafte Forderungen (pl. f)
All Saints' Day Allerheiligen
all-year round admission ticket Dauerausweis (m)
almond Mandel (f)
almond bar Mandelschnitte (f)
almond cake Mandelkuchen (m)
almond pastry Mandelgebäck (n)
almond pudding Mandelpud-

ding (m)
almond tart Mandeltorte (f)
alpine climber Alpinist (m)
alpine hut Berghütte (f)
alpine meadow Almwiese (f)
alpine road Alpenstraße (f)
altar Altar (m)
alter (ver)ändern
alternating current Wechselstrom (m)
alternative offer Ausweichangebot (n)
alteration Änderung (f), Veränderung
altitude of a pass Paßhöhe (f)
amateur Amateur (m)
amber Bernstein (m)
ambulance Krankenwagen (m), Rettungswagen (m)
amend ergänzen, ändern, verbessern
amenit Annehmlichkeit (f)
a.m. vormittags (bei Zeitangabe)
America Amerika (n)
American Amerikaner (m), Amerikanerin (f), amerikanisch
American breakfast üppiges Frühstück (n) (Schinken, Eier, Pfannkuchen, Toast, Fruchtsaft etc.)
American Hotel and Motel Association Amerikanischer Hotel- und Motelverband (m)
American Society of Travel Agents (ASTA) Amerikanische Gesellschaft (f) der Reiseagenturen (pl. f)
amino-acid Aminosäure (f)
amortize tilgen, abzahlen, amortisieren
amount betragen; Betrag (m)
amount carried over Übertrag (m)

amount to sich belaufen auf
amphie zweiter Rang am (m) (Theater)
ample reichlich
amplifier Verstärker (m)
amusement park Vergnügungspark (m), Rummelplatz (m)
amusing unterhaltend
analysis Analyse (f), Untersuchung (f)
analyze untersuchen, analysieren
ancestor Vorfahre (m)
ancestry Vorfahren (pl. m), Abstammung (f)
anchor vor Anker gehen
anchovy Sardelle (f)
anchovy-butter Anchovisbutter (f) (Sardellenbutter)
anchovy butter sauce Sardellenbuttersoße (f)
anchovy-paste Anchovispaste (f)
anchovy sauce Sardellensauce (f)
anchovy straws Sardellenstäbchen (pl. n)
angle angeln
angled publicity gezielte Werbung (f)
angler Angler (m)
angling Angeln (n)
angling club Anglerverein (m)
angling competition Wettangeln (n)
animal fat tierisches Fett (n)
animated belebt, lebhaft
anise Anis (n)
aniseed cooky Anisplätzchen (n)
ankle Knöchel (m)
annex beifügen, Nachtrag (m), Nebengebäude (n), Dependance (f)
anniversary Jahrestag (m), Festtag (m)

anniversary dinner Festessen (n)
anniversary present Jubiläumsgeschenk (n)
announce ankündigen, bekanntgeben
announcement Ankündigung (f), Bekanntmachung (f)
announcer Ansager (m), Sprecher (m)
annoy ärgern, belästigen
annoyance Störung (f), Belästigung (f)
annual jährlich
annual demand jährliche Nachfrage (f)
annual earnings Jahresverdienst (m)
annual financial statement Jahresabschluß (m)
annual holiday (or vacation) Jahresurlaub (m)
annual meeting Jahresversammlung (f), Hauptversammlung (f)
annual ordering costs jährliche Bestellkosten (f)
annual placing of orders Anzahl (f) der jährlichen Bestellungen (pl. f)
annual usage Jahresbedarf (m), Jahresverbrauch (m)
anodyne schmerzstillend
anorak Anorak (m)
antenna Antenne (f)
answer Antwort (f); antworten
anticipate vorwegnehmen
anticlockwise entgegen dem Uhrzeigersinn (m)
anticyclone Hoch (Wetter) (n)
antidote Gegengift (n)
anti-freezing mixture Frostschutzmittel (n)
antique Antiquität (f)
antique shop Antiquitätengeschäft (n)

antirabic vaccination Tollwutimpfung (f)
anxious besorgt
AP (American Plan) Zimmer (pl. n) mit Vollpension (f)
apart-hotel Appartementhotel (n)
apartment Wohnung (f)
apartment house Appartementhaus (n)
apartment house property Mietwohngrundstück (n)
aperitif Aperitif (m)
apologize sich entschuldigen
apology Entschuldigung (f)
appeal Anziehungskraft (f), Attraktion (f)
appear erscheinen
appearance Erscheinung (f), Erscheinen (n)
appendix Anhang (m), Anlage (f)
appetite Appetit (m)
appetizer Vorspeise (f), Vorgericht (n), Appetitanreger (m)
appetizing appetitlich
applause Beifall (m)
apple Apfel (m)
apple fritter Apfelspalte (f), Apfelküchlein (n)
apple jam Apfelkonfitüre (f)
apple jelly Apfelgelee (n)
apple juice Apfelsaft (m)
apple pie Apfelkuchen (m)
apple rice Apfelreis (m)
apple sauce Apfelmus (n)
apple soufflé Apfelauflauf (m)
apple strudel Apfelstrudel (m)
apple-stuffed turnover Apfeltasche (f)
apple tart Apfeltorte (f)
apple turnover Apfel (m) im Schlafrock (m)
appliance Gerät (n), Vorrichtung (f)

applicability Anwendbarkeit (f)
applicable anwendbar
applicant Bewerber (m)
application Bewerbung (f), Antrag (m)
application form Antragsformular (n), Bewerbungsbogen (m)
application for visa Visumsantrag (m)
application software Anwendersoftware (f)
appointed hotel Vertragshotel (n)
appointed office Vertragsbüro (n)
appointed restaurant Vertragsgaststätte (f)
appointment Verabredung (f)
appraisal Bewertung (f)
apprentice Auszubildender (m), Lehrling (m)
apprenticeship Ausbildungszeit (f), Lehrzeit (f)
approach road Zufahrtsstraße (f), Anfahrtsweg (m)
approval Einwilligung (f), Zustimmung (f), Genehmigung (f)
approve einwilligen, billigen, genehmigen
apres-ski Apres-Ski (n)
apricot Aprikose (f)
apricot dumplings Marillenknödel (pl. m)
apricot soufflé Aprikosenauflauf (m)
apron Schürze (f)
aqua-lunging Unterwassersport (m)
aqua-planing Wellenreiten (n)
aquatic sports Wassersport (m)
arcade Arkade (f), Laubengang (m)
archery Bogenschießen (n)

architecture Architektur (f)
area Bezirk (m), Gebiet (n)
area code Vorwahlnummer (f)
area congestion Verkehrsstau (m)
arena Arena (f)
Argentina Argentinien
argue streiten, argumentieren
argument Streit (m), Argument (n)
aria Arie (f)
arise aufstehen
arm Arm (m)
arm-chair Lehnstuhl (m), Sessel (m)
armpit Achselhöhle (f)
aroma Aroma (n)
aromatic aromatisch
aromatic vinegar Kräuteressig (m)
arrange anordnen, vereinbaren
arrangement Anordnung (f), Vereinbarung (f)
arrest verhaften, festnehmen, Arrest (m), Haft (f), Verhaftung (f)
arrival Ankunft (f)
arrival by air Flugzeugankunft (f)
arrival book Ankunftsbuch (n)
arrival hall Ankunftshalle (f)
arrival time Ankunftszeit (f)
arrival time-table Ankunftstafel (f)
arrivals and departures table Fahrplan (m) (Ankünfte - Abreisen)
arrival station Aussteigebahnhof (m)
arrive ankommen
art centre Kunstzentrum (n)
art collection Kunstsammlung (f)
art-dealer Kunsthändler (m)
art gallery Kunstgalerie (f)

180

art   **ass**

art historical journey   Kunstreise (f)
art museum   Kunstmuseum (n)
art shop   Kunsthandlung (f)
art treasure   Kunstschatz (m)
arterial road   Fernverkehrsstraße (f)
artichoke bottoms   Artischokenböden (pl. m)
artichokes   Artischocken (pl. f)
article not to be found   unauffindbarer Gegenstand (m)
articles for daily use   persönliche Gebrauchsgegenstände (pl. m)
artificial honey   Kunsthonig (m)
artist   Künstler (m)
Ascension Day   Himmelfahrtstag
ascent   Aufstieg (m), Besteigung (f)
ascertain   feststellen, ermitteln
ascertainment of damage   Schadensfeststellung (f)
ash   Asche (f)
ashore   an Land
ashtray   Aschenbecher (m)
ask for   verlangen nach, bitten um
asleep   schlafend
asparagus   Spargel (m)
asparagus salad   Spargelsalat (m)
asparagus soup   Spargelsuppe (f)
asparagus sticks   Stangenspargel (m)
asparagus tips   Spargelspitzen (pl. f)
aspic   Aspik (n), Sülze (f)
assault   tätliche Bedrohung (f)
assert   geltend machen, behaupten
assertion   Behauptung (f)
asset   Aktivposten (m), Aktivum (n), Vermögenswert (m), Wirtschaftsgut (n)
asset account   Aktivkonto (n)
assets   Betriebsvermögen (n)
assets and liabilities   Aktiva (pl.) und Passiva (pl.)
assign   übertragen, abtreten
assignment   Abtretung (f), Übertragung (f), Auftrag (m)
assist   helfen, beistehen, Hilfe (f) leisten
assistance   Hilfe (f), Unterstützung (f), Beihilfe (f)
assistant   Gehilfe (m), Assistent (m)
assistant cook   Hilfskoch (m), Jungkoch (m)
assistant driver   Beifahrer (m)
assistant head-waiter   Chef de rang (m)
assistant manager (front)   Assistent (m) der Geschäftsleitung (f) (Empfang)
associate   sich vereinigen, verbinden, Teilhaber (m)
associate advertising   Gemeinschaftswerbung (f)
associated airline   angeschlossene Luftfahrtgesellschaft (f)
association   Arbeitsgemeinschaft (f), Verein (m), Gesellschaft (f)
association of travel agencies   Reisebüroverband (m)
assort   sortieren
assorted   ausgesucht, gemischt
assorted biscuits   gemischte Plätzchen (pl. n)
assorted boiled meat   gekochtes Fleischallerlei (n)
assorted cold meat   Aufschnitt (m)
assorted sausage   Wurstplatte (f)
assorted stewed fruit   gemisch-

181

tes Kompott (n)
assortment Auswahl (f)
assume annehmen, voraussetzen
assumption Annahme (n), Voraussetzung (f), Übernahme (f)
assurance Versicherung (f), Erklärung (f)
assure versichern
asthma Asthma (n)
athletic ground Sportplatz (m)
athletics Leichtathletik (f)
athletics meeting Sportveranstaltung (f)
atmosphere Atmosphäre (f)
atmospheric pressure Luftdruck (m)
attach beifügen, pfänden
attack Anfall (m)
attend teilnehmen, beiwohnen, bedienen
attendance Anwesenheit (f), Bedienung (f)
attendant Platzanweiser (m)
attention Aufmerksamkeit (f), Achtung (f)
attentive aufmerksam
attic Dachkammer (f), Mansarde (f)
attitude Haltung (f), Einstellung (f)
attraction Anziehungskraft (f), Attraktion (f)
attribute of taste Geschmackseigenschaft (f)
audit prüfen; Buchführung (f)
auditor Buchprüfer (m), Leiter (m) des Rechnungswesens (n)
au gratin überbacken
aunt Tante (f)
au pair stay Au-pair-Aufenthalt (m)
Austrian Federal Railways Österreichische Bundes-

bahn (f)
authority Vollmacht (f), Befugnis (f), Kompetenz (f)
authorize bevollmächtigen, billigen
authorized
establishment Vertragshaus (n)
authorized hotel Vertragshotel (n)
authorized restaurant Vertragsgaststätte (f)
automate automatisieren
automatic cooker Garautomat (m)
automatic selling Automatenverkauf (m)
automatic ticket machine Fahrkartenautomat (m)
automatic transmission automatisches Getriebe (n)
automation Automation (f)
automobile service Automobildienst (m)
automobile traffic Autoverkehr (m)
autumn Herbst (m)
autumn holiday Herbstferien (pl.)
autumn trade-fair Herbstmesse (f)
auxiliary service Hilfsdienst (m).
availability Verfügbarkeit (f), Gültigkeit (f), Gültigkeitsdauer
available verfügbar, gültig
available cash Barliquidität (f)
avenue breite Straße (f), Allee (f)
average Durchschnitt (m)
average cost Durchschnittskosten (pl.)
average earnings Durchschnittsverdienst (m)

average food check Durchschnittsspeisenertrag (m) pro Gedeck (n)
average length of guest stay Durchschnittsaufenthaltsdauer (f) pro Gast (m)
average length of stay Durchschnittsaufenthaltsdauer (f)
average price Durchschnittspreis (m)
average ratio Durchschnittsverhältnis (n)
average receipt per food cover Durchschnittsertrag (m) pro Gedeck (n)
average revenue per guest, per day Durchschnittsumsatz (m) pro Gast (m) und Tag (m)
average room rate Durchschnittsbeherbergungsertrag (m) pro Gästezimmer (n); Durchschnittszimmerpreis (m)
average stock value Wert (m) des Durchschnittsbestandes (m)
average storeroom inventory Durchschnittsinventarbestand (m)
average value of the stock Durchschnittsbestand (m)
average working force Durchschnittsbeschäftigtenzahl (f)
aviation Luftfahrt (f)
aviation chart Flugkarte (f)
aviator Flieger (m)
avocado (pear) Avocado (birne) (f)
avoid aufheben, vermeiden, anfechten
avoidance Vermeiden (n), Anfechtung (f), Aufhebung (f)
await erwarten
awake wach

award belohnen, zubilligen, Belohnung (f), Zubilligung (f)
awful schrecklich
awning Plane (f), Markise (f)
axle Achse (Auto) (f)

B

babies' room Raum (m) für Säuglingsbetreuung (f)
baby care Säuglingsbetreuung (f)
baby chicken Hühnchen (n)
baby lamb Milchlamm (n)
baby pig Jungschwein (n)
baby-sitter Babysitter (m)
bachelor Junggeselle (m)
back-ache Rückenschmerzen (pl. m)
background music Hintergrundsmusik (f)
back pay Lohnnachzahlung (f)
back room Hofzimmer (n), rückwärtiges Zimmer (n)
bacon Speck (m)
bacon and eggs Eier (pl. n) mit Speck (m)
bad dept uneinbringliche Forderung (f)
badminton Federballspiel (n)
bag Tasche (f), Reisetasche (f)
baggage Gepäck (n)
baggage car Gepäckwagen (m)
baggage check Gepäckschein (m), Aufbewahrungsschein (m)
baggage compartment Gepäckraum (Bahn) (m)
baggage hold Gepäckraum (Flugzeug) (m)
baggage in excess Übergepäck (n)
baggage insurance Gepäckversicherung (f)

baggage label Gepäckanhänger (m), Kofferanhänger (m)
baggage locker Gepäckschließfach (n)
baggage office Gepäckaufgabestelle (f)
baggage platform Gepäckbahnsteig (m)
baggage rack Gepäckablage (f), Gepäcknetz (n)
baggage registration counter Gepäckabfertigung (f)
baggage room Gepäckraum (Schiff) (m)
baggage service Gepäckdienst (m)
baggage trailer Gepäckanhänger (Auto) (m)
bake backen (n)
baked Alaska Überraschungsomelett (n), Eisomelett (n)
baked apple im Ofen (m) gebackener Apfel (m)
baked apple dumplings Apfel (m) im Schlafrock (m)
baked apple in puff paste Apfel (m) im Schlafrock (m)
baked apricot roll warmes Aprikosenröllchen (n)
baked ham in bread crust Schinken (m) im Brotteig (m)
baked in their jackets in der Schale (f) gebacken
baked potatoes Pellkartoffeln (pl. f) amerikanische Art (f)
baked semolina dumplings gratinierte Grießklößchen
baked sultana pudding Rosinenpudding (m)
baker Bäcker (m)
balance ausgleichen, saldieren, Saldo (m), Überschuß (m), Restbetrag (m), Bilanz (f)
balance an account ein Konto

(n) saldieren
balance carried forward Saldovortrag (m), Schlußsaldo (m)
balance of payments Zahlungsbilanz (f)
balance sheet Bilanz (f)
balance sheet audit Bilanzprüfung (f)
balcony Balkon (m)
balcony facing south Südbalkon (m)
ballet performance Ballettaufführung (f)
ballroom Ballsaal (m) Tanzsaal (m)
balneation Heilbadekur (f), Heilbäderwesen (n)
balneology Bäderwesen (n)
balneotherapy Bäderbehandlung (f)
banana Banane (f)
band Kapelle (f)
bandage verbinden
bandleader Kapellmeister (m)
bandstand Konzertpavillon (m), Orchesterplatz (m)
bank Bank (f)
bank account Bankkonto (n)
band card Scheckkarte (f)
bank holiday Bankfeiertag (m)
banking hours Schalterstunden (pl. f) der Bank (f)
bankrupt zahlungsunfähig, bankrott
bankruptcy Zahlungsunfähigkeit (f), Konkurs (m), Bankrott (m)
banquet Bankett (n), Veranstaltung (f), Festessen (n)
banquet business Veranstaltungsgeschäft (n), Bankettgeschäft (n)
banquet extra waiter Aushilfskellner (m) für Veranstaltungen (pl. f)

banquet headwaiter Bankettoberkellner (m)
banqueting hall Festhalle (f), Festsaal (m)
banquet kitchen Bankettküche (f)
banquet manager Veranstaltungsleiter (m), Bankettleiter (m)
banquet room Festsaal (m), Veranstaltungsraum (m)
bar Schanktisch (m), Theke (f), Bar (f), Schenke (f)
barbecue Holzkohlen-Grillgericht (n)
barbecue braten auf dem Rost (m)
barbel Barbe (f)
barber Herrenfriseur (m)
bar counter Bartheke (f)
bargain Handel (m), handeln, vorteilhafter Kauf (m)
barkeeper Barmann (m), Buffetier (m)
barley Gerste (f)
barley soup Gerstenschleimsuppe (f)
barmaid Schankkellnerin (f), Büffetmädchen (n)
barman Barmann (m), Schankkellner (m), Buffetier (m)
barometer Barometer (n)
baron of lamb Rückenstück vom Lamm (n)
barrage Staudamm (m), Talsperre (f)
barrel Faß (n)
barrier Schranke (f), Sperre (f)
bartender Schankkellner (m), Büffetkellner (m), Büffetier (m)
bar utensil Bargerät (n)
basement Kellergeschoß (n)
base pay Grundlohn (m)
base salary Grundgehalt (n)

base snow Altschnee (m)
base terminal Talstation (f) (Bergbahn)
basic grundlegend
basic fare Grundfahrpreis (m)
basic price Grundpreis (m)
basic research Grundlagenforschung (f)
basil Basilikum (n)
basilica Basilika (f)
basis Grundlage (f), Basis (f)
bask in der Sonne (f) liegen, bräunen
bass Seebarsch (m)
baste begießen, mit Fett (n)
bath Bad (n) (Wanne)
bath attendant Bademeister (m) (Heilbad)
bath chair Rollstuhl (m)
bath Baden i. Bad (n) (im Freien)
bather Badegast (m)
bathing beach Badestrand (m)
bathing cabin Umkleidekabine (f)
bathing cap Bademütze (f), Badehaube (f)
bathing costume Badeanzug (m)
bathing establishment Badeanstalt (f)
bathing facilities Badeanlagen (pl. f)
bathing gown Bademantel (m)
bathing pier Badesteg (m)
bathing place Badeplatz (m), Freibad (n)
bathing prohibited Baden (n) verboten!
bathing resort Badeort (m)
bathing season Badesaison (f)
bathing shorts Badehose (f)
bathing suit Badeanzug (m)
bathing trunks Badehose (f)
bath mat Badematte (f)
bathrobe Bademantel (m)

bathroom Badezimmer (n)
bath towel Badetuch (n)
bathtub Badewanne (f)
batter Schlagteig (m)
Bavarian cream gestürzte Creme (f), Bayrische Creme (f)
bay Bucht (f)
bay leaf Lorbeerblatt (n)
beach Strand (m)
beach attendant Strandwärter (m)
beach-bag Badetasche (f)
beach-chair Strandkorb (m)
beach-guard Badewärter (m)
beach hotel Strandhotel (n)
beach mattress Schwimmatratze (f)
beach shoes Strandschuhe (pl. m)
beach-umbrella Strandschirm (m)
bean Bohne (f)
Béarnaise sauce Sauce Béarnaise
beautician Kosmetikerin (f)
beautification Verschönerung (f)
beauty contest Schönheitswettbewerb (m)
beauty culture Kosmetik (f)
beauty parlour Kosmetiksalon (m), Schönheitssalon (m)
beauty spot Naturschönheit (f), Sehenswürdigkeit (f)
béchamel sauce Béchamelsoße
bed Bett (n)
bed and breakfast Zimmer (n) mit Frühstück (n)
bed-couch Bettcouch (f)
bedding Bettzeug (n)
bed-linen Bettwäsche (f)
bedroom Schlafzimmer (n)
bedside rug Bettvorleger (m)
bedside-table Nachttisch (m)

bed-sitter, bed-sitting room Wohnschlafraum (m)
bedspread Bettüberzug (m)
beef Rind (n)
beef broth with egg Bouillon mit Ei (f)
beefburger Frikadelle (f)
beef fondue Fleischfondue (Rindfleisch) (n)
beef olive Rindsroulade (f)
beef pie Beefsteakpastete (f)
beefsteak Beefsteak (n)
beefsteak tartare style Beefsteak à la tartare (n)
beefsteak with fried egg Beefsteak à la Meier (n)
beef stew Rindsgulasch (n)
beef stew in juice Saftgulasch (n)
beef stew gipsy style Zigeunergulasch (n)
beef stew peasant style Bauerngulasch (n)
beef stew with onions Zwiebelfleisch (n)
beef Stroganoff Filetgulasch in Sauerrahmsauce (n)
beeftea Fleischbrühe (f)
beer Bier (n)
beer-cellar Bierkeller (m), Kellerlokal (n)
beer festival Bierfest (n)
beer-garden Biergarten (m)
beer on draft (draught) offenes Bier (n), Bier (n) vom Faß (n)
beer on tap Bier vom Faß (n)
beer saloon Bierstube (f)
beer-shop Bierausschank (m)
beet-root Rote Beete (f)
beet-root salad Rote Beete-Salat (m)
behave sich benehmen, sich verhalten
behaviou(u)r Verhalten (n), Benehmen (n)

bell Glocke (f), Klingel (f)
bellboy Hotelpage (m)
bellcaptain Portier (m), Getränkeautomat (m)
bellhop Hotelpage (m)
bellman Hausdiener, Hoteldiener (m)
bell tent Rundzelt (n)
belt highway Ringstraße (f)
belt line Ringbahn (f)
bend Kurve (f)
benefit gewinnen; Nutzen (m), Vorteil (m)
Berlin doughnut Berliner Pfannkuchen (m)
berry Beere (f)
berth Koje (f), Bett (n)
best buy vorteilhaftester Kauf (m)
betray betrügen
betrayal Betrug (m)
between-decks Zwischendeck (n)
beverage Getränk (n)
beverage control Getränkekontrolle (f)
beverage-tax Getränkesteuer (f)
beware of trains Vorsicht, Zug!
bi-annual zweijährlich
bicarbonate Natron (n)
bicycle Fahrrad (n)
bicycle excursion Fahrradausflug (m)
bicycle hire Fahrradvermietung (f)
bid anbieten, bieten, Angebot (n)
bidet Bidet (n)
bid price Nachfragepreis (m)
bifurcation Straßengabel (f)
big-game reservation Großwildreservat (n)
bike Rad (n)
bilberry Heidelbeere (f)
bilking Zechprellerei (f)

bill Rechnung (f), in Rechnung (f) stellen, berechnen
bill-board Anschlagbrett (n), Anschlagtafel (n), schwarzes Brett (n)
billiard-room Billardzimmer (n)
bill of fare Speisekarte (f)
bi-monthly zweimonatlich
bin card Lagerfachkarte (f)
binoculars Fernglas (n)
bird Vogel (m)
birds nest soup Schwalbennestersuppe (f)
birds on skewer with corn pie Vögel am Spieß mit Polenta (pl. m)
birth Geburt (f)
birth certificate Geburtsurkunde (f)
birthplace Geburtsort (m)
biscùit Plätzchen (n)
biscuit in wine sauce Biskuit mit Weinschaum (m)
bisque dicke Suppe (f)
bisque of crayfish Krebsrahmsuppe (f)
bitter bitter
bitter ale helles Ale (n)
bitters Magenbitter (m)
bi-weekly zweiwöchentlich
black bean schwarze Bohne (f)
blackberry Brombeere (f)
black coffee schwarzer Kaffee (m)
black coffee with whipped cream Einspänner (m)
black cock Auerhahn (m), Birkhahn (m)
black currant schwarze Johannisbeere
black grapes blaue Trauben (pl. f)
black grouse Birkhuhn (n)
black market Schwarzmarkt (m), Schleichhandel (m)

187

black pudding Blutwurst (f)
black radish Rettich (m)
blancmange Vanillepudding (m)
blank Formular (n)
blanket Wolldecke (f)
blank ticket Blankofahrschein (m)
blind alley Sackgasse (f)
blind bend unübersichtliche Kurve (f)
bloater Bückling (m)
block sperren
blocked period Sperrfrist (f)
block of flats Appartementhaus (n)
blood poisoning Blutvergiftung (f)
blood transfusion Blutübertragung (f)
blue boiled trout Forelle blau (f)
blue char Bodenrenke (f)
blue collar worker Arbeiter (m)
blue print Blaupause (f), Plan (m)
blue fish Goldmakrele (f)
bluff Steilküste (f)
blunt stumpf
board Verpflegung (f), Beköstigung (f), Pensionspreis (m), Bord (m) (Schiff)
board and lodging Vollpension (f), Kost (f) und Logis (f)
board and lodging voucher Aufenthaltsgutschein (m)
board and residence Vollpension (f)
board a plane sich an Bord eines Flugzeugs (n) begeben
boarding-house Pension (f), Fremdenheim (n)
boarding pass (card) Bordausweis (m), Bordkarte (f), Einsteigekarte (f)

board residence Vollpension (f)
boardwalk Strandpromenade (f)
boat Boot (n), Kahn (m)
boat deck Bootsdeck (n)
boat-hire Bootsverleih (m), Bootsvermietung (f)
boat-house Bootshaus (n)
boating Bootfahren (n)
boating-lake Rudersee (m)
boat-ride Bootsfahrt (f), Kahnfahrt (f)
boat trailer Bootsanhänger (m) (Auto)
boat train Zug (m) mit Schiffsanschluß (m)
boat-trip Bootsfahrt (f), Kahnfahrt (f)
bob Bob (m)
bon run Bobbahn (f)
bobsled Bobschlitten (m)
bobsledding Bobsport (m)
boccie, boccia Boccia (n)
boccie court Boccia-Bahn (f)
boiled gekocht
boiled beef gekochtes Rindfleisch (n)
boiled beef in broth Suppentopf mit Fleischeinlage (m)
boiled chicken Suppenhuhn (n)
boiled eel Aal grün (m)
boiled ham gekochter Schinken (m)
boiled pork with horseradish Suppenfleisch (n) mit Meerrettich (m)
boiled pork with pickled cabbage Krautfleisch (n)
boiled potatoes Salzkartoffeln (pl. f)
boiled rice gekochter Reis (m)
boiled round of beef Tafelspitz (m)
boiled salmon pochierter Salm (m)
boiled smoked bacon Silesian

style Schlesisches Himmelreich (n)
boletus Steinpilz (m)
bolster Keilkissen (n)
bone Knochen (m)
boned rips of beef Rostbraten (m)
bonus Gratifikation (f), Sondervergütung (f)
book buchen, vorbestellen, Buch (n)
book a room in advance ein Zimmer (n) im voraus bestellen
book a table einen Tisch (m) reservieren (Restaurant)
book by telephone telefonisch bestellen
booking Bestellung (f), Buchung (f)
booking charge Buchungsgebühr (f)
booking clerk Schalterbeamter (m)
booking department Buchungsabteilung (f)
booking hall Schalterhalle (f)
booking office Fahrkartenschalter (m), Fahrkartenausgabe (f), Vorverkaufsstelle (f)
booking of seats Platzbestellung (f)
book inventory Buchinventur (f)
bookkeeper Buchhalter (m)
bookkeeping Buchführung (f)
bookkeeping entry Buchung (f), Buchungsposten (m)
bookkeeping error Buchführungsfehler (m), Fehlbuchung (f)
bookkeeping machine Buchungsmaschine (f)
booklet Broschüre (f), Prospekt (m)

booklet of coupons (tickets) Fahrscheinheft (n)
book loss Buchverlust (m)
bookseller Buchhändler (m)
bookshop Buchhandlung (f)
book-stall Zeitschriftenkiosk (m)
book value Buchwert (m)
boom geschäftlicher Aufschwung (m), Hochkonjunktur (f), Boom (m)
boot Stiefel (m), Kofferraum (Auto) (m)
bootblack Schuhputzer (m)
boots Schuhputzer (Hotel) (m)
border Grenze (f), Landesgrenze (f), Pensionsgast (m), Hausgast (m)
border area Grenzgebiet (n)
border crossing Grenzübergang (m), Grenzübertritt (m)
border crossing point Grenzübergangsstelle (f)
border town Grenzstadt (f)
border traffic Grenzverkehr (m)
border zone Grenzzone (f)
borrow leihen, entleihen
borrowed capital Fremdkapital (n)
borrowing Kreditaufnahme (f)
Botanical Garden Botanischer Garten (m)
bottle Flasche (f)
bottled beer Flaschenbier (n)
bottled wine Flaschenwein (m)
bottleneck Engpaß (m)
bottle-opener Flaschenöffner (m)
bottle screw Korkenzieher (m)
bottoms of artichoke Artischokenböden (pl. m)
bottoms up Prost!
boulevard Allee (f)
bound (by contract) verpflich-

189

tet, vertraglich, gebunden
bouquet Blumenstrauß (m)
boutique Boutique (f)
bow Bug (m)
bowl kegeln, Schüssel (f)
bowling Bowling (n), Kegeln (n)
bowling-alley Kegelbahn (f)
box Loge (Theater) (f), Schachtel (f)
box meal Lunchpaket (n), Imbißpaket (n)
box office Kasse (Kino, Theater) (f)
boy Hotelboy (m)
brains Hirn (n)
braised gedünstet, geschmort
braised aitchbone Rinderschwanzstück geschmort (n)
braised beef Schmorbraten (m)
braised beef marinated Sauerbraten (m)
braised filet of beef with onions Zwiebelrostbraten (m)
braised ox-tongue Ochsenzunge gebraten (f)
braised veal cutlet in paprika sauce Paprikaschnitzel (n)
brambleberry Brombeere (f)
branch line Nebenstrecke (f)
branch manager Geschäftsstellenleiter (m)
branch office Nebenstelle (f), Zweigstelle (f), Filiale (f), Geschäftsstelle (f)
brand Marke (f), Sorte (f), Markenname (m)
brandy Weinbrand (m)
brandy-glass Weinbrandglas (n), Cognacschwenker (m)
brawn Eberfleisch (n), Schweinskopfsülze (f)
Brazilian bean-stew brasilianischer Bohnen-Eintopf (m)
Brazil nut Paranuß (f)

breach of contract Vertragsbruch (m)
bread Brot (n)
bread and butter Brot und Butter
bread and butter pudding Brotpudding (m)
bread-basket Brotkorb (m)
bread-crumbed paniert
breaded paniert
breaded veal steak paniertes Kalbsschnitzel (n)
bread-plate kleiner Teller (Brot) (m)
breakage Bruch (m) (Geschirr)
breakdown Unterteilung (f)
breakdown lorry Abschleppwagen (m)
breakdown service Pannenhilfe (f)
break-even chart Gewinnschwellen-Diagramm (n)
break-even point Gewinnschwelle (f), Nutzenschwelle (f)
breakfast Frühstück (n)
breakfast key Türanhänger (m) für die Frühstücksbestellung (f)
breakfast room Frühstückszimmer (n)
breakfast tray Frühstückstablett (n)
break of journey Fahrtunterbrechung (f)
breakwater Wellenbrecher (m)
bream Seebrasse (f)
breast Brust (f)
breast of chicken Geflügelbrust (f)
breast of pork Schweinsbrust (f)
breathing exercises Atemgymnastik (f)
breeze Brise (f)

brewery Brauerei (f)
bribe bestechen, Bestechung (f), Bestechungsgeld (n)
brick of ice-cream Eisschnitte (f)
bridge Brücke (f), Bridge (n)
bridge toll Brückenzoll (m)
bridle-path Reitweg (m)
brief instruieren, informieren
briefcase Aktenmappe (f), Aktentasche (f)
brill Meerbutt (m)
brine bath Solebad (n)
bring out veröffentlichen
bring up-to-date aktualisieren
brisket Brust (f)
brisket of beef Rinderbrust (f)
British Hotels and Restaurants Association Britischer Hotel- und Gaststättenverband (m)
British Travel and Holiday Association Britischer Verband (m) für Reise- und Urlaubswesen
broad bean dicke Bohne (f)
broadcast Rundfunk (m), durch Rundfunk (m) verbreiten
broadcast advertising Rundfunkwerbung (f)
broccoli Brokkoli (pl.), Kohlsprossen (pl. f)
brochure Prospekt (m), Broschüre (f)
broiled gegrillt
broiled potatoes geröstete Kartoffeln (pl. f)
broiler Brathähnchen (n)
brook-trout Bachforelle (f)
broom Besen (m)
broth Bouillon (f)
brother Bruder (m)
brother-in-law Schwager (m)
broth with rice Fleischbrühe (f) mit Reiseinlage (f)
broth with vermicelli Fleischbrühe (f) mit Nudeleinlage (f)

brown beef stew Rindsragout (n)
brown bread dunkles Brot (n), Schwarzbrot (n)
browned gratiniert
browned butter Nußbutter (f)
brown hazel-hen-stew Haselhuhnragout (n)
brown stew Gulasch (n)
brown veal stew Kalbsragout (n)
brunch Brunch (m) (aus breakfast = Frühstück und lunch = Mittagessen)
Brunswick sausage Braunschweiger Wurst (f)
brush Bürste (f)
Brussels sprouts Rosenkohl (m)
bubble-bath Schaumbad (n)
bucket Eimer (m), Eiskübel (m)
buckwheat Buchweizen (m)
buckwheat pancakes Plinsen (pl. f)
budget vorausplanen, Vorausplanung (f), Budget (n), Voranschlag (m), Finanzplan (m)
budgetary control Budgetkontrolle (f), Kontrolle (f) durch Planung (f)
budgeted cost geplante Kosten (pl.)
buffer stock Sicherheitsbestand (m)
buffer time Pufferzeit (f) (Netzplan)
buffet car Büffetwagen (m) (Eisenbahn)
building Gebäude (n)
building cost Bauwert (m)
building lot Bauplatz (m)
building permit Baugenehmigung (f)
building rentals Vermietungen

(pl. f)
building site Bauplatz (m)
built-in check eingebaute Kontrolle (f)
built-in control automatische Kontrolle (f)
built-in cupboard (wardrobe) Einbauschrank (m)
built-up area geschlossene Ortschaft (f)
built-up property bebautes Grundstück (n)
buiscuit Plätzchen (n)
bulb Glühbirne
bulk Masse (f), Hauptteil (m)
bulk purchase Massenkauf (m)
bulky baggage sperriges Gepäck (n)
bulky goods (or freight) Sperrgut (n)
bulletin board Anschlagbrett (n), schwarzes Brett (n)
bull-fight Stierkampf (m)
bull-fighter Stierkämpfer (m)
bun Brötchen (n)
bunch Bündel (n), Strauß (m)
bunch of flowers Blumenstrauß (m)
bungalow Bungalow (m)
bungalow village Bungalowdorf (n)
bunk Koje (Schiff) (f)
burbot Trüsche (f)
burglar Einbrecher (m)
burglary Einbruch (m)
burglary insurance Einbruchsversicherung (f)
Burgundy wine Burgunderwein (m)
burnt angebrannt
burnt butter gebrannte Butter (f)
bus Bus (m), Autobus (m), Omnibus (m)

bus-air service Flug-Bus-Verbindung (f)
bus and coach station Busbahnhof (m), Autobahnhof (m)
bus company Busunternehmen (n)
bus conductor Busschaffner (m)
bus connection Busverbindung (f)
bus driver Busfahrer (m)
bus hire Busvermietung (f)
business Geschäft (n), Betrieb (m), Unternehmung (f)
business car Geschäftswagen (m)
business consultant Betriebsberater (m)
business district Geschäftsviertel (n)
business expense Betriebsausgabe (f)
business friend Geschäftsfreund (m)
business hours Geschäftszeit (f)
business letter Geschäftsbrief (m)
business life Geschäftsleben (n)
businessman Geschäftsmann (m)
business policy Geschäftspolitik (f), Richtlinien (pl. f)
business premises Geschäftsräume (pl. m)
business recession Geschäftsrückgang (m)
business relation Geschäftsverbindung (f)
business suit Straßenanzug (m)
business trip (tour) Geschäftsreise (f)
business volume Geschäftsumfang (m)

bus line Buslinie (f), Busverbindung (f)
bus rental Busvermietung (f)
bus service Busverbindung (f)
bus service Zubringerdienst (Bus) (m)
bus station Busbahnhof (m)
bus stop Bushaltestelle (f)
bus travel Busreisen (pl. f)
bus trailer Busanhänger (m)
bus trip Busreise (f), Busfahrt (f)
busy belebt, belegt (Telefon), beschäftigt
butcher Metzger (m), Fleischer (m)
butcher's shop Metzgerei (f), Fleischerei (f)
butcher test Fleischzerlegungsbericht (m), Fleischtest (m)
butter Butter (f)
buttered in Butter zubereitet
buttered slice of bread Butterbrot (n)
butterfried potatoes Schmelzkartoffeln (pl. f)
butterfried potatoes with onions Bratkartoffeln (pl. f) mit Zwiebeln (pl. f)
butterfried sausage Bratwurst (f)
butterfried trout in Butter gebratene Forelle (f)
buttermilk Buttermilch (f)
butter with fine herbs Kräuterbutter (f)
button Klingelknopf (m)
buy kaufen, einkaufen, erwerben
buyer Käufer (m), Einkäufer (m)
buyer's market Käufermarkt (m)
buying decision Kaufentschluß (m)

buying habits Kaufgewohnheiten (pl. f)
buying power Kaufkraft (f)
by-pass Umgehungsstraße (f)
by-road Nebenstraße (f)
by-street Nebenstraße (f)

C

cab Taxi (n)
cabaret Kabarett (n), Nachtklub (m)
cabbage Kohl (m)
cabbage in wine Weinkraut (n)
cabbage lettuce Kopfsalat (m)
cabbage salad Krautsalat (m)
cabin Kabine (f), Kajüte (f)
cabin cable railway Kabinenseilbahn (f)
cabin cruiser Jacht (f)
cabin luggage Kabinengepäck (n)
cable kabeln, telegrafieren, Kabel (n), Telegramm (n)
cable car Gondel (f), Kabine (f)
cable railway Seilbahn (f)
cab stand Taxistand (m)
Caerphilly cheese Caerphilly-Käse (m)
café Imbißstube (f), Café (n), Gasthaus (n)
cafeteria Selbstbedienungsrestaurant (n), Snackbar (f)
cake Kuchen (m)
calculate rechnen, berechnen, kalkulieren
calculating machine Rechenmaschine (f)
calculation Rechnung (f), Berechnung (f), Kalkulation (f)
calculation of an economic order

193

quantity Berechnung der wirtschaftlichen Bestellmenge (f)
calculator Rechenmaschine (f), Taschenrechner (m)
calender of cases Terminkalender (m)
calf (veal) Kalb (n)
calf's brains Kalbshirn (n)
calf's brains fried Kalbshirn (n) gebacken
calf's brain soup Hirnsuppe (f)
calf's breast Kalbsbrust (f)
calf's feet Kalbsfüße (pl. m)
calfs' gristle Kalbsbrustknorpel (m)
calf's head Kalbskopf (m)
calf's head fried Kalbskopf (m) gebacken
calf's head vinaigrette Kalbskopf (m) in Essigsoße (f)
calf's head with turtle sauce Kalbskopf „en tortue" (m)
calf's heart Kalbsherz (n)
calf's knuckle Kalbshaxe (f)
calf's lights Kalbslunge (f)
calf's liver Kalbsleber (f)
calf's liver fried Kalbsleber gebacken (f)
calf's liver on skewers Kalbsleberspießchen (n)
calfs' liver roasted Kalbsleber (f) geröstet
calf's sweetbread baked Kalbsbries gebacken (n)
calf's tongue Kalbszunge (f)
call Abruf (m), Anruf (m), Vertreterbesuch (m), wecken
call at anlaufen (Seefahrt)
call-box Telefonzelle (f), Fernsprechzelle (f)
camera Kamera (f)
camomile Kamille (f)
camomile tea Kamillentee (m)
camp Lager (n), campen, zelten
campaign Werbekampagne (f), Aktion (f)
camp out Feldbett (n)
camper Camper (m), Campingtourist (m)
camp fire Lagerfeuer (n)
camping Camping (n), Campingtourismus (m)
Camping and caravaning Zelt- und Wohnwagenwesen (n)
camping equipment Campingausrüstung (f)
camping-ground Campingplatz (m), Zeltplatz (m)
camping permit Campingausweis (m)
camping-site offering full facilities eingerichteter Campingplatz (m)
can Konservenbüche (f)
canapé geröstete Brotschnitte (f) garniert
cancel stornieren, streichen, abbestellen
cancellation Abbestellung (f), Storno (m), Streichung (f)
cancellation fee Stornierungsgebühr (f), Anullierungsgebühr (f)
candied lemon peel Zitronat (n)
candied orange peel Orangeat (n)
candle light Kerzenlicht (n)
candlestick Kerzenständer (m)
candy Süßigkeiten (pl. f)
canned in Konservenbüchse (f)
canned bee Dosenbier (n)
canneloni Canneloni (pl.)
canoe Kanu (n), Paddelboot (n)
cantaloupe Zuckermelone (f)
canvas Segeltuch (n)
capability Fähigkeit (f), Taug-

lichkeit (f)
capable fähig, tauglich, in der Lage (f)
capable of contracting geschäftsfähig
capacity Kapazität (f), Fähigkeit (f), Leistungsvermögen (n)
capacity cost Kapazitätskosten (pl.)
capacity increase Betriebserweiterung (f), Kapazitätsausweitung (f)
capacity of accommodation Aufnahmekapazität (f)
caper Kaper (f)
caper sauce Kapernsauce (f)
capital Kapital (n), Betriebskapital (n), Hauptstadt (f)
capital assets Anlagevermögen (n)
capital demand Kapitalbedarf (m)
capital expenditure budgeting Investitionsrechnung (f)
capital requirements Kapitalbedarf (m)
capital turnover Kapitalumschlag (m)
capon Kapaun (m)
captain Schiffskapitän (m), Flugkapitän (m)
captain (waiter) Stationsoberkellner (m)
car Wagen (m), Auto (n)
carafe Karaffe (f)
carafe wine Schoppenwein (m)
caramel custard Karamelpudding (m)
caramel pudding Karamelpudding (m)
caravan Wohnwagen (m)
caravaner Wohnwagentourist (m)
caravan trailer Wohnwagenanhänger (m)
car-carrier train Autoreisezug (m)
care Betreuung (f), Sorgfalt (f)
careaway-seed Kümmel (m)
career Karriere (f), Laufbahn (f)
careful sorgfältig
careless fahrlässig
carelessness Fahrlässigkeit (f)
care of (c/o) per Adresse (f), bei
care fare Fahrtkosten (pl.)
car ferry Autofähre (f)
cargo Ladung (f), Schiffsladung (f), Fracht (f), Seefracht (f)
cargo aircraft Frachtflugzeug (n)
cargo book Frachtbuch (n)
cargo consignment Frachtsendung (f)
cargo office air Luftfrachtbüro (n)
car hire service Autoverleih (m), Leihwagendienst (m)
car key Autoschlüssel (m)
carload Waggonladung (f)
carload freight Waggonfracht (f)
car-loading Autoverladung (f)
carload rate Waggonfrachtrate (f)
carnival fritter Faschingskrapfen (m)
carnival season Karnevalszeit (f), Faschingszeit (f)
carp Karpfen (m)
car park Parkplatz (m)
carpet Teppich (m)
car rental service Autoverleih (m)
carriage Beförderung (f), Transport (m), Fracht (f), Wagen (m)
carriage door Wagentür (f)

195

carriage rates Transporttarif (m)
carriageway Fahrbahn (f)
car ride Autofahrt (f)
carrier Frachtführer (m), Spediteur (m), Transportunternehmen (n)
carriers Verkehrsgewerbe (n)
carrier's receipt Ladeschein (m)
carrot Karotte (f)
carry forward vortragen (Buchhaltung)
car-sleeper train Autoreisezug (m) (Schlagwagen)
cartage Rollgeld (n), Fuhrlohn (m)
car-tow Abschleppdienst (m)
car traffic Autoverkehr (m)
carve tranchieren, zerschneiden
case Koffer (m), Kiste (f)
cash kassieren, einlösen, bar, Bargeld (n), flüssige Mittel (pl. n)
cash audit Kassenprüfung (f)
cash balance Kassenbestand (m)
cash box Geldkassette (f)
cash flow betrieblicher Geldumlauf (m), Bargeldstrom (m)
cashier Kassierer (m)
cash on delivery (c.o.d.) Nachnahme (f)
cash payment Barzahlung (f)
cash purchase Bareinkauf (m)
cash sale Barverkauf (m)
cash short Kassenfehlbestand (m)
cash value Barwert (m)
casserole Tiegel (m), schmoren
cast anchor den Anker (m) werfen
castle Burg (f), Schloß (n)
castle ruins Schloßruine (f), Burgruine (f)

casualty department Unfallstation (f)
casual worker Gelegenheitsarbeiter (m)
catch Fang (m), fangen
catchup Ketchup (m)
category Klasse (f), Kategorie (f)
cater for versorgen, bewirten
catering Verpflegung (f)
catering arrangements Magenfahrplan (Luftfahrt) (m)
catering business Gastgewerbe (n)
catering industry Catering-Industrie (f)
catering trade Gastgewerbe (n), Gaststättengewerbe (n)
cathedral Dom (n), Kathedrale (f)
cattle Rindvieh (n), Vieh (n)
cauliflower Blumenkohl (m)
cauliflower browned Blumenkohl gratiniert (m)
cauliflower salad Blumenkohlsalat (m)
cauliflower soup Karfiolsuppe (f), Blumenkohlsuppe (f)
cause veranlassen, verursachen, Anspruch (m), Grund (m)
caution Vorsicht!
cautious vorsichtig
cave Höhle (f)
caviar Kaviar (m)
caviar sandwich Kaviarbrötchen (n)
Cayenne pepper Cayennepfeffer (m)
cease aufhören
ceiling Zimmerdecke (f)
celebrate feiern
celeriac Knollensellerie (m)
celery Sellerie (m)
celery salad Selleriesalat (m)
celery sticks Stangensellerie (m)

cellar Keller (m), Weinkeller (m)
cemetery Friedhof (m)
cenotaph Ehrenmal (n)
center Zentrum (n), Schwerpunkt (m)
central buying zentraler Einkauf (m)
central heating Zentralheizung (f)
Central Office of German Travel Deutsche Zentrale (f) für Fremdenverkehr (m)
central processing unit (CPU) Zentraleinheit (f)
central station Hauptbahnhof (m)
cep Steinpilz (m)
cereals Getreide (n), Getreideflocken (pl. f)
certificate Bescheinigung (f), Zeugnis (n)
certificate of antirabic vaccination Tollwutimpfzeugnis (n)
certificate of conduct Führungszeugnis (n)
certificate of vaccination Impfzeugnis (n)
certified check durch Bank (f) bestätigter Scheck (m)
chain Kette (f), Filialbetrieb (m)
chair Stuhl (m)
chairlift Sessellift (m)
chairman of the board Aufsichtsratvorsitzender (m)
challenge herausfordern; Herausforderung (f)
chamber-maid Zimmermädchen (n)
chamber-pot Nachttopf (m)
chamois Gemse (f)
champagne Sekt (m), Champagner (m)
chance guest Durchreisender (m), Passant (m), Übernachtungsgast (m)
change Kleingeld (n), Wechselgeld (n), Wechsel (m), wechseln, ändern, tauschen
change-giving machine Geldwechselautomat (m)
change in stocks Bestandsveränderung (f)
change in the program Programmänderung (f)
change in value of currency Geldwertänderung (f)
change of carriage Umsteigen (n)
change of route Änderung (f) des Reiseweges (m), Streckenänderung (f)
change reservations umbuchen
changing a wheel Reifenwechsel (m)
changing room Umkleideraum (m)
chanterelle Pfifferling (m)
chapel Kapelle (f)
char Saibling (m)
charcoal Holzkohle (m)
charcoal broiled vom Holzkohlenfeuer (n)
charcoal broiled mixed grill Fleisch (n) vom Holzkohlengrill (m)
chard Mangold (m)
charge belasten, Berechnung (f), Spesen (pl.)
charge for bed and breakfast Zimmerpreis (m) mit Frühstück (n)
charge for handling Bearbeitungsgebühr (f)
charge for service Bedienungszuschlag (m), Bedienungsgeld (n)
charge per piece of baggage Gepäckgebühr (f) je Stück (n)

charges Kosten (pl.)
chart grafisch darstellen, Tabelle (f), Diagramm (n)
charter chartern
charter aircraft Chartermaschine (f)
charter flight Charterflug (m)
charter money Schiffsmiete (f)
chart of accounts Kontenplan (m)
Chateaubriand Filetsteak (n), Chateaubriand
cheap billig
cheap ticket ermäßigte Fahrkarte (f)
check (amerik.) Scheck (m)
checkbook Scheckbuch (n)
checked baggage aufgegebenes Gepäck (n)
check-in sich anmelden (Hotel)
check-in Abfertigung (Flug) (f)
check-in baggage Gepäck (n) aufgeben
check-in formality Abfertigungsformalität (f)
checking of baggage Gepäckabfertigung (f)
checking of the hotels Überprüfung (f) der Hotels (pl. n)
check-in time Meldeschluß (Luftfahrt) (m)
check list Kontroll-Liste (f), Prüfliste (f), Checkliste (f)
check-out sich abmelden, abreisen (Hotel), Abfertigung (f)
checkroom Garderobe (f), Gepäckaufbewahrung (f), Aufbewahrungsstelle (f)
checkroom girl Garderobenfrau (f)
Cheddar cheese Cheddarkäse (m)
cheerio Prosit!
cheers Zum Wohl! Prosit!

cheese Käse (m)
cheese- and ham stuffed veal steak gefülltes Kalbsschnitzel (n), Cordon bleu (n)
cheese cake Käsekuchen (m)
cheese fondue Käsefondue (n)
cheese pie Käsekuchen (m)
cheese sandwich Käsebrot (n)
cheese soufflé Käseauflauf (m)
cheese spread Schmelzkäse (m)
cheese tartlet Käsetörtchen (n)
chef Küchenchef (m), Chefkoch (m)
chef de partie Abteilungskoch (m)
chemist's shop Apotheke (f)
chequé (brit.) Scheck (m)
cheque book Scheckbuch (n), Scheckheft (n)
cherry Kirsche (f)
cherry brandy Kirschlikör (m)
cherry cake Kirschkuchen (m)
cherry tart Kirschtorte (f)
chervil Kerbel (m)
Cheshire cheese Chesterkäse (m)
chestnut Edelkastanie (f)
chestnut-vermicelli Kastanienpüree (n)
chest of drawers Kommode (f)
chew kauen
chicken Huhn (n)
chicken á la King Geflügelrahmragout (n)
chicken breast Hühnerbrust (f)
chicken curry indisches Geflügelgericht (n)
chicken, fried Backhuhn (n)
chicken in broth Suppentopf mit Geflügeleinlage (m)
chicken in jelly Huhn in Aspik (n)
chicken leg Hühnerkeule (f)
chicken liver Geflügelleber (f)
chicken noodle soup Geflügel-

suppentopf (m)
chicken pie warme Geflügelpastete (f)
chicken rice Geflügelreis (m)
chicken, roast Brathuhn (n)
chicken salad Geflügelsalat (m)
chicken stew Huhn in Tomatensauce mit Pilzen und Eiern (n)
chicken winglet Flügelspitze vom Huhn (f)
chicken wing Flügelspitze vom Huhn (f)
chick-pea Kichererbse (f)
chicory Zichorie (Salat) (f)
chief accountant Hauptbuchhalter (m), Buchhaltungsleiter (m)
chief conductor Zugführer (m)
chief engineer Technischer Leiter (m)
chief steward Chefsteward (m)
child care Kinderbetreuung (f)
children's dining-room Kinderspeisesaal (m)
children's menu Speisekarte (f) für Kinder (pl. n)
children's playground Kinderspielplatz (m)
children's playroom Kinderspielzimmer (n)
children's pool Kinderbecken (n)
child's bed Kinderbett (n)
child's ticket Kinderfahrkarte (f)
childs's travel document Kinderausweis (m)
chili con carne Hackfleisch (n) mit braunen Bohnen (pl. f)
chill kühlen
chilled grapefruit Grapefruit (f) eisgekühlt
chilled melon geeiste Melone (f)

chilled vegetable soup gekühlte Gemüsesuppe (f)
chilly kühl, frostig
chimney Kamin (m)
china Porzellan (n)
china and glassware Porzellan- und Glaswaren (pl. f)
chinese cabbage Chinakohl (m)
chipped veal geschnetzeltes Kalbfleisch (n)
chip Chip (Elektronik) (m)
chips Pommes frites (pl. f)
chives Schnittlauch (n)
chocolate Schokolade (f)
chocolate cake Schokoladentorte (f)
chocolate cake Sacher style Sachertorte (f)
chocolate ice-cream Schokoladeeis (n)
chocolate-meringue Schokoladebaiser (n)
chocolate pudding Schokoladenpudding (m)
chocolates Pralinen (pl. f)
choice Auswahl (f)
chop Kotelett (ohne Knochen) (n)
chopped gehackt
chopped veal cutlet Hackfleischkotelett vom Kalb (n)
chopping board Hackbrett (n)
chopping knife Hackmesser (n)
chopper Hackmesser (n)
chowder dicke Suppe (f)
Christian name Vorname (m)
Christmas Weihnachten (n)
Christmas bonus Weihnachtsgratifikation (f)
Christmas holidays (vacation) Weihnachtsferien (pl.)
Christmas period Weihnachtszeit (f)
Christmas pudding Weihnachts-

199

pudding (m)
church concert Kirchenkonzert (n)
church tax Kirchensteuer (f)
churchyard Friedhof (m)
cider Apfelwein (m)
cigar Zigarre (f)
cigarette Zigarette (f)
cigarette lighter Feuerzeug (n)
cinema program Kinoprogramm (n), Filmprogramm (n)
cinema ticket Kinokarte (f)
cinnamon Zimt (m)
circle railway Ringbahn (f)
circle trip Rundreise (f)
circle trip ticket Rundreisefahrschein (m)
circular Rundschreiben (n)
circular road Ringstraße (f)
circular tour Rundfahrt (f), Rundreise (f)
circular tour of port Hafenrundfahrt (f)
circular trip Rundreise (f)
circulation Umlauf (m)
circumstances beyond control unabwendbarer Zufall (m)
circus-ring Arena (f)
citadel Zitadelle (f)
citizen Bürger (m), Staatsangehöriger (m)
citizenship Staatsbürgerschaft (f)
city Stadt (f), Innenstadt (f)
city-airport transfer Zubringerdienst (m)
city hall Rathaus (n)
city railway Stadtbahn (f)
city sightseeing flight Stadtrundflug (m)
city sightseeing tour Stadtrundfahrt (f)
city zone Stadtgebiet (n)
clam Venusmuschel (f)
clam broth Muschelsuppe (f)

clam chowder Muschelsuppe (f)
claim fordern, beanspruchen, Anspruch (m), Forderung (f)
claim for damages Schadenersatzanspruch (m)
claret Bordeauxwein (m)
claret-cup Bowle (f)
classification Klassifizierung (f), Einstufung (f)
classification of accounts Kontenplan (m)
classification of hotels Hoteleinstufung (f), Hotelklassifizierung (f)
classified telephone directory Branchentelefonbuch (n)
classify klassifizieren, einstufen, kontieren
clause Klausel (f), Vertragsbestimmung (f)
clean reinigen, rein, sauber
cleaning Reinigung (f), Säuberung (f)
cleaning personnel Reinigungspersonal (n)
cleaning supplies Reinigungsmittel (pl. n)
cleanse reinigen
clean-up aufräumen
clear klären, verzollen, räumen
clearance Verzollung (f), Räumung (f)
clearance charges Zollabfertigungsgebühren (pl. f)
clear away abräumen, wegräumen
clearing Verzollung (f) einer Schiffsladung (f)
clearing account Verrechnungskonto (n)
clearing office Abrechnungsstelle (f)
clear mock turtle soup falsche Schildkrötensuppe (f)
clear oxtail soup klare Ochsen-

schwanzsuppe (f)
clear port auslaufen (Schiffahrt)
clear soup Bouillon (f), Kraftbrühe (f)
clear soup royal klare Suppe (f) mit Eierstich (m)
clear soup with beaten egg Einlaufsuppe (f)
clear soup with vegetables klare Gemüsesuppe (f)
clear turtle soup klare Schildkrötensuppe (f)
clear up aufklären (Wetter)
clerk Büroangestellter (m)
climate Klima (n)
climatic conditions Klimaverhältnisse (pl. n)
climatic health resort Luftkurort (m), Klimakurort (m)
climatological station Klimastation (f)
climbing boot Bergschuh (m)
climbing equipment Bergausrüstung (f), Kletterausrüstung (f)
climbing tour Klettertour (f)
clinic Klinik (f)
clipper Atlantikflugboot (n)
cloakroom Garderobe (f)
cloakroom attendant Garderobenfrau (f)
cloakroom ticket Garderobenmarke (f)
clock Uhr (f)
close control genaue (scharfe) Kontrolle (f)
closed abgeschlossen
closed season Schonzeit (f)
closing Abschluß (m)
closing hour Geschäfts- oder Betriebsschluß (m)
closing inventory (Waren) Endbestand (m)
closing of an account Kontoabschluß (m)
closing time Sperrstunde (f)
cloth Tuch (n)
clothes-brush Kleiderbürste (f)
clothes-hanger Kleiderbügel (m)
clothing Kleidung (f)
cloud Wolke (f)
cloudy bewölkt, wolkig
cloves Gewürznelke (f)
club Verein (m)
club evening Klubabend (m)
clubhouse Klubhaus (n)
club membership Vereinsmitgliedschaft (f)
club-table Couchtisch (m)
coach Bus (m), Omnibus (m), Trainer (m), trainieren
coach-air service Flug-Bus-Verbindung (f)
coach conductor Busschaffner (m)
coach connection Busverbindung (f)
coach driver Busfahrer (m)
coach line Buslinie (f), Busverbindung (f)
coach stop Bushaltestelle (f)
coach travel Busreisen (pl. f)
coal fish Seehecht (m)
coast Küste (f)
coastal area Küstengebiet (n)
coastal cruise Küstenkreuzfahrt (f)
coastal road Küstenstraße (f), Uferstraße (f)
coastal shipping Küstenschiffahrt (f)
coasting slide Rodelhang (m)
coat-hanger Kleiderbügel (m)
coat-rack Kleiderständer (m)
cock Hahn (m)
cock-a-leekie Hähnchen (n) oder Suppenhuhn (n) und Lauch (m)

201

cockles Pilgermuscheln (pl. f)
cockpit Kanzel (f) (Flugzeug)
cocktail Cocktail (m)
cocktail bar tender Barkellner (m)
cocktail reception Cocktailempfang (m)
cocktail savory Vorspeise (f)
cocoa Kakao (m)
coconut Kokosnuß (f)
cod Dorsch (m)
code number Schlüsselzahl (f), Kodenummer (f)
cod fish Dorsch (m)
coffee Kaffee (m)
coffee break Kaffeepause (f)
coffee cup Kaffeetasse (f)
coffee ice-cream Eiskaffee (m)
coffee-mill Kaffeemühle (f)
coffee-pot Kaffeekanne (f)
coffee with cream Kaffee mit Sahne (m)
coffee with hot milk Milchkaffee (m)
coffee without caffeine Koffeinfreier Kaffee (m)
coin Münze (f)
cold kalt
cold beef in vinegar Rindfleisch (n) in Essig (m) und Öl (n)
cold buffet kaltes Büffet (n)
cold cuts kalter Aufschnitt (m)
cold cuts on plate Aufschnitt-Teller (m)
cold dishes kalte Speisen (pl. f)
cold fowl Geflügel kalt (n)
cold game pie Wildpastete (f)
cold meat kalter Aufschnitt (m)
cold punch Bowle (f)
cold semolina pudding kalter Grießpudding (m)
cold side dishes kalte Vorspeisen (pl. f)
cold-storage Kühlhaus (n), Kühlhauslagerung (f)

coldstore im Kühlhaus (n) lagern
cole slaw Krautsalat (m)
collar Kragen (m)
collared beef Roulade (f)
collared herring Rollmops (m)
collect sammeln
collection Eintreibung (f), Einzug (m), Inkasso (n)
collection account Sammelkonto (n)
collection of luggage Gepäckabholung (f)
collective agreement Tarifvertrag (m)
collective passport Sammelpaß (m)
collision Zusammenstoß (m)
collop Schnitzel (n)
colony Kolonie (f)
colour print Farbabzug (m) (Foto)
column Spalte (f)
comb Kamm (m)
combination sale Kopplungsverkauf (m)
comfort Bequemlichkeit (f)
comfortable bequem
comfortstation öffentliche Toilette (f)
commercial airport Zivilflughafen (m)
commercial travel(l)er Handelsreisender (m)
commissary store Kantine (mit großem Warenangebot) (f)
commission Provision (f), Vermittlungsgebühr (f), Auftrag (m), beauftragen
commission account Provisionskonto (n)
commissionaire Pförtner (m)
committee Ausschuß (m), Gremium (n)
commodity Ware (f), Artikel (m)

commodity rate Vorzugsfrachtrate (Luftverkehr) (f)
communal bath room Gemeinschaftsbadezimmer (n)
communal canteen Gemeinschaftsküche (f)
communal feeding Gemeinschaftsverpflegung (f)
communal kitchen Gemeinschaftsküche (f)
communal provisions Gemeinschaftsverpflegung (f)
communication Mitteilung (f), Nachricht (f), Verkehrsverbindung (f)
communication cord Notbremse (f)
community Gemeinde (f), Gemeinschaft (f)
community tax Gemeindesteuer (f)
commutation ticket Zeitkarte (f), Dauerkarte (f)
company Unternehmen (n), Betrieb (n), Gesellschaft (f)
company seniority Betriebszugehörigkeit (f), Dienstalter (n) im Betrieb (m)
compartment Abteil (n)
compartment for ramblers Touristenabteil (n)
compensate entschädigen, ersetzen, vergüten
compensation Ersatz (m), Entschädigung (f), Vergütung (f)
compensation for damages Schadenersatz (m)
compete konkurrieren, im Wettbewerb stehen (m)
competition Konkurrenz (f), Wettbewerb (m)
competitive market Wettbewerbsmarkt (m)
competitor Konkurrent (m), Wettbewerber (m)

compile sammeln, zusammenstellen
complain reklamieren, bemängeln, sich beschweren
complaint Beschwerde (f), Reklamation (f), Klage (f)
complaints book Beschwerdebuch (n)
complete breakfast komplettes Frühstück (n)
complimentary kostenlos
complimentary room Gratiszimmer (n) Zimmer (n) ohne Berechnung (f)
complimentary ticket Freifahrkarte (f)
comptroller Controller (m)
computer Computer (m)
computerize Elektronische Datenverarbeitung (f)
concern Unternehmung (f), Angelegenheit (f), Geschäft (n)
concert-hall Konzertsaal (m)
concierge Portier (m), Concierge (m, n)
condensed milk Kondensmilch (f)
condition bedingen, Bedingung (f)
condition of conveyance Beförderungsbedingung (f)
condition of participation Teilnahmebedingung (f)
conducted tour Gesellschaftsreise (f)
conductor Schaffner (m), Zugbegleiter (m)
confectioner Konditor (m)
confections Konfekt (n)
conference Sitzung (f), Konferenz (f), Besprechung (f)
conference hall Sitzungssaal (m)
conference room Konferenz-

203

raum (m), Sitzungsraum (m)
confidential vertraulich
confirm bestätigen
confirmation Bestätigung (f), Zusage (f)
conger-eel Meeraal (m)
congress Kongress (m)
conress hall Kongreßhalle (f)
congress information service Kongreßberatung (f)
connecting flight Flugverbindung (f), Anschlußflug (m)
connecting line (or route) Anschlußstrecke (f)
connecting point Umsteigepunkt (m)
connecting rooms ineinandergehende Zimmer (pl. n)
connecting station Umsteigebahnhof (m)
connecting train Anschlußzug (m)
connection Anschluß (m), Verbindung (f), Anschlußfahrt (f)
connector Stecker (m)
consecutive number fortlaufende Nummer (f)
consignment note Frachtbrief (m)
consignment note Gepäckschein (m)
consist of bestehen aus
consolidated balance sheet konsolidierte Bilanz (f), Konzernbilanz (f)
constable Polizist (m)
construction Bau (m), Auslegung (f)
construction site Baustelle (f)
consulate Konsulat (n)
consultant Berater (m)
consume verbrauchen, konsumieren
consumer Verbraucher (m), Konsument (m)

consumption Verbrauch (m), Konsum (m), Verzehr (m)
contagious disease ansteckende Krankheit (f)
container Behälter (m)
content zufrieden
continental breakfast einfaches Frühstück (n)
contingencies unvorhergesehene Aufgaben (pl. f)
continuation of one's journey Weiterfahrt (f)
contract vereinbaren, Vertrag (m), Vereinbarung (f)
contract of accommodation Beherbergungsvertrag (m), Gastaufnahmevertrag (m), Übernachtungsvertrag (m)
contract of apprenticeship Ausbildungsvertrag (m), Lehrvertrag (m)
contract of carriage Transportvertrag (m)
contract of employment Arbeitsvertrag (m)
contract of passage Passagevertrag (m)
contract of sale Kaufvertrag (m)
contractual vertraglich
contrast bath Wechselbad (n)
contribution margin Deckungsbeitrag (m)
contribution margin ratio Deckungsbeitragsfaktor (m) vom Umsatz (m) (DBU-Faktor)
control kontrollieren, überwachen, steuern, regeln, Kontrolle (f), Leitung (f)
controllable cost beeinflußbare Kosten (pl.)
controller Controller (m)
control of expenses Ausgabenkontrolle (f), Spesenkontrolle (f)

control system Steuerungs- und Überwachungssystem (n)
control tower Kontrollturm (m)
convalescence Erholung (f), Rekonvaleszenz (f)
convalescent home Erholungsheim (n)
convalescent leave Erholungsurlaub (m)
convalescent trip Erholungsreise (f)
convenience foods Fertiggerichtesysteme, (pl. n)
conventional landesüblich
convert umrechnen, umwandeln, konvertieren
convertible currency konvertierbare Währung (f)
conversion table Umrechnungstabelle (f)
conveyance Beförderung (f), Beförderungsmittel (n)
conveyance of cars Autobeförderung (f)
conveyance of luggage Gepäckbeförderung (f)
conveyer belt Förderband (n)
cook Koch (m), kochen
cooked gekocht
cokked in butter in Butter
cookie kleines Gebäck (n)
cookie sheet Backblech (n)
cooking Kochen (n), Kochkunst (f)
cooking-facilities Kochgelegenheit (f)
cooking-pot Kochtopf (m)
cooking stove Kochstelle (f)
cooking utensils Kochgeschirr (n)
cook's assistant Küchengehilfe (m)
cook-shop Garküche (f)
cooky kleines Gebäck (n)
cool kühl

cooling-water Kühlwasser (n)
cooperation Kooperation (f), Mitarbeit (f)
cooperative advertising Gemeinschaftswerbung (f)
coot Wasserhuhn (n)
co-pilot Kopilot (m)
coppers Kleingeld (n)
cork Kork (m)
corkscrew Korkenzieher (m)
corky taste Korkgeschmack (m)
corn Mais (m)
corn-cob Maiskolben (m)
corned beef Pökelfleisch (n)
corner seat Eckplatz (m)
cornflakes Maisflocken (pl. f), Cornflakes (pl.)
corn flour Maismehl (n)
Corpus Christi Fronleichnam
correct richtig, berichtigen, verbessern
correspondence Briefwechsel (m)
corridor Korridor (m), Gang (m)
cosiness Behaglichkeit (f), Gemütlichkeit (f)
cosmetics Kosmetikartikel (pl. m)
cosmetic therapy Schönheitskur (f)
cost Kosten (pl.)
cost accounting Kostenrechnung (f), Kostenträgerrechnung (f)
cost analysis Kostenanalyse (f)
cost centre Kostenstelle (f)
cost comparison Kostenvergleich (m)
cost control Kostenkontrolle (f)
cost estimate Vorkalkulation (f)
cost increase Kostenzuwachs (m), Kostenerhöhung (f)
cost of beverage sold Wareneinsatz (m) bei Getränken (pl. n)

205

cost of board and lodging Aufenthaltskosten (pl. f)
cost of food sold Wareneinsatz (m) bei Speisen (pl. f)
cost of goods sold Kosten (pl.) der verkauften Erzeugnisse (pl. n)
cost of living Lebenshaltungskosten (pl.)
cost of sales Wareneinsatz (m)
cost per order Kosten pro Bestellung (f)
cost-price Selbstkostenpreis (m)
cost reduction Kostensenkung (f)
cost saving Kosteneinsparung (f)
cost-volume-profit-analysis Deckungsbeitragsrechnung (f)
cosy behaglich, gemütlich
cot Kinderbett (n)
cottage Ferienhaus (n), Landhaus (n)
cottage cheese Hüttenkäse (m)
cotton wool Watte (f)
couch Couch (f), Liege (f)
couchette Liegeplatz (m)
couchette charge Liegeplatzgebühr (f)
cough Husten (m)
count zählen
counter Ladentisch (m), Theke (f)
country Land (n), Staat (m)
country air Landluft (f)
country ham Landschinken (m)
country house Landhaus (n)
country in development Entwicklungsland (n)
country inn Dorfgasthaus (n), Landgasthof (m)
country lane Feldweg (m)
country of destination Bestimmungsland (n), Zielland (n)

country of origin Ursprungsland (n)
country pub Dorfschenke (f)
country road Landstraße (f)
coupe (Eis-)becher (m)
couple Eheleute (pl.)
coupon Gutschein (m), Abschnitt (m), Bon (m)
courier Reiseleiter (m)
courier's office Reiseleitung (f)
course Kurs (m), Strecke (f), Gang (Essen) (m)
course of a journey Reiseverlauf (m)
course for beginners Anfängerkurs (m)
course of treatment Kur (f)
course of treatment at a spa Heilbadekur (f), Bäderkur (n), Badekur (f)
court Hof (m)
courtesy Höflichkeit (f)
courtyard Hof (m)
cove for bathing Badebucht (f)
cover Gedeck (n), Couvert (n)
cover charge Gedeckpreis (m), trockenes Gedeck (n)
covered apple pie Apfelstrudel (m)
covered-court tennis Hallentennis (n)
covering letter Begleitbrief (m)
CP (continental plan) Zimmer (n) mit Frühstück
crab Krabbe (f)
crabmeat Krabbenfleisch (n)
cracker dünner Keks (m)
craftsman Handwerker (m)
cranberry Preiselbeere (f)
crash landing Bruchlandung (f)
crawfish, crayfish Krebs (m)
crayfish cream soup Krebsrahmsuppe (f)
crayfish salad Krebsschwanzsalat (m)

crayfish soup Krebssuppe (f)
cream Rahm (m), Sahne (f)
cream cheese Rahmkäse (m), Weichkäse (m), Schmelzkäse (m)
cream cheese tart Rahmkäsetorte (f)
creamed potatoes Kartoffelbrei (m)
creamed veal collop Rahmschnitzel (n)
cream of asparagus Spargelcremesuppe (f)
cream of cauliflower Blumenkohlcremesuppe (f)
cream of chicken Königinsuppe (f)
cream of green pea soup grüne Erbsensuppe (f)
cream of mushroom Pilzcremesuppe (f)
cream of tomato Tomatencremesuppe (f)
cream of vegetable Gemüsecremesuppe (f)
cream of wheat Weizengrießbrei (m)
cream puff Windbeutel (m)
cream sauce Rahmsauce (f)
cream silice Cremeschnitte (f)
cream soup Rahmsuppe (f)
creativeness Kreativität (f)
credit gutschreiben, kreditieren, Gutschrift (f)
credit balance Habensaldo (m)
credit card Kreditkarte (f), Gutschriftskarte (f)
credit control Kreditüberwachung (f)
credit limit Kreditgrenze (f)
credit note Gutschriftsanzeige (f)
credit purchase Kreditkauf (m)
creole sauce Tomatensoße (spanisch) (f)
crescent Gipfel (m), (Gebäck) (n)
cress Kresse (f)
crevasse Gletscherspalte (f)
crew Besatzung (f), Bordpersonal (n)
crib Kinderbett (n)
cricket match Kricketspiel (n)
crisp knusprig
crisscross journey Kreuzundquerfahrt (f)
critical path kritischer Weg (m)
Critical Path Method Netzplantechnik (Methode des kritischen Weges) (f)
crockery Eßgeschirr (n)
crop Ernte (f)
croquettes Kroketten (pl. f)
croquettes of fowl Geflügelkroketten (pl. f)
croquette potatoes Kartoffelkroketten (pl. f)
cross-country drive Geländefahrt (f)
cross-country skiing Skilanglauf (m)
crossing Straßenkreuzung (f), Überfahrt (f)
crossing time Überfahrtsdauer (f)
cross-roads Straßenkreuzung (f)
cross the frontier die Grenze (f) überschreiten
crowded überfüllt
cruet-stand Essig- und Ölständer (m)
cruise Schiffsreise (f), Seereise (f), Kreuzfahrt (f), Vergnügungsfahrt (f)
cruising speed Reisegeschwindigkeit (f)
crustaceans Krustentiere (pl. n)
cucumber Gurke (f)
cucumber salad Gurkensalat (m)

207

cuisine Küche (f), Kochkunst (f)
cul-de-sac Sackgasse (f)
culinary delights kulinarische Genüsse (pl. m)
cultural centre Kulturzentrum (n)
cup Tasse (f)
cupboard Schrank (m)
cup custard Karamelpudding (m)
curative climate Heilklima (n)
curative factor Heilfaktor (m)
curative-mud Heilmoor (n), Heilschlamm (m)
curative power Heilkraft (f)
curd cheese Quark (m)
curdle gerinnen
curds and whey Dickmilch (f)
cure Kurbehandlung (f), Heilung (f)
cure at a spa Bäderkur (f), Badekur (f)
curler Lockenwickler (m)
curling Curling (n)
currant Johannisbeere (f), Korinthe (f)
currency Währung (f)
currency allowance Devisenfreigrenze (f)
currency control Devisenkontrolle (f), Devisenbewirtschaftung (f)
currency conversion Geldwechsel (m)
currency devaluation Geldabwertung (f)
currency regulations Devisenbestimmungen (pl. f), Devisenvorschriften (pl. f)
currency restrictions Devisenbewirtschaftung (f)
current account Kontokorrent (n)
current assets Umlaufvermögen (n)

current rate Tageskurs (m)
curriculum vitae Lebenslauf (m)
curried chickencream soup Geflügelrahmsuppe mit Curry (f), Mulligatawny-Suppe (f)
curry Curry (m)
curry powder Currypulver (n)
cursor Schreibmarke (f)
curtain Vorhang (m)
cushion Kissen (n)
custard pudding Karamelpudding
custard sauce Vanillesoße (f)
custom Sitte (f), Gewohnheit (f), Brauch (m)
customary gebräuchlich, üblich
customer Kunde (m)
customs Zoll (m), Zölle (pl. m)
customs assessment value Zollwert (m)
customs authorities Zollbehörde (f)
customs clearance (clearing) Zollabfertigung (f)
customs declaration Zollerklärung (f)
customs examination hall Zollabfertigungshalle (f)
customs inspection Zollkontrolle (f)
customs number Zollnummer (f) (Auto)
customs officer Zollbeamte (m)
customs regulations Zollvorschriften (pl. f)
customs tariff Zolltarif (m)
customs territory Zollgebiet (n)
cut schneiden, Schnitt (m)
cutlery Besteck (n)
cutlet Kotelett (n)
cut price Preis (m) drücken, Preis (m) senken
cuttle-fish Tintenfisch (m)
cycle path Fahrradweg (m)

cycle-stand Fahrradständer (m)
cycle track Radfahrweg (m)
cycling tourist Radtourist (m)

D

dab Rotzunge (f)
daily täglich
daily cash report Tageskassenbericht (m)
daily service täglicher Verkehr (m), verkehrt täglich
dairy Molkerei (f)
daisywheel Typenrad (n)
daisywheelprinter Typenraddrucker (m)
dam Staudamm (m), Talsperre (f)
damage schaden, schädigen, Schaden (m), Verlust (m)
damages Schadenersatz (m)
damages in transit Transportschäden (pl. m)
damp feucht
damson Zwetschge (f)
dance band Tanzorchester (n), Tanzkapelle (f)
dance bar Tanzbar (f)
dance hall Tanzsaal (m), Tanzlokal (n)
dancing Tanz (m)
dancing-floor Tanzfläche (f)
dancing-party Tanzabend (m)
dancing show Tanzvorführung (f)
danger Gefahr (f)
dangerous gefährlich
dark beer dunkles Bier (n)
darkness Dunkelheit (f)
darn stopfen, ausbessern
dash Prise (f), kleine Menge (f), Spritzer (m)
dash of soda Spritzer Soda (m)

data bank Datenbank (f)
data processing Datenverarbeitung (f)
date datieren, Datum (n), Dattel (f)
date of arrival Ankunftsdatum (n), Ankunftstermin (m)
date of birth Geburtsdatum (n)
date of booking Buchungstermin (m)
date of departure Abreisedatum (n)
date of expiry Verfalldatum (n)
daughter Tochter (f)
daughter in law Schwiegertochter (f)
dawn Dämmerung (f), Tagesanbruch (m)
daybreak Tagesanbruch (m)
day excursion Tagesausflug (m), Tagesfahrt (f), Tagestour (f)
day flight Tagesflug (m)
daylight colour film Tageslichtfilm (m)
daylight-saving time Sommerzeit (f)
day of arrival Ankunftstag (m), Anreisetag (m)
day of departure Abreisetag (m), Abflugtag (m)
day of issue Ausgabetag (m)
day of stay Aufenthaltstag (m)
day restaurant Tagesrestaurant (n)
day return ticket Tagesrückfahrkarte (f)
day-room Tagesraum (m), Aufenthaltsraum (m)
day ticket Tageskarte (f)
day-tripper Ausflügler (m)
day-trippers' goal Ausflugsziel (n)
deadline letzter Termin (m)
deal handeln, Handel (m),

Geschäft (n)
dealing Geschäft (n), Geschäftsverkehr (m)
debark an Land gehen, ausschiffen
debarkation Ausschiffung (f)
debit belasten, debitieren, Soll (n)
debit balance Sollsaldo (m)
debt Schuld (f)
debts Schulden (pl. f)
decanter Karaffe (f)
decide entscheiden
decision Entscheidung (f), Entschluß (m), Beschluß (m)
deck Deck (n)
deck-chair Liegestuhl (m)
deck game Bordspiele (n)
deck steward Decksteward (m)
declare anmelden, verzollen
declaration Erklärung (f), Anmeldung (f)
declaration of value Wertangabe (f)
decline Abnahme (f), Rückgang (m), Verminderung (f)
decorate schmücken, verzieren
decorations Dekoration (f)
decrease abnehmen, Abnahme (f)
decrease in costs Kostensenkung (f)
deduct abziehen, absetzen
deductible abzugsfähig
deduction Abzug (m), Absetzung (f)
deep-fried eggs in Öl (n) gebackene Eier (pl. n)
deep-fried fish in Öl (n) gebackener Fisch (m)
deep-frozen tiefgefroren
deer Hirsch (m), Reh (n)
default Verzug (m), Versäumnis (n)
defect Fehler (m), Mangel (m)

defective mangelhaft, fehlerhaft, schadhaft
defer aufschieben, stunden
deficit Ausfall (m), Fehlbetrag (m), Defizit (n), Verlust (m)
deficiency Mangel, Defizit (n), Fehlbetrag (m), Ausfall (m)
defile Bergpaß (m)
definite bestimmt, endgültig
deflation Deflation (f), Wertabnahme (f)
degree Grad (m)
degree of liquidity Liquiditätsgrad (m)
delay verzögern, verspäten, Verzögerung (f), Aufschub (m), Verspätung (f)
delay of a train Zugverspätung (f)
delay of payment Zahlungsverzug (m)
delays Wartezeiten (pl. f)
delegate delegieren, übertragen
delete what is not applicable Nichtzutreffendes (n) streichen
delicious köstlich
deliver liefern, überbringen
delivery Lieferung (f)
delivery date Liefertermin (m)
delivery note Lieferschein (m)
delivery of baggage Gepäckzustellung (f)
delivery service Zustelldienst (m)
delivery slip Lieferschein (m)
delivery time Lieferzeit (f)
de luxe Luxus (m)
demand verlangen, fordern, Anspruch (m), Nachfrage (f)
demand a deposit eine Anzahlung (f) verlangen
demi-pension Halbpension (f)
demi-tasse Mokka (m)
dentist Zahnarzt (m)

department Abteilung (f)
departmental expenses direkte Aufwendungen (pl. f)
departmental profit Bereichsgewinn (m) brutto, Bereichsergebnis (n)
department head Abteilungsleiter (m)
department store Warenhaus (n)
departure Abreise (f), Abfahrt (f), Abflug (m)
departure station Abgangsbahnhof (m)
departure time Abfahrtszeit (f), Abflugzeit (f)
departure timetable Abfahrtstafel (f)
depend on abhängen, sich verlassen auf
deplane das Flugzeug (n) verlassen, aussteigen
deposit einzahlen, deponieren, Hinterlegung (f), Einzahlung (f), Anzahlung (f)
deposit counter Gepäckschalter (m)
depreciate abschreiben, entwerten, abnutzen
depreciation Abschreibung (f), Abnutzung (f)
depression Tief (n)
depth Tiefe (f)
Derby-cheese Derby-Käse (m)
descent Abstieg (m)
describe bezeichnen, beschreiben
description Bezeichnung (f), Beschreibung (f)
desk Pult (n), Schreibtisch (m)
desk clerk Empfangsherr (m)
despatch absenden
dessert Dessert (n), Nachtisch (m), Nachspeise (f), Süßspeise (f)

dessert wine Dessertwein (m), Süßwein (m)
destination Bestimmungsort (m), Zielort (m), Reiseziel (n)
destination airport Zielflughafen (m)
destination station Bestimmungsbahnhof (m), Zielbahnhof (m)
deteriorate (sich) verschlechtern, an Wert (m) verlieren
determination Entscheidung
determine bestimmen, entscheiden, urteilen
detour Umleitung (f), Umweg (m), Abstecher (m)
devaluation Abwertung (f)
development Entwicklung (f)
deviled scharf gewürzt
dial wählen (Telefon)
diapositive Diapositiv (n)
diced apples gewürfelte Apfelstückchen (pl. n)
dictate diktieren
dictionary Wörterbuch (n)
diet Diät (f), Diätkost (f)
dietary cooking Diätkost (f), Diätküche (f)
dietary foods Diätkost (f), Diätnahrung (f)
diet cure Diätkur (f)
dietic treatment Diätkur (f)
diet kitchen Diätküche (f)
diet plan Diätplan (m)
difference Unterschied (m), Differenz (f)
digest verdauen
digestion Verdauung (f)
dike Deich (m), Damm (m)
dill Dill (m)
dilute verschneiden, verdünnen
dim matt, undeutlich (m)
dine speisen, zu Abend essen
diner Speisewagen (m)
dining-car Speisewagen (m)

dining-room Eßzimmer (n), Speisezimmer (n), Gastzimmer (n)
dining-saloon Speisesaal (m)
dinghy Jolle (f)
dinner Abendessen (n), Diner (n)
dinner dance Abendessen (n) mit Tanz (m), Tanzdiner (n)
dinner-jacket Smoking (m)
dinner wine Tischwein (m)
dinner with floor show Diner (n) mit Show (f)
dip eintauchen
dipsomaniac Trinker (m)
direct unmittelbar, anweisen, anordnen
direct cost Direktkosten (pl.), direkt zurechenbare (variable) Kosten (pl.)
direct costing Direkt-Kostenrechnung (f)
direct distance dialing Ferndurchwahl (f)
direction Anweisung (f), Anordnung (f), Richtung (f)
directional arrow Richtungspfeil (m)
directory Adreßbuch (n)
dirty schmutzig
disadvantage Nachteil (m), Schaden (m)
disagreeable unangenehm
disburse verauslagen
discerning anspruchsvoll
disconnect trennen
discount abziehen, diskontieren, Diskont (m), Rabatt (m), Abzug (m), Nachlaß (m)
discounts earned Skonto-Erträge (pl. m)
discovery Entdeckung (f)
discretion Verschwiegenheit (f), Ermessen (n)
disembarkation charge Ausschiffungsgebühr (f)

disengaged frei
diskette Diskette (f)
dish Gericht (n), Speise (f), Teller (m), Schüssel (f)
dishes Geschirr (n)
dishes prepared to order frischgemachte Speisen (pl. f)
dishwasher Spüler (m), Tellerwäscher (m), Spülmaschine (f)
dishwashing area Abwaschküche (f)
dishwashing machine Geschirrspülmaschine (f)
dislike nicht mögen
dismiss entlassen
dismissal Entlassung (f)
dispatch absenden
dispatch note Paketkarte (f)
display ausstellen, zur Schau (f) stellen
display case Schaukasten (m)
disposal Verfügung (f)
dispose of verfügen über
distance Entfernung (f), Strecke (f)
distance travelled zurückgelegte Strecke (f)
distant entfernt
distant view Fernblick (m)
distil destillieren
distilled water destilliertes Wasser (n)
distinctly deutlich
distinguished vornehm
distinguishing marks besondere Kennzeichen (pl.)
distort verdrehen, verzerren
distress Not (f), Notlage (f), Notstand (m)
distribute verteilen, ausschütten
distribution Verteilung (f), Vertrieb (m)
distribution channel Absatzweg (m)

district Bezirk (m)
distrust mißtrauen, Mißtrauen (n)
disturb stören, belästigen, beeinträchtigen
disturbance Störung (f), Belästigung (f), Beeinträchtigung (f)
divan Bettcouch (f)
dive tauchen
dive bar Kellerbar (f)
diversification Differenzierung (f), Angebotserweiterung (f), Diversifikation (f)
diversified abwechslungsreich
diversion Umleitung (f), Umgehungsstraße (f)
divine service Gottesdienst (m)
diving club Taucherclub (m)
diving equipment Taucherausrüstung (f)
diving-pool Tauchbecken (n)
diving-tower Sprungturm (m)
division Abteilung (f), Teilung (f), Verteilung (f)
dock area Hafenviertel (n)
dock quarter Hafenviertel (n)
docks Hafenanlagen (pl. f)
doctor in attendance behandelnder Arzt (m)
doctor on duty diensttuender Arzt (m)
doctor's certificate ärztliches Attest (n)
dog Hund (m)
dogs must be kept on the lead Hunde (pl. m) sind an der Leine (f) zu halten
doll Puppe (f)
domestic inländisch
domestic air traffic Binnenflugverkehr (m)
domestic flight Inlandsflug (m)
domestic route Inlandsstrecke (f)

domicile Wohnsitz (m)
donkey Esel (m)
do not disturb bitte nicht stören!
do not lean out nicht hinauslehnen!
do not open nicht öffnen!
don't touch nicht berühren!
door Tür (f)
door handle Türklinke (f)
door-keeper Pförtner (m)
door knob menu Zimmerfrühstückskarte (f)
door-to-door pick up and delivery service Haus-zu-Haus-Gepäckbeförderung (f)
dorado Goldbarsch (m)
dormitory Schlafraum (m), Schlafsaal (m)
double bed Doppelbett (n)
double-bedded room Zimmer (n) mit zwei Betten
double-berth compartment Zweibettabteil (n)
double-deck zweistöckig
double-entry bookkeeping doppelte Buchführung (f)
double room Doppelzimmer (n), Zweibettzimmer (n)
double-sized steak doppeltes Beefsteak (n)
double tenderloin Doppellendenstück (n)
double-track line zweigleisige Strecke (f)
doubt bezweifeln, Zweifel (m)
doubtful account dubiose Forderung (f)
douche medizinische Dusche (f)
dough Teig (m)
dough dumplings Spätzle (pl.)
doughnut Krapfen (m)
downhill course Abfahrt (f)
downhill race Abfahrtslauf (m)

downhill trail Abfahrt (f)
downpour Platzregen (m)
downtown Geschäftsviertel (n)
downward journey Talfahrt (f)
dozen (doz.) Dutzend (n)
draft Muster (n), Vorlage (f)
dragon fish Drachenfisch (m), Meerdrachen (m)
drain trocknen, Abfluß (m)
draper's Stoffgeschäft (n)
draught Luftzug (m)
draught beer Faßbier (n), offenes Bier (n)
drawing account Privatkonto (n)
draw out abheben
draw out of the bank account von der Bank (f) abheben
drawbridge Zugbrücke (f)
drawer Schublade (f)
drawers Unterhose (f)
dress Kleid (n), ankleiden
dress-circle erster Rang (Theater) (m)
dressing Garnierung (f), Salatsoße (f)
dressing gown Morgenrock (m)
dressings Verbandszeug (n)
dressing-table Frisiertisch (m), Toilettentisch (m)
dried getrocknet
dried cod Stockfisch (m)
dried meat Trockenfleisch (n)
drink Getränk (n), Drink (m), trinken
drinkable trinkbar
drink dispenser Getränkeautomat (m)
drinking water Trinkwasser (n)
drinks and snacks on board Getränke (pl. n) und kalte Speisen (pl. f) im Zug (m)
drinks extra Getränke (pl. n) nicht inbegriffen
drink the waters eine Trinkkur (f) machen

drip-dry bügelfrei
dripping Schmalz (n)
drive fahren (einen Wagen)
drive-in cinema Autokino (n)
driver's license Führerschein (m)
drive slowly langsam fahren!
driveway Autostraße (f), Einfahrt (f), Autobahn (f)
driving licence Führerschein (m)
drop Tropfen (m) fallen lassen
druggist Drogist (m)
drunkenness Trunkenheit (f)
dry trocken, herb, trocknen
dry-clean chemisch reinigen
dry cleaning chemische Reinigung (f)
drying-room Trockenraum (m)
dry wine trockener Wein (m)
dual carriageway zweispurige Fahrbahn (f)
duck Ente (f)
duckling junge Ente (f)
due fällig
dumping Preisdruck (m), Preisunterbietung (f), Dumping (n)
dumpling Kloß (m), Knödel (m)
dune Düne (f)
dunning Mahnung (f)
dunning letter Mahnbrief (m)
duration Dauer (f), Laufzeit (f)
duration of a journey Reisedauer (f)
duration of the stay Aufenthaltsdauer (f)
dust Staub (m)
dustbin Kehrichteimer (m)
duster Staubtuch (n)
Dutch Cheese Edamer Käse (m)
dutchess potatoes Herzoginnenkartoffeln (pl. f)
Dutch sauce holländische Soße (f)

dutiable zollpflichtig
duty Pflicht (f), Dienst (m), Zoll (m)
duty drawback Zollerstattung (f)
duty-free zollfrei, abgabefrei
duty-free shop Verkaufsstand (m) für zollfreie Waren (pl. f)
duty paid verzollt
dwell wohnen
dwelling house Wohnhaus (n)

E

early früh
early morning tea Tee (m) vor dem Aufstehen (n)
early vegetable Frühlingsgemüse (n)
earn verdienen
earnings Verdienst (m), Einkommen (n)
ear-warmers Ohrenschützer (pl. m)
Easter Ostern, Osterfest (n)
Easter holidays Osterferien (pl.)
east wind Ostwind (m)
easy-chair Sessel, Lehnstuhl (m)
easy to get to leicht erreichbar
eat essen, speisen
eating-place Eßlokal (n), Speiselokal (n)
economical wirtschaftlich, ökonomisch
economic analysis Wirtschaftlichkeitsanalyse (f)
economic system Wirtschaftssystem (n)
economize sparen, rationalisieren
economizing Rationalisierung (f)

economy class Touristenklasse (f)
Edam cheese Edamer Käse (m)
edge Rand (m)
edible snail Weinbergschnecke (f)
educate ausbilden, erziehen
education Ausbildung (f), Vorbildung (f)
educational holiday Bildungsurlaub (m), Studienurlaub (m)
educational stay Bildungsaufenthalt (m)
educational tour Bildungsreise (f), Schulausflug (m)
educational trip Studienreise (f)
eel Aal (m)
eel in dill-sauce Aal (m) in Dill (m)
eels jellied Aal (m) in Gelee (n)
effective wirksam
effectiveness Wirksamkeit (f)
effervescent bath Sprudelbad (n)
efficiency Leistung (f), Leistungsfähigkeit (f)
efficiency expert Rationalisierungsfachmann (m)
efficiency report Leistungsbericht (m)
efficient leistungsfähig
egg Ei (n)
egg and bacon Eier mit Speck (pl. n)
eggbeater Schneebesen (m)
egg-cup Eierbecher (m)
egg-dishes Eiergerichte (pl. n)
egg-plant Eierfrucht (f)
egg-salad Eiersalat (m)
egg sandwich Eiersandwich (n), Eierbrot (n)
eggs in a glass Eier im Glas (pl. n)
eggs in cocotte Eier im Näpf-

215

chen (pl. n)
eggs in mayonnaise Mayonnaiseeier (pl. n)
eggs Russian style russische Eier (pl. n)
egg yolk Eigelb (n)
eiderdown Daunendecke (f)
elbow macaroni Hörnchennudeln (pl. f)
elderberry-tea Holundertee (m)
electric bulb Glühbirne (f)
electrician Elektriker (m)
electric kettle elektrischer Kessel (m)
electric power Strom (m), Kraftstrom (m)
electric power consumption Stromverbrauch (m)
electric range elektrischer Herd (m)
electric rate schedule Stromtarif (m)
electric razor elektrischer Rasierapparat (m)
electric sign advertising Leuchtreklame (f), Leuchtwerbung (f)
electric storm Gewitter (n)
electric torch Taschenlampe (f)
Electronic Data Processing (EDP) Elektronische Datenverarbeitung (EDV) (f)
electrotherapy Elektrotherapie (f)
elegant elegant
elevator Fahrstuhl (m), Aufzug (m), Lift (m)
elevator boy Fahrstuhlführer (m), Liftboy (m)
elevator shaft Aufzugsschacht (m)
elevenses zweites Frühstück (n), Brotzeit (f)
eliminate eliminieren, ausscheiden

elimination Elimination (f), Ausscheidung (f)
embankment Uferstraße (f), Damm (m)
embargo Ausfuhrsperre (f), Handelssperre (f), Embargo (n)
embark einschiffen
embarkation Verladung (f), Einschiffung (f)
embassy Botschaft (f)
emergency Notfall (m)
emergency address Notadresse (f)
emergency brake Notbremse (f)
emergency chute Notrutsche (f)
emergency exit Notausgang (m)
emergency landing Notlandung (f)
emotion Gefühl (n)
emotional reaction gefühlsmäßige Reaktion (f)
emotional sales argument an das Gefühl (n) appellierendes Verkaufsargument (n)
employ beschäftigen, anstellen
employee Angestellter (m), Arbeitnehmer (m)
employee attitude Einstellung der Arbeitnehmer (pl. m) zum Betrieb (m)
employee moral Arbeitsmoral (f)
employee rating scale Mitarbeiter-Beurteilungsskala (f)
employees meals Angestelltenverpflegung (f), Personalverpflegung (f)
employees' opinion survey Mitarbeiterbefragung (f)
employees' representative Arbeitnehmervertreter (m)
employer Unternehmer (m), Arbeitgeber (m)
employers' association Arbeitge-

berverband (m)
employment Beschäftigung (f), Anstellung (f)
employment application Bewerbung (f)
employment contract Arbeitsvertrag (m)
empty leer
en brochette am Spießchen (n)
enclose beifügen
enclosure Anlage (f)
endive Endivie (f)
endive salad Endiviensalat (m)
engage anstellen, beschäftigen, verpflichten
engaged besetzt (Telefon)
engagement Anstellung (f), Beschäftigung (f), Verpflichtung (f), Verlobung (f)
engine driver Lokomotivführer (m)
engineer Ingenieur (m), technischer Leiter (m)
engineering department technische Abteilung (f)
engine noise Motorenlärm (m)
English breakfast englisches Frühstück (n)
English mustard englischer Senf (m)
enjoy genießen
enlargement Vergrößerung (f)
enquiry Erkundigung (f)
enroll eintragen
enrollment Eintragung (f)
en route unterwegs, auf der Fahrt (f)
enter betreten, buchen, eintragen, eintreten
enter a country in ein Land (n) einreisen
entertaining customers Kundenbewirtung (f)
entertainment Bewirtung (f), Unterhaltung (f)

entertainment centre Vergnügungszentrum (n)
entertainment expense Bewirtungsspesen (pl.)
entertainment tax Vergnügungssteuer (f)
enter without knocking eintreten ohne anzuklopfen
entity capital Eigenkapital (n)
entrance Eingang (m), Einfahrt (f)
entrance hall Hotelhalle (f)
entrance to a harbour Hafeneinfahrt (f)
entrée Zwischengericht (n)
entrepreneur of the hotel and catering trade gastgewerblicher Unternehmer (m)
entry Buchung (f), Eingang (m), Einreise (f), Eintragung (f), Eintritt (m)
entry into the country Einreise (f)
entry permit Einreisebewilligung (f), Einreisegenehmigung (f)
entry visa Einreisevisum (n)
enumerate aufzählen
envelope Briefumschlag (m)
environment Umwelt (f)
equal gleich, gleichmäßig
equestrian sport Pferdesport (m)
equipment Einrichtung (f), Ausstattung (f), Gerätschaften (pl. f)
equipped with ausgestattet mit
equivalent gleichwertig, gleichbedeutend, Gegenwert (m)
erect errichten
err irren
errand Botengang (m)
error Fehler (m), Irrtum (m)
errors and alterations excepted Irrtümer (pl. m) und

217

Änderungen (pl. f) vorbehalten
escalator Rolltreppe (f)
escalope Schnitzel (n)
escape period Rücktrittsfrist (f)
escarole Winterendivie (f)
escorted tour Gesellschaftsreise (f)
espresso bar Espressobar (f)
espresso coffee Espresso (m)
establish gründen
establishment Gründung (f), Unternehmen (n), Niederlassung (f)
establishment of the hotel trade Beherbergungsbetrieb (m)
establishment of the tourist trade Fremdenverkehrsbetrieb (m)
estate agent Grundstücksmakler (m)
estate car Kombiwagen (m)
esteem schätzen
estimate schätzen, voranschlagen, Schätzung (f), Voranschlag (m)
estimated cost Budgetkosten (pl.), geschätzte Kosten (pl.), Sollkosten (pl.)
estimate of demand Bedarfsschätzung (f)
estimating-cost system Prognosekostenrechnung (f)
European plan Zimmerpreis (m) ohne Pension (f)
evaluate bewerten, abschätzen
evaluation Bewertung (f), Auswertung (f)
evasion of customs Zollhinterziehung (f)
evening by candlelight Kerzenabend (m)
evening concert Abendkonzert (n), Musikabend (m)
evening dance Tanzabend (m)

evening dress Abendkleidung (f)
evening entertainment Unterhaltungsabend (m)
evening gown Abendkleid (n)
evening performance Abendvorstellung (f), Theaterabend (m)
event Veranstaltung (f)
event of loss Schadensfall (m)
event order Veranstaltungsinformation (f)
everything included alles inbegriffen
eve-cheese Schafkäse (m)
exact genau
exaggerate übertreiben
examination of luggage Gepäckkontrolle (f)
examine prüfen, untersuchen
excavation Ausgrabung (f)
excellent ausgezeichnet
excess baggage Übergepäck (n), Mehrgepäck (n)
excess baggage fare Zuschlag (m) für Übergepäck (n)
excess capacity Überkapazität (f)
excessive überhöht, übertrieben
excessive charge Überpreis (m)
excessive price Überpreis (m)
exchange wechseln, tauschen, Austausch (m)
exchange control Devisenkontrolle (f), Devisenbewirtschaftung (f)
exchange loss Kursverlust (m)
exchange office Wechselstube (f)
exchange of money Geldwechsel (m)
exchange profit Kursgewinn (m)
exchange rate Wechselkurs (m)
exchange regulations Devisenvorschriften (pl. f)
exchange voucher Austausch-

gutschein (m)
exclusive agency Alleinvertretung (f)
excursion Ausflug (m), Tour (f)
excursion area Ausflugsgebiet (n)
excursion facilities Ausflugsmöglichkeiten (pl. f)
excursion fare Ausflugsfahrpreis (m), Ferienflugpreis (m)
excursion flight Rundflug (m)
excursionist Ausflügler (m)
excursionists' goal Ausflugsziel (n)
excursion program Ausflugsprogramm (n)
excursion rate Ausflugstarif (m)
excursion steamer Ausflugsdampfer (m)
excursion ticket Ausflugskarte (f)
excusable entschuldbar
excuse entschuldigen, Entschuldigung (f)
executive Führungskraft (f), leitender Angestellter (m)
executive assistant manager stellvertretender Direktor (m)
executive board Vorstand (m)
executive chef Küchenchef (m)
executive development Ausbildung (f) von Führungskräften (pl. f)
executive housekeeper Leiterin der Hausdamenabteilung, Hausdame (f)
executive secretary Chefsekretärin (f)
exemplary musterhaft, vorbildlich
exempt ausgenommen, befreit, ausnehmen
exemption from duty Zollfreiheit (f)
exeption Ausnahme (f)

exercise Übung (f)
exhibit ausstellen, zeigen
exhibition Ausstellung (f)
exhibition grounds Ausstellungsgelände (n), Messegelände (n)
exhibition stand Ausstellungsstand (m)
exhibitor Aussteller (m)
exit Ausgang (m), Ausfahrt (f)
exit drive Autoausfahrt (f)
exit-interview Entlassungsinterview (n), Ausgangsinterview (n)
exit road Autobahnausfahrt (f)
exit visa Ausreisevisum (n), Ausreisesichtvermerk (m)
expand erweitern, expandieren
expansion Erweiterung (f), Expansion (f)
expect erwarten, voraussehen
expenditure Ausgabe (f), Aufwand (m)
expenditure account Aufwandskonto (n)
expenditure control Ausgabenkontrolle (f)
expense account Aufwandskonto (n), Spesenkonto (n)
expenses Kosten (pl.), Aufwand (m)
expensive teuer, aufwendig
expiration date Verfalltag (m)
expire ablaufen, verfallen
explore erforschen
exploration Entdeckungsfahrt (f)
export ausführen, exportieren, Ausfuhr (f), Export (m)
export duty Ausfuhrzoll (m)
export permit Ausfuhrbewilligung (f)
expose belichten (Foto)
exposed to avalanches lawinengefährdet

219

exposure meter Belichtungsmesser (m)
express Express, Schnellzug (m)
express coach Schnellbus (m)
express railcar Schnelltriebwagen (m)
express road Schnellstraße (f)
express traffic Schnellverkehr (m)
express train Schnellzug (m), D-Zug (m)
exquisite auserlesen
ex ship ab Schiff (n)
extend verlängern, erweitern
extension Verlängerung (f), Erweiterung (f)
extension cord Verlängerungsschnur (f)
extension of stay Aufenthaltsverlängerung (f)
exterior äußerlich, außerhalb
extinction Tilgung (f)
extra Zuschlag (m), Nebengebühr (f), besonder (er, e, es, s)
extra bed Zusatzbett (n)
extra charge Aufschlag (m)
extra charge for service Bedienungszuschlag (m)
extra cost Nebenkosten (pl.), Sonderaufwendungen (pl. f), Sonderkosten (pl.)
extra flight Sonderflug (m)
extra help Aushilfe (f)
extra pay Zulage (f)
extra pay for sunday and holiday work Sonn- und Feiertagsvergütung (f)
extras Nebenausgaben (pl. f)
extra shift Sonderschicht (f)
extra tour Sondertour (f)
extra train Sonderzug (m)
extra wages Löhne (pl. m) für Aushilfen (pl. f)

extra waiter Extrakellner (m), Aushilfskellner (m)
extra week Verlängerungswoche (f)
eye appeal Blickfang (m)
eye catching ins Auge (n) fallend
eye opener Wachmacher (m)
eye-witness Augenzeuge (m)

F

F (= first) Erste Klasse (Vermerk auf Flugscheinen)
face cloth Waschlappen (m)
facilitate erleichtern
facilitation Erleichterung (f)
facilities for hydropathic treatment Kneippanlagen (pl. f)
facilities planning Einrichtungsplanung (f)
facility Einrichtung (f), Möglichkeit (f)
facing gegenüber
facing inland zur Landseite (f)
facing south nach Süden gehend
fact Tat (f), Tatsache (f), Angelegenheit (f)
fail unterlassen, nicht erfüllen, versagen, mißlingen
failure of performance Nichterfüllung (f)
fair Messe (f), angemessen, gerecht
fair authorities Messeleitung (f)
fair-ground Messegelände (n), Festwiese (f)
fair-ground tent Festzelt (n)
fair information office Messe-Informationsstelle (f)
fall Herbst (m)

fall due fällig werden
fall off abfallen, absinken
falling stones Steinschlag (m)
fallow-deer Damhirsch (m)
fall vacation Herbstferien (pl.)
faltboat Faltboot (n)
family allowance Familienzulage (f)
family boardinghouse Familienpension (f)
family budget Haushaltsrechnung (f)
family business Familienbetrieb (m)
family guesthouse Familienferienhotel (n)
family holiday Familienferien (pl.)
family holiday resort Familienferienort (m)
family income Familieneinkommen (n)
family rate Spezialpreis (m) für Familien
family-run firm Familienbetrieb (m)
family status Familienstand (m)
family ticket Familienkarte (f)
family tourism Familientourismus (m)
family vacation Familienferien (pl.)
family size package Haushaltspackung (f)
fan Ventilator (m)
fancy Phantasie (f), Mode (f), Luxus (m), Laune (f)
fancy-cake Torte (f)
fancy-cake of biscuit Biskuittorte (f)
fancy cake with almonds Mandeltorte (f)
fancy cake with caramel Dobostorte (f)
fancy-cake with coffee cream Kaffeecremetorte (f)
fancy-cake with cream Cremetorte (f)
fancy-cake with chocolate Sachertorte (f)
fancy-cake with Linz nut Linzer Torte (f)
fancy cake with nuts Nußtorte (f)
fancy-dress ball Kostümball (m), Maskenball (m)
fancy goods Modewaren (pl. f), Geschenkartikel (pl. m)
far weit, entfernt
fare Fahrgeld (n), Fahrgast (m), Fahrpreis (m)
fare reduction Fahrpreisermäßigung (f)
fare reductions for tourist parties Fahrpreisermäßigungen (pl. f) für Reisegesellschaften (pl. f)
farewell Abschied (m)
farewell dinner Abschiedsessen (n)
farinaceous food Teigwaren (pl. f)
farinaceous dish Mehlspeise (f)
farinaceous sidedish Teigwaren – Vorgericht (n)
farm Bauernhof (m)
farmer's ham Bauernschinken (m)
farmhouse Bauernhaus (n)
farmhouse room Bauernstube (f)
farm trout Zuchtforelle (f)
fashion Mode (f)
fashionable modisch, elegant
fashion contest Modewettbewerb (m)
fashion magazine Modezeitschrift (f)
fashion show Modeschau (f)

221

FAS price Preis (m) einschließlich sämtlicher Kosten (pl.) bis zum Schiff (n)
fasten seat belts bitte anschnallen!
fast freight train Eilgüterzug (m)
fast local train Nahschnellverkehrszug (m)
fast moving goods Waren (pl. f) mit hoher Umschlagsgeschwindigkeit (f)
fast steamer Schnelldampfer (m)
fast train Schnellzug (m)
fat Fett (n)
father-in-law Schwiegervater (m)
fatigue Ermüdung (f), Erschöpfung, ermüden
fattened chicken Masthuhn (n)
fatty fett
fault Fehler (m), Mangel (m)
faulty fehlerhaft, mangelhaft
favourite bevorzugt
favourite dish Lieblingsgericht (n)
favourite pub Stammlokal (n)
feasibility Durchführbarkeit (f)
feasibility study Rentabilitätsstudie (f), Durchführbarkeitsstudie (f)
feasible durchführbar
feast Festmahl (n), festlich bewirten, schmausen
feathered game Federwild (n)
feature Attraktion (f), Einrichtung (f), Merkmal (n), Spielfilm (m)
Federation of Travel Agencies (FIAV) Internationaler Verband (m) der Reisebüros (pl. n)
fee Gebühr (f), Honorar (n), Kosten (pl.)

feed ernähren, speisen
feed-back Rückinformation (f)
feeder road Autobahnzubringer (m)
feeder-service aircraft Zubringerflugzeug (n)
feedway Zubringerstraße (f)
feet (pl.), siehe foot
Felchen from Lake Constance Bodenseefelchen (n)
fellow-passenger Mitreisender (m)
female weiblich
fennel Fenchel (m)
ferment gären (lassen)
ferry Fähre (f)
ferry-boat Fähre (f)
ferryman Fährmann (m)
ferry over übersetzen
festival Festspiele (pl. n), Festwochen (pl. f)
festival committee Festausschuß (m)
festival hall Festhalle (f), Festsaal (m)
festival week Festwoche (f)
festive illumination Festbeleuchtung (f)
festive procession Festzug (m)
festivity on board ship Bordfest (n)
fever Fieber (n)
field of activity Tätigkeitsgebiet (n)
field path Feldweg (m)
field survey Marktuntersuchung (f)
field trip Betriebsbesichtigung (f)
field work Außendienst (m)
fig Feige (f)
figure Zahl (f), Ziffer (f), Abbildung (f)
figure skating Eiskunstlauf (m)
filbert Haselnuß (f)

file ablegen, Akte (f), Kartei (f)
file card Karteikarte (f)
filing cabinet Registratur (f), Aktenschrank (m)
filled gefüllt
filled puff pastry Blätterteigpastete (f)
fillet Filet (n)
fillet-mignon Filetsteak (n), Lendenschnitte (f)
fillet of beef Lendenschnitte (f)
fillet of beef, tenderloin Rindsfilet (n)
fillet of beef with cream-soup Filetbraten in Rahmsauce (m)
fillet of fish Fischfilet (n)
fillet of pork roasted Jungfernbraten (m)
fillet of veal Kalbsfilet (n)
fill in ausfüllen
filling-station Tankstelle (f)
filling-station attendant Tankwart (m)
film Film (m), filmen
film actor Filmschauspieler (m)
film festival Filmfestspiele (pl. n)
filter coffee Filterkaffee (m)
filter-tipped cigarette Filterzigarette (f)
final endgültig, abschließend
final account Schlußabrechnung (f)
final day Endtermin (m)
final holiday registration Reiseanmeldung (f)
final payment Restzahlung (f)
finance in advance vorfinanzieren
financial accounting Geschäftsbuchhaltung (f), Finanzbuchhaltung (f)
financial aid Finanzhilfe (f)

financial analysis Finanzanalyse (f)
financial distress finanzielle Notlage (f)
finder's reward Finderlohn (m)
fine Geldstrafe (f), fein
fines herbes feingehackte Kräuter (pl. n)
finished goods Fertigerzeugnisse (pl. n)
finished product Fertigerzeugnis (n)
fire fristlos entlassen, Feuer (n)
fire-alarm Feuermelder (m)
fire-brigade Feuerwehr (f)
fire department Feuerwehr (f)
fire escape Feuerleiter (f)
fire-extinguisher Feuerlöscher (m)
fire insurance Feuerversicherung (f)
fireplace Kamin (m)
fire regulations Brandschutzbestimmungen (pl. f)
fire-side Kamin (m)
fire-works Feuerwerk (n)
firm service Firmenbetreuung (f)
firn Firn (m)
first aid erste Hilfe (f)
first-aid kit Verbandszeug (n), Verbandskasten (m)
first-aid post Unfallstation (f)
first class erste Klasse (f), erstklassig
first class category erste Kategorie (f)
first class fares Ersteklassetarif (m)
first class hotel Hotel (n) erster Klasse (f)
first course erster Gang (m)
first performance Erstaufführung (f)

223

fish angeln, fischen, Fisch (m)
fish and chips gebratener Fisch (m) mit Pommes frites (pl.)
fish and chip shop Fischrestaurant (n)
fishcake Fischfrikadelle (f)
fisherman Fischer (m)
fishes and crustaceous animals Fische (pl. m) und Schalentiere (pl. n)
fishing Angeln (n), Fischen (n), Angelsport (m)
fishing-boat Fischerboot (n)
fishing club Anglerverein (m)
fishing facilit Angelgelegenheit (f)
fishing-gear Angelgerät (n)
fishing licence Angelschein (m)
fishing-tackle Angelgerät (n)
fishing village Fischerdorf (n)
fish knife and fork Fischbesteck (n)
fishmonger Fischhandlung (f)
fishpond Weiher (m)
fish salad Fischsalat (m)
fish soup Fischsuppe (f)
five-o'clock tea Fünfuhrtee (m)
fix feststellen, festsetzen
fixed fest, festgesetzt, festgelegt
fixed assets Anlagevermögen (n)
fixed cost fixe Kosten (pl.)
fixed price Festpreis (m)
fix the route of a journey Reiseroute (f) festlegen
fixture Inventarstück (n), Zubehör (n), Einrichtungsgegenstand
fizz Fizz (m), Schampus (m)
fizzi lemonade Brauselimonade (f)
flag Flagge (f)
flageolet Bohne (f), grüne
flambé flambiert

flamed flambiert
flamed bananas flambierte Bananen (pl. f)
flamed saddle of venison flambierter Rehrücken (m)
flaming Flambieren (n)
flaming rum-omelet Omelett mit Rum (n)
flan Obstkuchen (m)
flannel board Flanell-Tafel (f)
flash bulb Blitzlichtbirne (f)
flash cube Blitzwürfel (m)
flashing signal Lichthupe (f)
flash light Taschenlampe (f)
flat pauschal, Wohnung (f)
flat price Einheitspreis (m)
flat sum Pauschalbetrag (m)
flavour Aroma (n), Geschmack (m)
fleet Flotte (f)
fleet of trucks Fuhrpark (m)
flexibility Anpassungsfähigkeit (f)
flight Flug (m)
flight captain Flugkapitän (m)
flight engineer Bordmechaniker (m)
flight information Fluginformation (f)
flight schedule Flugplan (m)
flight time Flugzeit (f)
flipper Flosse (f)
float schwimmen
floating hotel schwimmendes Hotel (n)
floodlight anstrahlen
floor Stock(werk) (n), Etage (f)
floor cloth Scheuertuch (n)
floor housekeeper Etagenbeschließerin (f), Etagenhausdame (f), Etagengouvernante (f)
floor houseman Etagendiener (m), Etagenhausdiener (m)
floor staff Etagenpersonal (n)

floor waiter Etagenkellner (m)
floppy disk Floppy disk (f)
florist Blumenhändler (m)
flounder Flunder (f)
flour Mehl (n)
flow chart Ablaufdiagramm (n)
flower shop Blumenladen (m)
flower stand Blumenstand (m)
flow of cost Kostenfluß (m)
flow of work Arbeitsablauf (m)
flow process chart Arbeitsablaufbogen (m), Arbeitsablaufanalyse (f)
fluctuate schwanken
fluctuation Schwankung (f)
fluctuation of price Preisschwankung (f)
fluctuations of the exchange rate Wechselkursschwankungen (pl. f)
fluffy flaumig, locker
fluke Flunder (f)
flyer Flugzettel (m)
flying safety Flugsicherheit (f)
flying speed Fluggeschwindigkeit (f)
flying time Flugzeit (f)
foam Schaum (m), schäumen
fog Nebel (m)
foggy neblig
fold-away bed Klappbett (n)
fold-away table Klapptisch (m)
folder Hefter (m), Prospekt (m)
folding bed Klappbett (n)
folding screen Wandschirm (m), Paravent (m)
folding seat Klappsitz (m), Notsitz (m)
folding table Klapptisch (m)
folio Blatt (n), Folio (n)
folk art Volkskunst (f)
folk dance Volkstanz (m)
folklore Folklore (f), Brauchtum (n)

folkloristic evening Heimatabend (m)
folk song Volkslied (n)
follow up verfolgen
follow-up file Wiedervorlagemappe (f)
follow-up system Wiedervorlageverfahren (n), Nachfaßsystem (n)
food Speisen (pl. f), Verpflegung (f), Nahrung (f)
food and beverage controller Leiter (m) der Wareneinsatzkontrolle (Speisen und Getränke)
food and beverage cost Wareneinsatzkosten (pl.) (Speisen und Getränke)
food and beverage department Wirtschaftsabteilung (f), Verpflegungsbereich (m), Gastronomiebereich (m)
food and beverage management Wirtschaftsdirektion (f)
food and beverage manager Wirtschaftsdirektor (m), Food and Beverage-Manager (m)
Food and Beverage Manager Association (FBMA) Verband (m) der Wirtschaftsdirektoren (pl. m)
food and beverage prices Verkaufspreise (pl. m) für Speisen und Getränke
food and beverage profit Bereichsergebnis (n) Speisen und Getränke (Verpflegungsbereich), Bruttoabteilungsgewinn (m), Verpflegung (f)
food average check durchschnittlicher Speisenertrag (m) pro Gast (m)
food control Wareneinsatzkontrollbüro (n), Wareneinsatzkontrolle (Speisen) (f)

225

food cost Wareneinsatz (m), Speisen (pl. f)
food cost controller Leiter (m) der Wareneinsatzkontrolle (Speisen) (f)
food festival Spezialitätenwochen (pl. f)
food inventory control record Lebensmittelinventarkontrollbuch (n)
food pack Imbißpaket (n)
food-poisoning Lebensmittelvergiftung (f)
food revenue Speisenertrag (m), Umsatz (m) bei Speisen (pl. f)
food service betrieblicher Mittagstisch (m)
food store Lebensmittellagerraum (m)
food storekeeper Lagerverwalter (m) für Lebensmittel
food supply Verpflegung (f)
food supply capacity Verpflegungskapazität (f)
food test Qualitätsüberprüfung (f) der Speisen (pl. f)
foot Fuß (= 0,3048 m) (m)
football match Fußballspiel (n)
footbridge Steg (m), Fußgängerbrücke (f)
footpath Gehweg (m), Bürgersteig (m), Fußweg (m)
foot pump inflator Tretblasebalg (m)
forced landing Notlandung (f)
forcemeat Füllung (f), Füllsel (n)
forcemeat, roasted falscher Hase (m)
forecast vorausplanen, Prognose (f), Plan (m), Vorausschau (f)
forecast factor Prognosefaktor (m)

forecastle Vorderdeck (n)
fore deck Vordeck (n)
foreign ausländisch
foreign country Ausland (n)
foreign currency Devisen (pl. f)
foreign currency control Devisenkontrolle (f)
foreigner Ausländer (m)
foreign exchange Devisen (pl. f)
foreign exchange adjustment Kursdifferenz (f)
foreign exchange office Wechselstube (f)
foreign guest Auslandsgast (m)
foreign rate Auslandstarif (m)
foreign tourist Auslandstourist (m)
foreign visitor Auslandsgast (m)
forenoon Vormittag (m)
forest Wald (m)
forester's house Forsthaus (n)
forest path Waldweg (m)
for hire zu vermieten
fork Gabel (f)
form formulieren, gründen; Formular (n)
formal förmlich, formal
formal dress Gesellschaftskleidung (f)
formality Formalität (f)
formula Formel (f)
for sale zu verkaufen
fortnight Vierzehntage (pl.)
fortress Festung (f), Burg (f)
forward befördern, senden
forwarding agency Spedition (f)
forwarding agent Spediteur (m)
found article gefundener Gegenstand (m)
foundation Gründung (f), Stiftung (f)
fountain Quelle (f), Springbrunnen (m), Brunnen (m)
fowl Geflügel (n)

226

foyer Foyer (n)
fragrance Geruch (m)
France Frankreich
franchise Konzession (f), Vorrecht (n)
Frankfurters Frankfurter Würstchen (pl. n)
Frankfurter sausage Frankfurter Würtschen (n)
franking machine Freistempler (m), Frankiermaschine (f)
free frei, unentgeltlich
free baggage allowance Freigepäck (n)
free currency konvertierbare Währung (f)
free economy Verkehrswirtschaft (f)
free enterprise system freie Marktwirtschaft (f)
free from fog nebelfrei
free from ice eisfrei
free gift Zugabe (f)
free gift advertising Werbung (f) durch Zugaben (pl. f), Zugabewerbung (f)
free lance selbständig
free of charge ohne Berechnung (f)
free on board (f. o. b.) frei an Bord (m)
free on quay (f. o. q.) frei Kai (m)
free on rail (f. o. r.) frei Eisenbahn (f)
free on truck (f. o. t.) frei Waggon (m)
free parking gebührenfreies Parken (n)
free port Freihafen (m)
free ticket Freikarte (f)
Free Trade Area Freihandelszone (f)
freeway Autobahn (f)
freight Fracht (f)

freightage Frachtgebühr (f)
freight aircraft Frachtflugzeug (n)
freight bill Frachtrechnung (f)
freight car Güterwagen (m)
freigth charges Frachtkosten (pl.)
freight elevator Lastenaufzug (m)
freighter Frachtschiff (n)
freightliner train Containerzug (m)
freight service Luftfrachtspedition (f)
freight station Güterbahnhof (m)
freight traffic Güterverkehr (m)
freight train Güterzug (m)
French bean grüne Bohne (f)
French beans salad grüner Bohnensalat (m)
French dressing französische Salatsoße (f)
French fish soup Fischsuppe (f)
French fried potatoes Pommes frites (pl.), gebackene Kartoffelstäbchen (pl. n)
French pepper-stew Pfefferschoten-Mischgericht (n)
frequency Häufigkeit (f)
frequent häufig
frequented vielbesucht
fresh frisch, kühl
fresh egg Trinkei (n)
fresh fruit cup Obstsalat (m)
fresh water Frischwasser (n)
fresh water crayfish Süßwasserkrebs (m)
fresh-water fish Süßwasserfisch (m)
fresh-water swimming pool Süßwasserschwimmbad (n)
fricadelle Frikadelle (f)
fricandeau of veal Kalbsfricandeau (n)

227

fricassee Frikassee (n), Ragout (n)
fricasséed gehackt
fricassee of veal Kalbsfrikassee (n)
fridge Kühlschrank (m)
fried gebraten, in Öl gebacken
fried button mushrooms gebackene Champignongs (pl. m)
fried chicken Backhuhn (n)
fried eggs Setzeier (pl. n), Spiegeleier (pl. n)
fried kipper gebratener Räucherhering (m)
fried pork cutlet gebackenes Schweinekotelett (n)
fried potato balls Pariser Kartoffeln (pl. f)
fried potatoes Bratkartoffeln (pl. f)
fried potato wafers Waffelkartoffeln (pl. f)
fried sausage Bratwürstchen (n)
fried sippets Röstbrotwürfelchen (pl. n)
fried slice of veal Vienna style Wiener Schnitzel (n)
fringe benefits Sozialleistungen (pl. f)
fritter Fettgebackenes (n), Krapfen (m), Küchlein (n)
fritters arme Ritter (pl. m)
frog Frosch (m)
frog fish Seeteufel
frog-leg Froschschenkel (m)
front desk Empfangspult (m)
front door Haustür (f)
frontier Grenze (f), Landesgrenze (f)
frontier area Grenzgebiet (n)
frontier crossing Grenzübergang (m), Grenzübertritt (m)
frontier crossing point Grenzübergangsstelle (f)
frontier formalities Grenzformalitäten (pl. f)
frontier station Grenzbahnhof (m)
frontier town Grenzstadt (f)
frontier zone Grenzzone (f)
front office department Empfangsabteilung (f)
front office manager Empfangschef (m)
front office staff Empfangspersonal (n)
front-room Vorderzimmer (n)
front seat Vordersitz (m)
frost Frost (m),
frozen goods Tiefkühlerzeugnisse (pl. n)
fruit Frucht (f), Früchte (pl. f), Obst (n)
fruit-basket Früchtekorb (m)
fruit bowl Obstschüssel (f)
fruit cake Obstkuchen (m)
fruiterer Obsthändler (m)
fruit flan Obsttorte (f)
fruit jelly Obstgelee (n)
fruit juice Fruchtsaft (m)
fruit pie Obstkuchen (m)
fruits Früchte (pl. f)
fruit salad Obstsalat (m)
fruit savarin Hefeteigkuchen mit Früchten (m)
fruit sundae Fruchteiscreme (f)
fruit tart Obsttorte (f)
fruity fruchtig
fry braten, backen
frying-pan Bratpfanne (f)
fuel Heizöl (n), Treibstoff (m), Benzin
fuel tank Bezintank (m)
fulfill erfüllen, vollziehen
fulfillment Erfüllung (f), Vollziehung (f)
full besetzt, ausgebucht, ausverkauft
fullage volljährig
full bath Vollbad (n)

full board Vollpension (f)
full board and lodging Vollpension (f)
full-bodied schwer (Wein) (m)
full coverage volle Risikoübernahme (f)
full-flavoured voll im Geschmack (m)
full liability Vollhaftung (f)
full massage Vollmassage (f)
full moon Vollmond (m)
full pension Vollpension (f)
full ship beladenes Schiff (n)
fully airconditioned vollklimatisiert
fully licensed Ausschankberechtigung (m) alkoholischer Getränke (pl. n)
fun Spaß (m)
function Tätigkeit (f), Funktion (f)
function room Veranstaltungsraum (m), Gesellschaftszimmer (n)
function sheet Bankettinformation (f)
funds Kapital (n), Fonds (m), Mittel (pl.)
fun-fair Rummelplatz (m), Jahrmarkt (m)
funnel Trichter (m)
fur coat Pelzmantel (m)
furnish bereitstellen, möblieren
furnished apartment möblierte Wohnung (f)
furnished house möbliertes Haus (n)
furnished selfcontained flat möbliertes Appartement (n)
furnish meals without charge kostenlos Essen (n) ausgeben
furniture Mobiliar (n)
furniture and fixtures Einrichtungsgegenstände (pl. m)
furred game Haarwild (n)

furrier Pelzgeschäft (n)
fuse Sicherung (f)
fuselage Flugzeugrumpf (m)

G

gaiety Heiterkeit (f), Fröhlichkeit (f)
gain Gewinn (m), Vorteil (m); gewinnen
gala dinner Festessen (n)
gala performance Festvorstellung (f)
gallery Galerie (f)
gallon Gallone (f)
gamble spielen
gambler Spieler (m)
gambling Glücksspiel (n)
gambling debt Spielschuld (f)
game Wildbret (n), Wildfleisch (n)
gamekeeper Jagdaufseher (m)
game licence Jagdschein (m)
game of cards Kartenspiel (n)
game of chance Glücksspiel (n)
game reserve Jagdreservat (n)
games deck Sportdeck (n)
games room Spielzimmer (n)
gaming casino Spielkasino (n), Spielbank (f)
gaming table Spielbank (f), Spieltisch (m)
gammon Räucherschinken (m)
gangway Landungsbrücke (f)
gap Lücke (f)
garage Garage (f), Reparaturwerkstätte (f)
garage assistant Tankwart (m)
garage-parking lot Garage (f), Parkplatz (m)
garden city Gartenstadt (f)
gardener Gärtner (m)
garden party Gartenfest (n)

229

gardens Liegewiese (f)
garlick Knoblauch (m)
garlick sauce Knoblauchsoße (f)
garment Gewand (n)
garnish garnieren, Suppeneinlage (f)
garnished garniert
garnishing Garnierung (f)
garret Dachkammer (f)
gas cooker Gasherd (m)
gas-cooker range Gasherd (m)
gas lighter Gasfeuerzeug (n)
gasoline Benzin (n)
gasoline can Benzinkanister (m)
gasoline coupon Benzinschein (m)
gas tap Gashahn (m)
gastronomy Gastronomie (f)
gate Tor (n), Flugsteig (m)
gateway Flugsteig (m)
gathering Beisammensein (n)
gear-change Gangschaltung (f)
gear lever Schalthebel (m)
geese Gänse (pl. f)
general administrative expenses allgemeine Verwaltungskosten (pl.)
general delivery postlagernd
general journal Hauptjournal (n), Sammeljournal (n)
general ledger Hauptbuch (n)
general manager Generaldirektor (m)
general profit and loss statement Gewinn- und Verlustrechnung (f)
general store Gemischtwarenhandlung (f), allgemeines Lager (n)
general tariff Regeltarif (m)
general-tariff ticket Fahrkarte (f) zum vollen Preis (m)
general travel conditions allgemeine Reisebedingungen (pl. f)
generous freigiebig, großzügig
gentlemen's cloak-room Herrentoilette (f)
gentlemen's hairdresser Herrenfriseur (m)
gentlemen's lavatory Herrentoilette (f)
German Automobile Club Allgemeiner Deutscher Automobilclub ADAC (m)
German Camping Club Deutscher Camping-Club DDC (m)
German Federal Railways Deutsche Bundesbahn DB (f)
German Hotel and Catering Association Deutscher Hotel- und Gaststättenverband DEHOGA (m)
German light (dark) beer deutsches helles (dunkles) Bier (n)
German pot roast Sauerbraten (m)
German Sleeping and Dining Car Company Deutsche Schlaf- und Speisewagengesellschaft DSG (f)
German-speaking guide deutschsprechender Fremdenführer (m)
German Tourist Association Deutscher Fremdenverkehrsverband, DFV (m)
get in einsteigen
get in lane sich einordnen
get lost sich verirren
get off aussteigen
get rid of loswerden
get up aufstehen
get well again sich erholen
gherkin Essiggurke (f)
gherkin in picca-lilli Senfgurke (f)

giant slalom Riesenslalom (m)
giblets of chicken Geflügelklein (n)
giblets of goose Gänseklein (n)
giblet soup Geflügelkleinsuppe (f)
gift Geschenk (n), Schenkung (f)
gift article Geschenkartikel (m)
gift shop Geschenkladen (m)
gift token Geschenkgutschein (m)
gilt head Goldmakrele (f)
gin Gin (m)
Gin and French Martini dry Cocktail ähnlich
Gin and It englischer Cocktail, Martini sweet ähnlich
ginger Ingwer (m)
gingerale Ingwerlimonade (f)
ginger beer Ingwerbier (n)
gingerbread Lebkuchen (m), Pfefferkuchen (m)
ginger pudding Ingwerpudding (m)
gipsy Zigeuner (m)
giro Postscheck (m)
give-away weggeben; Werbegeschenk (n), Gutschein (m)
give notice kündigen
give up aufgeben, preisgeben, verzichten
give way Vorfahrt beachten!
glacial ice Gletschereis (n)
glacial lake Gletschersee (m)
glacier Gletscher (m)
glacier lake Gletschersee (m)
glacier travel Gletscherwanderung (f)
glass Glas (n)
glass fibre ski Glasfaserski (m)
glass-ware Glaswaren (pl. f)
glass-washing machine Abwaschmaschine (f) für Gläser (pl. n)

glazed frost Glatteis (n)
glide segelfliegen, segeln
glider Segelflugzeug (n)
gliding Segelfliegen (n), Segelflugsport (m)
globetrotter Weltenbummler (m), Globetrotter (m)
glossy glänzend
glove Handschuh (m)
glue Klebstoff (m)
glutton Vielfraß (m)
go gehen
go abroad ins Ausland (n) reisen
goal Ziel (n), Tor (Sport) (n)
goalkeeper Torwart (m)
go ashore an Land (n) gehen
goat Ziege (f)
goat cheese Ziegenkäse (m)
go away on holiday verreisen
goby Gründling (m)
go by car mit dem Auto (n) fahren
golden mackerel Goldmakrele (f)
golf course Golfplatz (m)
golfer Golfspieler (m)
golf equipment Golfausrüstung (f)
gondola Gondel (f)
gondola ride Gondelfahrt (f)
good afternoon Guten Tag!
good-bye auf Wiedersehen
good evening Guten Abend
good faith guter Glaube (m)
Good-Friday Karfreitag (m)
good morning guten Morgen
good night gute Nacht
goods Waren (pl. f), Güter (pl. n)
goods afloat schwimmende Ware (f)
goods elevator Lastenaufzug (m)
goods in bond Waren (pl. f)

231

unter Zollverschluß (m)
goods in process Halbfabrikate (pl. n)
goods in hand Warenvorrat (m)
goods station Güterbahnhof (m)
goods tariff Frachttarif (m)
goods traffic Güterverkehr (m)
goods train Güterzug (m)
goods waggon Güterwagen (m)
goodwill ideeller Firmenwert (m)
go on board an Bord gehen
goose Gans (f)
gooseberry Stachelbeere (f)
goose liver Gänseleber (f)
goosliver-mousse Gänselebermousse (n)
gooseliver patty Gänseleberpastete (f)
goose liver pie Gänseleberpastete (f)
Gorgonzola Gorgonzola (m)
gossip Gerücht (n), Tratsch (m), Geschwätz (n)
go straight on gehen Sie geradeaus!
goulash Gulasch (n)
goulash soup Gulaschsuppe (f)
gourmand Vielfraß (m)
gourmet Feinschmecker (m)
gourmet restaurant Feinschmekkerrestaurant (n)
gourmet's meal Feinschmeckeressen (n)
government controlled economy Zentralverwaltungswirtschaft (f)
gown Kleid (n)
grade Güteklasse (f), Steigung (f)
grade crossing Bahnübergang (m)
grade labelling Qualitätskennzeichnung (f)

gradient Steigung (f)
grading klassifizieren, Klassifikation (f)
gramophone record Schallplatte (f)
grandchild Enkel (m)
granddaughter Enkeltochter (f)
grandfather Großvater (m)
grandmother Großmutter (f)
grandparents Großeltern (pl.)
grand piano Flügel (m)
grandson Enkel (m)
grand-stand Tribüne (f)
grand total Endsumme (f), Abschlußsumme (f)
grant gewähren; Bewilligung (f)
grant a commission Provision (f) gewähren
grape Traube (f)
grape cure Traubenkur (f)
grapefruit Pampelmuse (f), Grapefruit (f)
grapefruit juice Pampelmusensaft (m), Grapefruitsaft (m)
grape juice Traubensaft (m)
grape-nuts Teiggraupen (pl. f)
grapevine Gerücht (n)
grasp Arbeitsgriff (m)
grate reiben
grated cheese geriebener Käse (m)
grater Reibeisen (n)
gratinated gratiniert, überbacken
gratuitous freiwillig, grundlos, kostenlos, unentgeltlich
gratuity einmalige Zahlung (f), Geschenk (n), Gratifikation (f), Trinkgeld (n)
gravy Bratensoße (f)
grayling Äsche (f)
grease einfetten
greaseproof paper Fettpapier (n)

greasing Abschmieren (n)
greasing service Abschmierdienst (m)
great bustle Hochbetrieb (m)
greedy gierig, gefräßig
green beans grüne Bohnen (pl. f)
green belt grüner Gürtel (m)
green cabbage Grünkohl (m)
green cheese Kräuterkäse (m)
greengage Reineclaude (f)
greengrocer Obst- und Gemüsehändler (m)
green noodles grüne Nudeln (pl. f)
green pea grüne Erbse (f)
green pepper grüne Paprikaschote (f)
green salad grüner Salat (m)
green vinegar sauce grüne Essigsoße (f)
Greenwich mean time Weltzeit (f)
greeting Gruß (m)
greetings card Grußkarte (f), Ansichtskarte (f)
grief Kummer (m)
grievance Beschwerde (f), Arbeitsstreitigkeit (f)
grill Grill (m), Rost (m)
grill-bar Grillbar (f)
grilled vom Grill (m)
grilled bread Toast (m), Röstbrot (n)
grilled fillet of wild boar gegrilltes Wildschweinfilet (n)
grilled meat Fleisch vom Grill (n)
grilled pork chop gegrilltes Schweinekotelett (n)
grilled pork cutlet gegrilltes Schweineschnitzel (n)
grilled sausages with sauerkraut Bratwürstchen (pl. n) mit Sauerkraut (n)

grilled snipes gegrillte Schnepfen (pl. f)
grill-room Grillstube (f), Grillrestaurant (n)
grits gekühlte Gemüsesuppe (f)
grocer Lebensmitteleinzelhändler (m)
grocery story Kolonialwarengeschäft (n)
grog Grog (m)
gross brutto
gross amount Bruttobetrag (m)
gross income Bruttoeinkommen (n)
gross operating profit Bruttobetriebsgewinn (m)
gross pay Bruttolohn (m)
gross price Bruttopreis (m)
gross profit Bruttogewinn (m), Rohgewinn (m)
gross profit on sales Rohertrag (m)
gross sales Bruttoumsatz (m)
gross weight Bruttogewicht (n)
grotto Grotte (f)
ground Boden (m), Grund (m)
ground coffee gemahlener Bohnenkaffee (m)
ground-floor Erdgeschoß (n)
ground hostess Bodenstewardeß (f)
ground meat Hackfleisch (n)
group advertising Gemeinschaftswerbung (f)
group business promotion Gemeinschaftsverkaufsförderung (f)
group buying Sammeleinkauf (m)
group discount Mehrheitsnachlaß (m)
group insurance Gruppenversicherung (f)
group journey Gruppenreise (f)

group leader Gruppenleiter (m)
group passport Sammelpaß (m)
group travel Gesellschaftsreiseverkehr
group visa Sammelvisum (n)
group visit Gruppenbesichtigung (f)
grouse Auerhahn (m)
grouse, black Birkhuhn (n)
grow wachsen (größer werden)
grow-up Erwachsener (m)
growth Wachstum (n)
growth rate Wachstumsrate (f)
gruel Haferschleim (m)
Gruyére cheese Gruyérekäse (m)
guarantee garantieren; Garantie (f)
guard Bewachung (f), Schaffner (m), Zugbegleiter (m), Zugschaffner (m)
guarded camping-site bewachter Campingplatz (m)
guarded car park bewachter Parkplatz (m)
guest Gast (m)
guest count Gästeanzahl (f), Gästezählung (f)
guest-house Gästehaus (n), Fremdenheim (n), Pension (f)
guest pass Feriennetzkarte (f)
guest performance Gastspiel (n)
guest questionnaire Gästefragebogen (m)
guest-room Gästezimmer (n), Fremdenzimmer (n), Logierzimmer (n)
guest laundry Gästewäsche (f)
guest registration Gästeregistrierung (f)
guests' supplies Gästegeschenke (pl. n), Aufmerksamkeiten für Gäste (pl. m)
guide Reiseführer (m), Fremdenführer (m), Ratgeber (m),

Leitkarte (f)
guide-book Reiseführer (m)
guided tour Gesellschaftsreise (f)
guided visit Führung (f)
guidepost Wegweiser (m)
guide service Lotsendienst (m)
guinea-fowl Perlhuhn (n)
gulp verschlingen
gum boots Gummistiefel (pl. m)
gurnard Knurrhahn (m)
gurnet Knurrfisch (m)
gust Bö (f), Windstoß (m)
guzzle saufen
gym Sporthalle (f), Turnhalle (f)
gymnasium Turnhalle (f)
gymnastics Gymnastik (f)
gym shoes Turnschuhe (pl. m)

H

haberdasher Kurzwarenladen (m)
habit Gewohnheit (f)
hacking Pferdeverleih (m)
hackney-cab Pferdedroschke (f)
haddock Schellfisch (m)
hail insurance Hagelversicherung (f)
hairbrush Haarbürste (f)
hair-cut Haarschnitt (m)
hairdresser at the hotel Hotelfriseur (m)
hairdresser's saloon Frisiersalon (m)
hair-grip Haarklemme (f)
hair lotion Haarwasser (n)
hair-net Haarnetz (n)
hairpin bend Haarnadelkurve (f)
hairpin Haarnadel (f)
hair-slide Spange (f)

hair-style Frisur (f)
hake Kabeljau (m), Seehecht (m)
half a bottle eine halbe Flasche (f)
half a fried chicken ein halbes Backhuhn (n)
half a portion eine halbe Portion (f)
half-day halbtags
half-day excursion Halbtagsausflug (m)
half-fare halbe Preis (m)
half moons Hörnchen (n) (Gebäck)
half-pension Halbpension (f)
half-price zum halben Preis (m)
half-timbered house Fachwerkhaus (n)
halibut Heilbutt (m)
hall porter Hotelportier (m)
hall-stand Kleiderablage (f)
halt Aufenthalt (m), Halt (m), halten
halt at major road ahead Halt-Vorfahrt (f) beachten
ham Schinken (m)
ham and eggs Spiegeleier (pl. n) mit Schinken (m)
ham, boiled gekochter Schinken (m)
Hamburger Hamburger (m), Hackbeefsteak (n)
Hamburger steak Hamburger (m), Hackbeefsteak (n)
ham cured Schinken gepökelt (m)
hammock Hängematte (f)
ham omelet Schinkenomelett (n)
ham raw roher Schinken (m)
ham smoked geräucherter Schinken (m)
hand Hand (f) aushändigen

handbag Handtasche (f)
hand bellows Handblasebalg (m)
hand brake Handbremse (f)
handicraft Handwerk (n)
handing out of baggage Gepäckausgabe (f)
handkerchief Taschentuch (n)
handle anfassen, Griff (m), handhaben
hand luggage Handgepäck (n)
hand-napkin Handserviette (f)
hand-operated handbetrieben
hand out Unterlage (f), Pressemitteilung (f)
handover aushändigen, übergeben
handsome hübsch
hangar Flugzeughalle (f), Hangar (m)
hanger Kleiderbügel (m)
hangover Kater (m), Katzenjammer (m)
hangover breakfast Katerfrühstück (n)
harbour (harbor) Hafen (m)
harbour dues Hafengebühren (pl. f)
harbour mouth Hafenausfahrt (f), Hafeneinfahrt (f)
harbour police Hafenpolizei (f)
harbour station Hafenbahnhof (m)
harbour tug Hafenschlepper (m)
hard hart
hard-boiled hartgekocht
hard-boiled eggs hartgekochte Eier (pl. n)
hard cider Apfelwein (m)
hard-cooked hartgekocht
hard currency harte Währung (f)
hard disk Plattenlaufwerk (m)
hard liquor Schnaps (m)

235

hard sausage Dauerwurst (f)
hard-shell crabs Krabben (pl. f)
hardware Maschinen (pl. f) eines elektronischen Datenverarbeitungssystems (n), Hardware (f)
hare Hase (m)
haricot bean grüne Bohne (f)
haricot soup Bohnensuppe (f)
harm verletzen; Verletzung (f)
harpoon Harpune (f)
harvest Ernte (f)
harvest thanksgiving Erntedankfest (n)
hash Ragout (n)
hash brown potatoes Rösti (f)
hashed gehackt
hashed meat Hackbraten (m)
hashed steak Russian style Hackbeefsteak (n) in Rahmsoße (f)
haste Eile (f), Hast (f)
hatbox Hutkoffer (m)
hatch Luke (f)
haunch Keule (f)
haunch of vension Rehkeule (f)
hay Heu (n)
haystack Heuhaufen (m)
hazard Risiko (n), Gefährdung (f)
hazel-hen Haselhuhn (n)
hazelnut Haselnuß (f)
hazelnut tart Haselnußtorte (f)
hazy dunstig, verschwommen
head Kopf (m)
headache Kopfschmerz (m)
head cheese Preßkopf (m)
heading Überschrift (f)
headlight Scheinwerfer (m)
head for ansteuern
head of a train Zugspitze (f)
head of wild boar Wildschweinskopf (gefüllt)
head office Hauptbüro (n), Zentrale (f)

headquarter Hauptverwaltung (f)
head waiter Oberkellner (m)
health Gesundheit (f), Gesundheitszustand (m)
health insurance Krankenversicherung (f)
health certificate Gesundheitszeugnis (n)
health insurance for abroad Auslandskrankenversicherung (f)
health resort Kurort (m), Heilbad (n)
health resort patient Kurpatient (m)
hearsay Hörensagen (n)
heart Herz (n)
heart of artichoke Artischokkenherz (n)
hearts of palm Palmenmark (n)
hearty stark, herzhaft, herzlich
heat Hitze (f)
heath Heide (f)
heath cock Birkhahn (m)
heath hen Birkhuhn (n)
heating Heizung (f)
heat, light and power expenses Strom- und Heizungskosten (pl.), Strom-, Gas-, Wasserkosten (pl.)
heat therapy Bestrahlung (f)
heavy wine schwerer Wein (m)
hedge Hecke (f)
height Höhe (f)
height of the season Hochsaison (f)
height restriction Höhenbegrenzung (f)
helicopter Helikopter (m), Hubschrauber (m)
helicopterport Hubschrauberflugplatz (m)
heliotherapy Sonnenkur (f)
helm Steuer (n)

helmsman Steuermann (m)
help Hilfe (f), helfen
hem Saum (m)
hen Henne (f)
hen-chicken Hühnchen (n)
herb Kraut (n)
herring salad Heringssalat (m)
hidden offer verstecktes Angebot (n)
high altitude Höhenlage (f)
high altitude climber Hochtourist (m)
high altitude health resort Höhenluftkurort (m)
high-class hotel 1a-Hotel (n), erstklassiges Hotel (n)
high-diving tower Sprungturm (m)
highest bid Höchstgebot (n)
highlight Schlaglicht (n), hervorheben
highly seasoned scharf
high mountains Hochgebirge (n)
high plateau Hochplateau (n)
high seas hohe See (f)
high season Hochsaison (f)
high-speed bus Schnellbus (m)
high-speed road Schnellstraße (f)
high tea Nachmittagstee (m) und Abendessen (n) kombiniert
high value hochwertig
highway Hauptverkehrsstraße (f)
highway carrier Straßentransportunternehmen (n)
hijacking Flugzeugentführung (f)
hike wandern, Fußwanderung (f)
hike on skis Skiwanderung (f)
hiker Wanderer (m)
hikers' guide Wanderführer (m)

hiking Wandern (n), Wandertourismus (m), Wandersport (m)
hiking region Wandergebiet (n)
hill Steigung (f), Gefälle (n)
hinterland Hinterland (n)
hip Hagebutte (f), Hüfte (f)
hip-bath Sitzbad (n)
hip-tea Hagebuttentee (m)
hire mieten, Miete (f)
hire charge Verleihgebühr (f)
hired car Leihwagen (m), Mietwagen (m)
hire purchase agreement Mietkaufvertrag (m)
hirer Vermieter (m)
hire service Verleih (m)
hiring policy Einstellungspolitik (f)
hiring procedure Einstellungsverfahren (n)
historical building historisches Bauwerk (n)
hitch-hike per Anhalter reisen
hitch-hiker Autostopper (m)
hock Rheinwein (m)
hodge-podge Eintopfgericht (n)
hoist hissen, hochziehen
hold Laderaum (m)
hold accountable verantwortlich machen
holder Inhaber (m)
holding company Dachgesellschaft (f), Besitzgesellschaft (f), Holding (f)
holding costs Lagerhaltungskosten (pl.)
hold on am Apparat (Telefon) bleiben
hold the line am Apparat (Telefon) bleiben
holiday Feiertag (m), Ferientag (m)
Holiday air travel Flugtouristik (f)
holiday camp Ferienlager (n)

holiday centre Urlaubsort (m)
holiday country Ferienland (n), Fremdenverkehrsland (n)
holiday course Ferienkurs (m)
holiday flat Ferienunterkunft (f), Ferienwohnung (f)
holiday gift Reisemitbringsel (n)
holiday guest Feriengast (m)
holiday guide Ferienführer (m)
holiday hotel Ferienhotel (n)
holiday house Ferienhaus (n), Sommerhaus (n)
holiday insurance Urlaubsversicherung (f)
holiday island Ferieninsel (f)
holiday leave Erholungsurlaub (m)
holiday-maker Urlaubsreisender (m), Urlauber (m)
holiday pay Feiertagslohn (m), Urlaubsgeld (n)
holiday place Urlaubsort (m)
holiday region Feriengebiet (n)
holiday resort Ferienort (m), Erholungsort (m)
holiday runabout ticket Feriennetzkarte (f)
holidays Urlaub (m)
holiday season Urlaubszeit (f), Ferienzeit (f)
holiday season ticket Feriennetzkarte (f)
holiday ticket Ferienfahrkarte (f)
holiday traffic Urlaubsverkehr (m), Ferienverkehr (m), Ausflugsverkehr (m)
holiday train Feriensonderzug (m)
holiday trip Ferienreise (f), Urlaubsreise (f)
holiday village Feriendorf (n)
holiday weather Urlaubswetter (n)

Holland Holland
hollandaise sauce Sauce Hollandaise (w)
home address Heimatanschrift (f)
home computer Heimcomputer (m)
home country Heimat (f)
home for old people Altersheim (n)
homeless obdachlos
homely gutbürgerlich (Küche)
home-made hausgemacht
home-made noodles hausgemachte Nudeln (pl. f)
home office Zentrale (f)
home port Heimathafen (m)
homeward journey Heimreise (f)
homeward tourist traffic Rückreiseverkehr (m)
hominy Maisbrei (m)
honest ehrlich
honey Honig (m)
honeymoon Hochzeitsreise (f), Flitterwochen (pl.)
honking Hupen (n)
hood Haube (f)
hook Haken (m)
hooter Autohupe (f)
hoover Staubsauger (m), staubsaugen
hop Hopfen (m)
hop sprouts Hopfensprossen (pl. f)
horn Hupe (f)
horsd'oeuvre Vorspeise (f), horsd'oeuvre (n)
horse-drawn vehicle Pferdewagen (m)
horse-race Pferderennen (n)
horse-radish Meerrettich (m)
horse-radish sauce Meerrettichsoße (f)
horses for hire Reitpferde (pl. n) zu vermieten

horse sleigh Pferdeschlitten (m)
horticultural show Gartenschau (f)
hospice Hospiz (n)
hospitable gastlich, gastfreundlich
hospital Krankenhaus (n)
hospital benefits Krankenhauskostenzuschuß (m)
hospitality Gastfreundschaft (f)
hospitalization insurance Krankenhauskostenversicherung (f)
host Gastgeber (m), Datenbankanbieter (m)
host country Gastland (n)
hostel Herberge (f), Heim (n)
hostess Hosteß (f), Gastgeberin (f)
host family Gastfamilie (f)
hot heiß
hot-air bath Schwitzbad (n), Heißluftbad (n)
hot-air heating Luftheizung (f)
hot bacon tart Lothringer Specktorte (f)
hot broth Bouillon (f)
hot broth with liver-dumplings Leberknödelsuppe (f)
hot claret with cinnamon and clove Glühwein (m)
hot dishes warme Speisen (pl. f)
hot dog Hot dog (m)
hotel Hotel (n), Gasthaus (n)
hotel accommodation Hotelunterbringung (f), Hotelunterkunft (f)
hotel and catering trade Hotellerie (f), Hotel- und Gaststättengewerbe (n)
hotel and restaurant business Gastgewerbe (n)
hotel and restaurant guide Hotel- und Gaststättenführer (m)

hotel and tourist industry Fremdenverkehrsindustrie (f)
hotel and tourist trade Fremdenverkehrsgewerbe (n)
hotel association Hotelverband (m)
hotel bed Hotelbett (n)
hotel bedrooms surplus Hotelbettenüberschuß (m)
hotel bill Hotelrechnung (f)
hotel bellboy Hotelboy (m), Page (m)
hotel booking Hotelreservierung (f)
hotel bookings Hotelbelegung (f)
hotel broker Hotelnachweis (m)
hotel building Hotelgebäude (n)
hotel business Hotelfach (n)
hotel capacity Hotelkapazität (f)
hotel car Schlafwagen (m) mit Speisewageneinrichtung (f)
hotel chain Hotelkette (f)
hotel contract Hotelvertrag (m)
hotel dining-room Hotelrestaurant (n)
hotel directory Hotelanzeiger (m)
hotel employee Hotelangestellter (m)
hotel entrance hall Hotelhalle (f)
hotel expenses Hotelkosten (pl.)
hotel foyer Hotelhalle (f)
hotel fraud Zechprellerei (f)
hotel guest Hotelgast (m)
hotel guide Hotelführer (m)
hotelhood Hoteleigenschaft (f)
hotel industrie Hotellerie (f)
hotelize in ein Hotel (n) verwandeln

hotel-keeper Hotelier (m), Gastronom (m)
hotel-keeping Hotelführung (f), Hotelwesen (n)
hotel label Hotelzettel (m) (Gepäck)
hotel lobby Hotelempfangshalle (f)
hotel lounge Aufenthaltsraum (m)
hotel management Hotelleitung (f), Hoteldirektion (f)
hotel manager Hoteldirektor (m)
hotel occupancy Hotelbelegung (f)
hotel office Hotelbüro (n)
hotel of international standard Hotel (n) internationaler Klasse (f)
hotel operation Hotelbetrieb (m)
hotel owner Hotelbesitzer (m)
hotel pageboy Hotelpage (m)
hotel register Gästeverzeichnis (n), Meldebuch (n), Fremdenregister (n)
hotel reservation Zimmerreservierung (f)
hotel room Hotelzimmer (n)
hotel rules and regulations Hotelordnung (f)
hotels information service Hotelnachweis (m)
hotel site Hotelgelände (n), Hotelgrundstück (n)
hotel size Hotelgröße (f)
hotel staff Hotelpersonal (n)
hotel trade Hotelwesen (n), Hotellerie (f)
hotel training school Hotelfachschule (f)
hotel under good management gutgeführtes Hotel (n)
hotel vestibule Hotelhalle (f)

hotel voucher Hotelgutschein (m)
hot milk heiße Milch (f)
hot rum grog Grog mit Rum (m)
hot slices of Swiss cheese heißer Schabkäse (m)
hot Swiss cheesemush Käsefondue (n)
hot water Warmwasser (n), Heißwasser (n)
hot-water bottle Wärmflasche (f)
hot wine Glühwein (m)
hourly rate Stundenlohnsatz (m)
hours absent Fehlstunden (pl. f)
hours of rest Ruhezeiten (pl. f)
hours of service Betriebszeit (f)
hours worked geleistete Arbeitsstunden (pl. f)
housebuilding Wohnungsbau (m)
housecoat Hausmantel (m)
household goods Haushaltsgüter (pl. n)
housekeeper Hausdame (f)
housekeeping department Hausdamenbereich (m), Hausreinigungsabteilung (f)
house key Hausschlüssel (m)
houseman Hoteldiener (m), Reinigungspersonal (n)
house number Hausnummer (f)
house of accommodation Absteigequartier (n)
house organ Hauszeitung (f)
house rules Hausordnung (f)
house telephone Haustelefon (n)
housing allowance Wohnungsgeldzuschuß (m)
hover schweben
hovercraft Luftkissenboot (n)
hull Schiffsrumpf (m)

human relations zwischenmenschliche Beziehungen (pl. f)
humid feucht, naß
humidity Feuchtigkeit (f)
Hungarian goulash ungarisches Gulasch (n)
Hungarian pork stew Szegediner Gulasch (n)
hunger Hunger (m)
hunt jagen, Jagd (f)
hunting Jagd (f)
hunting box Jagdhütte (f)
hunting ground Jagdrevier (n), Jagdgebiet (n)
hunting season Jagdsaison (f)
hurt verletzen, Verletzung (f)
husband Gatte (m), Mann (m)
hut Hütte (f)
hydrofoil Tragflächenboot (n)
hydropathic establishment Kurbadehaus (n), Thermalbadehaus (n)
hydropathic treatment Kneippkur (f)
hydroplane Wasserflugzeug (n)
hypnotherapy Schlafkur (f)

I

ice Eis (n), Speiseeis (n)
ice-bar Eisdiele (f)
ice-box Eisschrank (m)
ice-coated eisbedeckt
ice-cone Eistüte (f)
ice-cream Speiseeis (n)
ice-cream cake Eistorte (f)
ice-cream coffee Eiskaffee (m)
ice-cream cup Eisbecher (m)
ice-cream cup with hot chocolate-sauce Eisbecher mit heißer Schokoladensauce (m)
ice-cream meringue Eisbaiser (m), Eismeringe (f)
ice-cream parlour Eisdiele (f)
ice-cream soufflè Eisauflauf (m)
ice-cream sundae Eisbecher (m)
ice-cream wafer Eiswaffel (f)
ice-cube Eiswürfel (m)
iced eisgekühlt, gefroren, überzuckert, mit Zuckerglasur (f)
iced chocolata Eisschokolade (f)
iced tea Eistee (m)
ice-free eisfrei
ice-freezer Eismaschine (f)
ice-hockey Eishockey (n)
Iceland Island
ice machine Eismaschine (f)
ice man Eisverkäufer (m)
ice pail Eiskübel (m), Weinkühler (m)
ice-parlo(u)r Eisdiele (f)
ice-skating Eislauf (m), Eislaufen (n)
ice-soda Sodawasser (n) mit Speiseeis
ice stadium Eisstadion (n)
ice water Eiswasser (n)
ice-yachting Eissegeln (n)
icicle Eiszapfen (m)
icing Zuckerguß (m), Glasur (f)
icing sugar Puder-, Staubzucker (m)
icy eisig
identification Identifizierung (f)
identification card Ausweis (m)
identification paper Ausweispapier (n)
idiomatic spracheigentümlich
idle untätig, stillstehend, unproduktiv
idle time Leerlaufzeit (f)
ignore übersehen, nicht beachten, nicht erkennen

ill krank
illegal ungesetzlich, rechtswidrig
illicit work Schwarzarbeit (f)
illness Krankheit (f), Erkrankung (f)
illness frequency rate Krankheitsrate (f)
ill-treatment Mißhandlung (f)
illuminate beleuchten
illustrated booklet Bildprospekt (m)
immediate supervisor direkter Vorgesetzter (m)
immigrant Einwanderer (m)
immigrate einwandern
immigration Einwanderung (f)
immoral unsittlich
immorality Unsittlichkeit (f), Sittenwidrigkeit (f)
immovables Immobilien (pl. f)
impact Wirkung (f), Einwirkung (f)
impair vermindern, beeinträchtigen
implement Gerät (n), Werkzeug (n)
implied stillschweigend
import einführen, importieren, Import (m)
import duty Einfuhrzoll (m)
import license Einfuhrgenehmigung (f)
import restriction Einfuhrbeschränkung (f)
import trade Einfuhrhandel (m)
impose a fine upon eine Geldstrafe (f), auferlegen
impose on auferlegen
impracticable undurchführbar
improper falsch
improve verbessern, vervollkommnen
improvement budget Modernisierungsplan (m)

imputed cost kalkulatorische Kosten (pl.)
inadequate unzulässig, unangemessen
inadmissible unzulässig
in advance vorweg, im voraus, vorzeitig
in accordance with local customs ortsüblich, landesüblich
inaccuracy Ungenauigkeit (f)
inalienable unveräußerlich
inapplicable nicht anwendbar
in arrears rückständig
inattention Unaufmerksamkeit (f)
in bond unter Zollverschluß (m)
incapable unfähig
incentive Anreiz (m), Ansporn (m)
incentive system Prämiensystem (n)
incidental charges Nebenkosten (pl.)
include einschließen
inclusive einschließlich
inclusive air fare Flugpauschale (f)
inclusive air journey Flugpauschalreise (f)
inclusive arrangement Pauschalarrangement (n)
inclusive charge Pauschalgebühr (f)
inclusive fare Pauschalpreis (m)
inclusive holiday Pauschalpreisferien (pl.)
inclusive journey Pauschalreise (f)
inclusive of service and taxes einschließlich Bedienung (f) und Abgaben (pl. f)
inclusive price Pauschale (f), Pauschalpreis (m)
inclusive rates for self-drive car

hire Pauschalpreise (pl. m) für Selbstfahrer (pl. m)
inclusive single fare Einzelflugpauschale (f)
inclusive terms Pauschalarrangement (n)
inclusive trip Pauschalreise (f)
inclusive winter sports terms Wintersportarrangement (n)
incognito unerkannt, inkognito
income Einkommen (n), Ertrag (m), Einkünfte (pl. f)
income account Ertragskonto (n)
income and expense Ertrag (m) und Aufwand (m)
income tax Einkommensteuer (f)
incompatible unverträglich, unvereinbar
inconvertible unkonvertierbar
incorrect unrichtig
increase erhöhen, vermehren, Erhöhung (f), Aufschlag (m), Vermehrung (f)
increase in capacity Betriebserweiterung (f), Kapazitätsausweitung (f)
increase of customs Zollerhöhung (f)
increase of wages Lohnerhöhung (f)
incur debts Schulden (pl. f) machen
indebted verschuldet, verpflichtet
in default of mangels
indenture of apprenticeship Lehrvertrag (m)
independent unabhängig
index Verzeichnis (n)
index figure Kennzahl (f)
Indian corn Mais (m)
indication Heilanzeige (f)
indigestion Verdauungsstörung (f)
indirect advertising indirekte Werbung (f)
indispensable unerläßlich
individual einzeln, individuell
individual care persönliche Betreuung (f)
individual inclusive journey Einzelpauschalreise (f)
individual journey Einzelreise (f)
individually persönlich
individual return Einzelrückfahrt (f)
individual traveller Einzelreisender (m)
indoor sport Hallensport (m)
indoor swimmingpool Hallenschwimmbad (n)
induction Einführung (f)
induction training Einführungsschulung (f)
in due time termingerecht
industrial area Industriegebiet (n)
industrial fair Industrieausstellung (f)
industry fair Industriemesse (f)
ineffective außer Kraft (f), unwirksam
inefficient unwirtschaftlich, erfolglos
inexpensive billig, nicht teuer
inexperienced unerfahren
infant Minderjähriger
infant's carrying basket Babytragekorb (m)
inferior minderwertig
inflammable leicht entzündlich, feuergefährlich
inflatable beach mattress Schwimmluftmatratze (f)
influence beeinflussen, Einfluß (m)
influenza Grippe (f)

inform benachrichtigen, mitteilen, informieren, avisieren
informal zwanglos
information Information (f)
information apply to Auskunft (f) erteilt
information bureau Informationsbüro (n)
information on application Auskünfte (f) auf Anfrage (f)
information service Informationsdienst (m)
information trip Informationsreise (f)
infusion Aufguß (m)
infusion of herbs Kräutertee (m)
ingest Nahrung aufnehmen (f)
ingestion Nahrungsaufnahme (f)
inglenook Kaminecke (f)
ingredient Zutat (f)
inhabitant Einwohner (m)
inhalation Inhalation (f)
inhalation therapy Inhalationskur (f)
inhaler Inhalationsapparat (m)
initial Anfangsbuchstabe (m), unterzeichnen
initial advertising Einführungswerbung (f)
initial salary Anfangsgehalt (n)
injure schaden, beschädigen
inland carriage Binnenverkehr (m)
inland harbour Binnenhafen (m)
inland navigation Binnenschiffahrt (f)
inland postage rates Inlandspostgebühren (pl. f)
in lien of anstatt
inn Gasthaus (n), Gasthof (m), Gastwirtschaft (f)
inner courtyard Innenhof (m)

innkeeper Gastwirt (m), Gastronom (m)
innkeeping Hotelwesen (n)
inoculation Impfung (f)
inoculation requirement Impfbestimmung (f)
input Eingabe (f), Einsatz (m), Eingang (m)
inquiry Anfrage (f), Nachfrage (f), Untersuchung (f)
inquiry office Auskunftsstelle (f), Informationsbüro (n)
insanitary ungesund
insect Insekt (n)
insert Zeitungsbeilage (f)
insert advertising Beilagenwerbung (f)
inside room Innenkabine (f)
insipid fade, geschmacklos
insolation Sonneneinstrahlung (f)
insolvent zahlungsunfähig
inspect prüfen, besichtigen
installation cost Einbaukosten (pl.), Aufstellungskosten (pl.)
instalment Rate (f), Teilzahlung (f), Abschlagszahlung (f)
instant sofort, unverzüglich
instant coffee Sofortkaffee (m)
instead of anstatt, an Stelle von
instruct anweisen, unterweisen, instruieren
instruction Anweisung (f), Unterweisung (f)
instruction card Arbeitsanweisung (f)
instruction for use Gebrauchsanweisung (f)
instruction manual Dienstanweisungs-Handbuch (n)
insulated picnic bag Kühltasche (f)
insult beleidigen, Beleidigung (f)

insurance Versicherung (f)
insurance-building and contents Versicherung - Gebäude (n) und Einrichtungen (pl. f)
insurance charge Versicherungsbeitrag (m)
insurance company Versicherungsgesellschaft
insurance contribution Versicherungsbeitrag (m)
insurance-general Global-Versicherungspolice (f)
insurance protection Versicherungsschutz (m)
insure versichern
intensity verstärken, steigern
interavailable wechselweise gültig
Inter-City train Intercity-Zug (m)
intercontinental network interkontinentales Streckennetz (n)
interest Zins (m), Zinsen (pl.)
interest charge Zinssatz (m)
interest on investments Zins (m) auf Anlagevermögen (n)
interface Schnittstelle (f)
interfere einmischen, beeinträchtigen
interference Störung (f)
inter-hotel-accounts Verrechnungskonto (n) innerhalb der Hotels (pl. n)
interim vorläufig, einstweilig
interim bill Zwischenrechnung (f)
interim invoice Zwischenrechnung (f)
interior Innere (n), Binnenland (n)
interior equipment Inneneinrichtung (f)
intermediate port Zwischenhafen (m)

intermediate result Zwischenergebnis (n)
intermediate season Zwischensaison (f)
intermediate station Zwischenstation (f)
intermediate stop Fahrtunterbrechung (f), Zwischenaufenthalt (m)
internal communicating system internes Kommunikationssystem (n)
internal control interne Kontrolle (f)
internal reporting internes Berichtswesen (n)
internal tariff Binnentarif (m)
International Air Transport Association (IATA) Internationaler Luftverkehrsverband (m)
International Automobile Federation Internationaler Automobil-Verband (m)
International Civil Aviation Organization (ICAO) Internationale Zivil-Luftfahrt-Organisation (f)
international driving permit (IDP) internationaler Führerschein (m)
international exhibition Weltausstellung (f)
International Exhibition of the Hotel and Catering Trade Internationale Fachausstellung (f) für das Hotel- und Gaststättengewerbe (n)
International Federation of Travel Agencies Reisebüroverband (m)
international flight Auslandsflug (m)
International Hotel Association (IHA) Internationaler Hotelverband (m)

international hotel code internationaler Hoteltelegrafenschlüssel (m)
international money order internationale Postanweisung (f)
international motor insurance card internationale grüne Versicherungskarte (f)
international reply coupon internationaler Antwortschein (m)
international tourist traffic Ausländerfremdenverkehr (m)
International Union of Touristic Centers Internationale Vereinigung (f) der Fremdenverkehrszentralen (pl. f)
International Vaccination Certificate internationales Impfzeugnis (n)
International Youth Hostel Federation (IYHF) Internationaler Verband (m) der Jugendherbergen (pl. f)
interpreter Dolmetscher (m), Interpreter (m)
interrupt unterbrechen
interruption Unterbrechung (f)
intersection Straßenkreuzung (f)
interurban traffic Überlandverkehr (m)
interzonal traffic Interzonenverkehr (m)
interzonal train Interzonenzug (m)
in the long run langfristig
in the open sea auf hoher See (f)
in transit unterwegs
introduce einführen, vorstellen
introduction Einführung (f), Vorstellung (f)
invalid ungültig
inventory Inventar (n),

Bestandsverzeichnis (n)
inventory adjustment Inventurberichtigung (f)
inventory card Lagerkarte (f), Bestandskarte (f), Lagerfachkarte (f)
inventory control Bestandskontrolle (f)
inventory pricing Vorrätebewertung (f), Inventurbewertung (f)
inventory taking Bestandsaufnahme (f)
inventory turnover Lagerumschlag (m)
inventory variation Inventurabweichung (f)
invest investieren, anlegen
investment Geldanlage (f)
invitation Einladung (f)
invite einladen
invoice Rechnung (f), berechnen
invoice amount Rechnungsbetrag (m)
iodine spring Jodquelle (f)
Irish stew Hammelragout irische Art (n)
ironing-board Bügelbrett (n)
ironing service Büglerei (f)
irregular entry Falschbuchung (f)
island Insel (f)
isle Insel (f)
issue ausgeben, ausstellen, Ausgabe (f), Ausstellung (f)
issuing Warenausgabe (f)
issuing office Ausgabebüro (n)
Italian cornpudding Maisgrütze (f)
Italian salad Italienischer Salat (m)
item Posten (m)
itemize aufgliedern, spezifizieren

itineracy Umherreisen (n)
itinerary Fahrtroute (f), Reiseroute (f), Reiseplan (m), Reiseführer (m)
itinerate umherreisen

J

jack Wagenheber (m)
jacket Jacke (f), Sakko (m, n)
jack price Preis (m) anheben
jam Marmelade (f), Konfitüre (f)
jam-omelet Konfitürenomelett (n)
jam roll Marmeladenbrötchen (n)
janitor Hausmeister (m)
Japan Japan
jar Gefäß (n), Topf (m), Krug (m)
jardinière Blumenschale (f), Blumenständer (m)
jellied eingedickt, in Gelee (m), geliert
jellied eels Aal in Gelee (m)
jelly Aspik (m), Gelee (n), Sülze (f)
jellyfish Qualle (f)
jelly of pork Schweinesülze (f)
jeopardize gefährden
jeopardy Gefahr (f), Gefährdung (f)
jerk Fleisch (n) in Streifen (pl. m) schneiden und dörren
jerkin Jacke
jersey dress Strickkleid (n)
jersey shirt Strickhemd (n)
jet Düsenflugzeug (n), Düsenmaschine (f)
jet liner Düsenverkehrsflugzeug (n)
jet plane Düsenflugzeug (n)

jet propulsion unit Düsentriebwerk (n)
jetty Landungsbrücke (f), Landungssteg (m), Mole (f)
jeweller, jeweler Juwelier (m)
jewellery, jewelry Schmuck (m), Juwelen (pl. m)
job Tätigkeit (f), Arbeit (f), Verrichtung (f)
job analysis Arbeitsstudie (f)
job analyst Arbeitsanalytiker (m)
job attribute Tätigkeitsmerkmal (n)
job breakdown Tätigkeitsbeschreibung (f)
job category Stellengruppe (f)
job description Stellenbeschreibung (f), Tätigkeitsbeschreibung (f), Arbeitsplatzbeschreibung (f)
job enlargement Arbeitserweiterung (f)
job enrichment Arbeitsanreicherung (f)
job evaluation Arbeitsbewertung (f)
job holder Stelleninhaber (m)
job instruction Arbeitsunterweisung (f)
job instruction training Betriebliche Unterweisung (f)
job knowledge Fachwissen (n)
job rotation Arbeitsplatzrotation (f)
job satisfaction Arbeitszufriedenheit (f)
job security Arbeitsplatzsicherheit (f)
job specification Arbeitsplatzbeschreibung (f)
job standardization Arbeitsplatzstandardisierung (f)
job title Stellenbezeichnung (f), Tätigkeitsbezeichnung (f)

jogging Dauerlauf (m), Langlauf (m), Joggen (n)
John Dory (fish) Petersfisch (m)
johnny-cake amerik. Maiskuchen (m)
join vereinigen, eintreten, beitreten
joint gemeinsam, gemeinschaftlich, Braten (m)
joint of beef Rindsbraten (m)
joint owner Mitbesitzer (m)
joint passport Familienpaß (m)
joint proprietor Miteigentümer (m)
joke Spaß (m), Scherz (m)
jolly lustig, fröhlich
joule Joule (n)
journal entry Journalbuchung (f)
journal voucher Buchungsbeleg (m)
journey Reise (f), Fahrt (f), Anreise (f)
journey abroad Auslandsreise (f)
journey home Heimreise (f)
journey time Fahrzeit (f)
joy Freude (f)
joys of winter Winterfreuden (pl. f)
jug Kännchen (n), Krug (m)
jugged game Wildfleischragout (n)
jugged hare Hasenpfeffer (m)
jugged meat Peffer Fleischgericht (m)
juice Saft (m)
juicy saftig
juke-box Musikbox (f)
julienne Gemüsesuppe (f)
jumble sale Ramschverkauf (m)
jumbo jet Jumbo Jet (m)
junction Straßenkreuzung (f), Verkehrsknotenpunkt (m)

junior cook Jungkoch (m), Hilfskoch (m)
juniper Wacholder (m)
junket Milchgelee (n)
justifiable vertretbar
justification Berechtigung (f), Rechtfertigung (f)
justify berechtigen, rechtfertigen
juvenile jugendlich

K

kaki Kakifrucht (f)
kale Grünkohl (m)
kangaroo tail soup Känguruhschwanzsuppe (f)
karting Go-kart-Sport (m)
kayak Kajak (n)
kedgeree Kedgeree (Reisgericht mit Fisch, Eiern, Zwiebeln) (n)
keelage Hafengebühren (pl. f)
keen competition scharfe Konkurrenz (f)
keep books Bücher (pl. n) führen
keep clear freihalten!
keeper Inhaber (m)
keep in stock lagern, bevorraten
keep left links fahren!
keep off the grass Rasen (m) nicht betreten!
keep out Eintritt (m) verboten!
keep right rechts fahren!
keep the change Wechselgeld (n) behalten!
keep track of cost Kosten (pl.) kontrollieren
keep up-to-date auf dem laufenden bleiben
kefir Kefir (m)

keg Fäßchen (n)
kernel Kern (m), Nuß (f), Samenkorn (n)
kernel of veal Kalbsnuß (f)
kerosene Petroleum (n), Brennöl (n)
ketchup Ketchup (m, n)
kettle (Koch-)Kessel (m)
key Schlüssel (m), Taste (f)
key board Tastatur (f), Tastenfeld (n)
key button Tastenkopf (m)
keying mit Kennziffern (pl. f) versehen
key number Kennziffer (f)
key personnel Schlüsselarbeitskräfte (pl. f)
key position Schlüsselposition (f), Schlüsselstellung (f)
kid-goat Zicklein (n)
kidney Niere (f)
kidney bean Wachsbohne (f)
kidney steak Kalbsnierensteak (n)
kidneys of veal Kalbsnieren (pl. f)
kill time Zeit totschlagen, vertreiben
kilometre Kilometer (m)
kilt Schottenrock (m)
kind Art (f), Gattung (f), Sorte (f), nett, freundlich
kindle anzünden
kindness Freundlichkeit (f)
kipper Bückling (m)
kippered herring Räucherhering (m)
kitchen Küche (f)
kitchen-boy Küchenjunge (m)
kitchen brigade Küchenbrigade (f)
kitchen cupboard Küchenbuffet (n)
kitchen dresser Küchenbuffet (n)

kitchenette Kochnische (f), Kochschrank (m)
kitchen help Küchenhilfe (f)
kitchen layout planning Küchenplanung (f)
kitchenmaid Küchenmädchen (n)
kitchen personnel Küchenpersonal (n)
kitchen privileges Küchenbenutzung (f)
kitchen range Küchenherd (m)
kitchen smell Küchengeruch (m)
kitchen staff Küchenpersonal (n)
kitchen utensil Küchengerät (n)
kitty Kartenspiel (gemeinsame Kasse) (n)
knickers Schlüpfer (m)
knife Messer (n)
knit stricken, verknüpfen
knock Klopfen (n), schlagen, klopfen
knot Knoten (m), Seemeile (f)
know-how Fachwissen (n), Sachkenntnis (f), praktisches Wissen (n)
knowingly wissentlich
knowledge Wissen (n), Kenntnis (f), Kenntnisse (pl.)
knuckle Haxe (f)
knuckle of veal Kalbshaxe (f)
kohlrabi Kohlrabi (m)
kosher koscher (nach jüdischen Speisegesetzen)
kosher-function jüdische Veranstaltung (f)
kosher party jüdische Veranstaltung (f)
kraft paper Packpapier (n)

L

label Etikett (n), etikettieren
labor Arbeit (f)
labor committee Betriebsrat (m)
labor contract Tarifvertrag (m)
labor force Arbeitskräfte (pl. f)
labor market Arbeitsmarkt (m)
labor productivity Arbeitsproduktivität (f)
labor saving Arbeitsersparnis (f)
labor turnover Personalumschlag (m), Kündigungsrate (f)
labor union Gewerkschaft (f)
lace Schuß (m), Branntwein (m) in Getränken (pl. n)
lace-coffee Kaffee (m) mit einem Schuß (m) Branntwein (m)
lack mangeln, nicht haben, Mangel (m)
Ladies Damen(toilette) (f)
ladies-choice Damenwahl (f)
ladies' hair-dresser Damenfriseur (m)
ladies' lavatory Damentoilette (f)
ladies' room Damentoilette (f)
ladle Schöpflöffel (m)
lady fingers Biskotten (pl. f)
lady finger cake Biskottentorte (f)
lager Bier (Lager) (n)
lagoon Lagune (f)
lake See (m)
lake trout Seeforelle (f)
lamb Lamm (n)
lamb breast Lammbrust (f)
lamb cutlet Lammkotelett (n)
lamb shoulder Lammschulter (f)
lamb's lettuce-salad Rapunzelsalat (m)
lamb stew Lammragout (n)

lamp Lampe (f)
lamprey Neunauge (n)
Lancashire-(cheese) Lancashire-Käse (m)
Lancashire hot-pot Hammel-, Rindfleisch und Kartoffel-Eintopf (m)
land and buildings Grundstücke (pl. n) und Gebäude (pl. n)
land at anfliegen, landen in
landing Landung (f)
landing dock Anlegeplatz (m)
landing-field Landeplatz (m)
landing-gear Fahrgestell (n)
landing-pier Landungsbrücke (f)
landing-place Anlegestelle (f)
landing runway Landebahn (f)
landing speed Landgeschwindigkeit (f)
landing-stage Bootssteg (m), Landungsbrücke (f)
landing-strip Landeplatz (m)
landlady Besitzerin (f), Wirtin (f)
landlord Hauseigentümer (m), Gastwirt (m), Vermieter (m), Quartiergeber (m)
land safely sicher landen
landscape Landschaft (f)
lane Fahrspur (f), Gasse (f)
langlauf Skilanglauf (m)
language Sprache (f)
lantern Laterne (f)
lapwing Kiebitz (m)
lard Schmalz (m)
larded gespickt mit Speck (m)
larded veal collops gespickte Kalbsschnitzelchen (pl. n)
larder Speisekammer (f)
larding-needle Spicknadel (f)
larding-pin Spicknadel (f)
lardon Speckstreifen zum Spicken (m)
large-capacity garage Sammel-

garage (f)
large patty   Blätterteigpastete (f)
large puff-paste patty stuffed with chicken and mushrooms (vol-au-vent)   Blätterteigpastete mit Geflügelfüllung (f)
large puff-paste pie   Blätterteigpastete (f)
large-scale public transport   Massenverkehrsmittel (n)
large-scale tourism   Massentourismus (m)
lark   Lerche (f)
late   spät, verspätet
late booking   Spätbuchung (f)
late passenger arrival   verspätete Ankunft (f) eines Fluggastes (m)
late payment   Nachzahlung (f)
latest check-in time   Meldeschluß (m)
Latin America   Lateinamerika
launch   Barkasse (f)
laundry   Wäsche (f), Wäscherei (f)
laundry bag   Wäschesack (m)
laudry-chute   Wäscheschacht (m)
laundry manager   Wäschereileiter (m)
laurel   Lorbeer (m)
lavatory   Toilette (f), Waschraum (m)
lawful   rechtlich, rechtmäßig, gesetzlich
lawful age   Volljährigkeit (f)
lawless   ungesetzlich
lawyer   Rechtsanwalt (m)
lay-by   Rastplatz (m)
layday   Liegetag (m)
layer   Schicht (f)
layer-cake   Schichttorte (f)
layman   Laie (m)
layout   räumliche Anordnung (f)

lay the table   Tisch (m) decken
lazy   faul
lazy Susan   amerik. drehbares Tablett (n)
leadership   Führerschaft (f)
leadership ability   Führungsfähigkeit (f)
leading   führend
leaf   Blatt (n)
leaflet   Merkblatt (n), Prospekt (m)
leak   auslaufen, lecken
lean   mager
lean bacon   Magerspeck (m)
leap year   Schaltjahr (n)
learner   Lernender (m)
lease   mieten, vermieten, pachten, Pachtvertrag (m), Mietvertrag (m)
leasehold   Pacht (f), Pachtbesitz (m)
leaseholder   Mieter (m), Pächter (m)
leasing   Leasing (n)
leave   Urlaub (m)
leaven   Sauerteig (m), Hefe (f)
leave port   auslaufen
leave schedule   Urlaubsplan (m)
leave the ship   von Bord (m) gehen
leave-train   Urlauberzug (m)
leberkaese   Leberkäse (m)
lecture   Vortrag (m)
lecture tour   Vortragsreise (f)
lecture with slides   Lichtbildervortrag (m)
ledger account   Sachkonto (n)
leek   Lauch (m), Porree (m)
leeks   Lauchgemüse (n)
leek soup   Lauchsuppe (f)
left-hand traffic   Linksverkehr (m)
left-luggage office   Gepäckaufbewahrung (f)
left-luggage ticket   Gepäck-

251

schein (m)
left-over Speiserest (m)
leg Bein (n), Keule (Fleisch) (f), Unterschenkel (m)
legal rechtsgültig, gesetzlich
legal aid Rechtshilfe (f)
legal aid insurance Rechtsschutzversicherung (f)
legal claim Rechtsanspruch (m)
legal fees and expenses Rechtsanwaltsgebühren (pl. f)
legal form Rechtsform (f)
legal holiday gesetzlicher Feiertag (m), gesetzlicher Urlaub (m)
legend Zeichenerklärung (f)
legitimate gesetzmäßig, gesetzlich, rechtsmäßig
legitimation Ausweis (m), Legitimation (f)
leg of lamb Lammkeule (f)
leg of mutton Hammelkeule (f)
leg of pork Schweineschlegel (m)
leg of veal Kalbskeule (f), Kalbsschlegel (m)
leg of venison Rehschlegel (m)
legume Hülsenfrucht (f)
Leicester Leicester-Käse (m)
Leipzig hodge-podge Leipziger Allerlei (n)
leisure Muße (f)
leisureliness Gemütlichkeit (f)
leisure time Freizeit (f)
leisure time activity Freizeitbeschäftigung (f)
lemon Zitrone (f)
lemonade Limonade (f)
lemon-ice Zitroneneis (n)
lemon juice Zitronensaft (m)
lemon meringue pie Zitronenbaiserpudding (m)
lemon rind Zitronenschale (f)
lemon-sole Rotzunge (f)
lemon squash Zitronenlimonade (f)
lemon-squeezer Zitronenpresse (f)
lend leihen, verleihen, ausleihen
lending-fee Leihgebühr (f)
length Länge (f)
length of service Diensthalter (n)
length of stay Aufenthaltsdauer (f)
lens Objektiv (n)
Lent Fastenzeit (f)
lentil Linse (f)
lentil soup Linsensuppe (f)
less weniger
less discount abzüglich Skonto (n)
lessee Mieter (m), Pächter (m)
lessor Vermieter (m), Verpächter (m)
let gestatten, lassen, vermieten, Vermietung (f), verpachten
letter-box Briefkasten (m)
letter file Briefordner (m), Schnellhefter (m)
letter of invitation Einladungsbrief (m)
letter of recommendation Empfehlungsbrief (m)
letter-paper Briefpapier (n)
letter punch Brieflocher (m)
letter quality Korrespondenzqualität (f)
letter service Briefversand (m), Schreibbüro (n)
letting Vermietung (f)
lettuce Kopfsalat (m)
level Niveau (n)
level crossing Bahnübergang (m)
level of prices Preisniveau (n)
leveret Häschen (n), junger Hase (m)
levy a charge Gebühr (f),

erheben
liability Schuld (f), Verbindlichkeit (f), Haftung (f), Verantwortung (f)
liability account Passivkonto (n)
liability for damages Schadenshaftung (f)
liability insurance Haftpflichtversicherung (f)
liability insurance coverage Haftpflichtdeckung (f)
liability of the carrier Transporthaftung (f)
liability under the contract Vertragshaftung (f)
liable verantwortlich, haftpflichtig
liable to charges gebührenpflichtig
liable to customs zollpflichtig
liable to duty zollpflichtig
library Bibliothek (f)
licence Ausschanklizenz (f), Konzession (f)
licence plate Autonummernschild (n)
licensee Lizenzinhaber (m)
licensed hours Alkoholausschankzeiten (pl. f)
licenses and inspections Schankerlaubnis (f) und Gewerbeaufsicht (f)
licensing hours Alkoholausschankzeiten (pl. f)
licensor Lizenzgeber (m)
lid Deckel (m)
lido Freibad (n), Strandbad (n)
lie awake wach liegen
life-belt Rettungsgürtel (m)
life-boat Rettungsboot (n)
life-guard Badewärter (m)
life-guard station Rettungsstation (f)
life insurance Lebensversicherung (f)
life-jacket Schwimmweste (f)
life-saving station Rettungsstation (f)
life vest Schwimmweste (f)
lift Aufzug (m), Fahrstuhl (m)
lift-boy Fahrstuhlführer (m), Liftboy (m)
lift up aufheben
light leicht, Licht (n), anzünden, Beleuchtung (f)
light beer heller Bier (n)
lighter Feuerzeug (n)
lighter fuel Feuerzeugbenzin (n)
light food leichte Kost (f)
lighthouse Leuchtturm (m)
lighting effect Lichteffekt (m)
lightning Blitz (m)
lights Lunge (f)
light wine leichter Wein (m)
like gern haben, mögen, wie
lime Limone (f)
lime juice Limonensaft (m)
limestone cave Tropfsteinhöhle (f)
lime tea Lindenblütentee (m)
limit begrenzen, Limit (n), Grenze (f)
limitation Begrenzung (f), Einschränkung (f)
limited express train Fernschnellzug (m)
limited liability company Gesellschaft (f) mit beschränkter Haftung (f)
limited number of seats begrenzte Platzanzahl (f)
limited parking zone Kurzparkzone (f)
line Linie (f), Strecke (f), Gleis (n); Teleph.: Leitung (f), Apparat (m), Nummer (f)
line and staff organization Stablinienorganisation (f)

253

line cord Kabel (n)
line-fishing Angelfischerei (f)
line function Linienfunktion (f)
linen Wäsche (f), Weißzeug (n)
linen-closet Wäscheschrank (m)
linen hire Wäscheverleih (m)
linen keeper Wäschebeschließerin (f)
linen room attendant Wäschebeschließerin (f)
line position Linienstelle (f)
liner Passagierdampfer (m), Linienschiff (n), Verkehrsflugzeug, Linienflugzeug
liner company Schiffahrtsgesellschaft (f)
linguist-courier sprachkundiger Reiseleiter (m)
link Dünen (pl. f)
links Golfplatz (m)
linseed Leinsamen (m)
linseed-cake Leinkuchen (m)
lionize jemanden die Sehenswürdigkeiten eines Ortes zeigen
lipstick Lippenstift (m)
Liptauer, garnished Liptauer-Käse garniert (m)
liqueur Likör (m)
liquid flüssig, verfügbar
liquid assets flüssige Mittel (pl. n)
liquidity Flüssigkeit (f), Liquidität (f)
liquo(u)r Spirituose (f), Alkohol (m)
liquor shop Spirituosengeschäft (n)
list verzeichnen; Liste (f), Verzeichnis (n)
list of beverages Getränkekarte (f)
list of participants Teilnehmerliste (f)

list of travel agencies Agenturverzeichnis (n)
list of vacant rooms Vakanzliste (f)
list price Listenpreis (m)
live leben, wohnen
lively abwechslungsreich
liver Leber (f)
liver dumpling Leberknödel (m)
liveried livriert
liver of veal Kalbsleber (f)
liver puree soup Leberpüreesuppe (f)
liver sausage Leberwurst (f)
liver sausage with pickled cabbage Leberwurst (f) mit Sauerkraut (n)
living habit Lebensgewohnheit (f)
living-room Wohnzimmer (n), Wohnraum (m)
living standard Lebensstandard (m)
loading charges Verladegebühr (f)
loading hatch Ladeluke (f)
loading platform Verladebahnsteig (m)
loading point Verladestelle (f)
loading station Talstation (f)
loaf of bread Brotlaib (m)
loaf sugar Hutzucker (m)
lobby Empfangshalle (f), Foyer (n), Hotelhalle (f)
lobster Hummer (m)
lobster cocktail Hummercocktail (m)
lobster mayonnaise Hummermayonnaise (f)
lobster shift Nachtschicht (f)
local lokal, örtlich
local advertising lokale Werbung (f)
local advertisement postmark

Ortswerbestempel (m)
local call Ortsgespräch (n)
local carriage Ortsverkehr (m)
local colour Lokalkolorit (n)
local custom Ortsgebrauch (m)
local fair Kirchweih (f)
local festival Heimatfest (n)
locality Örtlichkeit (f), Lage (f)
local speciality Landesspezialität (f)
local tax Ortstaxe (f)
local time Ortszeit (f)
local tourist association Verkehrsverein (m)
local tourist office Verkehrsamt (n)
local traffic Ortsverkehr (m), Nahverkehr (m)
local wine Landwein (m)
locate errors Fehler (pl. m) aufdecken
location Standort (m)
location of goods Lagerort (m)
lock Schloß (Türen) (n), Schleuse (f)
lock box Schließfach (n)
locker Schließfach (n)
lock off absperren
lock-up garage verschließbare Garage (f)
lodge beherbergen, unterbringen, Jagdhütte (f)
lodger Mieter (m)
lodging Unterkunft (f), Quartier (n), Logis (n)
lodging-house Hotel garni (n), Logierhaus (n)
loganberry Logan-Beere (f)
log-book Bordbuch (n), Reservations- und Beschwerdebuch (n) im Restaurant (n)
log-hut Blockhütte (f)
loin Lendenstück (n), Lende (f)
long lang

long-dinstance call Ferngespräch (n)
long-distance express Fernschnellzug (m)
long-distance flight Langstreckenflug (m)
long-distance lorry Fernlaster (m)
long-distance service Langstreckendienst (m)
long-distance time-table Fernfahrplan (m)
long-distance traffic Fernverkehr (m)
long-range langfristig
long-range plane Langstreckenflugzeug (n)
long-range profit planning langfristige Erfolgsplanung (f)
long-term langfristig
look Blick (m), schauen, blicken
looking-glass Spiegel (m)
loose-leaf card record Lose-Blatt-Buchführung (f)
lorry Lastkraftwagen (m)
lose verlieren, einbüßen
loss Verlust (m), Schaden (m)
loss and damage to guest property Verlust (m) und Beschädigung (f) von Gasteigentum (n)
loss of earnings Verdienstausfall (m)
loss settlement Schadensregulierung (f)
lost discount Skontoverlust (m)
lost luggage fehlendes Reisegepäck (n)
lost profit entgangener Gewinn (m)
lost-property office Fundbüro (n)
lost time Verlustzeit (f)
lot size Losgröße (f), Auftrags-

255

größe (f)
lounge Aufenthaltsraum (m), Gesellschaftsraum (m), Hotelhalle (f)
lounge suit Straßenanzug (m)
lovely köstlich, lieblich, schön
lower berth Unterbett (n)
lower deck Unterdeck (n)
lowest bid Mindestgebot (n)
low-priced billig
low season Vorsaison (f), Nachsaison (f)
low valued geringwertig
loyal treu, pflichttreu
loyality Treue (f), Pflichttreue (f)
lucrative einträglich
luge Schlitten (m)
luggage Gepäck (n)
luggage compartment Gepäckraum (m)
luggage insurance Gepäckversicherung (f)
luggage label Gepäckanhänger (m), Kofferanhänger (m)
luggage locker Gepäckschließfach (n)
luggage office Gepäckabfertigung (f), Gepäckaufgabestelle (f)
luggage platform Gepäckbahnsteig (m)
luggage porter Gepäckträger (m)
luggage rack Gepäckablage (f), Gepäcknetz (n), Autogepäckträger (m)
luggage receipt Gepäckschein (m)
luggage registration counter Gepäckabfertigung (f)
luggage room Gepäckraum (m)
luggage service Gepäckdienst (m)
luggage-ticket Gepäckschein (m)

luggage transfer Gepäcktransfer (m)
luggage van Gepäckwagen (m), Packwagen (m)
luging Rodeln (n), Rodelsport (m)
lukewarm lauwarm
lump Klumpen (m), Stück (n)
lump sugar Würfelzucker (m)
lump sum Pauschale (f), Pauschalbetrag (m)
lunch(eon) Mittagessen (n)
lunch break Mittagspause (f)
lunch business Mittagsgeschäft (n)
lunch-counter Imbißbar (in Restaurants) (f)
luncheon-bar Mittagsrestaurant (n)
luncheon-basket Proviantkorb (m)
luncheonette Imbiß (m), Imbißstube (f)
luncheon meat Frühstücksfleisch (n)
luncheon voucher Essenbon (m), Essengutschein (m), Mahlzeitengutschein (m)
luncheon voucher arragement Esseabonnement (n)
lunch-hour Mittagszeit (f), Mittagspause (f)
lunch packet Lunchpaket (n), Imbißpaket (n)
lunch-room Mittagsrestaurant (n)
lungs Lunge (f)
luxurious fittings moderner Komfort (m)
luxury Luxus (m)
luxury bus Luxusbus (m)
luxury cabin Luxuskabine (f)
luxury goods Luxusgüter (pl. n)
luxury hotel Luxushotel (n)

luxury liner Luxusdampfer (m)
luxury restaurant Luxusrestaurant (n)
luxury trip Luxusreise (f)
luxury yacht Luxusjacht (f)

M

ma'am (umgangsspr. für madam)
macaroni Makkaroni (pl. f)
macaroon Makrone (f)
mace Muskatblüte (f), Muskatblatt (n)
machinery and equipment Maschinen (pl. f) und Ausrüstungen (pl. f)
mackerel Makrele (f)
mackintosh Regenmantel (m)
madam gnädige Frau (Anrede) (f), gnädiges Fräulein (n)
Madeira Madiera (m) (Wein)
Madeira cake Sandkuchen (m)
Madeira sauce Madeira-Sauce (f)
Mae West aufblasbare Schwimmweste
maffick lärmend feiern, johlen
magazine Zeitschrift (f)
magnificent prächtig, großartig
maid Dienstmädchen (n), Zimmermädchen (n)
maiden name Mädchenname (m), Geburtsname (m)
mail aufgeben (Post), Post (f)
mailbox Briefkasten (m)
mail flight Postflug (m)
mailing list Postliste (f), Adressenliste (f)
mailman Briefträger (amerik.) (m)
mail plane Postflugzeug (n)
main course Hauptgang

(Speisen) (m), Hauptgericht (n)
main deck Hauptdeck (n)
main dish Hauptgericht (n), Hauptspeise (f)
main entrance Haupteingang (m)
main joint Hauptfleischgang (m), Hauptgang (m)
main mast Großmast (m)
main meal Hauptmahlzeit (f)
main meat course Hauptgang (m), Hauptfleischgang (m)
main office Hauptbüro (n), Zentrale (f)
main road Hauptstraße (f)
main sail Großsegel (n)
main station Hauptbahnhof (m)
main street Hauptstraße (f)
maintain instandhalten, unterhalten, erhalten, aufrechterhalten
maintain records Bücher (pl. n) führen
maintenance Instandhaltung (f), Unterhalt (m), Erhaltung (f), Wartung (f)
maintenance and repair Instandhaltung (f) und Reparaturen (pl. f)
maintenance work order Instandhaltungsauftrag (f), Reparaturauftrag (m)
maitre Oberkellner (m)
maize Mais (m)
maizena Maisstärkemehl (n)
major road Vorfahrtsstraße (f)
make an entry buchen
make fast anlegen
make up Aufmachung (f), Ausstattung (f)
make use of gebrauchen, verwerten
male männlich
mall Laubenpromenade (f)

257

mallow Malve (f)
malt Malz (n)
Maltese Malteser (m)
manage leiten, verwalten
management Geschäftsleitung (f), Betriebsführung (f), Geschäftsführung (f)
management consultant Unternehmensberater (m), Betriebsberater (m)
management decision Führungsentscheidung (f)
management development Führungskräfteentwicklung (f)
management fees Managementgebühren (pl. f)
management training Führungsausbildung (f), Managementtraining (n)
manager Leiter (m), Direktor (m), Geschäftsführer (m), Manager (m)
managerial disease Managerkrankheit (f)
managerial responsibility Führungsverantwortung (f)
mandarine Mandarine (f)
mandatory obligatorisch, zwingend
man-day Arbeitstag (m), Tagewerk (n)
mango Mangopflaume (f)
man hour Arbeitsstunde (f)
man hour output Leistung (f) pro Arbeitsstunde (f)
manicure Maniküre (f)
manners Sitten (pl. f), Bräuche (pl. m), Lebensart (f)
manning guide Personalplanungsleitfaden (m)
manning table Stellenbesetzungsplan (m)
manpower Arbeitskraft (f)

manpower budget Personalbudget (n)
mansard Mansarde (f)
manual Handbuch (n), manuell
manual of instructions Dienstanweisungshandbuch (n)
map Landkarte (f), Karte (f)
maple syrup Ahornsirup (m)
map of the town Stadtplan (m)
marbled meat durchwachsenes Fleisch (n)
marchpane Marzipan (n)
Mardigras Fastnachtsdienstag (m)
margarine Margarine (f)
margin Spanne (f), Rohgewinn (m)
marginal cost Grenzkosten (pl.)
marginal costing Grenzkostenrechnung (f), Direktkostenrechnung (f)
marginal income Grenzertrag (m)
marina Jachthafen (m)
marinade Marinade (f)
marinated mariniert
marinated herring Bismarckhering (m)
marine cray fish Meereskrebs (m)
marine railway station Hafenbahnhof (m)
marinotherapy Seebadekur (f)
marital status Familienstand (m)
maritime shipping Seeschiffahrt (f)
marjoram Majoran (m)
mark kennzeichnen, Zeichen (n), Marke (f)
mark down Preissenkung (f)
market verkaufen, absetzen, Markt (m), Absatzgebiet (n)
market analyses Marktanalyse (f)

market coverage Marktanteil (m)
market-hall Markthalle (f)
marketing Absatzlehre (f), Marketing (n)
marketing manager Verkaufsleiter (m), Vertriebsleiter (m), Marketing-Manager (m)
market list Marktliste (f), Frischwarenverzeichnis (n)
market-place Marktplatz (m)
market price Marktpreis (m)
market-research Marktforschung (f)
market saturation Marktsättigung (f)
market study Marktstudie (f)
markup Gewinnaufschlag (m)
marmelade Orangenmarmelade (f)
married verheiratet
marrow Mark (n)
marrow-bone Markbein (n), Markknochen (m)
marrow dumplings Markklößchen (pl. n)
masked ball Maskenball (m)
mash Brei (m)
mashed potatoes Kartoffelbrei (m)
mason Maurer (m)
mass (heilige) Messe (f)
massage Massage (f)
masseur Masseur (m)
masseuse Masseuse (f)
mast Mast (m)
master scheduling Gesamtplanung (f)
master-key Hauptschlüssel (m)
mat Untersetzer (m)
match Zündholz (n), Streichholz (n), dazu passen, entsprechen, passend machen
match-box Streichholzschachtel (f), Zündholzschachtel (f)

matchstick potatoes Zündholzkartoffeln (pl. f)
material cost Materialkosten (pl.)
matrix printer Matrixdrucker (m)
matron Hausdame (f), Beschliesserin (f)
matter Angelegenheit (f)
mattress Matratze (f)
mature reif
matured coupon noch nicht eingelöster Gutschein (m)
mature wine abgelagerter Wein (m)
Maundy Thursday Gründonnerstag (m)
maximum capacity Betriebsmaximum (n)
maximum inventory Höchstbestand (m)
maximum manning Personalhöchstbestand (m), Höchstbesetzung (f) mit Personal (n)
maximum price Höchstpreis (m)
maximum speed Höchstgeschwindigkeit (f)
mayonnaise Mayonnaise (f)
mayonnaise eggs Russische Eier (pl. n)
mayonnaise of fish Fischmayonnaise (f)
mayonnaise of lobster Hummermayonnaise (f)
mayonnaise salad Mayonnaisesalat (m)
mayonnaise sauce Mayonnaisensoße (f)
mayor Bürgermeister (m)
Maypole Maibaum (m)
meadow Wiese (f)
meagre mager
meal Mahlzeit (f), Speise (f), Gericht (n), Essen (n)

meals á la carte Esse(n) á la carte
meals on board (a) ship Mahlzeiten (pl. f) an Bord
meal ticket Essensbon (m), Essensgutschein (m)
meal ticket arragement Essenabonnement (n)
meal-time Essenszeit (f), Tischzeit (f)
mean annual temperature mittlere Jahrestemperatur (f)
meaning Bedeutung (f)
means Mittel (pl. n)
means of transportation Beförderungsmittel (pl. n)
meanwhile inzwischen
measure Maßnahme (f), Maß (n)
measurement of performance Leistungsmessung (f)
meat Fleisch (n)
meat-ball Fleischklößchen (n)
meat-ball in withe caper sauce Königsberger Klops (m)
meat broth Fleischbrühe (f)
meat croquette Frikadelle (f)
meat dish Fleischspeise (f)
meat dumpling Fleischknödel (m)
meatless dish fleischloses Gericht (n)
meat-loaf Hackbraten (m)
meat pie Fleischpastete (f)
meat-pudding Fleischkäse (m)
meat rice Reisfleisch (n)
meat tag Fleischanhänger (m)
meaty fleischig, gehaltvoll
mechanic Mechaniker (m)
mechanical mechanisch, maschinell
mechanical kitchen equipment Küchenausstattung (f)

mechanical-sundry equipment Maschinen-sonstige Einrichtungen (pl. f)
mechanize mechanisieren
medallion of veal Kalbsmedallion (n)
medical care ärztliche Betreuung (f)
medical certificate ärztliches Zeugnis (n)
medical indentification card Unfallschutzkarte (f)
medicinal bath medizinisches Bad (n)
medicinal mineral water Heilwasser (n)
medicinal spring Heilquelle (f)
Mediterranean Mittelmeer (n), mittelmeerisch
medium mittel
medium done rosig gebraten
medium priced in mittlerer Preislage (f)
medium-range flight Mittelstreckenflug (m)
medium term mittelfristig
medlars Mispel (f)
meet treffen, sich versammeln, erfüllen
meeting Konferenz (f), Sitzung (f), Versammlung (f)
meeting-place Sammelstelle (f), Sammelpunkt (m), Treffpunkt (m)
meet with an accident verunglücken
Melbatoast hartgeröstete Brotscheiben (pl. f)
melon Melone (f)
melted ausgelassen, geschmolzen, zerlassen
melted butter zerlassene Butter (f)
member Mitglied (n)
membership Mitgliedschaft (f)

260

membership card Mitgliedskarte (f), Ausweis (m)
membership fee Mitgliederbeitrag (m)
memorandum Notiz (f), Vermerk (m)
memorial Denkmal (n)
men's hairdresser Herrenfriseur (m)
men's lavatory Herrentoilette (f)
menu Speisenfolge (f), Menü (n), Speisekarte (f)
menu at fixed prices Menü (n) zu festen Preisen (pl. m)
menu for motorists Menü (n) für Autofahrer (pl. m)
menu planning Menüplanung (f), Planung (f) der Speisekarte (f)
menu and wine list Speise- und Weinkarte (f)
merchandise Ware (f), Handelsware (f)
merchandising policy Verkaufsgrundsätze (pl. m)
merchant ship Handelsschiff (n)
merge fusionieren, verschmelzen, mischen
merger Fusion (f)
meringue Sahnebaiser (n), Baiser (n)
meringue cake Windtorte (f)
merit Verdienst (n)
merit rating Leistungsbeurteilung (f)
merry-go-round Karussell (n)
mess Verwirrung (f), Durcheinander (n)
message Nachricht (f), Botschaft (f)
mess-tin Kochgeschirr (n)
meteorological office Wetteramt (n)

meteorological services Wetterdienst (m)
meter maid Politesse (f)
method and procedures Ablauforganisation (f)
method of treatment Heilmethode (f)
metropolis Metropole (f), Hauptstadt (f)
meuniére sauce Soße (f) mit gebräunter Butter (f), Zitrone (f), Petersilie (f)
mew eggs Möwenei (n)
mezzanine Zwischenstock (m)
microbus Kleinbus (m)
micro computer Mikrocomputer (m)
micromotion study Griff- und Bewegungsstudie (f)
middle management mittleres Managment (n)
midnight Mitternacht (f)
mid-morning break Frühstückspause (f)
mid-morning snack zweites Frühstück (n), Brotzeit (f)
mid station Mittelstation (f)
mignonette kleines Filetstück (n)
milage Meilenzahl (f), Entfernung (f) in Meilen (pl. f)
mild mild, leicht
mild ale dunkles Ale (n)
mild climate mildes Klima (n)
mild diet Schonkost (f)
milestone Meilenstein (m), Markstein (m)
milk Milch (f)
milk bar Milchbar (f)
milk-dish Milchspeise (f)
milk-jug Milchkännchen (n)
milkman Milchhändler (m)
milk-rice Milchreis (m)
milk roll Milchbrötchen (n)
milk shake Milchmixgetränk (n)

millet Hirse (f)
mince hacken, durchdrehen
minced kleingehackt
minced beef Hackfleisch (n)
minced meat Hackfleisch (n)
minced raw beef Tatar (n)
mincemeat gehackte Früchte zur Pastetenfüllung (pl. f)
mince-pie Pastetchen (n) mit gehackten Früchten (pl. f) gefüllt
mincer (Fleisch-)Hackmaschine (f)
mincing machine (Fleisch-)Hackmaschine (f)
mind beachten
mineral bath Mineralbad (n)
mineral Mineralie (n)
mineral spring Mineralquelle (f), Heilquelle (f)
mineral water Mineralwasser (n)
minestrone Gemüsesuppe mit Einlagen (f), Minestrone (f)
mingle sich mischen, mengen
miniature golf Minigolf (n)
miniature golf course Minigolfplatz (m)
minibus Kleinbus (m)
minicab Kleintaxi (n)
mini computer Minicomputer (m)
minimum inventory Mindestbestand (m)
minimum manning Personalmindesbestand (m), Mindestbesetzung (f) mit Personal (n)
minimum number of participants Mindestteilnehmerzahl (f)
minimum stay Mindestaufenthalt (m)
minimum stock Lagermindestbestand (m), eiserne Reserve (f)

minimum wage Mindestlohn (m)
mint Pfefferminze (f)
mint sauce Minzensoße (f)
mint tea Pfefferminztee (m)
minutes Protokoll (n)
mirabelle plum Mirabelle (f)
mirror Spiegel (m)
miscellaneous vermischt, verschiedenartig
miscellaneous expenses sonstiger Aufwand (m)
misconduct Mißverhalten (n)
misguide fehlleiten
midleading irreführend
mismanagement Mißwirtschaft (f)
miss verfehlen, vermissen
missing fehlend, vermißt
miss the train Zug (m) versäumen
mist Nebel (m)
mistake irren, Irrtum (m)
mistry neblig, unklar
misunderstanding Mißverständnis (n)
misuse mißbrauchen, Mißbrauch (m)
mitten Fausthandschuh (m)
mix mischen, vermischen, Mischung (f)
mixed gemischt
mixed bathing Familienbad (n)
mixed boiled meat gekochtes Fleischallerlei (n)
mixed fruit gemischtes Obst (n)
mixed grill Mixed Grill (m)
mixed ice gemischtes Eis (n)
mixed ice-cream gemischtes Eis (n)
mixed meat-stew with vegetables Pichelsteiner Fleisch (n)
mixed pickles Essiggemüse (n)
mixed salad gemischter Salat (m)

mixed vegetable gemischtes Gemüse (n)
mixture (of food) Allerlei (n), Mischgericht (n)
mix-up Verwechslung (f)
moat Graben (m)
mock turtle soup falsche Schildkrötensuppe (f)
mode of payment Zahlungsmodus (m), Zahlungsweise (f)
moderate climate gemäßigtes Klima (n)
modernize modernisieren
modest bescheiden
modesty Bescheidenheit (f)
modification Abänderung (f), Modifizierung (f)
Modified American Plan (MAP) Zimmer (n) mit Halbpension (f)
modify abändern, modifizieren
moist feucht, naß
moisture Feuchtigkeit (f)
molasses Sirup (m)
molded cream bayrische Creme (f)
mole Mole (f)
molest belästigen
molestation Belästigung (f)
mollusk Weichtier (n)
monastery Kloster (n)
monetary system Geldsystem (n), Währung (f)
money order Zahlkarte (f)
money transfer Überweisung (f)
monthly closing Monatsabschluß (m)
monthly consumption Monatsverbrauch (m)
monthly programme Monatsprogramm (n)
monthly season ticket Monatskarte (f)
month-to-date kumuliert zum Datum (n)
monument Denkmal (n)
mood Stimmung (f)
mood music Stimmungsmusik (f)
moon Mond (m)
moonlight boat-trip Mondscheinbootsfahrt (f)
moor anlegen
mooring Anlegen (n)
mooring pier Anlegestelle (f)
moral sittlich, moralisch
morale Moral (f)
morel Morchel (f)
morning concert Frühkonzert (n)
morning performance Matineevorstellung (f)
morning train Frühzug (m)
Moselle wine Moselwein (m)
mosque Moschee (f)
mosquito net Moskitonetz (n)
moss Moos (n)
motel Motel (n)
mother-in-law Schwiegermutter (f)
motion study Bewegungsstudie (f)
motivate motivieren
motor accident Autounfall (m)
Motorail Autoreisezug-Service (m)
motor ambulance Krankenwagen (m), Rettungswagen (m)
motor boat Motorboot (n)
motor car Auto (n), Wagen (m)
motor caravan Campingbus (m)
motor carrier Transportunternehmer (m)
motor-car service Wagenpflege (f)
motor-club Automobilclub (m)
motor coach Bus (m), Omnibus (m)
motor-cycle Motorrad (n)

263

motor hotel Motel (n)
motoring guide Autoführer (m)
motoring journey Autoreise (f)
motoring offence Verkehrsdelikt (n)
motoring tourist Autoreisender (m)
motoring trip Autofahrt (f), Autoreise (f), Autotour (f)
motor inn Stadtmotel (n)
motor insurance Kraftfahrzeugversicherung
motorist Autofahrer (m), Kraftfahrer (m)
motorists' roadside assistance service Autohilfe (f)
motor launch Motorboot (n), Barkasse (f)
motor lorry Zugwagen (m)
motor race Autorennen (n)
motor ride Autofahrt (f)
motor road Autostraße (f)
motor scooter Motorroller (m)
motorship (MS) Motorschiff (n)
motor sleigh Motorschlitten (m)
motor traffic Autoverkehr (m)
motor vehicle Kraftfahrzeug (n)
motor vehicle insurance Kraftfahrzeugversicherung (f)
motor vehicle licence Zulassung (f)
motor vehicle user Kraftfahrzeugbenutzer (m)
motor-vessel (MV) Motorschiff (n)
motorway Autobahn (f)
motorway feeder road Autobahnzubringer (m)
motorway hotel Autobahnhotel (n)
motorway restaurant Autobahnraststätte (f)
motorway toll Autobahngebühr (f)

mountain Berg (m)
mountain air Höhenluft (f)
mountain cabin Berghütte (f)
mountain climate Höhenklima (n), Gebirgsklima (n)
mountain climber Bergsteiger (m)
mountain-climbing Klettern (n), Klettersport (m)
mountain-cock Auerhahn (m)
mountaineer Bergsteiger (m)
mountaineering Bergsteigen (n), Hochtouristik (f)
mountaineering eqiupment Bergsteigerausrüstung (f)
mountaineering school Bergsteigerschule (f)
mountain guide Bergführer (m)
mountain hike Bergwanderung (f)
mountain hotel Berghotel (n)
mountain hut Berghütte (f)
mountain inn Berggasthof (m)
mountain lake Bergsee (m)
mountain lodge Hüttenhotel (n)
mountain meadow Bergwiese (f)
mountain pass Bergpaß (m)
mountain peak Berggipfel (m)
mountain railway Bergbahn (f)
mountain rescue service Bergwacht (f)
mountain restaurant Höhenrestaurant (n), Bergrestaurant (n)
mountain road Bergstraße (f), Hochstraße (f)
mountains Gebirge (n), Gebirgswelt (f)
mountain top Berggipfel (m)
mountain tour Bergtour (f)
mountain village Bergdorf (n)
mousse Cremespeise (f), Creme (f)

mouth wash Mundwasser (n)
movable beweglich
move bewegen, beantragen
movie Film (m)
movie performance Filmvorführung (f), Filmvorstellung (f)
movie program Kinoprogramm (n), Filmprogramm (n)
movie room Kinosaal (m)
movie show Filmvorstellung (f)
movie theater Filmtheater (n), Kino (n)
movie ticket Kinokarte (f)
moving expense Umzugskosten (pl.)
mow mähen
much-frequented vielbesucht
mud bath Moorbad (n), Schlammbad (n)
mud pack Fangopackung (f), Schlammpackung (f)
mud therapy Fangotherapie (f)
mud treatment Moorbehandlung (f), Fangobehandlung (f)
muffin Muffins (engl. Teegebäck) (pl.)
mug Krug (m), Becher (m)
mulberry Maulbeere (f)
mule Maultier (n), Maulesel (m)
mulled claret Glühwein (m)
mulled wine Glühwein (m)
mullet Meerbarbe (f), Seebarbe (f), Meeräsche (f)
mulligatawny Geflügelrahmsuppe (f) mit Curry (m), Mulligatawny-Suppe (f)
multi-car garage Sammelgarage (f)
multi-lateral vielseitig, multilateral
multilingual guide sprachkundiger Führer (m)
multiple vielfach
multiple-unit train Triebwagenzug (m)
multiplier Multiplikator (m)
multiply multiplizieren
multi-purpose room Mehrzwekkraum (m)
multi-story car park Parkhochhaus (n)
multi-storey garage Hochgarage (f)
multi-uses system Mehrbenutzersystem (n)
municipal städtisch
municipal district Stadtbezirk (m)
municipal museum Stadtmuseum (n)
municipal theatre Stadttheater (n)
muscatel (wine) Muskateller-Wein (m)
museum Museum (n)
mushroom Edelpilz (m), Pilz (m)
mushroom sauce Pilzsoße (f)
mushrooms on toast Pilze (pl. m) auf Toast (m), Pilzschnitte (f)
mushroom soup Pilzsuppe (f)
musical Musical (n)
musical evening Musikabend (m)
music and entertainment Musik (f) und Unterhaltung (f)
musician Musiker (m)
mussel Muschel (f)
mussel soup Muschelsuppe (f)
mustard Senf (m)
mustard pot Senfglas (n)
mustard sauce Senfsoße (f)
mutton Hammel (m)
mutton chop Hammelrippchen (n)
mutton on skewers Hammelspießchen (n)
mutton-stew Hammelragout (n)

mutual gegenseitig, wechselseitig
mutual agreement gegenseitiger Vertrag (m)
mystery tour Fahrt (f) ins Blaue (n)

N

name nennen, benennen, Name (m)
napkin Serviette (f)
narrow eng, schmal
narrow film Schmalfilm (m)
narrow seas Ärmelkanal (n) und Irische See (f)
nasturtium Kapuzinerkresse (f), Brunnenkresse (f)
natation Schwimmen (n)
national einheimisch, Staatsangehörige (f), Staatsangehöriger (m)
national costume Nationaltracht (f), Volkstracht (f)
national currency Landeswährung (f)
national holiday Nationalfeiertag (m)
nationality Staatsangehörigkeit (f), Nationalität (f)
nationality sign Nationalitätszeichen (n)
nationalize verstaatlichen
national language Landessprache (f)
national park Reservat (n), Nationalpark (m)
national tourist Inlandsgast (m)
native eingeboren, einheimisch, Einheimische (r) (f), (m)
native language Muttersprache (f)
national park Nationalpark (m)

native town Heimatstadt (f)
natron kohlensaures Natron (n)
natural curative factor natürlicher Heilfaktor (m)
natural resources Naturschätze (pl. m)
nature Natur (f), natürliche Landschaft (f)
nature conservation Naturschutz (m)
nature cure Naturheilbehandlung (f)
nature reserve Naturschutzgebiet (n), Reservat (n)
naturism Freikörperkultur (f)
naturopath Heilpraktiker (m), Naturheilkundige (m)
naturopathy Naturheilmethode (f), Naturheilverfahren (n)
nausea Übelkeit (f), Brechreiz (m), Seekrankheit (f)
nautical chart Seekarte (f)
nautical mile Seemeile (1.852 km) (f)
navel orange Navelorange (f)
navigability Befahrbarkeit (f), Schiffbarkeit (f)
navigable schiffbar
navigable river schiffbarer Fluß (m)
navigate schiffen, befahren
navigation Nautik (f), Navigation (f), Schiffahrtskunde (f), Navigationskunde (f), Schiffahrt (f)
navigation channel Fahrrinne (f)
navigation guide Navigationskarte (f)
navigation light Positionslicht (n)
navigator Steuermann (m)
naze Landspitze (f)
neap zurückgehen (Flut) (f)
near nahe, in der Nähe (f)

near at hand nahe, in der Nähe (f), dicht dabei
near beer Dünnbier (n)
Near East Naher Osten
nearest nächster (Entfernung)
neat unverdünnt, pur, rein, sauber
necklace Halskette (f)
need Bedarf (m)
need of money Geldbedarf (m)
negative Negativ (n)
neglect vernachlässigen, versäumen
negotiate verhandeln, abschließen
negotiation Verhandlung (f), Abschluß (m)
neighbourhood Nachbarschaft (f)
neighbouring country Nachbarland (n)
nephew Neffe (m)
net amount Nettobetrag (m)
net earnings Nettoverdienst (m)
net income Reingewinn (m)
net loss Verlust (m), Reinverlust (m)
net profit Reingewinn (m)
net rooms revenue Nettozimmereinkünfte Nettobeherbergungsertrag (m) (pl. f)
net sales Nettoumsatz (m), Netto-Verkaufserlöse (pl. m)
net weight Reingewicht (n)
net worth Eigenkapital (n)
névé Firnschnee (m)
new-fallen snow Neuschnee (m)
new potaoes neue Kartoffeln (pl. f)
newspaper Zeitung (f)
newspaper advertising Zeitungswerbung (f)
newsreel Wochenschau (f)
news stall Zeitschriftenkiosk (m)
news stand Zeitungsstand (m), Kiosk (m)
new wine junger Wein (m)
New Year cruise Neujahrskreuzfahrt (f), Silvesterreise (f)
New Year's Day Neujahrstag (m)
New Year's dinner Silvesterdiner (n)
New Year's Eve celebration Silvesterfeier (f)
next of kin nächster Verwandter (m)
niece Nichte (f)
night and sunday duty Nacht- und Sonntagsdienst (m)
night-cleaner Nachtreinigungspersonal (n)
night club Nachtklub (m), Nachtlokal (n), Nachtbar (f)
night concierge Nachtportier (m)
nightdress Nachthemd (n)
night flight Nachtflug (m)
night life Nachtleben (n)
night manager Direktionsvertreter (m) während der Nacht (f)
night rate Nachttarif (m)
night rest Nachtruhe (f)
night run Nachtpiste (f)
night service Nachtverkehr (m)
night shift Nachtschicht (f)
night shift bonus Nachtschichtvergütung (f)
night shirt Herrennachthemd (n)
night's lodging Übernachtung (f), Schlafstelle (f)
night-telephone operator Nachttelefonistin (f)
night traffic Nachtverkehr (m)

night train Nachtzug (m)
night trip Nachtfahrt (f)
night-watchman Nachtwächter (m)
nightwork Nachtarbeit (f)
ninepin Kegel (m)
no admittance kein Eintritt (m)
no entry Eintritt verboten (m), Einfahrt (f) verboten!
no honking (no hooting) hupen verboten!
noise Lärm (m), Geräusch (n)
noise control Lärmbekämpfung (f)
non-alcoholic alkoholfrei
non-alcoholic beverage alkoholfreies Getränk (n)
nondeductible nicht abzugsfähig
nondelivery Nichtlieferung (f)
nondurable goods Verbrauchsgüter (pl. n)
non-dutiable nicht zollpflichtig
nonfulfillment Nichterfüllung (f)
non-malted nicht gemälzt
nonproduction group produktionsunabhängige Stelle (f)
non-scheduled flight Sonderflug (m)
non-smoker Nichtraucher (m)
non-smoker compartment Nichtraucherabteil (n)
non-stop flight Non-Stop-Flug (m), Flug (m) ohne Zwischenlandung (f)
non-swimmer Nichtschwimmer (m)
non-swimmers' pool Nichtschwimmerbecken (n)
noodle-dish with grated cheese Teigwaren mit geriebenem Käse (pl. f)
noodle Nudel (f)
noodle soup Nudelsuppe (f)
noon Mittag (m)

no overtaking Überholverbot (n)
no right turn Rechts abbiegen verboten (n)
normal-fare ticket Vollpreisfahrkarte (f)
normal performance Normalleistung (f)
north wind Nordwind (m)
Norway Norwegen
Norway lobster Langustinen (pl. f)
nose-to-tail collision Auffahrunfall (m)
no stopping Halteverbot (n)
no stopping this side today Halteverbot (n) heute auf dieser Straßenseite (f)
note aufzeichnen, vermerken, notieren, Mitteilung (f), Aufzeichung (f), Notiz (f)
note-paper Briefpapier (n), Schreibpapier (n)
no trough road keine Durchfahrt (f)
notice bekanntgeben, wahrnehmen, Bekanntgabe (f)
notice of accident Unfallmeldung (f)
notice of claim Schadensanzeige (f)
notice of defects Mängelanzeige (f)
notice of departure Abmeldung (f)
notifiable meldepflichtig, anzeigepflichtig
notification Benachrichtigung (f), Bekanntgabe (f)
notification of a loss Verlustanzeige (f)
notify avisieren
nourish ernähren
nourishment Nahrung (f), Nahrungsmittel (m)
no u-turn wenden (n) verboten

novelty Neuheit (f)
no waiting Parkverbot (n)
nudism FKK, Freikörperkultur (f)
nuisance Belästigung (f), Unfug (m), Störung (f)
null and void null und nichtig
number plate Nummernschild (n)
number of arrivals Anzahl (f) der Ankünfte (pl. f)
number of food covers Anzahl (f) der Essensgedecke (pl. n)
number of participants Teilnehmerzahl (f)
nurse Krankenschwester (f)
nursemaid Kindermädchen (n)
nursey Kinderzimmer (n), Spielzimmer (n)
nut Nuß (f)
nut bun Nußbeugel (n)
nut butter Nußbutter (f), braune Butter (f)
nut ice Nußeis (n)
nutmeg Muskatnuß (f)
nut pudding Nußpudding (m)
nutrition Ernährung (f)
nut tart Nußtorte (f)

O

oak Eiche (f)
oar Ruder (n)
oasis Oase (f)
oat Hafer (m)
oat flakes Haferflocken (pl. f)
oatmeal Hafermehl (n)
oatmeal cream soup Haferschleimsuppe (f)
oats Haferflocken
object Gegenstand (m)
objection Beanstandung (f)
objective Ziel (n), Zielsetzung (f)

object to beanstanden
obligate verpflichten
obligation Verpflichtung (f), Schuld (f), Verbindlichkeit (f)
obligation to register with the police polizeiliche Meldepflicht (f)
obligatory verpflichtend, bindend
oblige verpflichten, verbinden
observation Beobachtung (f)
observation platform Besucherbalkon (m)
observation tower Aussichtsturm (m)
observation window Aussichtsfenster (n)
observatory Sternwarte (f), Observatorium (n)
observe beobachten
occasion Gelegenheit (f)
occasional customers Laufkundschaft (f)
occupancy Belegung (f), Hotelbelegung (f), Aneignung (f)
occupancy percentage Belegungsprozentsatz (m)
occupation Beruf (m), Beschäftigung (f)
occupational illness Berufskrankheit (f)
occupied besetzt
ocean Ozean (m)
ocean-going hochseetüchtig
ocean liner Ozeandampfer (m)
odour Geruch (m), Duft (m)
of age mündig, volljährig
offals Innereien (pl. f)
offend beleidigen
offer anbieten, offerieren, Angebot (n), Offerte (f)
offer of employment Stellenangebot (n)
office Büro (n), Service-Office (n)

269

office equipment Büroausstattung (f)
office hours Geschäftszeit (f)
office supplies Büromaterial (n)
official offiziell, amtlich
off-licence inn Gassenschenke (f)
off limits Zutritt verboten (m)
off-peak fare Vor- und Nachsaisonfahrpreis (m)
off-peak period verkehrsarme Zeit (f)
off-peak season Vor- und Nachsaison (f)
off-season tote Saison (f)
off the beaten track abgelegen
off the peg von der Stange
off the road abseits der Straße (f)
off-time Freizeit (f)
oil Öl (n)
oil-changing Ölwechsel (m)
oil-fired central heating Ölzentralheizung (f)
oil heating Ölheizung (f)
oil level Ölstand (m)
old alt
old-fashioned altmodisch
old snow Altschnee (m)
old town Altstadt (f)
old wine alter Wein (m)
olive Olive (f)
olive oil Olivenöl (n)
olives, stuffed Oliven (pl. f) gefüllt
Olympic city Olympiastadt (f)
Olympic Games Olympische Spiele (pl. n)
omelet Omelett (n)
omelet soufflé Auflaufomelett (n)
omelet with fine herbs Kräuteromelett (n)
omelet with ham Schinkenomelett (n)

omelet with mushrooms Champignonomelett (n)
omnibus Omnibus (m)
on behalf of namens
on board an Bord
on board ship auf dem Schiff (n)
oncoming traffic entgegenkommender Verkehr (m), Gegenverkehr (m)
on demand auf Verlangen (n)
one-armed bandit Spielautomat (m)
one man operation Einmannbetrieb (m)
one-room flat Einzelzimmerappartement (n)
one-way street Einbahnstraße (f)
on hand vorrätig, vorhanden
onion Zwiebel (f)
onion mash Zwiebelmus (n)
onion sauce Zwiebelsoße (f)
on lease pachtweise, mietweise
on leaving the country bei der Ausreise (f)
on payment of the fees gegen Zahlung der Gebühren (pl. f)
on schedule planmäßig
on shore ans Land (n)
on short routes auf kurzen Strecken (pl. f)
on the high seas auf hoher See (f)
on the job training Ausbildung (f) am Arbeitsplatz (m)
on the quay am Kai (n)
on the rocks Getränk mit Eis (-würfel)
on the sea zur See (f), an der See (f)
on the spit am Spieß gebraten (m)
on trial auf Probe (f)
onward air journey Weiterflug (m)

open offen, geöffnet, öffnen
open-air bath Freibad (n)
open-air café Straßencafé (n), Gartencafé (n)
open-air dance Tanz (m) im Freien
open-air restaurant Gartenlokal (n), Gartenrestaurant (n)
open-air rest cure Liegekur (f)
open-air stage Freiluftbühne (f)
open-air swimmingpool Freibad (n), Sommerbad (n)
open-air theatre Freiluftbühne (f), Freilufttheater (n)
open-air ticket offener Flugschein (m)
open-air veranda Liegehalle (f)
open all the year round ganzjährig geöffnet
open check Barscheck (m)
open-door policy Politik (f) der offenen Tür (f)
opening freie Stelle (f), Eröffnung (f)
opening inventory Warenanfangsbestand (m), Eröffnungsinventur (f)
open market freier Mark (m)
opening of the season Saisoneröffnung (f)
open price freier Preis (m)
open sandwich belegtes Brot (einfach) (n)
open season Jagdsaison (f), Jagdzeit (f)
open space Grünfläche (f)
open vegetable pie Pizza (f)
open-water port Hafen (m) am offenen Meer (n)
open wine offener Wein (m)
opera Oper (f)
Opera Ball Opernball (m)
opera house Opernhaus (n)
operate verkehren, funktionieren, in Betrieb (m) halten, Reisen (pl. f) abwickeln, Gäste (pl. m) bedienen
operated departments Umsatzbereich (m)
operates daily verkehrt täglich
operating all the year round ganzjährig in Betrieb (m)
operating budget Budget (n) der betrieblichen Aufwendungen
operating cost Betriebskosten (pl.)
operating efficiency betriebliche Leistungsfähigkeit (f), Wirtschaftlichkeit (f)
operating expenses Betriebskosten (pl.)
operating loss Betriebsverlust (m)
operating months Betriebszeit (f)
operating profit Betriebsergebnis (n), Betriebsgewinn (m)
operating rate Beschäftigungsgrad (m)
operating results Betriebsergebnis (n)
operating statement Betriebsergebnisrechnung (f)
operating supplies Hilfs- und Betriebsstoffe (pl. f)
operating system Betriebssystem (n)
operational einsatzbar, einsatzbereit
operational control Betriebskontrolle (f)
operational management Operational Management (n), praktisches Hotelmanagement (n), Betriebsführung (f) in den Bereichen: Food und Beverage, Beherbergung, Wirt-

schaftsanalyse
operations analysis Wirtschaftsanalyse (f), Operations Analysis (f), Betriebsanalyse (f)
operations analyst Wirtschaftsanalytiker (m), Operations Analyst (m), Betriebsanalytiker (m)
operations research Planungsforschung (f), Verfahrensforschung (f), Unternehmensforschung (f)
operator Telefonistin (f)
operetta house Operettentheater (n)
opinion survey Meinungsuntersuchung (f)
opportunity advertising Gelegenheitswerbung (f)
opposite gegenüber, entgegengesetzt, Gegenteil (n)
optical optisch
optimal lot size optimale Losgröße (f)
optional wahlfrei, fakultativ, freigestellt
oral mündlich
orange Orange (f), Apfelsine (f)
orangeade Orangeade (f), natürliche Orangenlimonade (f)
orange ice-cream Orangeneis (n)
orchestra Orchester (n)
order bestellen, beauftragen, Bestellung (f), Auftrag (m), Ordnung (f)
order by telephone telefonische Bestellung (f)
order copy Bestellkopie (f)
order form Bestellformular (n)
ordering procedure Bestellverfahren (n)
ordering rate Bestellhäufigkeit (f)

orderly ordentlich, ordnungsgemäß
order pad Bestellscheinblock (m)
order quantity Bestellmenge (f)
order taking Bestellaufnahme (f)
ordinary gewöhnlich
organization Organisation (f), Einrichtung (f), Betrieb (m)
organization chart Organigramm (n), Organisationsplan (m)
organize organisieren, einrichten
organized tour Gesellschaftsreise (f)
organizer Veranstalter (m), Organisator (m)
orient Osten (m)
orientation plan Orientierungstafel (f)
orientation training Einführungsschulung (f)
origin Herkunft (f), Ursprung (m)
ornamental fountains Wasserspiele (pl. n)
other assets sonstige Aktiva
other catering operations sonstige Dienstleistungen (pl. f)
other current liabilities sonstige kurzfristige Verbindlichkeiten (pl. f)
other expenses sonstiger Aufwand (m)
other income sonstige Erträge (pl. m)
other operated departments Nebenbetriebe (pl. m), sonstige Betriebsabteilungen (pl. f)
other revenue sonstige Einkünfte (pl. f)
ounce, o. z. Unze (f), 28,350 g

outboard motor boat Außenbord-Motorboot (n)
outdoor advertising Außenwerbung (f)
outdoor bath Freibad (n)
outdoor dress Straßenkleidung (f)
outfit Ausstattung (f), Ausrüstung
outing Ausflug (m), Ausfahrt (f), Exkursion (f)
outing in the country Landausflug (m)
outlet Betriebsstätte (f), Absatzmarkt (m), Großabnehmer (m), Auslaß (m), Steckdose (f)
outline umreißen, Umriß (m)
out of date verfallen
out-of-line abweichend vom Üblichen (n)
out-of-pocket expense Barauslage (f)
out of the way abgelegen
output Produktionsmenge (f), Arbeitsleistung (f)
outsider Außenseiter (m)
outside representative Außenvertreter (m)
outside room Außenkabine (f)
outstanding hervorragend, offenstehend
outward auswärts
outward and homeward voyage Hin- und Rückreise (f)
outward and inward flight Hin- und Rückflug (m)
outward and inward journey Hin- und Rückreise (f), Hin- und Rückfahrt (f)
outward and return flight Hin- und Rückflug (m)
outward flight Hinflug (m)
outward journey Hinreise (f), Hinflug (m), Hinfahrt (f)

outward voyage Hinfahrt (f), Hinreise (f)
oven Bratofen (m), Backofen (m)
oven-baked im Ofen gebacken (m)
oven-baked apple im Ofen gebackener Apfel (m)
overage Überschuß (m), Mehrbetrag (m)
overall labor agreement Manteltarifvertrag (m)
overcapacity Überkapazität (f)
overcharge überfordern, zuviel berechnen
overcoat Mantel (m), Überzieher (m)
overcook zu stark braten
overcrowded überfüllt, überlaufen
overdone übergar
overdraw überziehen
overdue überfällig
overestimate überschätzen, Überschätzung (f)
overflow Überlauf (m)
overhead cost Gemeinkosten (pl.)
overhead department Gemeinkostenstelle (f)
overhead expenses Gemeinkosten (pl.)
overhead railway Hochbahn (f)
overland transportation Überlandverkehr (m)
overlap überlappen, überlagern
overload überladen
overlooking mit Blick (m) auf
overnight accommodation Übernachtungsmöglichkeit (f), Schlafstelle (f)
overnight bag Stadtkoffer (m)
overnight charge Übernachtungspreis (m)
overnight express Nachtschnell-

273

zug (m)
overnight stay Übernachtung (f)
overnight stay en route Zwischenübernachtung (f)
overpay überzahlen
overproduction Überproduktion (f)
oversea(s) in (nach) Übersee
overseas shipment Überseetransport (m)
overseas telegram Auslandstelegramm (n)
overseas tourist Auslandstourist (m)
overseas visitor Auslandsgast (m)
oversleep oneself verschlafen
overstaffed personell überbesetzt
overstocking Überbevorratung (f)
overtake überholen, einholen
overtime Überstunden (pl. f)
overture Ouvertüre (f)
overwhelm überwältigen, überwinden
owe verdanken, schuldig sein
own consumption Eigenverbrauch (m)
owner Eigentümer (m)
owner-driver Selbstfahrer (m)
ownership Eigentum (n)
owning company Eigentümergesellschaft
ox Ochse (m)
oxfords Straßenschuhe (pl. m)
ox-muzzle salad Ochsenmaulsalat (m)
ox-palate Ochsengaumen (m)
ox-tail Ochsenschwanz (m)
oxtail soup Ochsenschwanzsuppe (f)
oxtail stew Ochsenschwanzragout

ox-tongue Ochsenzunge (f)
oxygen bath Sauerstoffbad (n)
oyster Auster (f)
oyster-bank Austernbank (f)
oysterbed Austernbank (f)
oyster-farm Austernpark (m)
oz. (= ounce) Unze (28,350 g) (f)
ozone Ozon (n), reine Luft (f)
ozonic ozonisch
ozonic bath Ozonbad (n)
ozoniferous ozonhaltig

P

pace Schritt (m), Tempo (n), Leistung (f)
pack packen, verpacken, Packung (f)
package Paket (n), Packung (f), Programm (n)
package freight Stückgutfracht (f)
package tour Pauschalreise (f)
packaging Verpackung, verpakken
packed lunch Lunchpaket (n), Reiseproviant (m)
paddle paddeln, planschen, Paddel (n)
paddle-steamer Raddampfer (m)
paddling-boat Paddelboot (n)
paddling-pool Planschbecken (n)
paddy roher Reis (m)
pagan Heide (f)
pageant Festumzug (m), Trachtenfest (n)
page-boy Page (m)
paid holiday bezahlter Urlaub (m)
paid-up voll bezahlt, voll

eingezahlt
painting and decorating Malerarbeiten (pl. f) und Dekoration (f)
palate Gaumen (m)
pale ale helles Bier (n)
Palm Sunday Palmsonntag (m)
pamphlet Broschüre (f)
pan Pfanne (f), Topf (m)
pancake Pfannkuchen (m)
pancake Emperor style Kaiserschmarrn (m)
pancake soup Pfannkuchensuppe (f)
pane Fensterscheibe (f)
pan fried pork sausage Bratwurst (f)
panhandle Pfannenstiel (m)
pannikin Pfännchen (n), (Trink)-Kännchen (n)
panorama Panorama (n), Rundblick (m), Rundsicht (f)
pantry Speisekammer (f), Ausgabestelle (f) für Frühstück (n)
pantry girl Küchenhilfe (f)
pap (Kinder)-Brei (m)
paper bag cooking Kochen (n) in Folie (f)
paper napkin Papierserviette (f)
paper supplies Papierwaren (pl. f)
paper work Büroarbeiten (pl. f)
pappy breiig, pappig
paprika Paprika (m)
parasol Sonnenschirm (m)
parboil anbraten, ankochen
parcel Paket (n)
parcel post Paketpost (f)
parent company Muttergesellschaft (f)
parents-in-law Schwiegereltern (pl.)
parfait halbgefrorenes Eis (n)
parka Anorak (m), Parka (m)

park bench Ruhebank (f)
parking attendant Parkwächter (m)
parking disk Parkscheibe (f)
parking facilities Parkmöglichkeit (f), Parkgelegenheit (f)
parking lot Parkplatz (m)
parking meter Parkuhr (f)
parking place Parkplatz (m)
parlour Gastzimmer (n)
parlour game Gesellschaftsspiel (n)
parlour-maid Reinigungskraft (f)
Parmesan cheese Parmesankäse (m)
parsley Petersilie (f)
parsley potatoes Petersilienkartoffeln (pl. f)
parsley sauce Petersiliensoße (f)
par stock festgelegte Bestandsmenge
part teilen, auseinandergehen, einteilen, zuteilen, Stück (n), Teil (m), Bestandteil (m)
partial teilweise
partial board Teilverpflegung (f)
partial cancellation Teilstornierung (f)
partial massage Teilmassage (f)
partial payment Teilzahlung (f), Abschlagszahlung (f)
participant Teilnehmer (m), Teilhaber (m)
participate teilhaben, teilnehmen, sich beteiligen
participation Anteil (m), Teilnahme (f), Beteiligung (f)
particulars Einzelangaben (pl. f)
part-payment Teilzahlung (f)
partridge Rebhuhn (n), Schnepfe (f)
partridge pie Rebhuhnpastete (f)

275

part-timer Teilzeitarbeiter (m), Aushilfe (f), Kurzarbeiter (m)
party flight Gesellschaftsflug (m)
party game Gesellschaftsspiel (n)
party outing Gesellschaftsfahrt (f), Gruppenfahrt (f), Sammelfahrt (f)
party rate Gruppentarif (m)
party ticket Sammelfahrschein (m)
party tour Gesellschaftsreise (f), Gruppenreise (f)
party travel Gesellschaftsreisen (pl. f), Gruppenreisen (pl. f)
party trip Gesellschaftsfahrt (f), Gruppenfahrt (f)
pass übergeben, weiterreichen, übergehen, vergehen, Zugang (m), Paß (m), Durchgang (m)
passability Befahrbarkeit (f)
passable befahrbar
passage Durchfahrt (f), Gang (m)
passenger Fahrgast (m), Passagier (m)
passenger car Personenwagen (m)
passenger carriage Personentransport (m), Personenverkehr (m)
passenger density Reisedichte (f)
passenger fare Passagenpreis (m)
passenger ferry Personenfähre (f)
passenger plane Passagierflugzeug (n)
passenger ship Passagierschiff (n)
passenger's luggage Passagiergepäck (n)
passenger steamer Passagierdampfer (m)
passenger traffic Personenverkehr (m)
passenger train Reisezug (m), Personenzug (m)
passing-place Ausweichstelle (f)
pass in the Alps Alpenpaß (m)
pass-key Hauptschlüssel (m)
pass on abwälzen
pass over übergehen, übergeben
passport Reisepaß (m)
passport and customs examination Zoll- und Paßabfertigung (f)
passport inspection Paßkontrolle (f), Paßabfertigung (f)
passport office Paßstelle (f)
passport regulations Paßvorschriften (pl. f)
past due überfällig
paste Teig (m)
pasteurization Pasteurisierung (f)
pasteurized milk pasteurisierte Milch (f)
pastries Gebäck (n)
pastry Gebäck (n)
pastry board Nudelbrett (n)
pastry cook Patissier (m), Zuckerbäcker (m)
pastry envelopes Teigtaschen (pl. f)
pastry envelopes filled with white cheese Quarktaschen (pl. f)
pasturage Weideland (n)
pasture Weide (f)
patchboard Schalttafel (f)
patchcord Steckschnur (f)
paté Pastete (f)
paté de foie gras Gänseleberpastete (f)
patron Gast (m), Kunde (m), Stammkunde (m)

pattern Muster (n), Probe (f)
patt Blätterteigpastetchen (n), Pastetchen (n)
pavement Bürgersteig (m)
pawn pfänden
pawpaw Baummelone (f)
pax Gast (m), Passagier (m)
pay zahlen, bezahlen, Lohn (m), Gehalt (n)
payable zahlbar, fällig
pay as you go Zahlung (f) nach Wunsch
pay cash bar bezahlen
pay check Lohn/Gehaltsscheck (m)
pay damages Schadenersatz (m) leisten
pay day Zahltag (m)
paying guest zahlender Gast (m)
paying habit Zahlungsgewohnheit (f)
pay load Nutzlast (f)
pay-load capacity Ladefähigkeit (f)
paymaster Zahlmeister (m), Lohnbuchhalter (m)
payment Zahlung (f), Bezahlung (f), Auszahlung (f)
payment in advance Vorauszahlung (f)
payment in kind Naturalleistung (f)
payment of balance Restzahlung (f)
payments of travellers Reisezahlungsverkehr (m)
payment terms Zahlungsbedingungen (pl. f)
payroll Lohnliste (f), Lohnaufwand (m)
payroll and performance control system Lohn- und Leistungskontrollsystem (n)
payroll control Personalkostenkontrolle (f), Lohnkostenkontrolle (f)
payroll department Lohnbüro (n)
payroll taxes and employees relations übriger Personalaufwand (m), Personalgemeinkosten (pl.), Lohnsteuer (f) und Sozialleistungen (pl. f) für das Personal n
pea Erbse (f)
peaceful friedlich, ungestört
peach Pfirsich (m)
peaches ice-cream Pfirsich-Eis (n)
peach Melba Pfirsich Melba (m)
peacock Pfau (m)
peak days Verkehrsspitze (f)
peak hour Zeit (f) der Spitzenbelastung (f), Stoßzeit (f)
peak hour traffic Stoßverkehr (m), Spitzenverkehr (m)
peak load Stoßarbeit (f), Belastungsspitze (f), Arbeitshäufung (f)
peak period Stoßzeit (f)
peak season Hochsaison (f)
peak season fare Hauptsaisonflugpreis (m)
peak tourist season Hauptreisezeit (f)
peak tourist traffic Hauptreiseverkehr (m)
pea mash Erbsenpüree (n)
peanut butter Erdnußbutter (f)
peanut Erdnuß (f)
pear Birne (f)
pea soup Erbsensuppe (f), dichter Nebel (m) (scherzhafter Ausdruck), Waschküche (f)
pebbly beach Kiesstrand (m)
pedestrian crossing Fußgängerübergang (m)

peel schälen, Schale (f)
peeled geschält
peeling Haut (f), Rinde (f), Schale (f)
pem(m)ican Pemmikan (n)
penalty Geldstrafe (f), Vertragsstrafe (f), Strafstoß (Sport) (m)
peninsula Halbinsel (f)
penknife Taschenmesser (n)
penny-in-the-slot Automat (m), Verkaufsautomat (m)
pension scheme Pensionsplan (m)
Pentecost Pfingsten (n)
penthouse Dachwohnung (f), Nebengebäude (n)
pepper Pfeffer (m)
pepper-box Pfeffergefäß (n)
pepper cake Ingwerkuchen (m)
pepper-castor Pfefferstreuer (m)
pepper-corn Pfefferkorn (n)
pepper mill Pfeffermühle (f)
peppermint Pfefferminze (f)
pepper-pot Pfefferstreuer (m)
pepper Pfefferschote (f)
pepper-steak Pfeffersteak (n)
perambulate durchwandern, bereisen, besichtigen
perambulation Durchwanderung (f), Besichtigungsreise (f)
per annum im Jahr (n), jährlich
percentage of occupancy Belegungsprozentsatz (m)
perch Barsch (m)
perch-pike Fogosch (Zander) (m)
percolate Kaffee etc. filtern (m)
percolator Perkolator (m), Kaffee (filter)maschine (f)
per day pro Tag (m), täglich
per diem allowance Reisespesen-Tagesatz (m)

peregrinate wandern, umherreisen
peregrination Wandern (n), Wanderung (f)
performance Leistung (f), Leistungsgrad (m)
performance appraisal Arbeitsplatzbewertung (f), Leistungsbewertung
performance control Leistungskontrolle (f)
performance standard Leistungsmaßstab (m)
periodical Zeitschrift (f)
period of stay Aufenthaltsdauer (f)
perishable leicht verderblich (Lebensmittel) (f)
perishable goods verderbliche Waren (pl. f)
permanent dauernd, ständig
permantly open durchgehend geöffnet
permanent residence ständiger Wohnsitz (m)
permanent resident Dauergast (m)
permission Erlaubnis (f)
permit erlauben, gestatten, Erlaubnis (f), Genehmigung (f), Passierschein (m)
perpendicular senkrecht
perpetual inventory Buchinventur (f), permanente Inventur (f)
Persian blinds Jalousien (pl. f)
persimmon Kakipflaume (f)
personal belonging persönliche Gebrauchsgegenstände (pl. m)
personal computer Personalcomputer (m)
personal data Personenbeschreibung (f)
personal expenses persönliche Ausgaben (pl. f)

personal selling persönlicher Verkauf (m)
personal status Familienstand (m)
personnel Personal (n)
personnel department Personalabteilung (f)
personnel manager Personalchef (m)
personnel requisition Personalanforderung (f)
PERT, Program Evaluation and Review Technique Netzplantechnik (f), Projektfortschrittsplanung (f)
pet Haustier (n)
petrol Benzin (n)
petrol can Benzinkanister (m)
petrol consumption Benzinverbrauch (m)
petrol station Tankstelle (f)
petrol tank Benzintank (m)
petrol voucher Benzinschein (m)
pettitoes Schweinsfüße (pl. m)
petty cash kleine Kasse (f), Bargeldkasse (f)
pewit Kiebitz (m)
pharmacy Apotheke (f)
pheasant Fasan (m)
photo Foto (n)
photographic equipment Fotoausrüstung (f)
photographing not allowed Fotografieren (n) verboten!
photo safari Fotosafaria (f)
physical inventory körperliche Bestandsaufnahme (f)
physiotherapist Krankengymnast (m)
physiotherapy Heilgymnastik (f), Krankengymnastik (f)
piano Klavier (n)
piccalilli scharf gewürztes Essiggemüse (n)

pickerel Hecht (m)
picking-up point Zusteigemöglichkeit (f)
pickle Essigsoße (zum Einlegen) (f), Gewürzgurke (f), Essiggurke (f)
pickled gepökelt
pickled beef's muzzle Ochsenmaulsalat (m)
pickled cabbage Sauerkraut (n), Weinkraut (n)
pickled cucumber saure Gurke (f)
pickled fish marinierter Fisch (m)
pickled fruit Senfobst (n), Senffrüchte (pl. f)
pickled gherkin Gewürzgurke (f)
pickled onion Perlzwiebel (f)
pickled pork Pökelfleisch (n), Eisbein (n)
pickled shank of pork Eisbein (n)
pickles in Essig eingelegtes Gemüse (n)
pick-me-up (Magen)-Stärkung (f), Schnäpschen (n)
pickpocket Taschendieb (m)
picnic Picknick (n)
picnic bag Picknicktasche (f)
picture gallery Gemäldegalerie (f)
picture postcard Ansichtskarte (f)
picturesque malerisch schön
pimento Jamaikapfeffer (m)
piddock Dattelmuschel (f)
pie Pastete (f)
piece Stück (n)
piece of cake Stück Kuchen (n)
piece of the ribs of beef Mittelrippenstück (n) (Rind)
pie-crust Pastetenkruste (f), Teigdecke (f)

279

pie-plant Rhabarber (amerik.) (m)
pier Mole (f)
pig Schwein (n)
pigeon Taube (f)
pigeon hole Postfach (n), Ablagefach (n)
pig's head Schweinskopf (m)
pig's trotters Schweinsfüße (pl. m)
pike Hecht (m)
pike dumplings Hechtklößchen (pl. m)
pikelet engl. Teegebäck (n)
pike-perch Zander (m)
pilchard große Sardine (f)
pilfer stehlen, entwenden
pilferage Diebstahl (m)
pilgrimage Pilgerreise (f)
pilgrimage church Wallfahrtskirche (f)
pillow Kopfkissen (n)
pillow-case Kissenbezug (m)
pillow-slip Kissenbezug (m)
pilot Lotse (m), Pilot (m), steuern, lotsen
pilotage Lotsengebühr (f)
pilot's licence Flugschein (m)
pinch Prise (f)
pineapple Ananas (f)
pineapple ice Ananaseis (n)
pineapple-juice Ananassaft (m)
ping-pong Tischtennis (n)
ping-pong room Tischtennishalle (f)
pint ca. ½ Liter (m)
pintail Wildente (f)
piquant sauce pikante Soße (f)
pitcher Kanne (f), Krug (m)
pitch a tent zelten
pizza Pizza (f)
place a longdistance call ein Ferngespräch (n) anmelden
place an order einen Auftrag (m) erteilen

place-card Tischkarte (f)
place-name sign Ortstafel (f)
place on deck Deckplatz (m)
place of assembly Sammelstelle (f), Treffpunkt (m)
place of birth Geburtsort (m)
place of delivery Erfüllungsort (m)
place of departure Abfahrtsstelle (f)
place of destination Bestimmungsort (m)
place of dispatch Versandort (m)
place of entertainment Vergnügungslokal (n)
place of interest Ausflugsort (m), Sehenswürdigkeit (f)
place of issue Ausstellungsort (m)
place of payment Zahlungsort (m)
place of performance Erfüllungsort (m)
place of pilgrimage Wallfahrtsort (m)
place of residence Wohnort (m)
plaice Scholle (f)
plaid Plaid (n)
plain einfach, gutbürgerlich
plain boiled aus dem Wasser gezogen (gekocht)
plain boiled potatoes Salzkartoffeln (pl. f)
plain circle cake Gugelhupf (m)
plain cooking gutbürgerliche Küche (f)
plain fare Hausmannskost (f)
plain omelet einfaches Omelett (n)
plain sausage Knackwurst (f)
plain veal cutlet Kalbskotelett natur (n)
plain veal steak Naturschnitzel (n)

plan Plan (m), planen
plane Flugzeug (n), Maschine (f)
plane crash Flugzeugabsturz (m)
plane load Flugzeugladung (f)
plane ticket Flugkarte (f), Flugschein (m)
plank Steg (m)
planning Planung (f)
plant oil Pflanzenöl (n)
plastic bag Plastikbeutel (m)
plate Teller (m), Platte (f)
platform Bahnsteig (m)
platform ticket Bahnsteigkarte (f)
platter (Braten)-Platte (f)
player Spieler (m)
playgoer Theaterbesucher (m)
playground Spielplatz (m)
playhouse Schauspielhaus (n)
playing-field Spielwiese (f)
play ninepins kegeln
playroom Spielzimmer (n)
play skittles kegeln
please close the door bitte Tür (f) schließen
please do not touch bitte nicht berühren
pleasure Vergnügen (n)
pleasure boat Vergnügungsdampfer (m)
pleasure drive Vergnügungsfahrt (f), Spazierfahrt (f)
pleasures of the table kulinarische Genüsse (pl. m)
pleasure trip Vergnügungsreise (f)
plimsolls Tennisschuhe (pl. m)
plot of land Grundstück (n)
plover Kiebitz (m)
plover's eggs Kiebitzeier (pl. n)
plug stecken, einstecken
plum Pflaume (f), Zwetschge (f)

plumber Klempner (m), Installateur (m)
plum dumpling Zwetschgenknödel (m)
plum flan Pflaumenkuchen (m)
plummy reich an Pflaumen (pl. f) oder Rosinen (pl. f)
plum pudding engl. Weihnachtspudding (m), Plumpudding (m)
pluvial regnerisch
p. m. nachmittags
pneumatic boat Schlauchboot (n)
poached eggs verlorene Eier (pl. n)
poached egg on toast verlorenes Ei auf Toast (n)
pocket-lamp Taschenlampe (f)
pocket money Taschengeld (n)
pocket train schedule Taschenfahrplan (m)
point of origin Ausgangsort (m)
point of sale Verkaufsort (m)
point of turnaround Zielort (m), Umkehrpunkt (m)
pointsman Verkehrspolizist (m)
poker Feuerhaken (m), Poker(-spiel) (n)
police Polizei (f)
police headquarters Polizeipräsidium (n)
policeman Polizist (m)
police station Polizeirevier (n)
policy Politik (f), Geschäftspolitik (f)
polish polieren
polite höflich
polyglot vielsprachig
pollution of the air Luftverschmutzung (f)
pollution of the waters Gewässerverschmutzung (f)
pomegranate Granatapfel (m)
pond Teich (m)

281

pone amerik. Maisbrot (n)
pop Brause (f), Popmusik (f)
pop-corn Puffmais (m)
poppy-seed bun Mohnbeugel (n)
popularity rate Beliebtheitsgrad (m)
population density Bevölkerungsdichte (f)
porcelain Porzellan (n)
porch (überdachte) Vorhalle (f), Portal (n)
pork Schweinefleisch (n)
pork chop Schweinskotelett (n)
pork cutlet Schweinskotelett (n)
pork cutlet breaded Schweinskotelett (n) gebacken
porker Mastschwein (n)
pork galantine Schwartenmagen (m)
pork kidneys Schweinsnieren (pl. f)
pork knuckles Schweinshaxe (f)
porkling Ferkel (n)
porridge Haferbrei (m), Porridge (n)
port Hafen (m), Portwein (m)
portable luggage Handgepäck (n)
portable medicine case Reiseapotheke (f)
portable radio Kofferradio (n)
port dues Hafengeld (n)
port entrance Hafeneinfahrt (f)
porter dunkles Bier (n), Hoteldiener (m), Gepäckträger (m)
porterhouse steak Zwischenrippenstück (n) mit Filet (n)
porthole Bullauge (n)
port installations Hafenanlagen (pl. f)
portion Portion (f), Teil (m)
portion chart Verzeichnis (n) der Soll-Portionsgrößen (pl. f)

portion control Portionsgrößenkontrolle (f)
portion cost factor Portionskostenfaktor (m)
portion size Portionsgröße (f)
port of call Anlaufhafen (m), Anlegehafen (m), Bestimmungshafen (m)
port of registry Heimathafen (m)
port of transshipment Umschlaghafen (m)
position Stellung (f), Position (f), Lage (f)
possibility of travelling Anreisemöglichkeit (f)
postage Porto (n)
postage meter Frankiermaschine (f)
postale check account Postscheckkonto (n)
postal delivery Postzustellung (f)
postal district Postbezirk (m)
postal giro office Postscheckamt (n)
postal money order Postanweisung (f)
postal order Postanweisung (f)
postal rate Portogebühr (f)
postal savings account Postsparkonto (n)
postal stamp Briefmarke (f)
postal zone number Postleitzahl (f)
postcard Postkarte (f)
poster Werbeplakat (n), Plakat (n), Poster (n)
poster advertising Plakatwerbung (f)
poster board Anschlagtafel (f)
poste restante postlagernd
poste restante railway station bahnpostlagernd
posting Übertragung (f)

postman Briefträger (m)
post-mark Poststempel (m)
post office Postamt (n)
post-office box Postfach (n)
post-office bus Postbus (m)
post-paid franko, frankiert
post payment Nachzahlung (f)
postpone aufschieben, verschieben, vertagen
postponement Verschiebung (f), Vertagung
pot Topf (m), Tiegel (m), einmachen
potage (dicke) Suppe (f)
potation Trinken (n), Zecherei (f)
potato Kartoffel (f)
potato basket Kartoffelkörbchen (n)
potato chips Kartoffelchips (pl.)
potato crisps gebackene Kartoffelscheiben (pl. f)
potato-croquettes Kartoffelkroketten (pl. f)
potato dumpling Kartoffelknödel (m)
potatoes, baked gebackene Kartoffeln (pl. f)
potatoes baked in their jackets gebackene Pellkartoffeln (pl. f)
potatoes, boiled Salzkartoffeln (pl. f)
potatoes, chipped Pommes frites (pl. f)
potatoes, fried Bratkartoffeln (pl. f)
potatoes in their jackets Kartoffeln in der Schale (pl. f)
potatoes, sauté Schwenkkartoffeln (pl. f)
potato-fritters Reibekuchen (m)
potato-mash Kartoffelbrei (m)
potato masher Kartoffelstampfer (m)

potato nest Kartoffelkörbchen(n)
potato pancake Kartoffelpuffer (m)
potato salad Kartoffelsalat (m)
potato soup Kartoffelsuppe (f)
potato straws Strohkartoffeln (pl. f)
potential food cost Soll-Wareneinsatz (m), Speisen (pl. f)
potential of accommodation Aufnahmepotential (n)
pot-herb Küchenkraut (n)
pot of broth with boiled meat Suppentopf mit Fleischeinlage (m)
pot roast Schmorbraten (m)
pot-stew of fish Fischeintopfgericht (n)
pot stew of tripes gedämpfte Kutteln (pl. f)
pottage dicke Gemüsesuppe (mit Fleisch) (f)
potted beef Rinderschmorbraten (m)
pottery Keramik (f)
poultry Geflügel (n)
pound engl. Pfund (n) (ca. 450 g)
pound-cake Napfkuchen (m)
pour gießen
pour over darübergießen
poussin Kücken (n)
powder Pulver (n), Puder (m), bestreuen
powder snow Pulverschnee (m)
power consumption Stromverbrauch (m)
power current Kraftstrom (m)
power supply Energieversorgung (f)
practise üben, trainieren
practice slope Übungshang (m)
prawn cocktail Krabbencock-

283

tail (m)
prawn Garnele (f), Krabbe (f)
precedence Priorität (f), Vorrang (m), Vorrecht (n)
precipitation Niederschlag (m)
pre-cook vorkochen
pre-cool vorkühlen
predominat vorherrschend
prefer bevorzugen, vorziehen
preference Vorzug (m), Vergünstigung (f), Vorliebe (f), Wahl (f)
preferential treatment Vorzugsbehandlung (f), Sonderbehandlung (f)
preheat vorwärmen
preliminary agreement Vorvertrag (m)
pre-opening management Voreröffnungsmanagement (n)
prepaid vorausbezahlt
prepaid taxes Steuervorauszahlung (f)
preparation Vor-, Zubereitung (f)
prepare vor-, zubereiten
prepared at (guest's) table am Tisch zubereitet (m)
prepared with butter in Butter zubereitet (f)
prepayment Vorauszahlung (f)
pre-preparation Grundzubereitung (f)
pre-season Vorsaison (f)
present Geschenk (n)
present a bill Rechnung (f) vorlegen
preservation of monuments Denkmalpflege (f)
preserved fruit Kompott (n)
preserves Eingemachtes (n), Konserve (n. pl. f), eingemachte Rüchte (pl. f), Konfitüren (pl. f)

press advertising Anzeigenwerbung (f)
pressed hog's head Presskopf (m)
pressing service Bügelservice (m), Büglerei (f)
press release Presseinformation (f), Presseerklärung (f)
prestige advertising Repräsentationswerbung (f)
pretzel (Salz-)Bretzel (f)
prevent verhindern, verhüten
prevention Verhinderung (f), Vorbeugung (f)
preventive vorbeugend
preview Vorschau (f)
previous year Vorjahr (n)
previous season vorherige Saison (f)
price allowance Preisnachlaß (m)
price category Preisklasse (f)
price ceiling Preisobergrenze (f)
price cut Preisermäßigung (f)
price estimate Preiskalkulation (f)
price for board and lodging Pensionspreis (m)
price increase Preiserhöhung (f)
price list Preisliste (f)
price policy Preispolitik (f)
prices include service charge and added-value tax Preis (pl. m) einschließlich Bedienungsgeld (n) und Mehrwertsteuer (f)
prices include the following services Preise schließen die folgenden Leistungen (pl. f) ein
prices on request Preise (pl. m) auf Anfrage (f)
prices per day and person Preise je Tag (m) und Person (f)

prices subject to alteration Preisänderung (f) vorbehalten
price structure Preisgefüge (n)
prices without guarantee Preise (pl.m) ohne Gewähr (f)
price tag Preisschild (n)
pricing Preisfestsetzung (f)
prickling wine Perlwein (m)
prime erstklassig
prime choice erste Wahl (f)
prime rib of beef Ochsenrippenstück (n)
print Abzug (m), drucken
printing and stationery Druck- und Büromaterial (n) und Drucksachen (pl.f)
printed matter Drucksache (f)
printer Drucker (m)
priority Vorzug (m), Vorrang (m), Priorität (f)
priority road Vorfahrtsstraße (f)
private bath Einzelbad (n)
private bathing-beach Privatbadestrand (m)
private car Privatwagen (m)
private hotel Hotelpension (f)
private house Privathaus (n)
private party geschlossene Gesellschaft (f)
private performance geschlossene Vorstellung (f)
private property Privatgrundstück (n), Privatbesitz (m)
private room Privatzimmer (n), Privatquartier (n), Gesellschaftsraum (m)
private yacht Privatjacht (f)
probable time of arrival voraussichtliche Ankunftszeit (f)
proceed to the waiting room in good time sich frühzeitig in den Warteraum (m) begeben
procedure Verfahren (n)
process chart Arbeitsablaufdiagramm (n)

procession Umzug (m)
procession in national costumes Trachtenumzug (m)
produce herstellen, vorlegen
product Produkt (n), Erzeugnis (n)
production control Steuerung (f) der Produkion
production planning Produktionsplanung (f)
production standard Leistungsmaßstab (m), Leistungseinheit (f)
productivity Leistung (f), Produktivität (f)
productivity report Leistungsbericht (m)
product mix Sortiment (n)
profession Beruf (m)
profit Gewinn (m)
profitability Ertragskraft (f), Rentabilität (f), Wirtschaftlichkeit (f)
profitable gewinnbringend
profit and loss statement Gewinn- und Verlustrechnung (f)
profit before depreciation Gewinn (m) vor Abschreibung (f)
profit before interest and depreciation Gewinn (m) vor Zinsen (pl.m) und Abschreibung (f)
profit from operated departments Bereichsergebnissumme (f), Bereichsdeckungsbeitrag (m)
profit margin Verdienstspanne (f)
profit multiplier Gewinnmultiplikator (m)
profit sensitivity study Analyse (f) der Gewinneinflußfaktoren (pl.m)
program (amerik.) Pro-

285

gramm (n)
programme (brit) Programm (n)
programming language Programmiersprache (f)
prohibit untersagen, verbieten
prohibited area Sperrgebiet (n)
prohibition of entry of vehicles Verkehrsverbot (n)
prohibition to overtake Überholverbot (n)
prohibition to park Parkverbot (n)
prohibition to stop Haltverbot (n)
prolong verlängern
prolongation Verlängerung (f)
promenade Promenade (f)
promenade deck Promenadendeck (n)
promise versprechen, Versprechen (n)
promontory Vorgebirge (n)
promote werben, fördern, Vorschub (m) leisten
promotion Werbung (f), Verkaufsförderung (f)
promotion of the tourist trade Förderung (f) des Fremdenverkehrs (m)
prompt Eingabeaufforderung (f)
proof Unterlage (f), Beweis (m), Nachweis (m)
property Eigentum (n)
propan gas Propangas (n)
proposal Vorschlag (m), Antrag (m)
propose vorschlagen, beantragen
prospectus Prospekt (m)
prosperity irregularity report, PIR Bestätigung (f) für abhanden gekommenes Gepäck (n)

protected against the wind windgeschützt
protected from geschützt gegen
protection of places of natural beauty Landschaftsschutz (m)
protective inoculation Schutzimpfung (f)
protective vaccination Schutzimpfung (f)
provisional vorläufig
provision dealer Feinkosthändler (m)
provision for operating equipment Rückstellung (f) für Betriebsmittel (pl. n)
provision for replacement of china, crockery, glassware and linen Rückstellung (f) für Ersatz von Geschirr (n), Steingut (n), Glaswaren (pl. f) und Wäsche (f)
provisions Lebensmittel (pl. n), Proviant (m)
prunelle Prünelle (f), (getrocknete entkernte Pflaume)
prune Pflaume (f), Zwetschge (f), Dörrpflaume (f), Backpflaume (f), Zwetschge (pl. f)
ptarmigan Schneehuhn (n)
pub Gasthaus (n), Kneipe (f), Ausschank (m), Pub (m)
pub crawl Kneipenbummel (m)
publican Wirt (m), Schankwirt (m)
publication Veröffentlichung (f), Publikation (f)
public bar Stehbierhalle (f)
public bath-room Etagenbad (n)
public call-room öffentliche Fernsprechzelle (f)
public convenience öffentliche Toilette (f)
public festival Volksfest (n)
public gardens öffentliche Anlagen (pl. f)

public health regulations Gesundheitsbestimmungen (pl. f)
public holiday gesetzlicher Feiertag (m)
public house Bierlokal (n), Ausschank (m), Wirtshaus (n)
publicity Publizität (f), Öffentlichkeit (f)
publicity campaign Werbefeldzug (m)
publicity campaign abroad Auslandswerbung (f)
publicity department Werbeabteilung (f)
public lavatory öffentliche Toilette (f)
public notices öffentliche Bekanntmachungen (pl. f)
public relations Öffentlichkeitsarbeit (f), Public Relations (PR) (pl. f)
public room rentals Erträge (pl. m) aus Vermietung (f) von Veranstaltungsräumen (pl. m)
public space and kitchen cleaning Reinigung (f) der Veranstaltungsräume (pl. m) und Küche (f)
public transport öffentliche Verkehrsmittel (pl. n)
publish veröffentlichen
pudding Pudding (m)
puffed potatoes Auflaufkartoffeln (pl. f)
puff omelet Omelette Soufflée (n)
puff-paste Blätterteig (m)
puff-paste patty Blätterteigpastetchen (n)
puff-paste stick Blätterteigstengelchen (n)
puff pastry Blätterteiggebäck (n)
pull ziehen

pull-down table Klapptisch (m)
pullet Hühnchen (n), Poularde (f)
Pullman(car) Pullmanwagen (m), Salon-Schlafwagen (m)
pull-out bed Ausziehbett (n)
pull the emergency brake Notbremse (f) ziehen
pulse Hülsenfrüchte (pl. f)
pumpkin Kürbis (m)
pump room Trinkhalle (f), Quellpavillon (m), Wandelhalle (f)
pump-room cure Trinkkur (f)
punch Punsch (m)
purchase erwerben, einkaufen, Kauf (m)
purchase requisition Bedarfsmeldung (f)
purchasing agent Einkäufer (m)
purchasing department Einkaufsabteilung (f)
purchasing policy Einkaufspolitik (f)
purchasing procedure Einkaufsverfahren (n)
purchasing specifications Einkaufsrichtlinien (pl. f)
puree of beans Bohnenpüree (n)
puree of peas Erbsenpüree (n)
purse Geldbeutel (m)
purser Zahlmeister (m)
push stoßen
pusher Schieber (Kinderlöffel) (m)
put off vertagen
put on a waitinglist auf eine Warteliste (f) setzen
put up absteigen, beherbergen
put up to sea auslaufen
put up with sich abfinden mit
PX (post exchange) Warenhaus (n) für amerik. für Armeeangehörige)

Q

quack doctor Kurpfuscher (m), Quacksalber (m)
quaff zechen, schlürfen
quagmire Morast (m)
quail Wachtel (f)
qualification Tauglichkeit (f), Qualifikation (f), Eignung (f)
qualified qualifiziert
qualify befähigen, qualifizieren
quality Güte (f), Beschaffenheit (f), Qualität (f)
quality assurance program Qualitätsüberprüfungsprogramm (n)
quality checker Qualitätskontrolleur (m)
quality control Qualitätskontrolle (f)
quality evaluation Qualitätsbewertung (f)
quality label Gütezeichen (n)
quality standard Qualitätsstandard (m)
qualmish übel, unwohl
quantitative analysis quantitative Untersuchung (f)
quantity Menge (f), Qualität (f)
quantit bonus Mengenprämie (f)
quantity discount Mengenrabatt (m), Rückvergütung (f)
quantitiy of available traffic Verkehrsaufkommen (n)
quantity standard Mengenstandard (m), Mengenvorgabe (f)
quarantine Quarantäne (f)
quarrel streiten, zanken, Streit (m)
quarry Wild (n), Beute (f)
quart Quast (1, 136 l) (n)
quarter Viertel (n), Vierteljahr (n), Stadtviertel (n), Himmelsrichtung (f)
quarterly vierteljährlich
quartermaster Quartiermeister (m), Steuermannsmaat (m)
quarters Quartier (n)
quasi gleichkommend, quasi
quay Kai (m)
quayage Kaigeld (n), Kaianlagen (pl. f)
quay dues Kaigebühren (pl. f), Liegegeld (n)
queasy unwohl, empfindlich
queen olive große, grüne Olive (f)
quenelle Fleischknödel (m)
querulous unzufrieden
question Frage (f), in Frage (f) stellen
questionary Fragebogen (m)
questionnaire Fragebogen (m)
queue Schlange (f), Reihe (f)
queue up Schlange (f) stehen
quick schnell
quick frozen tiefgekühlt
quick lunch restaurant Schnellgaststätte (f)
quick-service restaurant Schnellgaststätte (f)
quiet ruhig, still
quiet enjoyment ungestörter Besitz (m)
quietly located in ruhiger Lage (f)
quilt Steppdecke (f)
quince Quitte (f)
quit aufgeben, verlassen, verzichten
quitclaim verzichten, Verzicht (m)
quite ganz, ziemlich
quit rate Kündigungsquote (f)
quota Quote (f), Anteil (m), Kontingent (n)
quotation Kursnotierung (f),

Preisnotierung (f), Preisangabe (f)
quotation of prices Preisangabe (f)
quote notieren, quotieren, ein Preisangebot (n) machen
quotient Quotient (m)

R

rabbit Kaninchen (n)
race Rennen (n); rennen
race course Rennstrecke (f)
racing boat Rennboot (n)
rack Trockengestell (n), Gläsergestell (n)
racket Tennisschläger (m)
radiator Kühler (Auto) (m)
radio sets in every room Radio in allen Zimmern (pl. n)
radio taxi Funktaxi (n)
radish Radieschen (n), Rettich (m)
radon spring Radonquelle (f)
raft Floß (n)
rag Lappen (m)
ragout Ragout (n)
ragout of chicken Geflügelragout (n)
rail Reling (f)
rail and steamship travel kombinierte Zug-Schiffsreise (f)
rail and water terminal Schiff-Eisenbahn-Umladeplatz (m)
railcar Triebwagen (m)
rail connection Bahnverbindung (f), Zugverbindung (f)
railroad Eisenbahn (f)
railroad car Eisenbahnwagen (m)
railroad grade crossing Eisenbahnübergang (m)
railroad schedule Eisenbahnfahrplan (m)
railroad staff Bahnpersonal (n)
railroad terminal Eisenbahnendstation (f)
rails Gleise (pl. n)
rail-steamer journey Bahn-Schifffsreise (f)
rail ticket Eisenbahnfahrkarte (f)
rail-ticket office Bahnschalter (m)
rail traffic Eisenbahnverkehr (m)
rail transport Eisenbahngütertransport (m)
railway Eisenbahn (f)
railway bookstand Bahnhofsbuchhaltung (f)
railway bus Bahnbus (m)
railway carriage Eisenbahnwagen (m)
railway coach Eisenbahnwagen (m)
railway guard Zugschaffner (m)
railway guide Kursbuch (n)
railway inquiry office Zugauskunft (f)
railway journey Bahnfahrt (f), Bahnreise (f)
railway junction Eisenbahnknotenpunkt (m)
railway level Bahnübergang (m)
railway line Bahnstrecke (f), Schienenweg (m)
railway network Bahnnetz (n)
railway rates Eisenbahntarif (m)
railway staff Bahnpersonal (n)
railway station Bahnhof (m), Bahnstation (f)
railway system Eisenbahnnetz (n)
railway terminus Eisenbahnend-

289

station (f)
railway ticket Eisenbahnfahrkarte (f)
railway timetable Eisenbahnfahrplan (m)
railway traffic Eisenbahnverkehr (m)
rainbow trout Regenbogenforelle (f)
raincoat Regenmantel (m)
rainfall Niederschlag (m), Regen (m)
rain insurance Regenversicherung (f)
rainproof regendicht
rainy regnerisch
rainy season Regenzeit (f)
raise erhöhen, aufnehmen
raise price Preis (m) erhöhen
raisin Rosine (f)
rally Sammeln (n), Massenversammlung (f)
rallye Rallye (n), Sternfahrt (f)
ramble wandern, Wanderung (f), Spaziergang (m)
rambler Wanderer (m)
ramblers' guide Wanderführer (m).
rambling Wandern (n), Wandertourismus (m), Wandersport (m)
rambling association Wanderverein (m)
ramp Rampe (f)
rancid ranzig
random access memory (ram) Speicher (m) mit wahlfreiem Zugriff (m)
random sampling Zufallsstichprobenuntersuchung (f)
random test Stichprobenprüfung (f)
range Palette (f), Auswahl (f), Herd (m), Bereich (m), Zone (f)

range finder Entfernungsmesser (m)
rank rangieren, einordnen; Rang (m)
rare blutig gebraten, halb durch
raspberry Himbeere (f)
raspberry ice Himbeereis (n)
raspberry juice Himbeersaft (m)
raspberry syrup with soda water Soda-Himbeer (n)
rate schätzen; Rate (f), Preis (m), Anteil (m)
rate of exchange Devisenkurs (m), Kurs (m), Umrechnungskurs (m)
rate of interest Zinssatz (m), Zinsfuß (m)
rate of mark-up Zuschlagssatz (m)
rate of turnover Umschlagsgeschwindigkeit (f)
rates on application Preise (pl. m) auf Anfrage (f)
rate restriction Preisbeschränkung (f), Preiskontrolle (f)
ratio Verhältnis (n), Anteilzahl (f), Kennziffer (f)
rationalization Rationalisierung (f)
rationalize rationalisieren
rauigote sauce Rauigote-Soße (f)
raw roh
raw ham Rohschinken (m)
raw material Rohmaterial (n)
raw yield Rohertrag (m)
razor point Steckdose (f) für Elektrorasierer (pl. m)
reading-room Leseraum (m), Lesezimmer (n)
read-only memory (rom) Lesespeicher (m), Festwertspeicher
ready fertig, bereit

ready for mail postfertig
ready for occupancy bezugsfertig
ready for shipment versandfertig
ready for use betriebsfertig
ready reckoner Rechentabelle (f)
ready-to-serve-dish Fertiggericht (n), Tagesgericht (n)
ready-to-use gebrauchsfertig
real time Echtzeit (f)
real turtle soup Schildkrötensuppe (f)
rear of a train Zuganschluß (m)
rearrange umgruppieren
reason urteilen; Vernunft (f), Grund (m)
reasonable billig, angemessen
reasonable hour angemessene Stunde (f)
reasonable price angemessener Preis (m)
reasonable time angemessene Zeit (f)
rebate Preisnachlaß (m), Rabatt (m)
recapitulation Zusammenfassung (f)
receipt quittieren; Empfangsbestätigung (f), Quittung (f)
receipt for registered luggage Gepäckaufbewahrungsschein (m)
receipt of baggage to be deposited Gepäckannahme (f), Gepäckannahmeschalter (m)
receipts Einnahmen (pl. f)
receivables an payables Forderungen (pl. f) und Verbindlichkeiten (pl. f)
receiving clerk Warenannehmer (m)
receiving department Warenannahme (f)
receiving record Wareneingangsbuch (n)
receiving report Eingangsmeldung (f), Wareneingangsbuch (n)
reception Empfang (m), Anmeldung (f), Aufnahme (f)
reception and information office Information (f) und Betreuung (f)
reception-clerk Empfangssekretär (m)
reception desk Rezeption (f), Empfangspult (n)
reception hall Empfangshalle (f)
receptionist Empfangsdame (f), Empfangsherr (m)
reception office Empfangsbüro (n), Rezeption (f)
recipe Rezept (Küche) (n)
recipient Empfänger (m)
reckon back zurückrechnen
reclaim reklamieren
reclassification Neuklassifizierung (f)
recognition Anerkennung (f)
recognize anerkennen, erkennen
recommend empfehlen
recommendation Empfehlung (f)
reconcile abstimmen, zusammenstellen
reconciliation Abstimmung (f)
reconditioning Instandsetzung (f), Generalüberholung (f)
reconfirm bestätigen
reconfirmation Bestätigung (f)
record eintragen, Eintragung (f), Akte (f)
records Unterlagen (pl. f)
recover sich erholen
recovery Erholung (f)

recovery service Abschleppdienst (m)
recreation Erholung (f)
recreational area Erholungsgebiet (n)
recreational facilities Erholungsanlage (f), Erholungsmöglichkeiten (f)
recreational holiday Erholungsurlaub (m)
recreational park Erholungspark (m)
recreation centre Erholungszentrum (n)
recreation program Erholungsprogramm (n)
recreation room Gemeinschaftsraum (m)
red rot
red beans rote Bohnen (pl. f)
red beef tongue Pökelzunge (f)
red beet rote Rübe (f)
red bilberry Preiselbeere (f)
red cabbage Rotkohl (m)
redcap Gepäckträger (m)
red currant rote Johannisbeere (f)
red currant-tartlets Cremetörtchen mit Johannisbeergelee (n)
red grits rote Grütze (f)
red herring Matjeshering (m)
redirect nachsenden
red mullet Rotbarbe (f)
red pepper rote Pfefferschote (f)
reduce ermäßigen, herabsetzen, vermindern
reduced fare Fahrpreisermäßigung (f)
reduced fares for tourist groups Fahrpreisermäßigung (f) für Reisegesellschaften (pl. f)
reduced-fare ticket Fahrkarte (f) zu ermäßigtem Preis (m)

reduced rates ermäßigter Tarif (m), ermäßigter Preis (m), Vergünstigungen (pl. f)
reduce speed now langsam fahren
reducing diet Abmagerungskur (f)
reduction Herabsetzung (f), Ermäßigung (f), Kürzung (f)
reduction for children Kinderermäßigung (f)
reduction for hotel guests Ermäßigung für Hausgäste (pl. m)
reduction of the rates Tarifsenkung (f), Preissenkung (f)
red wine Rotwein (m)
red wine from the cask roter, offener Wein (m)
re-educate umschulen
re-education Umschulung (f)
re-embark (sich) wieder einschiffen
re-entry visa Wiedereinreisevisum (n)
refer sich beziehen auf
reference Bezugnahme (f), Hinweis (m)
refreshed erfrischt
refreshing erholsam, erfrischend
refreshment Erfrischung (f)
refreshment bar Büffet (n), Erfrischungsraum (m)
refreshment room Erfrischungsraum (m)
refreshment stall Erfrischungskiosk (m)
refrigerator Kühlschrank (m)
refrigerator car Kühlwagen (m)
refuel tanken
refuge Verkehrsinsel (f), Schutzhütte (f)
refund Rückerstattung (f), zurückerstatten, zurückzahlen

292

refusal Ablehnung (f), Weigerung (f)
refusal to pay Zahlungsverweigerung (f)
refuse ablehnen, zurückweisen
region Gegend (f)
register eintragen, anmelden, einschreiben, Verzeichnis (n)
registered letter Einschreibebrief (m)
registering of luggage Gepäckabfertigung (f)
register luggage Gepäck (n) aufgeben
register with the police sich bei der Polizei melden (f)
registration Abfertigung (f), Anmeldung (f), Eintragung (f)
registration fee Anmeldegebühr (f)
registration form Anmeldeformular (n), Meldeschein
registration office Meldeamt (n)
registration of luggage Gepäckabfertigung (f)
regret bedauern
regular fahrplanmäßig
regular customer Stammgast (m)
regular hotel guest Hotelstammgast (m)
regular time Normalarbeitszeit (f)
regular traffic Linienverkehr (m)
regulation Regel (f), Richtlinie (f), Ordnung (f)
regulations of the house Hausordnung (f)
reheat aufwärmen
rehire wiedereinstellen
reimburse zurückvergüten, zurückerstatten, ersetzen
reimbursement Rückvergütung

(f), Rückerstattung (f)
reimbursement of travel expenses Reisekostenvergütung (f)
reindeer Ren (n), Rentier (n)
rejuvenation cure Verjüngungskur (f)
related verwandt
relation Beziehung (f), Verhältnis (f)
relative Verwandter (m)
relax sich erholen, entspannen
relaxation Erholung (f), Ausspannen (n)
relaxation cure Entspannungskur (f)
relaxation time Erholungszeit (f)
relevant costing Rechnen (n) mit relevanten Kosten (pl.)
reliability Zuverlässigkeit (f)
reliable zuverlässig
relief Erleichterung (f), Abhilfe (f)
relief train Entlastungszug (m), Sonderzug (m)
relieve unterstützen, entlasten, befreien
relieve measure Abhilfemaßnahme (f)
relish gern essen, sich schmecken lassen
reloading charge Umladungsgebühr (f)
rely sich verlassen auf
remainder Rest (m)
remarkable sehenswert
remedial gymnastics Krankengymnastik (f)
remedy Medikament (n), Heilmittel (n)
remind erinnern, mahnen
reminder Erinnerung (f), Mahnung (f)
reminder advertising Erinnerungswerbung (f)

293

remit überweisen
remittance Überweisung (f)
remote entfernt, abgelegen
remove beseitigen, entfernen
render a service einen Dienst (m) leisten
renew erneuern, verlängern
renewal Erneuerung (f), Verlängerung (f)
renounce aufgeben, verzichten, zurücktreten
renovate erneuern
renovation Erneuerung (f)
rent mieten, pachten, vermieten, verpachten, Miete (f), Pacht (f)
rentable mietbar, pachtbar
rental Mieteinnahmen (pl. f), Pachteinnahmen (pl. f)
rental revenue Mietertrag (m)
rental service Verleih (m)
re-opening Wiedereröffnung (f)
reorder nachbestellen, Nachbestellung (f)
reorder system Bestellverfahren (n)
reorganization Umorganisation (f)
reorganize sanieren, umorganisieren
repair reparieren, instandsetzen, ausbessern
repair cost Reparaturkosten (pl.)
repair order Reparaturauftrag (m)
repairs and maintenance Reparaturen (pl. f) und Instandhaltung (f)
repair shop Reparaturwerkstätte (f)
repay zurückzahlen, zurückerstatten
repayable rückzahlbar
repayment Rückzahlung (f), Rückerstattung (f)
repeat wiederholen, Wiederholung (f)
repeat business Wiederholungsgeschäft (n)
repeat order Wiederholungsauftrag (m)
reply postcard Rückantwortkarte (f)
replace ersetzen
replacement Wiederbeschaffung (f), Ersatzbeschaffung (f)
replacement cost Wiederbeschaffungskosten (pl.), Wiederbeschaffungswert (m)
reply antworten, Antwort (f)
report berichten, Bericht (m)
reporting time Meldezeit (f)
report to unterstellt sein
represent vertreten
representation Vertretung (f), Stellvertretung (f)
representative Beauftragter (m), Vertreter (m), Bevollmächtigter (m)
reputation Ruf (m), Ansehen (n)
request bitten, auffordern, Bitte (f), Aufforderung (f)
request for overtime Überstundenanforderung (f)
request stop Bedarfshaltestelle (f)
require erfordern, verlangen, brauchen
requirement Erfordernis (n), Bedürfnis (n), Anspruch (m)
requisition Anforderung (f), Lageranforderung (f), Bestellung (f)
rescue expedition Rettungsexpedition (f)
rescue party Rettungsmannschaft (f)
research forschen; Forschung

(f), Untersuchung (f)
research and development Forschung (f) und Entwicklung (f)
research department Forschungsabteilung (f)
reseller Wiederverkäufer (m)
reservation Reservierung (f), Belegung (f), Vorbehalt (m), Reservat (n)
reservation charges Reservierungskosten (pl.)
reservation clerk Reservierungsdame (f)
reservation expense Reservierungskosten (pl.)
reservation number Buchungsnummer (f)
reservation of seats in advance Vorbestellung (f) von Plätzen (pl. m)
reservation supervisor Leiterin (f) der Reservierungsabteilung (f)
reserve reservieren, buchen, vorbestellen
reserve Rücklage (f), Reserve (f)
reserve a table einen Tisch (m) reservieren
reserve by telephone telefonisch bestellen
reserved seat ticket Platzkarte (f)
reserve for operating equipment Rückstellung (f) für Betriebsmittel (pl. n)
reservoir Stausee (m)
reside wohnen, seinen Wohnsitz (m) haben
residence Wohnort (m), Wohnsitz (m), Aufenthaltsort (m)
residence permit Aufenthaltserlaubnis (f), Aufenthaltsgenehmigung (f)
resident wohnhaft, Einwohner (m), Bewohner (m), Hausgast (m), Pensionsgast (m)
residential area Wohngebiet (n)
residential hotel Hotel garni (n), Frühstückspension (f), Familienpension (f)
resident manager Hoteldirektor (m)
residue Rest (m), Restbetrag (m)
resignation Kündigung (f)
resource Hilfsquelle (f), Reserve (f)
respectable seriös
responsibility Verantwortung (f), Haftung (f)
responsible verantwortlich, haftbar
rest after treatment Nachkur (f)
restaurant-car Speisewagen (m)
restaurant deck Restaurantdeck (n)
restaurant-keeper Gastwirt (m), Gaststättenbesitzer (m), Restaurateur (m)
restaurant manager Restaurantdirektor (m)
rest-cure Erholungskur (f), Erholungsaufenthalt (m), Liegekur (f)
rest-cure lawn Liegewiese (f)
rest-cure terrace Liegeterrasse (f)
restful erholsam
rest-home Erholungsheim (n)
restoration Wiederherstellung (f)
restore wiederherstellen
rest pause Erholungspause (f)
restraint of trade Wettbewerbsbeschränkung (f)
restriction Einschränkung (f), Beschränkung (f)

295

rest-room Ruheraum (m), amerik. Toilette (f), Waschraum (m)
result Resultat (n), Ergebnis (n)
results from operations Betriebsergebnis (n)
retain zurückbehalten
retardation Verzögerung (f)
retire in Pension (f) gehen, zurücktreten
retirement Ruhestand (m), Pension (f)
retraining Umschulung (f)
return Rückkehr (f), Rückgabe (f), zurückgeben, zurückkommen
return fare Fahrpreis (m) für die Hin- und Rückreise (f)
return flight Rückflug (m)
return home Heimkehr (f)
return journey Rückreise (f), Rückfahrt (f)
return on sales Gewinnspanne (f)
return ticket Rückfahrkarte (f), Hin- und Rückfahrschein (m)
return trip Rückreise (f), Rückfahrt (f)
return voyage Rückreise (f)
re-use wieder verwenden, Wiederverwendung (f)
revalidate erneuern
revel schlemmen
revenue Einkommen (n), Ertrag (m), Umsatz (m)
review nachprüfen, überprüfen, Überprüfung (f)
revise verbessern, durchsehen, revidieren
reward belohnen, Belohnung (f)
Rhine salmon Rheinsalm (m)
Rhine wine Rheinwein (m)

rhubarb Rhabarber (m)
rhum-baba Rumbaba (m)
rib Rippchen (n)
ribbon macaroni Bandnudeln (pl. f)
rib of beef Ochsenrippenstück (n)
rib of beef boiled Beinfleisch (n)
rib of pork Schweinskarree (n)
rib roast of veal Kalbskarreebraten (m)
ribs of veal Kalbskarreebraten (m)
rib steak Kotelett (n)
rice Reis (m)
rice dish with grated cheese Reisgericht mit Reibkäse (n)
rice of peas Reisgericht mit Erbsen (n)
rice pie Reisgericht in Form (n)
rice pudding Milchreis (m)
rice soup Reissuppe (f)
rice timbale Reisgericht in Form (n)
riding-club Reitklub (m)
riding-course Reitkurs (m)
riding-facilities Reitgelegenheit (f)
riding-ground Reitgelände (n)
riding-ring Reitbahn (f)
riding-school Reitschule (f)
riding-stable Reitstall (m)
riding-track Reitweg (m)
rigging Takelung (f)
right Recht (n), Anspruch (m), Berechtigung (f)
rightful rechtmäßig
rightfulness Rechtmäßigkeit (f)
right-hand traffic Rechtsverkehr (m)
right of rescission Rücktrittsrecht (n)
right of sublease Untervermie-

tungsrecht (n)
right-of-way Vorfahrt (f)
ring road Ringstraße (f)
rinse spülen
ripe reif
ripe olive reife Olive (f)
rise erhöhen, Erhöhung (f), Aufstieg (m)
risk riskieren, Gefahr (f), Risiko (n), Wagnis (n)
risk of conveyance Transportgefahr (f)
risky risikoreich, gefährlich
risotto with saffron Safranreis (m)
rissole Fleischklöße (gebraten) (pl. m)
river Fluß (m)
riverside hotel Flußhotel (n)
river map Flußkarte (f)
river port Binnenhafen (m)
river steamer Flußdampfer (m)
river traffic Flußschiffahrt (f)
river-trout Flußforelle (f)
roach Plötze (f)
road atlas Straßenatlas (m)
roadside café Ausflugslokal (n)
road cleared of snow schneegeräumte Straße (f)
road closed gesperrte Straße (f)
road conditions Straßenzustand (m)
road construction Straßenbau (m)
road ditch Straßengraben (m)
road fork Straßengabelung (f)
road haulage Güterkraftverkehr (m)
road-hole Schlagloch (n)
road-house Raststätte (f)
road junction Straßenkreuzung (f)
road map Straßenkarte (f), Autokarte (f)
road narrows Straßenverengung (f)
road network Straßennetz (n)
road-rail service Huckepackverkehr (m)
road report Straßenzustandsbericht (m)
road safety Verkehrssicherheit (f)
road sign Verkehrszeichen (n)
road site Straßenbaustelle (f)
road traffic Straßenverkehr (m)
road transport connection Zubringerverkehr (m)
road tunnel Straßentunnel (m)
road user Verkehrsteilnehmer (m)
roadway Fahrbahn (f), Fahrdamm (m)
road works Straßenbauarbeiten (pl. f)
roast geröstet, gebraten, Braten (m)
roast beef Ochsenbraten (m), Rostbraten (m)
roast beef English style englisches Roastbeef (n)
roast chicken Brathähnchen (n)
roast duck gebratene Ente (f)
roasted gebraten
roast fillet of beef Rindslendenbraten (m)
roast fillet of beef in puff-paste Filet Wellington (n)
roast goose Gänsebraten (m)
roast goose with sauerkraut Gänsebraten mit Sauerkraut (m)
roast hare Hasenbraten (m)
roast joint of pork Schweinebraten (m)
roast lamb Lammbraten (m)
roast loin of veal Kalbsbraten (m)
roast loin of veal with kidney Kalbsnierenbraten (m)
roast of veal Kalbsbraten (m)

297

roast pheasant Fasan (m) gebraten
roast pork Schweinebraten (m)
roast potatoes Schwenkkartoffeln (pl. f)
roast sausage Bratwurst (f)
roast sirloin Roastbeef (n)
roast sirloin of beef Nierstückbraten (m)
roast smoked spare rib of pork Kasseler Rippenspeer (m, n)
roast stuffed breast of veal gefüllte Kalbsbrust (f)
roast turkey Truthahn (m) gebraten
roast venison Rehbraten (m)
robe Morgenrock (m)
rock Felsen (m)
rock-climbing Bergsteigen (n)
rock garden Steingarten (m)
rock lobster Languste (f)
rock partridge Steinhuhn (n)
rocky felsig
roe Rogen (m)
roebuck Reh (n)
roll ausrollen (Teig)
roll Brötchen (n), Semmel
rolled beef Rollbraten (m)
rolled braised beef Rindsroulade (f)
rolled fillets of sole Seezungenröllchen (pl. n)
rolled ham Rollschinken (m)
rolled herring Rollmops (m)
rolled pancake Palatschinken (m)
rolled stuffed cabbage leave Kohlroulade (f)
rolled veal on skewers Kalbsröllchen (n) am Spieß
rolled veal steak Kalbsroulade (f)
roll film Rollfilm (m)
rolling pin Nudelholz (n)

rollmop herring Rollmops (m)
roll on - roll off Autoverladung (f) bei Schiffen (pl. n)
romaine Sommerendivie (f)
Roquefort Roquefort-Käse (m)
rotate wechseln, rotieren
rotating shift Wechselschicht (f)
rotten faul, verfault
roof garage Dachgarage (f)
roof-garden Dachgarten (m)
roof rack Autodachgepäckträger (m)
room Zimmer (n)
room charge Zimmerpreis (m)
room clerk Empfangsdame (f), Empfangsherr (m)
rooms division department Beherbergungsbereich (m)
rooms division manager Leiter (m) der Beherbergungsabteilung (f)
room facing south Südzimmer (n)
room facing the street Zimmer (n) zur Straße (f)
room number Zimmernummer (f)
room rate Zimmerpreis (m)
rooms department Beherbergungsabteilung (f)
room service Etagenservice (n)
room service headwaiter Etagenoberkellner (m)
room service ordertaking Bestellungsaufnahme (f) für das Etagenservice (n)
room service waiter Etagenkellner (m), Zimmerkellner (m)
rooms occupied and vacant belegte und freie Zimmer (pl. n)
rooms statistic Beherbergungs-

statistik (f)
rooms to let Zimmer (pl. n) zu vermieten, Fremdenzimmer (pl. n)
room telephone Zimmertelefon (n)
rooms vacant Zimmer (pl. n) frei
room volume Zimmerlautstärke (f)
room with a view of the sea Zimmer (n) mit Blick (m) aufs Meer (n)
room with balcony Balkonzimmer (n)
room with private bath or shower Zimmer (n) mit Bad (n) oder Dusche (f)
room with two beds Zweibettzimmer (n)
roomy geräumig
rooster Hahn (m)
rope down abseilen
rope-ladder Strickleiter (f)
rope railway Seilbahn (f)
rope tow Schlepplift (m)
rosé rosé
rosemary Rosmarin (m)
rose wine hellroter Wein (m)
rough stürmisch
rough calculation überschlägige Berechnung (f)
rough estimate grobe Schätzung (f)
round rund, Runde (f)
roundabout Kreisverkehr (m), Karussell (n)
roundabout ticket Rückfahrkarte (f), Hin- und Rückfahrschein (m)
roundabout way Umweg (m)
round off abrunden
round-trip Rundreise (f)
round up aufrunden
route map Streckenkarte (f)

route network Flugnetz (n), Streckennetz (n)
routine work Routinearbeit (f)
routing Streckenführung (f)
row rudern, Bootsfahrt (f)
rowboat Ruderboot (n)
rowing-boat Ruderboot (n)
rubber boots Gummistiefel (pl. m)
rubber dinghy Schlauchboot (n)
rubbish Müller (m), Abfall (m)
rubbish removal Abfallbeseitigung (f)
rudder Steuerruder (n)
rug Vorleger (m)
rugged rauh, wild, zerklüftet
ruin Ruine (f)
rule regeln, entscheiden; Vorschrift (f), Regel (f)
rules and regulations of a hotel Hotelordnung (f)
rules of residents Hausordnung (f)
rum Rum (m)
rumpsteak Rumpsteak (n)
rumpsteak grilled Rumpsteak (n) am Rost (m)
rumpsteak with fried onions Wiener Rostbraten (m)
run Abfahrt (f), Abfahrtsstrecke (f)
run at regular times fahrplanmäßig fahren
runner bean grüne Bohne (f)
running time Fahrzeit (f)
running water fließendes Wasser (n)
run the risk Gefahr (f) laufen
runway Rollbahn (f), Piste (f), Startbahn (f), Landebahn
rural ländlich
rural district Landbezirk (m)
rush Andrang (m), Zustrom (m), Eile (f)
rush hours Hauptverkehrs-

zeit (f), Stoßzeit (f)
rush hour traffic Stoßverkehr (m)
rush order Eilauftrag (m)
rusk Zwieback (m)
Russian bath Dampfbad (n)
Russian beetroot soup russische rote Rübensuppe (f)
Russian eggs russische Eier (pl. n)
rye Roggen (m)
rye-bread Roggenbrot (n)

S

sabayon warme Wein/Eiersoße (f), Chaudeau (n)
saddle Rückenstück (n), Rücken (m)
saddle of hare Hasenrücken (m)
saddle of veal Kalbsrücken (m)
saddle of venison Rehrücken (m)
saddle of mutton Hammelrücken (m)
safari Safari (f)
safe deposit box Stahlfach (n), Schließfach (n)
safe deposit of valuables Aufbewahrung (f) von Wertgegenständen (pl. m)
safe for avalanches lawinensicher
safety Sicherheit (f)
safety binding Sicherheitsbindung (f)
safety regulation Unfallverhütungsvorschrift (f)
saffron Safran (m)
saffron-risotto Safranreis (m)
sage Salbei (m)
sail Segele (n), segeln

sailing Abfahrt (f), Fahrt (f)
sailing-boat Segelboot (n)
sailing date Abfahrtstag (m)
sailing dinghy Jolle (f)
sailingplane Segelflugzeug (n)
sailing time Abfahrtszeit (f)
sail near to the wind hart am Wind segeln
sailor Matrose (m)
salad Salat (m)
salad bowl Salatschüssel (f)
salad dressing Salatsoße (f)
salad of boiled beef Rindfleischsalat (m)
salad of ox-palate Ochsenmaulsalat (m)
salad plate Rohkostplatte (f)
salami Salami (f)
salaries and wages Löhne (pl. f) und Gehälter (pl. n)
salary Gehalt (n)
sale Verkauf (m), Absatz (m), Ausverkauf (m)
sale of alcoholic drinks Ausschank (m) alkoholischer Getränke (pl. n)
sale of tickets Kartenverkauf (m)
sales Verkaufserlöse (pl. m), Erträge (pl. m), Umsatz (m)
sales analysis Verkaufsanalyse (f), Absatzuntersuchung
sales argument Verkaufsargument (n)
sales commission Umsatzprovision (f)
sales department Verkaufsabteilung (f)
sales forecast Absatzplan (m), Umsatzprognose (f)
sales letter Werbebrief (m)
sales literature Werbematerial (n)
salesman Verkäufer (m),

Vertreter (m), Reisender (m)
sales manager Verkaufsleiter (m)
sales mix Umsatzmix (m), Umsatzzusammensetzung (f), Sortiment (n)
sales price Verkaufspreis (m)
sales promotion Verkaufsförderung (f)
sales representative Verkaufsvertreter (m), Verkaufsrepräsentant (m)
salmon Salm (m), Lachs (m)
salmon cut Salmmittelstück (n)
salmon cutlet Salmmittelstück (n)
salmon mayonnaise Salmmayonnaise (f)
salmon-trout Lachsforelle (f)
saloon Ausschank (m), Gastwirtschaft (f)
saloon-bar Ausschank (m), Kneipe (f), Schenke (f)
saloon carriage Salonwagen (m)
saloonkeeper Wirt (m), Schankwirt (m)
salsify Schwarzwurzel (f)
salt Salz (n), salzen
salt-cellar Salzfäßchen (n), Salzstreuer (m)
salt cod Stockfisch (m)
salted codfish Stockfisch (m)
salted gesalzen, gepökelt
salted almonds Salzmandeln (pl. f)
salted beef Pökelrindfleisch (n)
salted cucumber Salzgurke (f)
salted pig's knuckle Eisbein (n)
salted pig's trotter Eisbein (n)
salt(ed) herring Matjeshering (m)
salt spring Solquelle (f)
salt water Sole (f)
salt-water bath Solbad (n)
salt-water fish Meerfisch (m)

salt-water resort Solbad (n) (Kurort) (m)
Salzburg sweet dumpling Salzburger Nockerl (n)
sanatorium Sanatorium (n), Kuranstalt (f), Heilstätte (f)
sandbank Sandbank (f)
sand-bath Sandbad (n)
sand-castle competition Sandburgenwettbewerb (m)
sand-dune Sanddüne (f)
sandstone rock Sandsteinfelsen (m)
sandwich belegtes Brot (n)
sandy beach Sandstrand (m)
sanitary facilities sanitäre Anlagen (pl. f)
sanitary regulations Gesundheitsvorschriften (pl. f)
Santa Claus Weihnachtsmann (m)
sap Saft (m)
sardines Ölsardinen (pl. f)
sardines in oil Sardinen (pl. f) in Öl (n)
satisfactory zufriedenstellend
satisfy befriedigen, bezahlen
sauce Soße (f), Tunke (f)
sauce-boat Sauciere (f)
saucepan Kochtopf (m), Tiegel (m)
saucer Untersetzer (m), Untertasse (f)
sauerbraten Sauerbraten (m)
sauerkraut Sauerkraut (n)
sauerkraut or string beans with meat and sausage Berner Platte (f)
sauerkraut with smoked meat, ham and sausage Sauerkrautplatte (f)
sauna Sauna (f)
sausage Wurst (f), Würstchen (n)
sauteed gebraten

301

sauté potatoes Bratkartoffeln (pl. f)
Sauterne Sauterne (m)
saveloy Zervelat (f), Zervelatwurst (f)
savoury schmackhaft; pikantes Vorgericht (n)
savoy cabbage Sommer- und Wirsingkohl (m)
scald brühen, abkochen (Milch) (f)
scale Waage (f), Skala (f), staffeln
scallion Schalotte (f)
scallop (of meat) Schnitzel (n)
scallop (mussel) Miesmuschel (f)
scallop Kammuschel (f)
scallop St. Jaques Jakobsmuschel (f)
Scandinavian salmon Nordsalm (m)
scenery Landschaft (f)
scenic malerisch, landschaftlich schön
schedule planen, Aufstellung (f), Zeitplan (m), Verzeichnis (n), Fahrplan (m), Flugplan (m)
scheduled fahrplanmäßig, planmäßig
scheduled air line Fluglinie (f) mit fahrplanmäßigem Dienst (m)
scheduled bus Linienbus (m)
scheduled flight planmäßiger Flug (m)
scheduled halt planmäßiger Halt (m)
scheduled plane Kursmaschine (f), Linienmaschine (f)
scheduled stop planmäßiger Halt (m)
scheduled train Regelzug (m)
school holidays Schulferien (pl.)

school of hotel management Hotelfachschule (f)
school outing Schulausflug (m)
scientific management wissenschaftliche Betriebsführung (f)
scone (dreieckiger) Weizen- oder Gerstenmehlkuchen (zum Tee) (m)
scones Teegebäck (n)
scooter Motorroller (m)
Scotch broth dicke Gemüsesuppe (f) mit Hammelfleisch (n)
Scotch egg hartgekochtes Ei (eingehüllt in Teig) (n)
scouring cloth Scheuerlappen (m)
scrambled eggs Rühreier (pl. n)
screen Bildschirm (m)
screw Schiffsschraube (f)
scuba diving Unterwassersport (m)
sea See (f), Meer (n)
sea air Seeluft (f)
sea-air voyage See-Luft-Reise (f)
sea bag Seesack (m)
sea bath Seebad (n), Seeheilbad (n)
sea-bream Brasse (f), Rotbrasse (f)
sea-captain Schiffskapitän (m)
sea-climate Seeklima (n)
sea-fish Meerfisch (m)
sea-food Meeresfrüchte (pl. f), Seetiere (pl. n)
sea-front hotel Seehotel (n)
sea glider Wassersegelflugzeug (n)
sea-gull Möwe (f)
seaman Seemann (m), Schiffer (m)
sea-perch Meerbarsch (m)
seaplane Wasserflugzeug (n)
seaport Seehafen (m)

sear Sengen (Geflügel) (n), versengen, anbrennen
search suchen, durchsuchen
sea route Seeroute (f), Seeweg (m)
seasick seekrank
seasickness Seekrankheit (f)
seaside Küste (f)
seaside gala Strandfest (n)
seaside health resort Seeheilbad (n)
seaside hotel Strandhotel (n), Seehotel (n)
seaside pleasures Badefreuden (pl. f)
seaside resort Seebad (n)
sea-shells Muscheltiere (pl. n)
sea-shore Strand (m)
season Jahreszeit (f), Saison (f), würzen (Speisen)
seasonal business Saisongeschäft (n)
seasonal employment saisonale Beschäftigung (f)
seasonal establishment Saisonbetrieb (m)
seasonal fluctuation Saisonschwankung (f)
seasonal hotel Saisonhotel (n)
seasonal hotel trade Saisonhotellerie (f)
seasonal peak Saisonspitze (f)
seasonal price increase Saisonaufschlag (m)
seasonal service Saisonbetrieb (m)
seasonal surcharge Saisonzuschlag (m)
seasonal variation Saisonschwankung (f)
season's salad Jahreszeitsalat (m)
season ticket Zeitkarte (f), Dauer-Abonnement (n)
seat Platz (m), Sitz (m), Sessel (m)
seat belt Sicherheitsgürtel (m), Sicherheitsgurt (m)
seating-capacity Sitzplatzkapazität (f)
sea tourism Seetourismus (m), Seetouristik (f)
sea tourist Seetourist (m)
seat reservation Platzreservierung (f), Platzbestellung (f)
seat reservation fee Platzkartengebühr (f)
seats should be reserved in advance Platzkarten (pl. f) erforderlich
seat taken besetzter Platz (m)
sea-water Meerwasser (n)
seawater bathing pool Seewasser-Badebecken (n)
seawater cure Meerwasserkur (f)
second class zweite Klasse (f)
second-class compartment Abteil (n) zweiter Klasse (f)
second course zweiter Gang (m)
second hand gebraucht
secretarial compartment Schreibabteil (n)
secretary rail Zugsekretärin (f)
secure sichern, decken, schützen
sedative factor Schonfaktor (m)
sediment Bodensatz (m)
select auswählen
selection Auswahl (f)
selection of cheese Käseplatte (f)
selection of cold cuts gemischter Aufschnitt (m)
selection of cold meat gemischter Aufschnitt (m)
self-contained flat Appartement (n)
self-drive car hire service Auto-

vermietung (f) an Selbstfahrer (pl. m)
self employed selbständig
self-service Selbstbedienung (f)
self-service cafeteria Selbstbedienungsrestaurant (n)
self-service restaurant Selbstbedienungsrestaurant (n)
self-service restaurant with slot-machines Automatenrestaurant (n)
self-service snack bar Schnellimbißstube (f)
self-service store Selbstbedienungsladen (m)
sell verkaufen
sellers' market Verkäufermarkt (m)
selling price Verkaufspreis (m)
sell out ausverkaufen, (Lager) räumen
send senden
semiannual halbjährlich
semimonthly halbmonatlich
semivariable cost Mischkosten (pl.), halbveränderliche Kosten (pl.)
semolina Grieß (m)
semolina pie Grießstrudel (m)
semolina pudding Grießpudding (m)
semolina soup Grießsuppe (f)
send luggage in advance Gepäck (n) aufgeben
separate trennen
serve dienen, servieren, auftragen, bedienen
service Dienst (m), Dienstleistung (f), Verbindung (f), Service (m), Servierleistung (f), servieren (n), Bedienungsgeld (n), Gottesdienst (m)
service and taxes included Bedienung (f) und Steuern (pl. f) inbegriffen

service charge Bedienungsgeld (n), Tronk (m), Bedienungszuschlag (m)
serviced hut bewirtschaftete Hütte (f)
service included Bedienung (f) inbegriffen
service lift Speisenaufzug (m)
service on board Service (m) an Bord (m)
service program Dienstprogramm
service staff Bedienungspersonal (n)
service station Reparaturdienst (m), Tankstelle (f)
service-station attendant Tankwart (m)
service trade Dienstleistungsgewerbe (n)
servicing Wartung (f)
serving dish Platte (f)
set down passengers Fahrgäste (pl. m) aussteigen lassen
set off aufbrechen
set off again weiterfahren
set the table Tisch decken (m)
setting-up exercises Gymnastik (f)
settle an account ein Konto ausgleichen (n)
severe climate rauhes Klima (n)
sewing kit Nähzeug (n)
shad Maifisch (m), Alse (f)
shadow Schatten (m)
shady schattig
shaft Welle (f)
shake schütteln
shallot Schalotte (f)
shandy Schorle (f), Radlermaß
shared bathroom gemeinsames Badezimmer (n)
shark's fins Haifischflossen (pl. f)

shark's fins soup Haifischflossensuppe (f)
sharp bend scharfe Kurve (f)
shaved cheese Hobelkäse (m)
shaver point Steckdose (f) für Elektrorasierer (m)
sheat-fish Wels (m)
shed Schuppen (m)
sheep's cheese Schafskäse (m)
sheet Laken (n)
shellfish Schalentier (n)
shelter Unterkunft (f)
sheltered geschützt
shepherd's pie Auflauf (m) aus Hackfleisch (n) und Kartoffeln (pl. f)
sherbet Scherbett (m), Sorbett (m)
sherry Sherry (m)
shift Schicht (f)
shin of pork Schopfbraten (m)
ship versenden, Schiff (n)
shipbuilding Schiffsbau (m)
ship game Bordspiel (n)
shipment Versendung (f), Verfrachtung (f)
ship owner Reeder (m)
shipping charges Verladekosten (pl.)
shipping clerk Expedient (m)
shipping company Reederei (f)
shipping cost Versandkosten (pl.)
shipping space Schiffsraum (m)
ship's cook Schiffskoch (m)
ship's doctor Schiffsarzt (m)
ship's newspaper Bordzeitung (f)
shirred eggs Spiegeleier (pl. n)
shoeblack Schuhputzer (m)
shoe cleaning schuhputzen (n)
shoehorn Schuhanzieher (m)
shoe-shining cloth Schuhputzlappen (m)
shoestring potatoes Streichholzkartoffeln (pl. f)
shoot schießen, jagen, Jagdrevier (n)
shooting Jagd (f)
shooting box Jagdhütte (f)
shooting licence Jagdschein (m)
shooting lodge Jagdhütte (f)
shooting-match Schützenfest (n)
shooting season Jagdsaison (f), Jagdzeit (f)
shooting trip Jagdreise (f)
shopping Einkaufen (n)
shopping center Geschäftsvietel (n), Einkaufszentrum (n)
shopping street Geschäftsstraße (f)
shore Strand (m), Küste (f), Ufer (n)
shore excursion Landausflug (m)
shortage Manko (n), Fehlbetrag (m), Minus (n)
shortcake Mürbeteigkuchen (m)
short cut Abkürzung (f)
short-distance flight Kurzstreckenflug (m)
short-distance traffic Nahverkehr (m)
shortening Fett (n), Pflanzenfett (n)
short-range kurzfristig
short term kurzfristig
short-term parker Kurzparker (m)
shoulder Schulter (f)
shoulder of pork Schweinsschulter (f)
shoulder of veal Kalbsschulter (f)
show Vorführung (f), Show (f), zeigen
shower Brause (f), Dusche (f)
shower-bath Dusche (f)

shower-bath cubicle Duschkabine (f)
shower of rain Regenschauer (m)
shower-room Duschraum (m)
showers Duschanlage (f)
shower stall Duschnische (f)
show of national costumes Trachtenfest (n)
shredded calf's liver geschnetzelte Kalbsleber (f)
shredded neat Geschnetzeltes (n)
shrimp Garnele (f), Krabbe (f)
shrink schrumpfen, sich vermindern
shrinkage Schwundverlust (m), Schwund (m)
Shrovetide Fastnachtszeit (f), Karnevalszeit (f)
Shrove Tuesday Fastnacht (f), Faschingsdienstag (m)
shrub Strauch (m)
shuffleboard Shuffleboard (Unterhaltungsspiel auf Kreuzfahrt-Schiffen) (n)
shunt rangieren
shutter Verschluß (m)
shutter-release Auslöser (m)
shuttle Flughafenbus (m)
shuttle cock Federball (m)
shuttle service Pendelverkehr (m)
sick leave Krankenurlaub (m)
sickness insurance Krankenversicherung (f)
side dish Beilage (f), Vorspeise (f), Vorgericht (n)
sidewalk Bürgersteig (m)
sidewalk café Straßencafé (n)
side-wheeler Raddampfer (m)
siesta Mittagsschlaf (m)
sieve Sieb (n)
sift sieben
sight Anblick (m), Sehenswürdigkeit (f)
sight-seeing Besuchen (n) von Sehenswürdigkeiten (pl. f)
sight-seeing excursion Besichtigungsfahrt (f)
sight-seeing flight Rundflug (m)
sight-seeing tour Stadtrundfahrt (f)
signature Unterschrift (f)
signpost Wegweiser (m)
signs and symbols Zeichenerklärung (f)
silver hake Seehecht (m)
silver trout Silberfelchen (m)
simmer brodeln lassen, leicht sieden
simple einfach
simple breakfast einfaches Frühstück (n)
single Einzelzimmer (n), ledig, einfach
single bedroom Einbettzimmer (n)
single-berth compartment Einbettabteil (n)
single cabin Einzelkabine (f)
single-engined aircraft einmotoriges Flugzeug (n)
single file traffic einspurige Fahrbahn (f)
single passenger Einzelreisender (m)
single room Einzelzimmer (n), Einbettzimmer (n), Einzelkabine (f)
single ticket einfache Fahrkarte (f)
single tourist Einzelreisender (m)
single track eingleisig
sip nippen, schlürfen
sirloin Zwischenrippenstück (n)
sirloin steak with green pepper Zwischenrippenstück (n) mit

grünem Pfeffer (m)
sirloin steak with onions Zwiebelrostbraten (m)
sister-in-law Schwägerin (f)
site Schauplatz (m)
sitting Besetzung (f) des Restaurants (n)
sitting-room Wohnzimmer (n), Gästezimmer (n), Tagesraum (m)
skate eislaufen, Schlittschuh (m) laufen, Rochen (m)
skateboard Skatebord (n)
skater Eisläufer (m)
skating Eislauf (m), Eislaufen (n)
skating-rink Eishalle (f), Rollschuhbahn (f)
skewer Spießchen (n), Spieß (m)
ski Ski (m), Ski fahren
ski binding Skibindung (f)
skibob Skibob (m)
ski boot Skistiefel (m)
ski carrier Skiträger (m)
ski center Skiort (m), Skizentrum (n)
ski-coach Skilehrer (m)
skid schleudern
ski equipment Skiausrüstung (f)
skier Skifahrer (m), Skiläufer (m)
ski grounds Skigelände (n)
ski hire Skiverleih (m)
ski hotel Skihotel (n)
ski hut Skihütte (f)
skiing Skifahren (n), Skilauf (m), Skisport (m)
skiing club Skiklub (m)
skiing exercises Skigymnastik (f)
skiing guide Skiführer (m)
skiing holidays Skiurlaub (m), Skiferien (pl.)
skiing instruction Skiunterricht (m)
skiing instructor Skilehrer (m)
skiing lessons Skiunterricht (m)
skiing trip Skireise (f)
skiing village Skidorf (n)
skiing-weekend Skiwochenende (n)
ski jump Sprungschanze (f)
ski-jumping Skispringen (n)
ski-lift day ticket Skitagespaß (m)
ski-lift season ticket Skipaß (m)
skill Fachkenntnis (f), Fähigkeit (f)
skilled manpower gelernte Arbeitskräfte (pl. f)
skillet Bratpfanne (f)
ski lodge Skihütte (f)
skimmed milk Magermilch (f)
skimmer Schaumlöffel (m)
skim milk Magermilch (f)
skim off abschöpfen
skin Haut (f)
skins ski Steigfelle (pl. n)
ski nursery slope Anfängerhang (m)
ski pole Skistock (m)
ski race Skirennen (n)
ski rental Skiverleih (m)
ski resort Skiort (m)
ski run Piste (f)
ski run maintenance Pistenpflege (f)
ski school Skischule (f)
ski slope Skihang (m), Abfahrtshang (m)
ski stick Skistock (m)
ski tour Skitour (f)
ski tourist Skitourist (m)
ski tow Skischlepplift (m)
ski trousers Skihose (f)
skittle Kegel (m)
skittle-alley Kegelbahn (f)

ski wax Skiwachs (n)
ski wear Skikleidung (f)
sky Himmel (m)
skyline Horizont (m)
sled Schlitten (m)
sledge tow Rodellift (m), Schlittenlift (m)
sleep Schlaf (m), schlafen
sleep late verschlafen
sleeper Schlafwagen (m)
sleeper section Schlafabteil (n)
sleeping accommodation Schlafgelegenheit (f)
sleeping-bag Schlafsack (m)
sleeping-berth Bett (n), Schlafplatz (m)
sleeping-car attendant Schlafwagenschaffner (m)
sleeping-car charge Schlafwagenzuschlag (m)
sleeping-car ticket Schlafwagenkarte (f)
sleeping-compartment Schlafabteil (n)
sleeping-cure Schlafkur (f)
sleigh-ride Schlittenfahrt (f)
slice Scheibe (f), Schnitte (f)
sliced calf's liver Kalbsleberscheiben (pl. f)
sliced knuckle of veal Kalbshaxenscheiben (f)
slice of grilled (beef) meat grillierte Fleischschnitte (f)
slices of sausage Wurstaufschnitt (m)
sliding roof Schiebedach (n)
slimming diet treatment Abmagerungskur (f)
slipper Hausschuh (m)
slippery glatt, rutschig
slippery when wet Schleudergefahr (f)
slips Badehose (f)
slope Abhang (m), Hang (m), Piste (f)

slope grooming Pistenpflege (f)
slopy abschüssig
slot machine Automat (m), Spielautomat (m)
slow down Schritt (m) fahren!
slow train Bummelzug (m)
sluice Schleuse (f)
slush Schneematsch (m)
small cream puff Windbeutel (m)
small dumpling Klößchen (n)
small veal sausage Kalbfleischwürstchen (n)
small veal steak Kalbsnüßchen (n)
smell Geruch (m), riechen
smelt Stint (m)
smoked geräuchert
smoked beef Rauchfleisch (n)
smoked beef tongue Rindszunge (f), geräuchert
smoked eel Räucheraal (m)
smoked ham Räucherschinken (m)
smoked herring Hering (m) geräuchert
smoked meat Rauchfleisch (n)
smoked pig's ears geräucherte Schweinsohren (pl. n)
smoked (stuffed) pig's trotter Eisbein (n)
smoked pork ribs Kasseler Rippenspeer (m, n)
smoked pork with pickled cabbage Rauchfleisch (n) mit Kraut (n)
smoked rib of pork with sauerkraut Schweinsrippchen (n) mit Sauerkraut (n)
smoked salmon Räucherlachs (m)
smoked sausage Mettwurst (f)
smoker Raucher (m), Raucherabteil (n)
smoke room Rauchsalon (m)

smuggle schmuggeln
snack Imbiß (m)
snack-bar Imbißstube (f), Snackbar (f)
snack-counter Imbißstube (f)
snail Weinbergschnecke (f)
snapshot Schnappschuß (m)
sneakers Turnschuhe (pl. m)
snipe Moorschnepfe (f)
snook Seebarsch (m)
snorkel Schnorchel (m)
snowball Schneeball (m)
snow-bound eingeschneit
snow break Schneeschmelze (f)
snow-chains Schneeketten (pl. f)
snow-cleared schneegeräumt
snow-clearing Schneeräumung (f)
snow conditions Schneelage (f), Schneeverhältnisse (pl. n)
snow-covered schneebedeckt, verschneit
snowdrift Schneewehe (f)
snowed up eingeschneit, verschneit
snow-fall Schneefall (m)
snowfield Schneefeld (n)
snow-goggles Schneebrille (f)
snow-man Schneemann (m)
snowmobile Motorschlitten (m)
snow-plough Schneepflug (m)
snowplow Schneepflug (m)
snow report Schneebericht (m)
snowstorm Schneesturm (m)
snow train Wintersportzug (m)
snowy schneereich
snowy season Schneesaison (f)
snuff Schnupftabak (m)
snug behaglich, gemütlich
soak einweichen
sober nüchtern
soccer Fußballspiel (n)
social activity gesellschaftliche Veranstaltung (f)
social evening Gesellschafts-
abend (m)
social insurance Sozialversicherung (f)
social tourism Sozialtourismus (m)
society Gesellschaft (f)
socket Steckdose (f), Fassung (f)
soda Soda (n)
soda fountain Erfrischungshalle (f)
soda-water Selterswasser (n)
sodium sulphate spring Glaubersalzquelle (f)
soft weich
soft boiled egg weichgekochtes Ei (n)
soft drink alkoholfreies Getränk (n)
software Software (f)
solar radiation Sonnenstrahlung (f), Sonnenbestrahlung (f)
sold out ausverkauft
sole Seezunge (f)
sole agent Alleinvertreter (m)
son-in-law Schwiegersohn (m)
sorrel Sauerampfer (m)
S.O.S. message Reiseruf (m)
soufflé Auflauf (m)
soufflé of chocolate Schokoladenauflauf (m)
soufflé of rice Reisauflauf (m)
soufflé of vanilla Vanilleauflauf (m)
soufflé-potatoes Auflaufkartoffeln (pl. f)
sound-proof schalldicht
soup Suppe (f)
soup-ladle Schöpflöffel (m)
soup-plate Suppenteller (m)
soup-tureen Suppenschüssel (f)
soup with dumpling Knödelsuppe (f)
soup with egg dough drops Eintopfsuppe (f)
soup with fowl Geflügelsuppe (f)

soup with fried peas Bouillon (f) mit gehackten Erbsen
soup with ham dumplings Schinkenknödelsuppe (f)
soup with liver dumpling Leberknödelsuppe (f)
soup with liver rice Leberreissuppe (f)
soup with mushrooms Pilzsuppe (f)
soup with potatoes Kartoffelsuppe (f)
soup with semolina dumplings Grießklößchensuppe (f)
soup with tapioca Tapiocasuppe (f)
soup with tomatoes Tomatensuppe (f)
soup with white beans Bohnensuppe (f)
sour sauer
source of information Informationsquelle (f)
sour cream saurer Rahm (m)
sous-chef stellvertretender Küchenschef (m)
souse Marinade (f)
soused herring Bismarckhering (m)
souvenir shop Andenkengeschäft (n)
soy bean Sojabohne (f)
spa Mineralquelle (f), Heilquelle (f), Kurort (m), Badeort (m), Heilbad (m)
spa ballroom Tanzkasino (n)
spa concert Kurkonzert (n)
spa doctor Kurarzt (m), Badearzt (m)
spaghetti with minced meat-sauce Spaghetti (pl.) mit Hackfleischsoße (f)
spaghetti with tomato sauce Spaghetti (pl.) mit Tomatensoße (f)

spa house Kurhaus (n)
Spanish fish stew spanischer Fischeintopf (m)
Spanish meat-pot spanischer Suppentopf (m)
Spanish rice dish with fish and meat spanisches Reisgericht mit Fisch und Fleisch (n)
span of control Kontrollspanne (f)
spa open all the year round ganzjähriger Kurbetrieb (m)
spa orchestra Kurorchester (n)
spa park Kurpark (m)
spare bed Reservebett (n)
spare part Ersatzteil (n)
spare-rib Rippenspeer (m, n), Schopfbraten (m)
spare-room Fremdenzimmer (n), Gastzimmer (n), Gästezimmer (n)
spare time Freizeit (f)
sparkling schäumend, perlend
sparkling hock Schaumwein (m), Sekt (m)
spa treatment Kurbehandlung (f)
speaker Sprecher (m)
special arrangement Spezialarrangement (n)
special brochure Sonderprospekt (m)
special bus Sonderbus (m)
special folder Sonderprospekt (m)
speciality of the house Spezialität (f) des Hauses (n)
special leave Sonderurlaub (m)
special quota Sonderkontingent (n)
special plane Sonderflugzeug (n)
special price Vorzugspreis (m)
special rate Sondertarif (m), Sonderpreis (n)

special slalom Spezialslalom (m)
special weekend price Wochenend-Spezialpreis (m)
specification Spezifikation (f), Beschreibung (f)
specify spezifizieren
speed Geschwindigkeit (f), Tempo (n)
speed limit Geschwindigkeitsbegrenzug (f)
speed skating Eisschnellauf (m)
spend ausgeben
spice Gewürz (n)
spicy pikant, scharf, würzig
spinach Spinat (m)
spinach beets Mangold (m)
spiny lobster Languste (f)
spirits Spirituosen (pl. f), Alkohol (m)
spirit stove Spirituskocher (m)
spit-roasted am Spieß (m) gebraten
splash planschen
split 1/2 Flasche (f) Mineralwasser (n)
spilt shift unterbrochene Arbeitsschicht (f)
spoil verderben
spoilage Verderb (m) von Waren (pl. f)
sponge Schwamm (m)
sponge ice-cream Schaumgefrorenes (n)
sponge (Swiss)roll Biskuitrolle (f)
spoon Löffel (m)
sporting event Sportveranstaltung (f)
sporting goods Sportartikel (pl. m)
sporting plane Sportflugzeug (n)
sports car Sportwagen (m)
sport clothes Sportkleidung (f)

sports equipment Sportausrüstung (f)
sports facilities Sportanlagen (pl. f)
sports field Sportplatz (m)
sports hall Sporthalle (f)
sports hotel Sporthotel (n)
sportsman Sportler (m)
sportswear Sportkleidung (f)
spot check Überraschungsinventur (f), Prüfung (f) an Ort (m) und Stelle (f)
spotted dick Sultaninenpudding (m)
sponses Eheleute (pl.)
sprat Sprotte (f)
spring Quelle (f), Brunnen (m), Frühling (m), Frühjahr (n)
spring-board Sprungbrett (n)
spring chicken Masthähnchen (n), Hähnchen (n)
spring cleaning Frühjahrsputz (m), Hausreinigung (f)
spring holiday Frühjahrsferien (pl.)
spring onion kleine Zwiebel (f)
spring trade-fair Frühjahrsmesse (f)
spring water Quellwasser (n)
sprinkle bestreuen
spritzer gespritzter Wein (m)
sprouts Kohlsprossen (pl. f), Brokkoli (pl.)
squab Taube (f)
square Platz (m)
squash Fruchtbrei (m), Fruchtsaft (m), Squash (Spaß) (n)
squid Tintenfisch (m)
stadium Stadion (n)
staff function Stabsfunktion (f)
staff holiday Betriebsferien (pl.)
staffing schedule Stellenbesetzungsplan (m)
staff position Stabsstelle (f)
staff responsibility Verantwor-

311

tungsbereich (m) einer Stabstelle (f)
stag Hirsch (m)
stage Teilstrecke (f), Bühne (f)
stage of journey Reiseetappe (f)
staggered holidays Ferienstaffelung (f)
staggering of tourist traffic Streuung (f) des Fremdenverkehrs (m)
staggering scheduling gestaffelter Dienstplan (m)
staircase Treppenhaus (n)
stairs Treppe (f)
stale bread altbackenes Brot (n)
stall Sperrsitz (m), Parkett (n)
stamp Briefmarke (f), Stempel (m), stempeln, frankieren
stamp machine Briefmarkenautomat (m)
standard Standard (m), Vorgabe (f), Wertmesser (m)
standard class Einheitsklasse (f)
standard-cost system Plankostenrechnung (f)
standardization Normung (f), Standardisierung (f), Vereinheitlichung (f)
standardize standardisieren, vereinheitlichen
standardized menu item standardisierter Speiseartikel (m)
standard of living Lebensstandard (m)
standard of performance Leistungsstandard (m), Leistungsmaßstab (m)
stand-by Warteliste (Abflug ohne feste Reservierung) (f)
stand-by position Wartestellung (f)
standing order Dauerauftrag (m)

standing-place Stehplatz (m)
starfish Seestern (m)
start Reisebeginn (m), Abflug (m), Start
starting-point Ausgangsort m, Ausgangspunkt (m)
state forest Staatswald (m)
state frontier Staatsgrenze (f)
statement Aufstellung (f), Verzeichnis (n), Übersicht (f), Behauptung (f), Erklärung (f)
statement analysis Bilanzanalyse (f)
stationary stationär
stationery Bürobedarf (m)
station hall Bahnhofshalle (f)
station hotel Bahnhofshotel (n)
station locker Gepäckschließfach (n)
station-master Bahnhofvorstand (m), Bahnhofsvorsteher (m)
station post office Bahnpostamt (n)
station restaurant Bahnhofsgaststätte (f)
station superintendant Bahnhofsaufsicht (f)
station wagon Kombiwagen (m)
statistic Statistik (f)
statistical statistisch
status Status (m), Stand (m)
stay Aufenthalt (m)
stay abroad Auslandsaufenthalt (m)
stay at a spa Kuraufenthalt (m)
stay in the country Landaufenthalt (m)
steak gebratene Ochsenfleischschnitte (f), Beefsteak (n), Steak (n)
steak and kidney pie warme Steak- und Nierenpastete (f)
steak, Vienna style Wiener Rostbraten (m)
steamed gedämpft, gedünstet

steamed noodles with vanilla-cream Dampfnudeln (pl. f)
steamed potatoes Dampfkartoffeln (pl. f)
steamed rice with chopped pork (beef) Reisfleisch (n)
steamer Dampfer (m)
steamer service Schiffsverbindung (f)
steamer ticket Schiffskarte (f)
steam-ironing Dampfbügeln (n)
steamship Dampfer (m)
steamship connection Schiffsanschluß m
steep steil
steep coast Steilküste (f)
steeple Kirchturm (m)
steep slope Steilhang (m)
steer steuern
steerage Zwischendeck (n)
stencil Matrize (f)
stern Heck (n)
stew Ragout (n)
steward Steward (m), Schiffskellner (m), Leiter (m) der Spülküche (f)
stewardess Stewardeß (f)
stewarding department Spülküche (f), Reinigungsabteilung (f)
stewed gedämpft
stewed apples Apfelkompott (n)
stewed beef Rinderschmorbraten (m)
stewed chicken in paprika (cream) sauce Paprikahühnchen (n)
stewed fruit Kompott (n)
stewed pork and sauerkraut in paprika sauce Szegedinergulasch (n)
stewed veal eingemachtes Kalbfleisch (n)
stew of pork Hungarian style Schweinsgulasch (n)

stew of veal with dumplings Kalbsgulasch (n) mit Klößen (pl. m)
stew of venison Rehragout (n)
stew of white beans Weißbohnengericht (n)
sticker Aufklebezettel (m)
sticky snow Pappschnee (m)
Stilton (cheese) Blauschimmelkäse (m)
stock Lager (n), Vorrat (m), Lagerbestand (m)
stock control Bestandsüberwachung (f)
stock on hand Vorräte (pl. m), Lagerbestand (m)
stocktaking Bestandsaufnahme (f)
stomach Bauch (m)
stone Stein (m), Kern (m), auskernen, entsteinen
stool Barhocker (m)
stop Station (f), Aufenthalt (m), Haltestelle (f), halten
stop en route Zwischenlandung (f), Unterwegsaufenthalt (m)
stopover Reiseunterbrechung (f), Zwischenlandung (f)
stoppage Stockung (f)
storage Lagerung (f)
storage cost Lagerkosten (pl.)
storage space Lagerraum (m)
store lagern, speichern, Lager (n)
storekeeper Lagerhalter (m)
storeroom Lager (n), Vorratsraum (m)
storeroom-book inventory Lagersollbestand (m), Buchinventur (f)
storeroom inventory control record Lagerkontrollbuch (n)
storeroom inventory turnover Lagerumschlagsgeschwindigkeit (f)

storeroom requisition Lageranforderung (f)
storing Lagerhaltung (f)
stout beer dunkles (schwächeres) Bier (n)
stove heating Ofenheizung (f)
strain durchseien
stranger Fremder (m)
strategy Strategie (f)
straw Strohhalm (m), Trinkhalm (m)
strawberry Erdbeere (f)
strawberry ice-cream Erdbeereis (n)
straw potatoes Strohkartoffeln (pl. f)
stream trout Flußforelle (f)
streetcar Straßenbahn (f)
streetcar line Straßenbahnlinie (f)
street hawker Straßenhändler (m)
street island Verkehrsinsel (f)
street-lamp Straßenlaterne (f)
street plan Stadtplan (m)
street sign Straßenschild (n)
stretch Strecke (f)
strike streiken, Streik (m)
string bean Stangenbohnen (f), junge Brechbohnen (f)
strips of chicken breast Bruststreifen (pl. m) vom Huhn (n)
strips of sole fillets Streifen (pl. m) von Seezungen (pl. f)
stroll Bummel (m)
strong stark
stronghold Festung (f), Burg (f)
structure bauliche Anlage (f), Struktur (f), Aufbau (m)
strudel Strudel (m)
student travel Studentenfahrt (f), Studentenreiseverkehr (m)
student trip Studentenfahrt (f)
studio couch Bettcouch (f)
study trip Studienreise (f),

Exkursion (f)
stuff füllen (mit Füllsel)
stuffed gefüllt
stuffed boar's head Wildschweinskopf (gefüllt) (m)
stuffed breast of veal Kalbsbrust gefüllt (f)
stuffed eggs gefüllte Eier (pl. n)
stuffed fritters Teigtaschen (pl. f)
stuffed green (sweet) peppers gefüllte Paprika (pl. f)
stuffed half-moon patty gefülltes Halbmondpastetchen (n)
stuffed olive gefüllte Olive (f)
stuffed pancakes Palatschinken (m)
stuffed shoulder gefüllte Schulter (f)
stuffed tomatoes Tomaten gefüllt (pl. f)
stuffed veal collop gefülltes Kalbsschnitzel (n)
stuffing Füllung (f), Füllsel (n)
sturgeon Stör (m), Sterlet (m)
subcontract Untervertrag (m)
subdivide unterteilen, aufteilen
subdivision Unterteilung (f), Aufteilung (f)
subject to alteration Änderungen (pl. f) vorbehalten
sublease Untervermietung (f)
sublessee Untermieter (m), Unterpächter (m)
sublessor Untervermieter (m), Unterverpächter (m)
sublet untervermieten, unterverpachten
subletting Untermiete (f), Unterpacht (f)
subordinate unterordnen, Untergebener (m)
subscribe abonnieren
subscription Abonnement (n)

subsequent payment Nachzahlung (f)
subsidiary company Tochtergesellschaft (f)
substantial meal reichliche Mahlzeit (f)
substitute ersetzen, Ersatz (m), Stellvertreter (m)
subtenant Untermieter (m), Unterpächter (m)
subtotal Zwischensumme (f)
subtract abziehen
subtraction Abzug (m)
suburban train Vorortzug (m)
subway U-Bahn (f), Fußgängertunnel (m)
suckling pig Spanferkel (n)
sudatory bath Schwitzbad (n)
sue klagen, verklagen
suet Fett (n)
sugar Zucker (m)
sugar-basin Zuckerdose (f)
sugar-bowl Zuckerschale (f)
sugared gezuckert
sugar pea Zuckererbse (f)
sugar-tongs Zuckerzange (f)
suggest vorschlagen, anregen
suggestion Vorschlag (m), Anregung (f)
suit Anzug (m), Kostüm (n)
suitcase Handkoffer (m)
suitcase label Kofferaufkleber (m)
suite Suite (f), Zimmerflucht (f)
sulphur spring Schwefelquelle (f)
sultana Sultanine (f)
sultana (fruit) cake Englischer Kuchen (m)
sultry schül
summary Zusammenfassung (f)
summer fair Sommermesse (f)
summer festival Sommerspiele (pl. n)

summer health resort Sommerfrische (f), Sommerkurort (m)
summer holiday resort Sommerfrische (f)
summer holidays Sommerferien (pl.)
summer holiday village Sommerferiendorf (n)
summer party Sommerfest (n)
summer residence Sommersitz (m)
summer resort Sommeraufenthalt (m)
summer school Ferienkurs (m)
summer season Sommersaison (f)
summer-squash Zwergkürbis (m)
summer terrace Sonnenterrasse (f)
summer time Sommerzeit (f)
summer timetable Sommerfahrplan (m)
summer tourist traffic Sommerreiseverkehr (m), Sommerfremdenverkehr (m)
summer vacation Sommerferien (pl.)
summer visitor Sommergast (m)
sum up zusammenfassen, summieren
sunbath Sonnenbad (n)
sun-bathe ein Sonnenbad (n) nehmen
sun-bathing lawn Liegewiese (f)
sunburn Sonnenbrand (m)
sundae Eisbecher (m)
Sunday excursion Sonntagsausflug (m)
Sunday excursion ticket Sonntagsfahrkarte (f)
sun deck Sonnendeck (n)
sundry verschiedene, sonstige

sun glasses Sonnenbrille (f)
sun-light treatment Heliotherapie (f)
sunny sonnig
sunrise Sonnenaufgang (m)
sunset Sonnenuntergang (m)
sunshade Sonnenschirm (m)
sunstroke Sonnenstich (m)
sunterrace Sonnenterrasse (f)
sun treatment Sonnenkur (f)
sun umbrella Sonnenschirm (m)
supper Abendessen (n)
superior Vorgesetzter (m)
supermarket Selbstbedienungsladen (m)
supervise beaufsichtigen
supervision Aufsicht (f)
supervisor Aufsichtsperson (f), Vorgesetzter (m)
supervisory training Vorgesetztenschulung (f)
supplement Zuschlag (m), Ergänzung (f)
supplementary charge Zuschlag (m)
supplementary course of treatment zusätzliche Kur (f)
supplementary cure zusätzliche Kur (f)
supplementary fare Zuschlag (m)
supplementary ticket Zusatzfahrkarte (f)
supplementary treatment Ergänzungsbehandlung (f)
supplier Lieferant (m), Lieferer (m)
supply liefern, versorgen, Lieferung (f), Angebot (n)
supplying industry Zulieferindustrie (f)
support unterstützen, Unterstützung (f)
supreme Gericht (n) aus den feinsten Stücken (Geflügel n)
surcharge Aufschlag (m)
surf Brandung (f)
surface connection Anschluß (m) mit Bahn (f) oder Bus (m)
surface transport Bahn-Bus-Verkehr (m)
surfboard Surfbrett (n)
surf-riding Brandungsreiten (n)
surname Zuname (m), Familienname (m)
surpass übersteigen, übertreffen
surplus Überschuß (m), Mehrbetrag (m), Gewinn (m)
surroundings Umgebung (f)
survey Untersuchung (f), Erhebung (f), überblicken
survey sheet Erhebungsbogen (m), Fragebogen (m)
suspension railway Schwebebahn (f)
sustain a loss einen Verlust (m) erleiden
swamp Sumpf (m)
swap tauschen, vertauschen, austauschen
sweat Schweiß (m), schwitzen
swede weiße Rübe (f)
sweet süß
sweetbreads Kalbsbries (n)
sweet cheese cake süßer Käsekuchen (m)
sweet cider Süßmost (m), Apfelsaft (m)
sweetcorn Mais (m)
sweet cream Rahm (m), Sahne (f)
sweet curd-cheese strudel Topfenstrudel (m)
sweet curds pie Topfenstrudel (m)
sweet dish Dessert (m), Süßspeise (f)
sweeten zuckern

sweet potato süße Kartoffeln (f), Süßkartoffel (f)
sweets Süßigkeiten (pl.f), Nachtisch (m), Nachspeise (f)
sweet shop Konditorei (f)
sweet water fish Süßwasserfisch (m)
sweet wine Süßwein (m), süßer Wein (m)
swimmer Schwimmer (n)
swim schwimmen
swimming schwimmen (n)
swimming-bath Schwimmbad (n)
swimming-hall Schwimmhalle (f)
swimming instructor Schwimmlehrer (m)
swimming-lessons Schwimmunterricht (m)
swimming master Bademeister (m)
swimming-pool Schwimmbad (n), Badeanstalt (f)
swimsuit Badeanzug (m)
Swiss Central Office of Tourism Schweizerische Fremdenverkehrszentrale (f)
Swiss chard Mangold (m)
Swiss cheese Schweizer Käse (m)
Swiss Hotel-Proprietors' Association Schweizer Hotelier-Verein (m)
Swiss porridge with fresh fruit Birchermüsli (n)
switch Lichtschalter (m)
switchback road Serpentinenstraße (f)
switchboard Telefonzentrale (f)
swordfish Schwertfisch (m)
symbol Symbol (n), Zeichen (n)
syrup Sirup (m)
system System (m)

T

table Tisch (m), Tafel (f), Tabelle (f), Schema (n)
table-cloth Tischtuch (n), Tischdecke (f)
table-cover Tischdecke (f)
table-d'hote nach festem Menü (n) und Preis (m)
table d'hote meal Tagesgericht (n), gemeinsame Mahlzeit (f)
table-knife Tafel-Tischmesser (n)
table-lamp Tischlampe (f)
table-linen Tischzeug (n)
table-mat Untersatz (m)
table-napkin Serviette (f)
table number Tischnummer (f)
table of calorific values Kalorientabelle (f)
table of distances Entfernungstabelle (f)
table reservation Tischreservierung (f)
table reserved for regular customers Stammtisch (m)
table-salt Tafelsalz (n)
table-spoon Eßlöffel (m)
table-talk Tischgespräch (n)
tabletennis Tischtennis (n)
tabletennis room Tischtennishalle (f)
table-top Tischplatte (f)
table-ware Tischgeschirr (n)
table-water Tafelwasser (n), Mineralwasser (n)
table wine Tischwein (m)
tag Etikette (f), Anhängezettel (m)
tail Schwanz (m)
tailcoat Frack (m)
tail-light Schlußlicht (n)
tailor Schneider (m)
tail-wind Rückenwind (m)
take a holiday Ferien (pl.)

317

machen
take a photo fotografieren
take a supplementary ticket nachlösen
take care Vorsicht!
take care of sorgen für
take in petrol tanken
take in tow abschleppen
take inventory Inventur (f) machen
taken besetzt
take off ausziehen
take-off Start (m), Abflug (m)
take-off board Sprungbrett (n)
take part in teilnehmen an
take place stattfinden
take security precautions Sicherheitsvorkehrungen (pl. f) treffen
take shippings an Bord (m) nehmen, laden
take the lead Führung (f) übernehmen
takink of inventory Inventur (f)
tally Strichliste (f)
tang Beigeschmack (m)
tangerine Mandarine (f)
tankard Deckelkrug (m)
tap Faßhahn (m), Wasserhahn (m)
taproom Bierstube (f), Schankstube (f)
tapster Schankkellner (m)
tardy säumig
target Soll (n), Vorgabe (f), Planziel (n)
target inventory Sollbestand (m), Planbestand (m)
target stock Sollbestand (m)
tariff Zolltarif (m), Tarif (m)
tariff provision Tarifvorschriften (f)
tarragon Estragon (m), Beifuß (m)
tart (cake) Torte (f)

tart (of taste) herb
tartare sauce Tartarensoße (f)
tartare steak Beefsteak Tartar (n)
tartlet (Obst-)Törtchen (n)
task Aufgabe (f)
taste Geschmack (m)
tasteful geschmackvoll
tastefulness Geschmacksreichtum (m)
tasteless fade, unschmackhaft, geschmacklos
tastelessness Geschmacklosigkeit (f)
taster Probiergläschen (n) für Wein (m)
tastiness Schmackhaftigkeit (f)
tasty schmackhaft
tat-too Zapfenstreich (m), Abendparade (f) mit Musik (Vorführungen)
tavern Lokal (n), Wirtshaus (n), Ausschank (m)
tavern-keeper Schankwirt (m)
tax Steuer (f), besteuern
taxation Besteuerung (f)
tax de séjour Kurtaxe (f)
taxi Taxi (n)
taxi-driver Taxifahrer (m), Taxichauffeur (m)
taxi-rank Taxistand (m)
tax paid versteuert
T-bar tow Schlepplift (m)
T-bone steak kleines Porterhousesteak (n)
tea Tee (m)
tea-caddy Teebüchse (f)
tea cakes Teegebäck (n)
tea-cart Teewagen (m)
teaching method Lehrmethode (f)
tea-cloth kleine Tischdecke (f), Geschirrtuch (n)
tea-cosy Teewärmer (m)
teacup Teetasse (f)

tea-dance Tanztee (m)
tea garden Gartenrestaurant (n)
tea-house Teehaus (n) (in China und Japan)
tea-kettle Teekessel (m)
teal Krickente (f)
team Arbeitsgruppe (f), Team (n)
teamwork Gemeinschaftsarbeit (f)
tea-party Teegesellschaft (f)
tea-pot Teekanne (f)
tea-room Frühstückszimmer (n), Teestube (f)
tea set Teeservice (n)
tea-shop Teerestaurant (n), Imbißstube (f)
tea-spoon Teelöffel (m)
tea-things Teegeschirr (n)
tea-time Teestunde (f)
tea-trolley Teewagen (m)
tea-urn Teemaschine (f), Warmhaltegerät für das Teewasser (n)
tea with lemon Tee mit Zitrone
tea with milk Tee mit Milch
technician Techniker (m)
tee Ziel (n) (Sport), Golf: künstlich erhöhte Abschlagstelle (f), Golf: Ball auf die Abschlagstelle legen
tee off Golf: abschlagen, Spiel eröffnen (n)
teetotaller Abstinenzler (m)
TEE train, Trans-Europe-Express TEE-Zug (m)
telegram Telegramm (n)
telegram charges Telegrammkosten (pl.)
telegram form Telegrammformular (n)
telegraphic telegrafisch
telegraphic address Telegrammadresse (f)
telegraphic moneyorder telegrafische Anweisung (f)
telegraph office Telegrafenamt (n)
telephone Telefon (n)
telephone booth Fernsprechzelle (f), Telefonzelle (f)
telephone box Telefonzelle (f), Fernsprechzelle (f)
telephone directory Telefonbuch (n), Telefonverzeichnis (n)
telephone exchange Telefonvermittlung (f), Fernsprechamt (n)
telephone on the train Zugtelefon (n)
telephone operator Telefonistin (f)
telephone-receiver Telefonhörer (m)
telephoto lens Teleobjektiv (n)
teleprinter Fernschreiber (m)
teleprinter code Fernschreibercode (m)
teleregister elektronische Platzbelegung (f)
telescope Fernglas (n)
teletype Fernschreiber (m)
television (TV) Fernsehen (TV) (n)
television room Fernsehraum (m)
television set Fernsehgerät (n), Fernsehapparat (m)
television tower Fernsehturm (m)
telex Fernschreibnetz (n), Telex (n)
temperature Temperatur (f), Fieber (n)
tempest Unwetter (n)
tempestuous stürmisch
template Schablone (f)
temporary vorläufig, vorübergehend, zeitweilig

319

temporary financing Zwischenfinanzierung (f)
temporary guest Logiergast (m)
temporary hotel guest Durchreisender (m), Passant (m)
temporary residence visa Aufenthaltsvisum (n)
tenant Mieter (m), Pächter (m)
tench Schleie (f)
tendency Tendenz (f), Entwicklungsrichtung (f)
tender zart
telecommunication Telekommunikation (f)
telegram by telephone ein Telegramm (n) telefonisch aufgeben
tenderloin Lendenstück (n), zartes
tenderloin of beef „Wellington" Rindsfilet im Blätterteig (n)
tenderloin steak Lendenschnitte (f)
tennis Tennis (n)
tennis ball Tennisball (m)
tennis club Tennisklub (m)
tennis court Tennisplatz (m)
tennis court fee Platzmiete (f)
tennis game Tennisspiel (n)
tennis racket Tennisschläger (m)
tennis tournament Tennisturnier (n)
tent Zelt (n)
tentative vorläufig
tent awning Zeltvordach (n)
tent camp Zeltlager (n)
tented city Zeltstadt (f)
tent-peg Zelthering (m)
tepid water lauwarmes Wasser (n)
terminal Endstation (f), Datenendstation (f)
terminal point Endhaltestelle (f), Endstation (f)
terminate kündigen, beenden
termination Kündigung (f), Beendigung (f)
terminus Endstation (f)
terms Vertragsbestimmungen (pl. f), Vertragsbedingungen (pl. f)
terms of delivery Lieferbedingungen (pl. f)
terms of payment Zahlungsbedingungen (pl. f)
terrace facing south Südterasse (f)
terrace restaurant Terrassenrestaurant (n)
terrain treatment Terrainkur (f)
territorial waters Hoheitsgewässer (pl. n)
territory Gebiet (n)
test prüfen, untersuchen, Prüfung (f), Untersuchung (f)
thached strohgedeckt
thalassotherapy Meerwasserkur (f)
Thanksgiving Day Erntedankfest (n)
thaw (auf)tauen, schmelzen, (Auf)Tauen (n), Tauwetter (n)
theatre festival Bühnenfestspiele(pl. n)
theatre ticket Theaterkarte (f)
theatrical performance Theatervorstellung (f)
theatrical season Theatersaison (f)
the days dish Tagesplatte (f)
the days soup Tagessuppe (f)
theft Diebstahl (m)
theft insurance Diebstahlversicherung (f)
therapeutical therapeutisch
therapeutical facilities Kureinrichtungen (pl. f)
thermal baths Thermalbad (n)

thermal indoor swimming-pool Thermalhallenbad (n)
thermal water Thermalwasser (n)
thermal-water pool Thermalbecken (n)
thermos flask Thermosflasche (f)
thermotherapy Thermotherapie (f)
thick ox-tail soup gebundene Ochsenschwanzsuppe (f)
thick soup legierte Suppe (f)
thin pancakes filled with jam Palatschinken (m)
third-party insurance Haftpflichtversicherung (f)
third-party liability Haftpflicht (f)
thirst Durst (m)
thirsty durstig
thoroughfare Durchgangsstraße (f)
three-bed room Dreibettzimmer (n)
three-berth compartment Dreibettabteil (n)
three-berth room Dreibettkabine (f)
three-mile zone Dreimeilenzone (f)
three-minute egg Dreiminutenei (n)
threshold Schwelle (f)
thrifty sparsam
throng of people Andrang (m)
through connection Direktverbindung (f)
through-carriage Kurswagen (m)
through fare Gesamtstreckenfahrpreis (m)
through flight Direktflug (m)
through passenger Durchgangsreisender (m)

through traffic Durchgangsverkehr (m)
through train durchgehender Zug (m)
throw overboard über Bord werfen
thunder donnern
thunderstorm Gewitter (n)
thyme Thymian (m)
ticket Fahrkarte (f), Fahrschein (m), Verwarnung (f), Billett (n)
ticket barrier Bahnsteigsperre (f)
ticket clerk Schalterbeamter (m)
ticket-collector Bahnsteigschaffner (m)
ticket for reserved seat Platzkarte (f)
ticket inspection Fahrscheinkontrolle (f)
ticket inspector Kontrolleur (m)
ticket machine Fahrkartenautomat (m)
ticket of admission Eintrittskarte (f)
ticket office Fahrkartenschalter (m), Bahnschalter (m), Stadtbüro (n)
ticket office window Fahrkartenschalter (m)
tides Gezeiten (pl.)
tidy sauber, ordentlich
tie-in sale Kopplungsverkauf (m)
tilsit cheese Tilsiter Käse (m)
time Zeit (f)
time allowance Zeitvorgabe (f)
time and motion study Zeit- und Bewegungsstudie (f)
time exposure Zeitaufnahme (f)
timekeeper Personalpförtner (m)
time limit Frist (f)

321

time of arrival Ankunftszeit (f)
time of day Tageszeit (f)
time of delivery Lieferzeit (f)
time of departure Abfahrtszeit (f), Abflugzeit (f)
time of sailing Abfahrtszeit (f)
time of stay Aufenthaltsdauer (f)
time signal Zeitansage (f), Zeitzeichen (n)
timetable Fahrplan (m), Kursbuch (n), Flugplan (m)
timing Zeitnahme (f), Terminierung (f)
tin Konservenbüchse (f)
tinned beer Dosenbier (n)
tinned food Konserve (f)
tinned meat Büchsenfleisch (n)
tin opener Büchsenöffner (m)
tiny flour dumplings Spätzle (pl.)
tip Trinkgeld (n), Trinkgeld (n) geben
tips included Bedienungsgeld eingeschlossen (im Preis) (n)
tip-up seat Klappsitz (m), Notsitz (m)
tissue paper Seidenpapier (n)
T-junction Straßeneinmündung (f)
toad-in-the-hole Schweinswürstchen (n) in gebackenem Eierteig (m)
toast Röstbrotschnitte (f), Toast (m)
toast (to propose a toast) Trinkspruch (m)
toasted geröstet
toasted cheese Käseschnitte (f)
toaster Toaströster (m), Toaster (m)
toastmaster Toastmeister (m)
tobacco Tabak (m)
tobacconist Zigarettenverkäufer (m)

tobacconist's shop Tabakladen (m)
tobacco pipe Tabakspfeife (f)
tobacco tax Tabaksteuer (f)
toboggan Schlitten (m), rodeln
tobogganing Rodeln (n), Rodelsport (m)
toboggan run Rodelbahn (f)
toboggan slide Rodelbahn (f), Rodelhang (m)
toboggan tow Rodellift (m), Schlittenlift (m)
toby jug Bierkrug (in Form eines Mannes) (m)
today heute
today's bill of fare Tageskarte (f)
today's menu Tageskarte (f)
today's programm Tagesprogramm (n)
today's special dish Tagesspezialität (f)
today's speciality Tagesspezialität (f)
toddy Grog (m)
toilet Toilette (f)
toilet-paper Toilettenpapier (n)
toilet soap Toilettenseife (f)
toll Straßenzoll (m), Maut (f), Straßenbenutzungsgebühr (f), Autobahngebühr (f)
toll road gebührenpflichtige Straße (f)
tomato Tomate (f)
tomato juice Tomatensaft (m)
tomato ketchup Tomatenketchup (m)
tomato salad Tomatensalat (m)
tomato sauce Tomatensoße (f)
tomato-soup Tomatensuppe (f)
tomorrow morgen
tongue Zunge (f)
tonic(water) Tonic(wasser) (n)
tonnage Schiffstonnage (f)
too zu, allzu

tool Handwerkszeug (n), Gerät (n)
tooth brush Zahnbürste (f)
tooth-paste Zahnpaste (f)
tooth-pick Zahnstocher (m)
top cut roast Rindsrostbraten (m)
tope trinken, saufen
top executive leitender Angestellter (m)
topic Gesprächsstoff (m)
top management Betriebsführung (f), Geschäftsleitung (f)
top salary Spitzengehalt (n)
top secret streng geheim
top speed Höchstgeschwindigkeit (f)
top terminal Bergstation (f)
top up the radiator Kühlwasser (n) nachfüllen
tornado Wirbelsturm (m)
tossed salad gemischter Salat (m)
tot Gläschen (n), Schlückchen (n)
total Endsumme (f)
total cost Gesamtkosten (pl.)
to zu (Richtung)
tough zäh
tour Tour (f), Reise (f)
tour conductor Reiseleiter (m)
touring area Reisegebiet (n)
touring centre Ausgangsort (m), Ausgangspunkt (m)
touring exhibition Wanderschau (f)
touring facilities Ausflugmöglichkeiten (pl. f)
touring itinerary Reisestrecke (f), Reiseroute (f), Reiseverlauf (m)
tourism Fremdenverkehr (m), Tourismus (m), Touristik (f), Touristenverkehr (m), Fremdenverkehrswesen (n)

tourist Tourist (m), Reisender (m), Ausflügler (m)
tourist abroad Auslandsreisender (m)
tourist advertising Fremdenverkehrswerbung (f)
tourist agency Reiseagentur (f), Reisebüro (n)
tourist agent Reiseagent (m), Reisemittler (m)
tourist area Reisegebiet (n)
tourist association Fremdenverkehrsverband (m)
tourist atlas Reiseatlas (m)
tourist-board Fremdenverkehrsamt (n)
tourist bus Reisebus (m)
tourist campaign Fremdenverkehrskampagne (f)
tourist card Touristenkarte (f), Touristenausweis (m)
tourist centre Fremdenverkehrsort (m)
tourist class Touristenklasse (f)
tourist country Fremdenverkehrsland (n)
tourist court Motel (n)
tourist economy Fremdenverkehrswirtschaft (f)
touristed überlaufen
tourist fare Touristenflugpreis (m)
tourist hotel Touristenhotel (n)
touristic touristisch
touristic map Tourenkarte (f)
touristic poster Reiseplakat (n)
tourist industry Fremdenverkehrsindustrie (f)
tourist information office Verkehrsamt (n), Verkehrsbüro (n)
tourist journal Fremdenverkehrszeitschrift (f)
tourist market Reisemarkt (m)
tourist office Fremdenverkehrs-

amt (n), Fremdenverkehrsbüro (n)
tourist party Reisegesellschaft (f)
tourist policy Fremdenverkehrspolitik
tourist publicity Fremdenverkehrswerbung (f)
tourist region Fremdenverkehrsgebiet (n), Reisegebiet (n), Touristengebiet (n)
tourist resort Fremdenverkehrsort (m)
tourist season Fremdenverkehrssaison (f), Reisezeit (f)
tourist's medicine-case Reiseapotheke (f)
tourist town Fremdenverkehrsstadt (f)
tourist trade Fremdenverkehr (m)
tourist trade establishment Fremdenverkehrsbetrieb (m)
tourist trade statistics Fremdenverkehrsstatisk (f)
tourist traffic Fremdenverkehr (m), Touristenverkehr (m), Reiseverkehr (m), Ausflugsverkehr (m)
tourist traffic institution Fremdenverkehrsträger (m)
tourist weather insurance Reisewetterversicherung (f)
tourist visa Touristenvisum (n)
tour management Reiseleitung (f)
tour manager Reiseleiter (m), Reiseleiterin (f)
tour operator Reiseveranstalter (m)
tour program Ausflugsprogramm (n)
tour region Ausflugsgebiet (n)
tour round Rundgang (m)
tour ticket Ausflugskarte (f)

tow abschleppen
towel Handtuch (n)
towel-rack Handtuchhalter (m)
tower Turm (m)
towing Abschleppen (n)
town Stadt (f), Ort (m)
town bus Linienbus (m)
town centre Innenstadt (f), Stadtzentrum (n)
town hall Rathaus (n)
town office Stadtbüro (n)
town plan Stadtplan (m)
town terminal Autoabfahrtsstelle (f), Flugplatzbahnhof (m)
town wall Stadtmauer (f)
tow-rope Abschleppseil (n)
toxic(al) giftig, toxisch
toy Spielzeug (n)
to your healthy Prosit!
trace zurückverfolgen, ausfindigmachen
track Gleis (n)
trade Handel (m), Gewerbe (n), handeln
trade custom Handelsbrauch (m)
trade fair Fachmesse (f)
trading vessel Handelsschiff (n)
traffic Geschäftsverkehr (m), Verkehr (m), Handel (m)
traffic accident Verkehrsunfall (m)
traffic artery Verkehrsader (f)
traffic block Verkehrsstockung (f)
traffic circle Kreisverkehr (m)
traffic Verkehrsstauung (f)
traffic control Verkehrsüberwachung (f)
traffic density Verkehrsdichte (f)
traffic flow Verkehrsfluß (m)
traffic hold-up Verkehrsstockung (f)

traffic jam Verkehrsstockung (f)
traffic light Verkehrsampel (f)
traffic police Verkehrspolizei (f)
traffic regulation Verkehrsregelung (f), Verkehrsordnung (f)
traffic restriction Verkehrseinschränkung (f)
traffic safety Verkehrssicherheit (f)
traffic warden Politesse (f)
trail Pfad (m), Spur (f), Rennstrecke (f), Abfahrt (Ski) (f)
trailer Autoanhäger (m), Wohnwagen (m)
trailerite Wohnwagenfahrer (m)
trailtourist Caravaner (m)
train ausbilden, anlernen, trainieren, Zug (m)
train conductor Zugbegleiter (m)
trainee Auszubildender (m), Praktikant (m)
trainer Ausbilder
train ferry Eisenbahnfähre (f)
train formation Zusammensetzung (f) der Züge (pl. m)
train indicator Aushangfahrplan (m)
training Ausbildung (f), Anlernen (n), Training (n)
training film Lehrfilm (m)
training ground Übungsgelände (n)
training hotel Schulungshotel (n)
training manager Ausbilder (m), Ausbildungsleiter (m)
training method Lehrmethode (f), Ausbildungsmethode (f)
training on the job Ausbildung (f) am Arbeitsplatz (m)
training suit Trainingsanzug (m)

train journey Bahnfahrt (f), Bahnreise (f)
train number Zugnummer (f)
train set Zugteil (m)
train timings Zugzeiten (pl. f)
tram Straßenbahn (f)
tramcar Straßenbahnwagen (m)
tram-line Straßenbahnlinie (f)
tramp trampen, Landstreicher (m), Tramper (m), Trampschiff (n)
tramping Wandern (n)
tram-stop Straßenbahnhaltestelle (f)
tram-ticket Straßenbahnkarte (f)
tramway Straßenbahn (f)
transaction Verhandlung (f), Geschäft (n), Geschäftsvorfall (m)
transatlantic flight Ozeanflug (m)
transatlantic liner Ozeandampfer (m)
transfer übertragen, Übertrag (m), Versetzung (f), Transfer m, Umsteigekarte (f)
transferable übertragbar
transfer free of charge kostenlose Zubringung (f)
transfer from airport to town terminal Transfer (m) vom Flughafen (m) zum Air-Terminal (m)
transfer ticket Umsteigekarte (f)
transfer to hotel Transfer zum Hotel (n)
transient (guest) Durchreisender (m), Passant (m), Übernachtungsgast (m)
transient hotel Hotel (n) für Durchreisende (pl. m), Passantenhotel (n), Übernachtungshotel (n)

transient rate Übernachtungspreis (m) für Durchreisende (pl. m)
transire Zolldurchlaßschein (m)
transit Transit (m)
transit country Durchgangsland (n)
transit goods Transitgut (n)
transition period Übergangszeit (f)
transit journey Transitreise (f)
transit passenger Transitreisender (m)
transit traffic Transitverkehr (m), Durchgangsverkehr (m)
transit visa Transitvisum (n), Durchreisevisum (n)
translate umrechnen, übersetzen
translation Übersetzung (f), Umrechnung (f)
transmission Getriebe (Fahrzeug) (n), Sendung (f), Radioübertragung (f)
transoceanic voyage Ozeanreise (f), Überseefahrt (f)
transport Transport (m), Beförderung (f), transportieren
transportable transportierbar
transportation Transport (m), Transportgewerbe (n)
transportation advertising Verkehrsmittelwerbung (f)
transportation cost Transportkosten (pl.), Versandkosten (pl.)
transportation industry Verkehrsgewerbe (n)
transport charge Beförderungspreis (m)
transport charges Beförderungskosten (pl.)
transport company Transportunternehmen (n)
transport contractor Transportunternehmer (m)

transport insurance Transportversicherung (f)
transport planning Verkehrsplanung (f)
transport policy Verkehrsplanung (f)
transshipement point Umschlagplatz (m)
trash Kitsch (m), Schund (m)
travel Reise (f), Reisen (n), Reiseverkehr (m), reisen
travel accident insurance Reiseunfallversicherung (f)
travel advance Reisespesenvorschuß (m)
travel agency Reisebüro (n)
travel allowance Reisekostenvergütung (f)
travel booklet Reiseprospekt (m), Fremdenverkehrsprospekt (m)
travel boom Reisewelle (f)
travel by train mit dem Zug (m) reisen
travel companion Reisebegleiter (m)
travel documents Reisepapiere (pl. n)
travel expense report Reisespesenabrechnung (f)
travel expenses Reisespesen (pl.)
travel information Reiseauskunft (f)
travel insurance Reiseversicherung (f)
traveller Handelsvertreter (m), Reisender (m)
Travellers' Air Office Bahnhofsmission (f)
travellers' cheque Reisescheck (m)
travellers' letter of credit Reisekreditbrief (m)
travelling-bag Reisetasche (f)

travelling charges Reisespesen (pl.)
travelling day Reisetag (m)
travelling expenses Reisekosten (pl.) Reisespesen (pl.)
travelling funds Reisekasse (f)
travelling provisions Reiseproviant (m)
travel market Reisemarkt (m)
travel organizer Reiseveranstalter (m)
travel poster Ferienplakat (n), Reiseplakat (n)
travel preparations Reisevorbereitungen (pl. f)
travel program Reiseprogramm (n)
travel research Fremdenverkehrsforschung (f)
travel service Reisebetreuung (f)
travel souvenir Reiseandenken (n)
travel statistics Fremdenverkehrsstatistik (f)
travel supervisor Reiseleiter (m)
travel supplement Reisebeilage (f)
travel time Reisezeit (f), Fahrzeig (f), Wegzeit (f)
travel voucher Reisegutschein (m)
tray Tablett (n), Ablagekorb (m)
treacle Sirup (m)
treatment Kur (f, Behandlung (f), Kurmittel (n)
treatment at a spa Brunnenkur (f)
trekking Karawanenreise (f), Safari (f), Trekking (n)
trellis cake Linzertorte (f)
trend Tendenz (f), Trend (m)
trend of operations Geschäftsentwicklung (f)
treatment with aerosols Aerosoltherapie (f)
trial run Probelauf (m)
trifle Mürbekuchen (m) (getaucht in Sirup, Sherry etc.)
trigger Auslöser (m)
trimmings Beilage (f)
trip Reise (f), Fahrt (f)
tripe Kuttel (pl. n)
tripe á la mode de Caen Kutteln gekocht in Weißwein (pl.n)
tripe and onions Rindsmagen (m) in Milch (f) und Wasser (n) gekocht mit Zwiebeln (pl. f)
tripes soup Kuttelnsuppe (f)
triple room Dreibettzimmer (n)
triplicate dreifach
tripod Stativ (n)
tripper Ausflügler (m), Ausflüglerin (f), Tourist (m), Touristin (f)
tropical tropisch
tropics Tropen (pl.)
trotting race Trabrennen (n)
trouble maker Streithahn (m), Querulant (m)
trouble-shooter Friedensstifter (m), Problemlöser (m)
trout Forelle (f)
trout fishing Forellenfischen (n)
trout in champagne Forelle in Champagner (f)
truck Lastwagen (m), Zugwagen (m)
truck trailer Lastwagenanhänger (m)
truffle Trüffel (f)
truffled getrüffelt
trunk Kabinenkoffer (m), Kofferraum (m)

327

trunk-call Ferngespräch (n)
trunk exchange Fernsprechamt (n), Telefonvermittlung (f)
trunk road Fernverkehrsstraße (f)
trunks Badehose (f)
trustworthiness Vertrauenswürdigkeit (f)
trustworthy vertrauenswürdig
try versuchen, probieren
tub Wanne (f)
tub-bath Wannenbad (n)
tube U-Bahn (f), Röhre (f)
tube post Rohrpost (f)
tugboat Schlepper (m)
tumbler Wasserglas (n)
tuna fish Thunfisch (m)
tunny Thunfisch (m)
turbo-ship, TS Turbinenschiff (n)
turbo-steamship, TSS Turbinendampfschiff (n)
turbot Steinbutt (m)
tureen Suppenschüssel (f)
turkey Truthahn (m), Puter (m)
Turkish bath türkisches Bad (n)
Turkish coffee Kaffee türkisch (m)
Turkish towel Frottiertuch (n)
turn back kehrtmachen
turning Straßenbiegung (f)
turnip weiße Rübe (f)
turn off abbiegen, abschalten
turn on einschalten
turnover Umsatz (m), Umschlag (m)
turnover tax Umsatzsteuer (f)
turnpike Schlagbaum (m)
turn round umkehren, wenden
turn upside down sich überschlagen
turtle Schildkröte (f)
turtle soup, real echte Schildkrötensuppe (f)
tuxedos Smoking (m)

twilight Zwielicht (n)
twin-bedded room Doppelzimmer (n)
two-berth compartment Zweibettabteil (n)
two-berth room Zweibettkabine (f)
two-lane road zweibahnige Straße (f), zweispurige Straße (f)
two-way traffic Gegenverkehr (m)
type of customers Kundenkreis (m), Kundengruppe (f)
typewriter Schreibmaschine (f)
typical typisch
tyre Reifen (m)
tyre chains Schneeketten (pl. f)
tyre pressure Reifendruck (m)

U

ugly häßlich
ultrasinics Ultraschall (m)
ultrasound Ultraschall (m)
ultra-violet lamp Höhensonne (f)
ultraviolet rays ultraviolette Strahlen (pl. m)
umber Umberfisch (m)
umbrella Schirm (m)
umbrella tent Hüttenzelt (n)
unaddressed mailing Postwurfsendung (f)
unattainable unerschwinglich
unauthorized unbefugt, unerlaubt, unberechtigt
unbreakable unzerbrechlich
uncle Onkel (m)
unclean unsauber
uncomfortable unbequem, ungemütlich
unconventional zwanglos

undated undatiert
under age minderjährig
under construction im Bau (m) befindlich
undercut unterschreiten, unterbieten
underdone blutig gebraten, fast roh
underground U-Bahn (f)
underground bar Kellerbar (f)
underground garage Tiefgarage (f)
underground restaurant Kellerlokal (n)
underpants Unterhose (f)
underpass Unterführung (f)
understand verstehen
undertake unternehmen
underwater equipment Unterwasserausrüstung (f)
underwater exercises Unterwassergymnastik (f)
underwater massage Unterwassermassage (f)
underwear Unterwäsche (f)
undisturbed ungestört
undress sich ausziehen
unemployed arbeitslos
unfriendly unfreundlich
uniform einheitlich, Uniform (f)
uniform system of accounts Kontenrahmen (m) für Hotels und Verkehrsbetriebe (USA)
union Gewerkschaft (f)
union agreement Tarifvertrag (m)
unit Einheit
unit price Preis (m) pro Einheit (f)
unknow unbekannt
unload ausladen
unloading station Bergstation (f)

unlock aufschließen
unmarried ledig, unverheiratet
unoccupied leerstehend, unbewohnt
unpack auspacken
unpaid unbezahlt
unripe unreif
unskilled manpower ungelernte Arbeitskräfte (pl. f)
uphill bergauf
upon arrival nach Ankunft (f)
upper berth Oberbett (n)
upper-bracket hotel Hotel (n) der gehobenen Mittelklasse (f)
upper circle zweiter Rang (m) (Theater)
upper deck Oberdeck (n)
up-to-date auf dem laufenden (n), bis heute, aktuell, zeitgemäß
uptrend steigende Tendenz (f)
up-value aufwerten
upware and downward journey Berg- und Talfahrt (f)
upward journey Auffahrt (f), Bergfahrt (f)
urban städtisch
urban area Stadtgebiet (n)
urban bus service städtischer Autobusbetrieb (m)
urban express road Stadtschnellstraße (f)
urban freeway Stadtautobahn (f)
urban traffic Stadtverkehr (m)
urgent dringend
usable brauchbar, befahrbar
usage Brauch (m)
usage of trade Handelsbrauch (m)
use Gebrauch (m)
used gebraucht
useful zweckmäßig, nützlich

329

user Verbraucher (m), Benützer (m)
usher Türsteher (m), Platzanweiser (m)
usherette Platzanweiserin (f)
usual üblich
utilities sonstige Raumkosten (pl.) (Strom, Gas, Wasser)
utilty program Dienstprogramm (n)
utilization of capacity Beschäftigungsgrad (m), Kapazitätsausnutzung (f)
utilize auslasten

V

vacancy offene Stelle (f)
vacant frei, unbesetzt
vacate räumen, freimachen
vacation Urlaub (m)
vacation apartment Ferienwohnung (f), Ferienunterkunft (f)
vacationer Urlauber (m)
vacation pay Urlaubsgeld (n)
vacation program Ferienprogramm (n)
vacation schedule Urlaubseinteilung (f), Ferienordnung (f)
vaccinate impfen
vaccination Impfung (f)
vacuum cleaner Staubsauger (m)
valet Hausdiener (m), Etagendiener (m), Bügel- und Reinigungsdienst (m)
valid wirksam, gültig
validity Gültigkeit (f), Geltungsdauer (f)
valley Tal (n)
valuables Wertsachen (pl. f)
value bewerten, Wert (m)
valve Ventil (n)

vanilla Vanille (f)
vanilla ice Vanilleeis (n)
vanilla ice-cream Vanilleeis (n)
vapour bath Dampfbad (n), Schwitzbad (n)
variable veränderlich, variable
variable cost variable Kosten (pl.), proportionale Kosten (pl.), veränderliche Kosten (pl.)
variance Abweichung (f), Veränderung (f)
varied diet abwechslungsreiche Kost (f)
variety Vielfalt (f), Verschiedenheit (f)
variolization Pockenschutzimpfung (f)
various verschiedenartig
vary abwechseln, verändern
vase Vase (f)
veal Kalbfleisch (n), Kalb (n)
veal bird Kalbfleischröllchen (n)
veal chop Kalbskotelett (n)
veal collop Kalbsschnitzel (n)
veal collop with fried egg Holsteiner Schnitzel (n)
veal cutlet Kalbskotelett (n)
veal olive Kalbsröllchen (n)
veal roll Kalbsroulade (f)
veal scallop Kalbsschnitzel (n)
veal steak Kalbssteak (n)
veal steak in sour cream Rahmschnitzel (n)
veal steak Hungarian style Paprikaschnitzel (n)
veal stew Kalbsragout (n)
veal stew with scrambled eggs Hoppel-Poppel (n)
veal with tuna kaltes Kalbfleisch (n) in Thunfischsauce (f)
vegetable Gemüse (n)
vegetable broth Gemüsesuppe (f)

vegetable dish Gemüsegericht (n)
vegetable marrow Speisekürbis (m)
vegetable plate Gemüseplatte (f)
vegetable salad Gemüsesalat (m)
vegetarian Vegetarier (m), vegetarisch
vegetarian diet vegetarische Kost (f)
vegetarian dishes vegetarische Kost (f)
vegetarian food Rohkost (f)
vegetarian restaurant Vegetarierrestaurant (n)
vehicle Fahrzeug (n), Verkehrsmittel (n)
vehicle traffic Fahrverkehr (m)
velouté sauce milde Sauce (f) (Hühner od. Kalbfleischbrühe mit Zusätzen)
vending machine Verkaufsautomat (m)
vension Reh (n), Rehbock (m), Hirsch (m)
ventilation Lüftung (f)
ventilator Ventilator (m)
veranda deck Verandadeck (n)
verbal mündliche, wörtlich
verify überprüfen, bestätigen
vermicelli Fadennudeln (pl. f)
vermin Ungeziefer (n)
verm(o)uth Wermut(wein) (m)
vertical drop Höhenunterschied (m)
vessel Schiff
vestibule Vorhalle (f)
via über
vice-president Vizepräsident (m)
vicinity Nähe
Vienna Wien
Vienna plum pudding Gugelhupf (m)
Vienna steak with fried onions Wiener Rostbraten (m)
Viennese Schnitzel Wiener Schnitzel (n)
view Aussicht (f), Blick (m), erblicken
view-finder Sucher (m)
view of Blick (m) auf
village Dorf (n), Ort (m)
village inn Dorfgasthaus (n)
village pub Dorfschenke (f)
vinaigrette(sauce) Vinaigrette-Sauce (f)
vine Rebstock (m), Weinrebe (f)
vinegar Essig (m)
vintage Weinlese (f)
vintage festival Weinlesefest (n)
vintagers' festival Winzerfest (n)
vintage wine Spitzenwein (m), naturreiner Wein (m)
vinyard Weinberg (m), Weingut (n)
violate verletzen, brechen, übertreten
VIP very important person besonders wichtige Gäste (pl. m)
virgin forest Urwald (m)
visa Visum (n), Sichtvermerk (m)
visa charge Visagebühr (f)
visibility Sicht (f)
visit Besuch (m), besuchen
visiting hours Besuchszeiten (pl. f)
visit of relatives Verwandtenbesuch (m)
visitor Besucher (m)
visitors' book Gästebuch (n), Fremdenbuch (n)
visitors' card Besucherkarte (f)

331

visitors' tax Kurtaxe (f)
visitor visa Besuchervisum (n)
visual aid optisches Lehrhilfsmittel (n)
visual merchandising Verkaufsförderung (f) durch Ausstellung (f) der Ware (f)
vocational training Berufsausbildung (f)
vodka Wodka (m)
void ungültig
vol-au-vent Blätterteigpastete (f)
voltage Spannung (f)
volume Volumen (n), Beschäftigung (f), Beschäftigungsgrad (m), Band (Buch) (m)
volume discount Mengenrabatt (m)
volume of tourist traffic Reiseintensität (f)
vomit sich übergeben
voucher Beleg (m), Gutschein (m)
voyage Seereise (f), Schiffsreise (f), Fahrt (f), Reise (f)
voyage distance Fahrkilometer (pl. m)
voyage home Heimreise (f)
voyager Seereisender (m), Reisender (m)

W

waffle Waffel (f)
wage Lohn (m)
wage advance Lohnvorschuß (m)
wage and salary sturcture Lohn- und Gehaltsstruktur (f)
wage incentive Lohnanreiz (m)
wage increase Lohnerhöhung (f)

wages according to agreement Tariflohn (m)
wage scale Lohntarif (m)
waggon Eisenbahnwagen (m)
waistcoat Weste (f)
wait warten
wait on bedienen
waiter Kellner (m)
waiter apprentice Kellnerlehrling (m), Jungkellner (m)
waiting limited to Parkdauer (f) höchstens
waiting line Warteschlange (f)
waiting list Warteliste (f)
waiting period Wartezeit (f)
waiting prohibited Parken (n) verboten
waiting-room Wartesaal (m)
waitress Kellnerin (f), Serviererin (f), Bedienung (f)
waits Wartezeiten (pl. f)
wake up wecken, aufwachen
wake-up call Weckruf (m)
waking service Weckdienst (m)
walk gehen, spazierengehen, wandern, Spaziergang (m), Spazierweg (m)
walking Wandern (n)
walking shoes Straßenschuhe (pl. f)
walking tour Wanderung (f), Wanderfahrt (f)
walk in the woods Waldspaziergang (m)
walk round Rundgang (m)
walkway Laufgang (m)
wall Mauer (f)
wallet Brieftasche (f)
wall map Wandkarte (f)
wall plug Steckdose (f)
wall socket Steckdose (f)
walnut Walnuß (f)
waltz Walzer (m)
want Bedürfnis (n), Mangel (m), wünschen, wollen

want ad Kleinanzeige (f)
wardrobe Garderobe (f), Kleiderschrank (m)
wardrobe trunk Schrankkoffer (m)
warehouse Lagerhaus (n)
warm wärmen, erwärmen, warm
warmth Wärme (f)
warning Verwarnung (f), Warnung (f)
warning sign Warnschild (n)
warranted garantiert
warrant officer Deckoffizier (m)
washable waschbar, waschecht
wash-basin Waschbecken (n)
washing and lavatory facilities Wasch- und Toilettenanlagen (pl. f)
washing basin Waschbecken (n)
washing-machine Waschmaschine (f)
washing-powder Waschpulver (n)
washing tub Waschwanne (f)
washroom Toilette (f)
washstand Waschtisch (m)
wash up spülen, abspülen
waste verderben, verfallen, Verderb (m), Abfall (m)
waste-disposer Müllschlucker (m)
waste-paper basket Papierkorb (m)
watchman Wächter (m)
water Wasser (n)
water-borne traffic Schiffahrtsverkehr (m)
water-bottle Feldflasche (f)
water-closet, W. C. Toilette (f)
water-cress Kresse (f)
water cure Wasserkur (f)
waterfall Wasserfall (m)
water gliding Wasserfliegen (n)

water-heater Heißwasserboiler (m)
water hen Bläßhuhn (n), Wasserhuhn (n)
watering-place Wasserstelle (f), Badeort (m)
watering-place visitor Badegast (m)
water level Wasserstand (m)
water-melon Wassermelone (f)
water pipes Wasserleitung (f)
water pollution Wasserverunreinigung (f)
water-polo Wasserball (m)
waterproof wasserdicht
water-ski Wasserski (m)
water sports Wassersport (m)
water-tap Wasserhahn (m)
water temperature Wassertemperatur (f)
water wave Wasserwelle (f)
wave Welle (f), winken, schwenken
wave damage insurance Hochwasserversicherung (f)
wavy wellig
wax wachsen, Wachs (n)
wax bean Wachsbohne (f)
wax-egg Wachsei (n)
way in Autoeinfahrt (f)
way out Ausgang (m), Ausfahrt (f)
wayside inn Dorfgasthaus (n)
way up Aufgang (m)
wear and tear Abnutzung (f) durch Gebrauch (m)
weary müde, ermüdet
weather bureau Wetteramt (n)
weather chart Wetterkarte (f)
weather forecast Wettervorhersage (f), Wetterbericht (m)
weatherproof wetterfest
weather station Wetterwarte (f)
wedding Hochzeit (f)
wedge strap Keilriemen (m)

week-day Wochentag (m)
week-end Wochenende (n)
week-end-exursion Wochenendausflug (m)
week-end guest-house Wochenendpension (f)
week-end-outing Wochenendfahrt (f)
week-end return ticket Sonntagsrückfahrkarte (f)
week-end ticket Wochenendfahrkarte (f)
week-end tourism Wochenendtourismus (m)
week-end tourist traffic Wochenendreiseverkehr (m)
week-end trip Wochenendfahrt (f)
weekly wöchentlich
weekly bill Wochenrechnung (f)
weekly market Wochenmarkt (m)
weigh wiegen
weigh anchor Anker (m) lichten
weight Gewicht (n)
weighted average gewogener Durchschnitt (m)
welcome willkommen
well gut, wohl
well-cooked mürbe
well-done durchgebraten
well-furnished gut eingerichtet
well-seasoned würzig
well-wooded waldreich
Welsh rabbit (rarebit) geröstetes Brot mit heißem Käse (n), Welsh rabbit, (walisische Käseschnitte) (n)
Wensleydale Wensleydale-Käse (m)
Western European time westeuropäische Zeit (f), (WEZ)
Westphalian rye-bread Pumpernickel (m)
wet naß
wetness Nässe (f)
wet paint frisch gestrichen
wharf Schiffsanlegestelle (f), Kai (m)
wheaten bread Weizenbrot (n)
wheelage Rollgeld (n)
wheel-chair Rollstuhl (m)
when shipped nach Verladung (f)
whereabouts Aufenthaltsort (m)
whet anregen (Appetit, Apetitanreger) (m)
whiff Zigarillo (m)
whipped cream Schlagsahne (f)
whisk Schneebesen (m)
whisky, Whiskey Whisky (m)
whistle pfeifen
whitebait Breitling (m)
whitebait Breitling (m)
white bass Meerbarsch (m)
white bean weiße Bohne (f)
white bean-soup weiße Bohnensuppe (f)
white beer Weißbier (n)
white bread Weißbrot (n)
white bread dumpling Semmelknödel (m)
white cabbage Weißkohl (m), Weißkraut (n)
white cheese dumpling Quarkknödel (m)
white coffee Milchkaffee (m)
white collar worker Büroangestellter (m)
white fish Felchen (m)
white grape weiße Traube (f)
white sausage Weißwurst (f)
white stew weißes Ragout (n)
white wine Weißwein (m)
white wine from the cask Weißwein (m) offen
whiting Kohlfisch (m), Weißling (m)

Whitsunday Pfingsten (n)
Whitsun holidays Pfingstferien (pl.)
whole-day tour Tagesausflug (m)
whole(meal) bread Vollkornbrot (n)
wholesale discount Großhandelsrabatt (m)
wholesome gesund
wholesome climate Heilklima (n)
wick Docht (m)
wide-vision window Aussichtsfenster (n)
width Breite (f)
Wieners Wiener Würstchen (pl. n)
wife Ehefrau (f)
wild wild
wild boar Wildschwein (n)
wild boar haunch Wildschweinkeule (f)
wild boar saddle Wildschweinrücken (m)
wilderness Wildnis (f)
wild duck Wildente (f)
wild goose Wildgans (f)
wildlife conservation Naturschutz (m)
wild rabbit Wildkaninchen (n)
wild strawbeery Walderdbeere (f)
windcheater Windjacke (f)
Winchester hard disk Winchesterplattenlaufwerk (n)
windfall Zufall (m)
wind force Windstärke (f)
winding road Serpentinenstraße (f)
window Fenster (n), Schalter (m)
window awning Markise (f)
window cleaner Fensterputzer (m)

window pane Fensterscheibe (f)
window screen Sonnenblende (f)
window seat Fensterplatz (m)
window shade Fensterladen (m)
window-shopping Schaufensterbummel (m)
window technique Fenstertechnik (f)
wind-screen Windschutzscheibe (f)
wind-shield Windschutzscheibe (f)
wind-shield wiper Scheibenwischer (m)
wind-surfing Windsurfen (n)
wind up aufziehen
windy windig
wine Wein (m)
wine bottle Weinflasche (f)
wine bouquet Weinblume (f)
wine-butler Weinkellner (m), Getränkekellner, Sommelier (m)
wine by the glass Schoppenwein (m), offener Wein (m)
wine-cellar Weinkeller (m), Weinlokal (n)
wine cooler Weinkühler (m)
wine cup Bowle (f)
wine district Weingegend (f)
wine festival Weinfest (n)
wine-glass Weinglas (n)
wine grower Winze (m)
wine growing Weinbau (m)
wine-house Weinschenke (f)
wine in a carafe offener Wein (m)
wine-list Weinkarte (f)
wine-merchant Weinhändler (m)
wine shop Weinhandlung (f)
wine-tavern Weinstube (f)
wine-test Weinprobe (f)
wine with sodawater Schorle (f)

335

wing Flügel (m)
winglet Flügelspitze vom Huhn (f)
winter cure Winterkur (f)
winter garden Wintergarten (m)
winter health resort Winterkurort (m)
winter holiday resort Winterfrische (f)
winter holiday village Winterferiendorf (n)
winter season Wintersaison (f)
winter sports Wintersport (m)
winter sports centre Wintersportort (m)
winter sports equipment Wintersportausrüstung (f)
winter sports event Wintersportveranstaltung (f)
winter sports facilities Wintersporteinrichtungen (pl. f)
winter sports resort Wintersportort (m)
winter sports season Wintersportsaison (f)
winter sports trip Wintersportreise (f)
winter stay Winteraufenthaltsort (m)
winter timetable Winterfahrplan (m), Winterflugplan (m)
winter tourism Wintertourismus (m)
winter tourist traffic Winterreiseverkehr (m)
winter tyre Winterreifen (m)
wintry winterlich
wipe abtrocknen, wischen
wire Telegramm (n), telegrafieren
wireless Radio (n), Rundfunk (m)
withdraw abheben, entnehmen, kündigen

within the radius of im Umkreis (m) von
without delay unverzüglich
without fat fettlos, ohne Fett (n)
without obligation unverbindlich
without salt salzlos, ohne Salz (n)
wood Wald (m), Holz (n)
wood cock Schnepfe (f)
wood fire Holzfeuer (n)
wood grouse Waldhahn (m), Waldhuhn (n), Auerhahn (m)
woodruff Waldmeister (m), Maikräuter (pl. n)
wool blanket Wolldecke (f)
word processing Textverarbeitung (f)
worcestersauce Worcestersoße (f)
work Arbeit (f)
work area Arbeitsbereich (m)
work flow analysis Arbeitsablaufanalyse (f)
work force Arbeitskräfte (pl. f), Belegschaft (f)
working capital Betriebskapital (n), Umlaufvermögen (n)
working climate Betriebsklima (n)
working condition Arbeitsbedingung (f)
working fund Betriebsmittel (n)
working instruction Dienstanweisung (f)
working papers Arbeitspapiere (pl. n), Arbeitsunterlagen (pl. f)
work load Arbeitsbelastung (f)
work permit Arbeitserlaubnis (f)
work place Arbeitsplatz (m)
work place layout Arbeitsplatzgestaltung (f)
work sampling study Multimomentaufnahme (f), Arbeitszufriedenheit (f)

work satisfaction Arbeitszufriedenheit (f)
work sheet Arbeitsunterlage (f), Arbeitsbogen (m)
worksheet calculation Tabellenkalkulation (f)
workshop Fortbildungsseminar (n), Werkstätte (f)
work simplification Arbeitsvereinfachung (f)
work terms Arbeitsbedingungen (pl. f)
World Association of Travel Agencies Weltverband der Reisebüros (pl. n)
world exihibition Weltausstellung (f)
World Fair Weltausstellung (f)
world-wide fame Weltruf (m)
worn out abgenutzt
worry sich sorgen
worthless wertlos
worth seeing sehenswert
wrapping paper Packpapier (n)
wreck Strandgut (n), Wrack (n)
wrecking car Abschleppwagen (m)
write off abschreiben
write out ausschreiben
writing case Schreibmappe (f)
writing kit Schreibzeug (n)
writing paper Schreibpapier (n)
written schriftlich
wrong falsch, verkehrt, Unrecht (n)
wrongly routed luggage verschlepptes Reisegepäck (n)

X

xenophobia Fremdenfeindlichkeit (f)
X-mas, Christmas Weihnachten

X-ray photo Röntgenaufnahme (f)
xylonite Zelluloid (n)
xylose Holzzucker (m)

Y

y Flugscheinvermerk (m) für Touristenklasse (f)
yacht Segelboot (n), Jacht (f)
yachting Segelsport (m)
yachting-school Segelschule (f)
yachting-season Segelsaison (f)
yacht-race Segelregatta (f)
yachtsman Sportsegler (m)
yard Hof (m)
yardstick Maßstab (m)
yarn Garn (n)
yawl Segeljolle (f)
yawn gähnen
yeanling Lamm (n), Zicklein (n)
year-end closing Jahresabschluß (m)
yearly jährlich
year-round service Ganzjahresbetrieb (m)
yeast Hefe (f)
yeast extract Hefeextrakt (m)
yeast-powder Backpulver (n)
yellow filter Gelbfilter (m)
yellow pea gelbe Erbse (f)
yellow plum Mirabelle (f)
yesterday gestern
yield Ertrag (m), Rendite (f), einbringen
yoghourt Joghurt (m, n)
yolk Eigelb (n), Eidotter (m)
Yorkshire pudding gebackener Eierteig (m)
Yorkshire relish pikante fertige Soße (f)
young jung

337

young chicken Kücken (n)
young wild boar Frischling (m)
youth Jugend (f), Jugendlicher (m)
youth club Jugendklub (m)
youth fare Jugendfahrpreis (m)
youth group jorney Jugendgruppenreise (f)
youth hostel Jugendherberge (f)
Youth Hostel Association Membership Card Jugendherbergsausweis (m)
youth travel Jugendreise (f)
yule Weihnachten (n)

Z

zealous eifrig, hitzig
zebra crossing Zebrastreifen (m)
zero Null (f)
zero balancing Nullkontrolle (f)
zest Würze (f), Reiz (m)
zigzag cruise Kreuzundquerfahrt (f)
zinc Zink (n)
zip Reisverschluß (m)
zip code Postleitzahl (f)
zitherit Zitherspieler (m)
zone Zone (f), Gebiet (n)
zoned street Kurzparkzone (f)
zone of rest Ruhezone (f)
zoo Tiergarten (m), Zoo (m)
zoological garden zoologischer Garten (m)
zoom Steilflug (m), steil hochziehen, zoomen
zoom lens Gummilinse (f), Zoomobjektiv (n)

Names of countries and nationality signs for cars

Ländernamen und Nationalitätskennzeichen für Automobile

Aden Aden ADN
Albania Albanien AL
Algeria Algerien DZ
Andorra Andorra AND
Argentinia Argentinien RA
Australia Australien AUS
Austria Österreich A
Belgium Belgien B
Betchuanaland Botswana BP
Bolivia Bolivien RB
Brasilia Brasilien BR
Bulgaria Bulgarien BG
Burma Birma BUR
Burundi Burundi RU
Cambodia Kambodscha K
Cameroons Kamerun TC
Canada Kanada CDN
Central African Republic
  Zentralafrikanische Republik
  RCA
Ceylon Ceylon CL
Chile Chile RCH
China China (Volksrepublik)
  TI
Colombia Kolumbien CO
Congo Kongo (Brazzaville)
  RCB
Congo Kongo (Lepoldville)
  CGO
Costa Rica Costa Rica CR
Cuba Kuba C

Cyprus Zypern CY
Czechoslovakia Tschechoslowakei CS
Dahomey Dahome DY
Denmark Dänemark DK
Dominican Republic Dominikanische Republik DOM
Ecuador Ecuador EC
Egypt Ägypten ET
Ethiopia Äthiopien ETH
Finland Finnland SF
France Frankreich F
Gambia Gambia WAG
Germany Deutschland D
Ghana Ghana GH
Gibraltar Gibraltar GBZ
Great Britain Großbritannien
  GB
Greece Griechenland GR
Guatemala Guatemala GCA
Haiti Haiti RH
Hong Kong Hongkong HK
Hungary Ungarn H
Iceland Island IS
India Indien IND
Indonesia Indonesien RI
Iran Iran (Persien) IR
Iraq Irak IRQ
Ireland (Eire) Irland IRL
Israel Israel IL
Italy Italien I
Ivory Coast Elfenbeinküste CI
Japan Japan J
Jordan Jordanien JOR
Kenya Kenia EAK
Laos Laos LAO
Lebanon Libanon RL
Liechtenstein Liechtenstein FL
Luxemb(o)urg Luxemburg L
Malawi Malawi RNY
Malaysia Malaysia RMM
Mali Mali RM
Mexico Mexiko MEX
Monaco Monaco MC
Morocco Marokko MA

339

Netherlands Niederlande NL
New Zealand Neuseeland NZ
Newfoundland Neufundland NF
Nicaragua Nicaragua NIC
Niger Niger NIG
Nigeria Nigeria WAN
Norway Norwegen N
Pakistan Pakistan PAK
Panama Panama PA
Paraguay Paraguay PY
Peru Peru PE
Philippines Philippinen PI
Poland Polen PL
Portugal Portugal P
Romania Rumänien R
Ruanda Ruanda RWA
San Marino San Marino RSM
Senegal Senegal SN
Sierra Leone Sierra Leone WAL
Singapore Singapur SGP
Somalia Somalia SP
South Africa Südafrika ZA
Southern Rhodesia Südrhodesien RSR
Soviet Union Sowjetunion SU
Spain Spanien E
Swaziland Swasiland SD
Sweden Schweden S
Switzerland Schweiz CH
Syria Syrien SYR
Taiwan (Formosa) Taiwan (Formosa) RC
Tanzania Tansania EAT
Thailand Thailand (Siam) T
Tunisia Tunesien TN
Turkey Türkei TR
USA USA USA
Uganda Uganda EAU
Uruguay Uruguay U
Vatican City Vatikanstadt V
Venezuela Venezuela YU
Vietnam Vietnam VN
Yugoslavia Jugoslawien YU
Zambia Sambia RNR

Notizen

Notizen

Edgar E. Schaetzing
**Handbuch
Food & Beverage
Management**

Deutscher Fachverlag

Edgar E. Schaetzing
1. Auflage 1985
Ringordner, ca. 277 Seiten
ca. DM 98,–
ISBN 3-87150-226-X

Leitfaden für die Gastronomie und Hotellerie

Dieses Trainingshandbuch enthält die vollständigen geschäftspolitischen Richtlinien für alle Bereiche und Formen der Gastronomie: Planung, Einkauf, Kalkulation, Produktion, Service, Kontrolle, Marketing, Qualitätsüberprüfung, Personaleinsatz und Training.

Jeder Abschnitt des Handbuchs hat eine systematische Gliederung:
- schrittweise beschriebene Management-Techniken
- Fallbeispiele aus der Praxis
- notwendige Formulare zum Selbstausfüllen
- Checklisten für alle gastronomischen Bereiche
- spezielle Literaturempfehlungen.

„Handbuch Food & Beverage Management" ist gleichermaßen ein Trainingshandbuch für den Gastronomen und Hotelier sowie ein Arbeitshandbuch für alle Food und Beverage Abteilungen. Es dient als Quelle zur Erarbeitung neuer Checklisten als auch als Richtlinie zur Kosten- und Qualitätsüberwachung.

Zielgruppen:
Führungskräfte des HOGA-Bereichs, Hotelfachschulen, Fachhochschulen und Seminarveranstalter.

Edgar E. Schaetzing
**Management in
Hotellerie und
Gastronomie**
3. Auflage

Deutscher Fachverlag

Edgar E. Schaetzing
3., überarbeitete und
erweiterte Auflage 1985
322 Seiten, kartoniert, DM 49,80
ISBN 3-87150-199-9

Mehr Umsatz durch gutes Management

Es ist im Hotel- und Gaststättengewerbe nicht mehr damit getan nur über Einnahmen und Ausgaben Buch zu führen. Erfolgreiches Management für alle Bereiche des Gastgewerbes wird heute mehr denn je gefordert.

„Management in Hotellerie und Gastronomie" vermittelt das nötige know-how zur Leistungsüberprüfung und Leistungssteigerung. Der Schwerpunkt liegt bei den modernen Kontrollinstrumenten mit Möglichkeiten der Kosteneinsparung – auch in der Beherbergungsabteilung.

Dieses Nachschlagewerk erscheint nun in der dritten, erweiterten und überarbeiteten Auflage. Bereits 1983 wurde dieses Buch von der Gastronomischen Akademie Deutschlands mit dem Prädikat „zu empfehlen" und einer Silbermedaille ausgezeichnet.

„Management in Hotellerie und Gastronomie", in der Ausbildung an Fachhochschulen und Hotelfachschulen unentbehrlich, gehört in die Bibliothek aller Führungskräfte des HOGA-Bereichs.

Zielgruppen:
Führungskräfte des HOGA-Bereichs